Curt Riess was born and raised in New York State. He rotates his residence between the East Coast and the Midwest. In addition to an AAS and an MBA, Curt holds a BS in Journalism. Having put his passion for writing on hold for many years while growing a niche food processing business, after selling it to a private equity group, Curt started his second career as a novelist. He writes non-fiction and fiction, often sharing personal experiences from his lifetime not just for the readers enjoyment and interest but in hopes of his novels being passed along to people who may benefit from hearing his life stories. Curt and his wife have a history of helping disadvantaged people on three continents. He refers to their retirement, being philanthropic, and writing his novels as a permanent vacation.

This book is dedicated to John and Joyce King and the other families (deceased and living) like them in the Villages of Spencer and Van Etten, NY who unknowingly served as role models to me as a young man.

To my teachers and professors.

To my dad, who unselfishly took his marriage vow for better or worse seriously the second time around.

To my wife Darcy, for whom my life as it is, without a doubt, would never have occurred.

To my Comet.

Curt Riess

A BOY AND HIS COMET:
DANCING THROUGH THE RAIN

AUSTIN MACAULEY PUBLISHERS®

LONDON * CAMBRIDGE * NEW YORK * SHARJAH

Ordering Information
Quantity sales: Special discounts are available on quantity purchases by corporations, associations, and others. For details, contact the publisher at the address below.

Publisher's Cataloging-in-Publication data
Riess, Curt
A Boy and His Comet: Dancing Through the Rain

ISBN 9798886937114 (Paperback)
ISBN 9798886937121 (Hardback)
ISBN 9798886937145 (ePub e-book)
ISBN 9798886937138 (Audiobook)

Library of Congress Control Number: 2023920273

www.austinmacauley.com/us

First Published 2024
Austin Macauley Publishers LLC
40 Wall Street, 33rd Floor, Suite 3302
New York, NY 10005
USA

mail-usa@austinmacauley.com
+1 (646) 5125767

I would like to thank the editors and publicists of Austin Macauley Publishers for producing this book and to New York Times Best Selling Novelist Caroline Leavitt for her editing assistance to me in my first draft.

Table of Content

Authors Note

All the characters in this memoir living or deceased were or are real people. Some of the names in this memoir have been changed to protect their identity.

Music can move the soul, it did mine. Playlists from different periods in my life accompany most chapters. They can help convey to the reader an experience of that era and time which I passed through. I recommend listening to the playlist after completing each chapter for reflection on the experience or time period just read. Public playlists can be found on most music streaming services searching for the title of the book.

Chapter One
Comet

1958

Playlist:

Puff, the Magic Dragon, Peter, Paul, and Mary

He's Got the Whole World In His Hands, Laurie London

Green Onion, Booker T. and the M.G.s

Goldfinger, Shirley Bassey

Hold On. I'm Coming, Sam and Dave

In late 1958, the Ford Motor Company's consolidated Mercury-Edsel-Lincoln division was struggling to recover from the poor sales numbers that followed the introduction of the unpopular Edsel. While Henry Ford the Second anguished over the failure of the car he named after his father, I was still in Loretta's womb. Ford had just authorized the production of the compact Falcon to compete with smaller foreign cars recently entering the United States market. And the management of the newly consolidated division of Mercury-Edsel-Lincoln and one of its chief engineers, Lee Iacocca, were designing and launching new smaller compact cars to bring Ford's sales back from the bowels of the car industry. The new division of Mercury Edsel Lincoln made an argument for their compact vehicle slated to be part of the Edsel line to bolster

Edsel's sales numbers. The car was kept secret and known as the Edsel B. The compact shared much of the Falcon's platform except for having a longer wheelbase. Otherwise, it would transfer most of the Falcon's major components, such as the engine, suspension, basic body shell, and many of its parts.

A year later, in 1959, the world brought the United States Alaska and Hawaii to become the 49th and 50th of the United States. Lesser history had happened too, Loretta gave birth to me, and Ford started production of the secretive compact concept car known as Edsel B and gave it its official name— Comet. It became a highly successful production car until the Mustang began production in 1965.

Little could I know as a newborn, toddler, and beyond then, that I would grow up with abundant secrets all about my life and that a Comet, both in the form of a Ford and cosmic spirit, would play a key role in saving my teen life.

Chapter Two
The Queen of Queens

Harry and The Queen of Queens.

1959 – 1964
Spotify Playlist:
Like A Rolling Stone, Bob Dylan
He's So Fine, The Chiffons
Smoke Gets In Your Eyes, The Platters
A Lovers Question, Clyde McPhatter
The End of the World, Skeeter Davis
Puff, The Magic Dragon, Peter, Paul, and Mary

Loretta was one of four children from a mother who lost custody of her family to her husband Matteo Stellato in a divorce. We suspected she was an alcoholic. He subsequently boarded three of his children to an East Islip extension of the Brooklyn Orphanage Asylum called Brookwood Hall. At nine years of age, Loretta, the oldest and two younger siblings, lived out their lives at Brookwood Hall until fifteen or sixteen. Matteo visited his children periodically and as often as he could, but his job kept him plenty busy trying to maintain the support he had to pay to board his children out. His youngest son was adopted by his sister Rose as he suffered from a learning disability, most likely caused by fetal alcohol syndrome. Margaret, the children's mother, rarely visited her children at the orphanage. Loretta could have stayed at Brookwood Hall until age sixteen, but at fifteen years and longing to know the mother who never visited, she moved into her flat in Brooklyn. Through survival circumstances and asked to help pay for the rent Loretta would get pregnant and have her first child at just the age of 16.

By 25, Loretta was pregnant with her sixth child, by a sixth man, though perhaps she had many more lovers than that in her young life thus far. Like her previous lovers, once she was pregnant, they fled. Alone again and now pregnant with her sixth child, Loretta was in a dire predicament.

Deeply concerned over her friends' pattern of life and choice of lovers, her best friend Tesse said to her, "I'm going to introduce you to an honest man. His name is Harry."

Like others before him, Harry fell head over heels in love with her even as she was pregnant by another man. As he would put it years later in discussion with me, she was a "hot tamale"—"a Queen!"

Harry was divorced. He was looking for a new mate and fell so severely for the queen that he had asked Loretta two times in less than six months if she'd marry him. Two times she declined. She didn't want to marry him, but at the third proposal, she agreed she would marry him with the condition that he would adopt the sixth child she was carrying. Harry said no, he couldn't. He had three children to support from his first marriage, and he wasn't going to keep…as he told me many years later, "some other bastards kid." Quite frankly, he was not a man of economic means to sufficiently support the family he already had.

So, with two children already to care for and not in love with Harry enough to marry him yet still blaming him for not being willing to adopt the baby she'd birthed, Loretta again sadly and very painfully put another one of her baby girls up for adoption. That sister of mine and her existence, as well as others, would never be mentioned. Before she signed the papers, she held her infant child for a few hours, kissing the child, whispering into its ears, and then tearfully handing the infant to the new parents. She felt enormous sorrow and grief, knowing and understanding she may never see the child again.

While she still slept with Harry, she refused to marry him. He wouldn't ever be able to satisfy her desire for the good life she saw in the movies and had, for a short run, experienced. He was a truck driver, a local Teamsters Union delivery man, and educated only to the eighth grade like her. They eventually lived together as Harry supported his and her family, and she ultimately found herself pregnant again, this time from Harry.

On May 6, 1959, she delivered a baby boy in Elmhurst, a Queen's Hospital, and that baby was me. I was the Queen of Queens' seventh illegitimate bastard. Because she couldn't bear to give up another baby for adoption and add to the grief she was already burdened with, she finally accepted Harry's proposal of marriage to be able to keep me.

After asking her to marry him four times, Harry got his queen, the Queen of Queens. She insisted that Harry adopt the two other children she had living with her, and he agreed though it never happened. Harry bought her a small diamond ring and a crown for his queen's head, and they were married on New Year's Day, 1960.

I was raised as a toddler in a section of Brooklyn called Greenpoint, full of immigrants who spoke broken English in close-knit neighborhoods of Italians and Poles intermingled with Jews, Irishman, and Germans. They all looked upon the others with suspicion, and sometimes the hate they carried with them from their home countries spilled over into street fistfights if not through the fathers themselves, their offspring brats.

I lived among a punky melting pot of crazies. Some people picked at the garbage in the evenings, people slept on the sidewalks, and many people didn't speak English. Men with large tattoos on their arms who flexed their muscles as they walked to work the wharves and shipping docks grimaced at me as I sat on the steps to the street in the mornings.

As a five-year-old looking on, they look like rough sailors or pirates from a comic book speaking with varying accents and dialects. Many boasted with coarse language and ease about whiskey, woman, and what they stole from the freight they handled at work that day. They often had something for sale or swap.

The authoritarian immigrant parents raised tough teens who played stickball, spat at you, and went barefoot on the hot cobblestone and tar as if their calloused feet were made of leather soles. They would just as soon beat you with their stick if you got in their face or interfered with their game, than use as a ball bat. Green Point was a challenging lower-class impoverished neighborhood, and almost everyone around us was poor and ragged. And I don't exclude myself or our family from the category as we lived among them.

Loretta brought her eighth child into the world a year and a half after I was born. We lived in a small flat with hardly enough room for the five of us already there. She was the only legitimate she had through marriage. It was so crowded that my older half-brother Gary, at 12 years old, was forced to move out and live with my great-grandma Hardy.

I spent most of my first two and a half years of life in a carriage because it served as a bed, playpen, and cage where I could be kept off the streets and in our crowded flat. I was told through stories I loved that carriage and wasn't ready to give it up to my new little sister. The great thing about the carriage was that it had wheels and was portable. Where-ever we went, my bed, playpen, my whole world went with me. It was a tiny motor home. I was told my brother Gary loved to race me up and down the sidewalks of Brooklyn, bobbing that carriage back and forth, giving me a mildly comparative thrill to the Coney Island Roller Coaster and making me laugh and giggle.

But I nearly lost my life, too, in that carriage. One day while shopping at a Woolworths store, Loretta parked me in my carriage outside while she and my older sister went in to enjoy a chocolate seltzer at the soda fountain. When she came out, I and the carriage were gone.

I was kidnapped and whisked off a half block away by some immigrant woman. While I can't remember the episode, my recollections are from hearing the story so many times throughout my childhood that I have vivid imagined images of me freewheeling at top speeds down a Brooklyn sidewalk with Loretta and my older half-sister Candice racing down the street after me screaming and yelling to the sidewalk crowds to stop the woman with her baby. As they caught up to her, she abandoned the carriage slipping into an alley, never to be seen again.

As for me in that carriage and growing up on Huron Street, the thrill of risk, danger, recklessness, speed, and wheels entered my bloodstream in more ways than the eye may have seen. I was promised a little red pedal car to bribe me to leave the carriage for the new brat in town. With it, I was coached to pretend to be the famed Scottish-born race car driver James Clark (Champion of 25 Gran Prix Formula One races), and the sidewalks of my neighborhood became my racetracks and parkways. I ruled over those parkways pedaling as fast as possible, dodging the walking folks.

Between the ages of three to five, I pedaled around the city block where I lived, abiding by the one law given to me never to cross the street lest I become a bad boy and get kicked out of the flat like my older brother. Space in the apartment was not a commodity, and I was threatened often. I'd scour the sidewalks for any loose change, stop at the penny candy store, and say hi to the corner grocer, the newsstand man, and they all knew me as "the kid with the pedal car." Mostly I was a damn nuisance to the walkers. The regular folks I'd visit always asked if my mother knew where I was, "Yep," I'd lie.

Before he was kicked out, my brother Gary would often come running home from a gang of hooligans fast at his heels, and I'd split the sons of bitches in two by racing straight into their ankles with my pedal car. I was like a bowling ball running into the pins trying to knock them down. They'd threaten to beat me, kicked the side of my pedal car, and shoved their fists in my face. They'd scare me to death, and I'd sometimes begin to cry, but when they came at my brother Gary again, I charged again and again, even with tears streaming down my cheeks. Then one day, one of those punks repeatedly took his foot and bashed the back end of my pedal car to the point he bent the rear wheel's axle to a nearly 90-degree angle. Shaken and trying to bite his leg as he smashed my car, I screamed when he shoved me to the sidewalk and began kicking me, and the punk was chased off by some adult passing by. I was devastated. My dad managed to bend it back into a wobbly wheel, but it had crippled my bravado, maneuverability among the walkers and slowed my speed in half.

It wasn't long after that Harry decided to move us further out on the south shore of Long Island to a town named Baldwin. He had our hungry mouths to feed, and his 9–5 truck driving job didn't make ends meet. Harry wanted a garage space to fix cars and sell them. And he wanted the queen out of Queens. While Loretta held a part-time job as a store clerk, she seemed to have a way of getting a lot of things for free that cost more than her and Harry's wages could afford. Harry always noticed something new from Macy's, where her friend worked. There seemed to be plenty of meat from the local butcher, too, more than we could afford. Harry would often ask her where she got the money for that? She always answered, "people owe me favors, and they just give to me."

Even as Loretta dragged me around at age five with her shopping, I couldn't help but notice the butcher wink at her as he handed her a second package of meat after she paid for and received the first one. There were others, clerks at Models, the A&S department store where she worked part-time, the grocery store… she always seemed to be able to afford much more than she earned for reasons not fully understood by me at the time. Harry seemed to understand, and it was evident he wanted his queen out of Queens, out of Green Point.

Chapter Three
79 Smith Street

1964

Playlist:

My Girl, The Temptations

King Of The Road, Roger Miller

This Diamond Ring, Gary Lewis and The Playboys

The Tracks of My Tears, The Miracles

You've Got Your Troubles, The Fortunes

The night before our big move, they placed my pedal car on top of a heap of stuff they put on the curb for the garbage haulers. I was five, and I cried for what seemed like an eternity that I had to give it up, but they promised me a new one once we moved. They said I was getting too big for that pedal car, and the axle was not repairable.

From our flat window, I watched the old Polish woman we called the Junk Lady who scoured the piles of discarded furniture and other trash placed on the streets as she pulled my pedal car from the pile and looked it over. She lifted it into her wagon and some other items, and it was gone forever. Loretta wouldn't let me out of the apartment and told me to let it go as I watched the Junk Lady disappear into the gray shadows down the street with my car.

We moved into a house…sort of. We didn't own much, and only one small stake truck of belongings from Brooklyn to Baldwin made a complete move. The house was split into two to make a duplex, and we rented the downstairs, which now afforded one bedroom and a dining room that could serve as a bedroom. It was still small but seemed huge compared to our tiny flat in Brooklyn, as it had a separate living room and kitchen.

My two sisters and I had to share the small bedroom split by a dresser and a curtain above it to form two sides. On one side was a single bed crammed in for my older sister, and on the other, bunk beds to which my younger sister and I slept. I wondered where Gary would sleep, but unknown to me at the time, he was left to remain in Brooklyn living with my aunt. Because he and Harry didn't get along, it was demanded by Loretta (and Harry) that he stay with my aunt.

I thought it would be best for him to escape Greenpoint and live out his high school years in the suburb. Maybe he'd get fewer black eyes? He was only fifteen, ten years, and one day older than me. We always celebrated our birthdays together, his being on May 5, and mine on May 6. When we moved, he was away at the camp, and I assumed we'd see him soon in our new home.

When we arrived in Baldwin, to my surprise was a slightly used but new to me red fire engine pedal car. Wow, I couldn't believe my eyes, and I fit perfectly. I guess Loretta was right. I had outgrown that old pedal car because this one was bigger, and my legs could stretch straight out to give a good thrust to the pedals.

When I was relieved of the liftgate duties on the truck my dad borrowed from his workplace, I hopped into that shiny new fire truck and pedaled off down my new parkway. The sidewalks were narrower here; unlike Brooklyn, hardly anybody was using them. They were clear raceways for me and with nobody to dodge. Our house was the only one on the block, nestled between a small warehouse and office building. It was a large house, at least to me. It had a green asphalt roof and was sided with pink asphalt shingles. It stood out on Smith Street across from a vast Baldwin Long Island Railroad station parking lot, which we could see from our front porch. Trains came and went about every ten to fifteen minutes. I pedaled to the east and followed the sidewalk past the small office complex and into a real neighborhood around the corner. A tree-lined neighborhood with real single-family houses. They looked like mansions to me. In my little mind at the time, it seemed ironic that this place was called Baldwin when there was nothing "Bald" about it. It was lush and greener than Greenpoint!

Standing up to my brothers' chasers, I'd become a hardened mouthy kid in Brooklyn. When the group of neighborhood boys walked up to me and asked me who I was, I told them my name was Curt Lee Riess, and I live around the corner in the big pink house, and if you touch my fire truck, I'll punch you in the mouth, and I meant it too! That was my introduction, and I would be reminded about it by those boys for the next six years as we became friends and foes all the way through elementary school. When they wanted to taunt or torment me toward brawls and skirmishes, they'd chant in a sing-song sort of tune at me, "Hey, my name is Curt Lee Riess, and I live around the corner in the big pink house; if you touch my little firetruck, I'll punch you in the mouth" and then they'd laugh and pedal their bikes on.

I was only five, so they laughed me off and returned to their stick ball game.

I watched for a while, pedaled up the street to look at all the tidy houses with front lawns which were amazing to me, and then pedaled back. For the first couple weeks in our new home, pedaling up the street and around the corner to watch the neighborhood boys play stickball and trying to get to know them became the norm.

After several weeks in our new home, just as I was pedaling back to the big pink house one day, my brother was crying his head off with Loretta screaming at him to go back to Brooklyn. Gary was crushed and felt abandoned. No one had informed him that we had moved to Baldwin until he returned to my aunt's flat. When Gary returned to Brooklyn from the summer boys camp, he learned his family and mother had moved away.

He was only 15. He hopped a train on the Long Island Railroad and found his way to our new address. He begged to come live with us on the front porch and lawn. He cried and cried and cried and begged Loretta to let him come. "How could you leave me," he yelled, reaching for Loretta's arm. She pushed him off.

"Go back!" she hollered. "Go to your Aunt Peggy's! There's no room for you here!" He begged again. "I want to live with you, I want to live with you, please," he cried. She took two steps forward and slapped him. That was when I started to cry.

The slap had its effect! Stunned, Gary stood erect, tears streaming down his face. He looked at me sitting in my fire engine, crying, and then I screamed at Loretta. "I want Gary!"

"Shut up, Curt, shut up!" She shouted. I wanted what Gary wanted for himself. For the first time in my short life, I felt if I could give up anything I had, even these cherished wheels, I'd do it for whatever Gary wanted and have him live with us, but I couldn't make that happen.

How could Loretta give up her child? How could they not even tell him we were all moving? How could she do that? How could she literally push and drag him out of the pink house and ask him to go live elsewhere?

Gary was gasping for air uncontrollably and moved across the street. I wanted to run to him and go with him, but I was frozen with fear. What if Loretta wanted to get rid of me next? "Please, please," Gary begged again, now brought to his knees by grief.

"Stop making a scene!" Loretta screamed. "You get going, Gary. Get back on that train and get your ass back to Brooklyn." Gary looked at me again with heavy red sore eyes. Crying, and because I loved him, I shouted, "Go, Go, Gary," not because I wanted him to go, but because I loved him, and I couldn't bear this scene of anguish and pain any longer. Both of our hearts were broken to pieces. "Go, Gary," I pleaded… As I couldn't bear it anymore. And then Gary did, turning and walking away.

I sat in that fire truck and watched him return across the parking lot to the train station while Loretta went inside. I watched him up on the platform. Every three to five minutes, he waved to me again, and I waved at him until the train came and obstructed our view of each other.

My brother was no longer there on the platform when it moved on. I pedaled to the other end of the block and sobbed my heart out. Those iron horses took my brother away. The day that train took my brother away, in many respects, took him away from me forever.

While I would see Gary in future visits, having him as a brother wasn't the same as seeing him every day, wrestling with each other, playing with me and my matchbox cars, there were no bike rides, piggyback, or handlebar rides. I genuinely missed everything about him except his gang fights.

Lost to Brooklyn, having lost a mother, Gary became a man at sixteen when he started hanging out with a girl a couple of years older than him and got her pregnant. To support himself and his soon to be born child he learned the art of cutting hair and became a barber, and I became a boy full of insecurity, hatred for Loretta for what I'd seen her do, and filled with fear that I'd be sent off next. She threatened me with eviction every time I may have disappointed her in any way…if not to the wayward boys camp, I'd be thrown out onto the street.

Our move to Smith Street is where my daily observances of Loretta began to become more astute. In what she thought was solitary times alone, I'd often happen upon her to find her crying. Sometimes it was just simple tears and sometimes rain poured from her eyelids. As a young boy my emotions were laden with confusion. Why the rain poured from her eyes I didn't know, and when I approached her with any solace, she'd snap so violently at me to go away she'd reinforce my hate.

Chapter Four
Baldwin

1964 – 1967

Playlist:

Mr. Tambourine Man, The Byrds

Help, The Beatles

Medley Aquarius, Let the Sunshine In, The Broadway Performers

Let It Be, The Beatles

Good Morning Starshine, Night Singers

Lucy In The Sky With Diamonds, The Beatles

Michelle, The Beatles

Yesterday, Beatles

Life in the big pink house became insane. If Harry thought it was far enough away for Loretta to give up the imagined lovers, he thought she might have had, it wasn't, and a new neighborhood just brought more opportunity.

Within a year of leaving Brooklyn, some guy named Jimmy was frequently visiting Loretta and hanging out in the kitchen at our house. Whenever he would be there when we came home from school, he'd give me five bucks to take my little sister to Nunley's amusement park to get lost and leave him and Loretta alone.

Soon I found myself riding with Loretta to scope out Jimmy's house in Levittown. As we drove back and forth to look at it, Loretta asked: "Would you like to live in a house like that?" *Whom was she kidding? I thought. Did she think I didn't know what she was referring because I was a seven-year-old?*

I asked her straight out… "Are you going to marry Jimmy? Do you want to live in that house?" She looked at me with disbelief that I would affront her like that…she never responded to my questions. She asked, "Would he make a nice dad?"

I said, "he is a nice guy… but I already have a dad."

"But maybe he would be a better dad?" she bargained. My inner emotions welled up. I knew better than to carry this conversation any further with Loretta lest her mood crazily turned on me, and she scolded or beat me. She constantly put my father down. He was "a good-for-nothing bastard," she'd tell everyone.

Loretta's moods changed almost as fast as the hours in a day. One minute she could be the sweetest, most loving mother; the next, she raged at you for the slightest misbehavior. She was verbally and physically abusive, and as if her hair pulling and slapping weren't enough when Harry got home, she'd tell him what awful kids we were and make him use the strap on us.

One day Harry drew me quietly to him. "Have you seen a guy named Jimmy at the house, he asked?" I was scared to answer, and he studied me and then said, "I promise you won't get into trouble for telling the truth."

I stared at him; he seemed so kind that I told him. "Jimmy seems like a nice guy. He gives us five bucks to go to Nunley's while he and Loretta visit."

Harry's face grew dark. His mouth became one thin line. "Thank you," he said, and then he went to his garage and stayed there, working on one of his cars.

The screaming and threats started as soon as Loretta came home from work. Harry threatened her with divorce at one point, and his fist went through the top of the stereo cabinet. The shattered top would remain a daily reminder to us for many more years to come of that day. Loretta was sobbing and fuming. "Go ahead!" she screamed at him, "Go work on your f…ing cars. That's what you love, not me!" I followed her as she walked from the garage to our house to her beloved stereo cabinet. "You bastard," she muttered. "You destroy everything I love." Then, what scared me most, was that she brightened as if she had an idea, and I knew, even then, that her thoughts were always dangerous.

Harry had six cars in the driveway, all of which he was repairing and fixing to earn extra money to support this family and three other children from his first. She turned to me and said, "Your father wants to break the things I like; well you watch this… I'll fix those damn cars." She sped out the front door to a rock garden she had made, picked up a small boulder, and smashed it through one windshield. I ran to the kitchen window and watched with horror. Harry was in the garage. By the time he heard the crash of glass, she had smashed small boulders from the rock garden into four of his car windshields. Harry ran to her and restrained her. She screamed obscenities and threatened to kill him. Harry let go of her, and Loretta fled to the kitchen where I stood frozen with fear and she grabbed a steak knife, he followed, and she lunged at Harry as he came through the door. He grabbed her and pinned her down to the floor to remove the knife from her grip.

Scared to death, I fled from the house, ran around the corner to a neighbor's house crying, and told Ginger what had happened. She told me to stay at her home and called the police. Ginger then ran around the corner to my house.

I stayed at Gingers' house with her son and husband, Dick. The pink house is crazy, I thought to myself. *It's crazy. It's crazy. Just crazy.*

After a short time, Ginger called her house and asked her husband, Dick to bring me home, and I walked home with Dick. The police were at my house in the kitchen.

When I entered, Harry was handcuffed, and he would be hauled off to jail. Loretta told the police he had attacked her, pulled a knife, and threatened to kill her. The police looked at me. "Did you see what happened?" they asked. I nodded yes.

"Don't say a word," Harry told me, but the police told him to shut up.

I knew the real story. Loretta pulled the knife, she threw the first slaps and punches, and Harry was only defending himself.

The police looked at me again. "Young man, tell us what you saw," they said, and Harry interrupted. "Curt, don't say anything."

I said nothing, tears streaming down my face.

The police hauled my dad away in their car while Dick and Ginger sat and consoled Loretta.

Harry was jailed for a few days, and Loretta and I were summoned into court.

Loretta was pressing charges and wanted to send Harry to prison. The judge heard both sides of their story and then turned to me. Can you tell me what you saw and what happened, young man? I teared up and choked. I didn't say a word. "It's OK to tell the story, now Curt," Harry said, and the judge stiffened. "You," he said, pointing to Harry. "Shut your mouth."

Harry asked the judge to approach the bench, and the judge nodded. They whispered, and then the judge asked one of the police officers to take Harry and Loretta out of the courtroom.

The judge then asked me again what had happened. And that was when I told the truth.

"Why didn't you tell this before?" the judge asked.

"My dad told me to say nothing."

"Ah, I see," the judge said.

The judge then summoned Loretta and Harry back into the courtroom. The judge told them both that he'd not be so lenient again if he saw them back in court. And then he told Harry he wouldn't go to prison, but he had to stay clear of our home for a month. He strongly suggested to Loretta that she seek some psychiatric help or counseling. Loretta froze with a stone-cold puzzled face, almost as if she wanted to slap the judge.

For almost a year, Harry and Loretta remained separated. My little sister and I could only see our dad on the weekends when we would go to his mother's house in East Meadow, and we would stay there with him for the weekend, sometimes with him trying to see his other children from his first marriage. At least for the weekends that year, we would have some semblance of peace hanging out with our Nanny. My older sister stayed with Loretta in the pink house and lived as we all did under the dark umbrella, where it rained most of the time.

After almost a year of separation, Jimmy learned what Loretta had done, began distancing himself from her, and stopped coming to visit. Harry had found another girlfriend, and when Loretta discovered who she was, she drove out to the Oyster Bay bar where his girlfriend worked and she attacked her in a fistfight. Her actions told Harry she wanted him to come back home. Loretta was once again at a loss and desperate to have support. He still loved her and had always wanted her, so he did.

I never told anyone what went on in that crazy house. Loretta's personality to those outside the family was fun, voracious and carefree, but she put vivid and life-threatening fear in our lives if we even dared to tell. I didn't think anyone would believe it.

One particular day of many bad memories is of Loretta and my older sister Candice getting into a spat. Loretta threw her out of the house and told her never to return. Late evening fell, and Candice hadn't returned home. With me and my little sister, Harry and Loretta drove through Baldwin neighborhoods to find her. After a few hours, we found her hanging on the front steps at a friend's house with other girlfriends and boys. Harry pulled up to the sidewalk in front of the home. "Get in the car!" Loretta screamed. Candice refused. "Get your damn ass in this car right now!" she called again. Her friends stood in awe and gathered around her. Loretta turned to Harry. "Fix this," she demanded. "Go grab that bitch by the hair and drag her into the car."

Harry shook his head no. Instead, he got out of the car and said normally, "Candice, please get into the car and come home."

Candice was braver than I had ever seen her be. She shook her head no. She and I both knew that the beating she'd received earlier would continue if she got into the car. My little sis and I sunk lower into the car's back seat and almost to the floor. I had one knee on the floor as I looked out the rear seat window. If I could have, I would have bolted from the scene. Finally, harassed by Loretta, Harry went over and grabbed her by her lengthy hair, dragged her danglingly awkward legs down the sidewalk, and shoved her in the car.

Her friends rushed to her aid, but Harry made a fist with his other hand motioning them to back off. "Leave her alone!" her friends shouted over and over. I was astonished, quivering, and then crying with my older sister.

I never forgot that day. No one, including my big sis, deserved verbal, physical, and emotional humiliation, especially in front of her friends. It was one thing to experience the violence at home in the confinement and shelter of our four walls where it was hidden and no one could see. It was another to display it and practice the insanity that we lived with so publicly. It was another leak under our roof where our private lives became public. It sent us all a message that there would never be an escape, even though Loretta would sometimes throw us into the street and tell us to find another home. If we did, trouble from Loretta would follow us to any household we might try to go to.

That day's message was clear: no one would ever be allowed to provide a safe harbor for us. If Loretta found out, trouble would come to that household. And that day, too, I knew Harry would be no real help. He would always do what Loretta wanted.

Is it any wonder I was still wetting the bed?

But Loretta didn't think it was because of the stress she caused. Instead, she took me to a doctor. I remember the last doctor's visit. After X-rays and some tests, the doctor told Loretta that her boy is ordinarily healthy. Loretta nodded. "How is his home life?" the doctor asked. Loretta stiffened. "It's just fine."

"Because sometimes bedwetting results from a stressful home life," he stated. I glared up at Loretta to see what her reaction was to be. She became cool and reiterated that we had an everyday home life. I waited and hoped for the doctor to do more, and ask more, but instead, he just dismissed us.

Besides being disgusted with waking up every morning soaking wet, the bedwetting kept me from the normal sleepover activities with friends. I was always too embarrassed to participate and would decline. The constant declines would eventually divert the friendship toward another kid who could participate. I was so hungry for a close friend. In winter months, when one couldn't play outside, and most folks would only allow their son to bring one friend inside at a time to play, I was always the last resort in my immediate neighborhood because I could never reciprocate and have someone over in my own house because of the reputation Loretta created for us all. The crazy family in the pink house. Steadfast, ordinary, familiar neighbors avoided us.

We all tried to find reprieve from the household in our own ways. While I would discover new neighborhoods with my new Stingray, my older sister found salvation with the boy named Tommy in the upstairs apartment. Increasingly she would hang out with Tommy, eventually escaping by marrying him. She soon had a baby, and for the third time, I was an uncle. I was ten.

Chapter Five
The Stingray

1967 – 1970

Playlist:

Love Is Blue, Paul Mauriat

Ticket To Ride, The Beatles

Born To Be Wild, Steppenwolf

Nobody But Me, The Human Beinz

With A Little Help From My Friends, The Beatles

At age seven and living only two years at 79 Smith Street, the pedal fire truck had to give way to a Stingray bicycle. Most of the kids in my new neighborhood laughed at me pedaling away on that fire truck. They all had bicycles, mostly cool Stingray bikes of various colors by Schwinn.

I'll never forget getting my third set of wheels…it was a gold metallic painted Schwinn Kent with three speeds and a banana seat. A Stingray! It was expensive. I'd saved birthday money and other money gifts from my grandparents and great uncle, up to $20. The bike cost forty-plus, and I had to give everything I had saved toward the payment. My dad paid the rest. From carriage wheels to pedal car wheels to bike wheels, mobility and freedom always seemed a desirable priority for me to have at my feet and fingertips—freedom from being at home and living with Loretta.

Since I got that Stingray, I was biking miles and miles to other towns to see how far I could go by bike if Loretta ever threw me out. Once, I arrived at my older sister's apartment in Valley Stream, to which she scolded me greatly for being so far from home and told me if I ever came to see her again, she'd tell Loretta. That was enough of a threat that stopping by her apartment never happened again. I didn't want to lose my freedom. Little did she know I'd traveled much further than her apartment. Over the next three years, at ages eight, nine, and ten, I'd biked to Hempstead, Baldwin Harbor, Freeport Harbor, and Lynbrook and canvassed more miles along Sunrise Highway and the Long Island Railroad to Long Island City than one might imagine a small boy would do at my age.

It was too bad that I was so enthralled with those wheels in some ways. The Long Island Railroad was tempting me a lot. Throughout my elementary years, though I was told I wasn't allowed up on the station platform, many a time, I would dare to stand inches from the edge of the deck as a train sped into the Baldwin station whipping air through my hair. If I had raised an arm in front of me, I would have lost it to the train. I wanted to board one and go where it was going, coming up just short of doing just that so many times out of lack of fair money, but primarily out of fear I'd be put in jail or sent to some wayward boys home which Loretta threatened me with all the time. I'd seen the brutality that had happened to my older brother and sister for less trouble than that.

As I got older, what I wanted most was money. I saw it as a source of freedom. A paper route was a chance to earn money, but I was too young. The Long Island Press and the Daily News required a kid to be twelve. I was ten, and not wanting to wait two more years, I convinced an older kid delivering the Long Island Press to take another route and give it to me. I'd give him a cut of my tips. The next route that came up, he took it on, and I was a paperboy.

He gave me the route information and addresses, and I would stop by his house and pick up bundles of papers every day and deliver them first thing after school and in the morning on weekends. The canvas bag to hold the newspapers between my handlebars would be stuffed. And on Sundays, it would require several trips to pick up and deliver the extra-thick Sunday editions.

No one seemed to care that I was doing this as long as we kept it secret from the route manager of the Long Island Press. I could earn about five or six dollars a week from tips.

After a year and a half, the boy who helped me get the route was going into Jr High school and wanted to switch to delivering the New York Daily News. He said he could make more money delivering fewer papers at the Daily. I didn't want to give up what I had, so I convinced him to keep the route, and I took on the rest, delivering to more than a hundred addresses. I was still eleven when the route manager caught on to what we were doing after he quit.

She asked me to come into her office and formally apply. So, I did, and I lied about my age, but I had to have a parent sign a permission form which I conveniently kept forgetting to give her. I wouldn't be twelve for another six months.

I made great money with this route, sometimes exceeding 16 or 17 dollars a week. I lived the perfect Baldwin kid life. I could afford Carlucci's Pizza for lunch instead of a bagged lunch at Coolidge elementary school. After pizza, I could afford several bags of penny candy at the Powers candy store across Grand Avenue from the school, and I'd buy them for my little sis. I often stopped for a malt at a soda fountain during my route deliveries, and I'd shower Loretta with costume jewelry to appease her moods and try to make her happy.

My tips would have been greater, except Loretta forced me to church every Sunday. For all the papers I had to deliver, I had to make several trips home to fill up my handlebar bag, and on Sundays, I had to put all the Sunday edition inserts into the papers. I could only deliver about two-thirds of my route early in the morning before church, and the last third would have to wait until after church. Some customers were unhappy that the paper came late on a Sunday morning. They didn't care about my excuse, and registered formal complaints to my manager. I soon learned to rotate the last third of the papers I had to deliver so that it would only be late one or two Sundays a month, and regardless of my church excuse, some of those tips fell off. Still, the money was good, and it was the only opportunity. I was saving some of it, too, hiding it in a dresser drawer until Loretta found it digging through my stuff one day.

"Where did you get this?" she shouted. I told her I had been saving it from my paper route. She was a bit surprised and asked how much I made each week. What are you saving it for? I was nervous as she still looked at me as if I had stolen it. And I could not tell her the real reason. To buy gifts, I said, as I buy you jewelry. She looked sternly at me and then became a bit proud of my nearly thirty to forty dollars, and she then took me to a bank, opened up my first savings account, and taught me how to use one. Little did she realize I was saving for the day I might have to run. And I continued to save until, finally, my route manager told me she had to cut my route in half or take it away altogether. Primarily because of those late Sunday paper deliveries, and no matter how much I had pleaded with Loretta, she wouldn't let me out of the house any earlier than I was leaving at six am.

I was only another month from turning twelve when suddenly, the papers stopped coming to me in the morning. All of them, not just half, and without notice. I was devastated. I biked down to the Long Island Press manager's office and pleaded with her to return them, but she already gave the route to someone else. When I asked her why all of the routes were taken, and she didn't just take half, she reminded me, "I'm the boss kid, and you still aren't twelve and shouldn't have had the route in the first place."

"Your customers aren't satisfied with your deliveries on Sundays, and I can get in trouble for you lying to me." I wanted to scream. It was as if my whole life was just taken away from me. I pleaded with her again and again. She looked upon me as a hapless, hopeless little troublemaker and turned away after demanding the money owed for last week's papers.

I still owed her around sixteen dollars, and she asked me again for the payment. I wouldn't give it to her. I told her I had to go and collect from my customers for what I had already delivered first, and that is precisely what I did the next day. As I began trying to collect payments, I was told by customer after customer that my "brother," who was delivering the papers now, had already collected. I told them I didn't have a brother delivering papers! A couple of years older than me, the new kid had collected on my route and stole it all from me. I ran into him while he was delivering papers and confronted him about it, but he was twice my size and threatened me by asking me what I would do about it. I wanted to crack the kid's face with something, but he and his buddy were no match for me. I hoped he'd get bitten as I did by a couple of my customers' dogs.

I returned to the route manager's office the next day and told her what had happened. "You hired a dishonest kid!" I complained. She looked at me and said, "You're the dishonest kid," and reminded me that I had lied about my age to get a paper route, and she insisted on my payment for the papers. I told her to collect from the kid she gave my route to that he had the money, and I dropped off my handlebar bags.

Good riddance, sort of. I was devastated, but it didn't matter very long as I was only two months away from leaving Baldwin forever. Soon I'd never have to wake up every day by a loud train nor look at that train station which was the first thing one saw when leaving our front door. We'd be moving upstate New York, hopefully to a better life. Anything I imagined would have to be better than Brooklyn and Baldwin and the life I've lived thus far.

The Long Island Press route manager called my house and stopped by to collect several times. I repeated my dilemma and told her to collect the payment from the new kid as he stole my last collections for those papers. While I justified the non-payment with her abrupt actions of canceling my routes on me, I left Long Island feeling guilty and asked my God for forgiveness, both for acquiring the routes when I shouldn't have and for not making the final payment. I prayed she got the payment from the bastard who took over my route and stole my collections because, frankly, none of it was her fault. She was just doing her job firing me, and I blamed Loretta for not allowing me to skip church to deliver the papers in the morning on time, which caused the dissatisfied customers in my performance. But the reality was it was all my fault. I took on too much, more than I could serve well.

Chapter Six
Leaving the Long Island Box

1970

Playlist:

Raindrops Keep Falling On My Head, B.J. Thomas

Bridge Over Troubled Water, Simon and Garfunkel

Yellow Submarine, The Beatles

I'll Be There, The Jackson 5

Everything Is Beautiful, Ray Stevens

Five years after leaving Huron Street, we were leaving Smith Street and moving again. My older brother Gary was now twenty-one years old with two children. He had grown into a man fast. My older sis escaped the house by marrying the boy upstairs. A few years after her marriage, our landlord came to ask us if we would end our lease on the big pink house. After the first two years Harry had renewed a five-year lease, but the landlord, Mr. Cohen, asked him if he would be willing to end it two years earlier. If they agreed, Mr. Cohen, enticed Loretta and Harry with six months' free rent. He had a buyer for the land, and the big pink house would be torn down for a parking lot and a new Burger King franchise.

For one of the few times in my short life, I saw Harry and Loretta working together to plan a future. Harry inherited land located in upstate New York from his father. We had often gone there on weekends, like going to a cabin, except we referred to it as Upstate! It had a 20 foot by 20-foot one-room cement block cabin with a queen bed and two bunk beds. There was no running water, but it had electricity. The bathroom was an outhouse. We'd take showers when it rained or go to a nearby creek to swim and bathe, dodging early evening bats and picking off blood-sucking leeches when we emerged from the water. Oddly enough, it was Loretta that liked going upstate. We would spend weeks up there in the summers while Harry would commute back to Long Island for work and return on the weekends. Being with her sleeping under the stars at night or in the one-room cabin seemed to bring her some peace; it brought us some peace too. Every evening we'd build a small campfire to keep the bugs away and gaze up at the incredible night sky of stars that we never saw in the city. Loretta would tell us stories until we fell asleep. As youngsters, she'd sing us songs to put us asleep. Those weekends and weeks in the summer upstate were the happiest times I remember with Loretta. I remember wishing we could always be there because it was the only place I felt safe and comfortable and saw Loretta seemingly happy. And with a weekly absence from Harry, she seemed glad to see him when he'd arrive on Friday nights for the weekend.

Harry had considered selling the upstate property, but Loretta saw the property as her happy place, a place in her future. With six months' potential rent savings and his savings from all the cars he'd fixed up without Loretta smashing them to bits, Harry and Loretta began to plan their future upstate. Without needing to buy a parcel, they saw their way toward building a small ranch home for themselves. Harry would have completed twenty years with the Teamsters Union and have a small retirement pension within a couple of more years. He planned to work on cars and possibly do some backhoe and small bulldozer work to supplement his income needs and hang up his truck driving career.

The landlord was asking us to move before the house would be finished. Harry convinced Loretta that if she and us kids moved up there while the house was being built that summer, the savings from not having rent for the next two years could be used to construct the home. She agreed, and it became a frantic summer of 1971 to get the structure up and weather-tight before winter.

We moved one month before I turned twelve and graduated from the sixth grade. My sixth-grade teacher Michael Yosha arranged a small classroom going away party for me. I got an autograph book, and my whole class wrote me odd stories and well wishes. It was nice.

Our first summer, we spent our time as we always had in the cement block cabin, using the outhouse and bathing in the rain or stream. I worked like a dog to provide help in whatever way I could to help those building our house. My older brother Gary put the roof on. I was up on the top at twelve carrying shingles to him as he nailed them down. Once the roof was on, we installed the exterior windows and doors. I remember them being a significant expense, and arguments ensued over the most expensive one. Loretta insisted on a bay window on the front of the home. Harry acquiesced to Loretta's desire but warned there might be some delay in other things being done, and she agreed.

Harry would remain back in Long Island during the week, continuing to work for two more years as he drove the eight-hour trip every weekend, giving me new tasks to complete the small unfinished ranch we lived in. One of the first things to finish was the bathroom to have a sink and running water as the kitchen was not yet installed. I watched and learned how to install a toilet, plumbing, and hook up sinks and faucets.

That first winter, we lived in the home without sheetrock walls, with only the bare insulation shielding us from the outer walls. I temporarily installed insulation on the interior walls for privacy in the primary bedroom and the bathroom until sheetrock could be had. I was instructed to insulate all the walls and ceiling of the home, and I would learn how to drill holes through the 2 x 4 structure wall and pull wiring.

The following summer, my great uncle Karl, from my dad's side, would help install the exterior split shingles that would side the home. I followed his lead and installed many of them following his direction. It wouldn't be until the following summer that we would nail up the sheetrock on the interior walls and finish with doors and trim. One more year after that, my older brother Gary would install the flooring and carpeting, and then came the kitchen. Finally, the main level of the house inside and out was completed except for the basement floor.

This was a big life move for Loretta and Harry, moving to a small town eight hours away in upstate NY. There was no internet then, and long-distance telephone calls were expensive. This distance would separate us all immensely in more ways than one.

Harry moved the queen out of the city to Baldwin, and now he was driving her to the country. The new home and town were physically far from everything Loretta knew and desired, except this was also her choice. The distance would create long periods of absence from my older siblings and the rest of our family. For the worse, though, the checks and balances…the stabilizers to Loretta's behavior, my Aunt Elisabeth and Uncle Eddy, Aunt Helen, her sister, and some cousins who visited Loretta on weekends, would now be twice-yearly visitors.

For me, I was so excited about the move. I hoped that the day I woke up in upstate New York in our new home would be a new birth. I was hoping to open my eyes one morning, and everything would be perfect. Moving upstate was an imaginary feeling of liberation, like getting out of the boxes I was trapped in.

Having avoided most opportunities for trouble as an elementary student, I was extremely anxious over the large Baldwin Jr. High school I'd be attending. A neighborhood kid a few years older than me, Jack would share horror stories about the drugged kids in the Jr. High he was attending. He told me about the bullies who pressured him and others into trying weed and speed. His stories scared me to death and made me anxious. Jack said he'd protect me if I went to Baldwin South Jr. High where he was, but he'd be in ninth grade and only there for me for one year.

I was looking to escape his box too. Jack was almost three years older than me. We had a non-sexual, although risky, relationship which started as show and tell in a refrigerator box behind our home when I was in third grade. Later years in the summer, we would strip to our shorts and lose our shirts to sunbathe naked along a wooded stream between Freeport and Baldwin. It was innocent enough until one day in the summer before I'd enter the sixth grade, and he in the eighth, he jumped me while we were sunbathing and started trying to kiss me on the lips. "Get off me, you queer," I demanded.

"I'm not queer," he retorted.

"Yes you are… what are you trying to do?" I blasted at him as I pushed him off.

"I just wanted to practice kissing a girl!" He pleaded.

"Well, I'm not a girl. Kiss someone else," I told him. His body was changing from mine. He had hair in his armpits and elsewhere. He scared me to death; it was the last time he and I sunbathed together again. While he invited me several times after the queer attack, I found some excuses to avoid hanging with Jack. My only regret was that I might lose his protection in Jr. High as, at the time, I still didn't know we were moving upstate.

Once I learned we were moving upstate, I was relieved not to go to Baldwin Jr. High School. Over the years, I'd seen riots, fights, and stabbings at the football games, and for all the other fear Jack had instilled in me, I could only imagine what my older sister had gone through. Most of all I was hoping the move upstate would help Loretta to be happy. Loretta seemed more content when we were up there; I thought life with her would dramatically improve, but that was not to be the case. I would know and experience more traumatic abuse and insecurity than I'd have ever known before. Harry wouldn't move up for two more years finishing his 20 years toward union retirement. While the Long Island routine was he'd come home to occasionally beat us in the evenings due to Loretta's rants and complaints, he was there every day to tame the beast inside her. Now he'd only arrive on weekends.

I also had to give up that part of life that seemed to be the only good part of my existence as a child: the likes of occasional visits to Nathan's Clam shack in Coney Island, a weekly stop at the local Jewish bakeries for their bagels, rye bread and poppy seed rolls; the Good Humor Truck, Five and Ten Dime Stores, Woolworths Soda Fountain, and most disappointing, the paper route which gave me my eleven-year-old version of financial independence. All of these adolescent food luxuries I found comfort in disappeared. Lost were the biweekly visits to my cousins, my aunts, my brother and sister, and other relatives, which seemed to, at the moments and time they visited, calm Loretta's behavior from day-to-day.

Van Etten had a population of 700, a Tasty Freeze, a Gulf gas station and laundromat, Ben's Food Mart, Ed's barbershop (I liked Ed, he was kind of like a grandpa), the Banfield Hardware store, Larison's Feed Mill, a couple of churches, and The Mchann and Van Etten Hotels from a bygone horse-drawn era which consisted of several guest rooms but were mainly just old saloons where plenty of the local drunks hung out.

Spencer, the next town to the east of Van Etten, was a dry town with no alcohol sold anywhere, no Tasty Freeze, just The Big M food mart, which gave Loretta an alternative to Ben's Food Mart with an additional five-mile drive. It had three churches, an ARCO gas station, a Tioga State Bank, a small Ford Dealer (with a car lot of about 15 and a repair shop), and a post office. In these two little towns, I would take on puberty, develop relationships, grow through my teen years and take the most formative rides of my life.

There was no Good Humor in our neighborhood… in more ways than one; we didn't even live in a community. We lived alone on a one-lane dirt road with weeds growing up the middle. We had to walk a mile to the school bus stop straddling muddy ruts from the tires of our car and the mailman's truck, the only daily traffic. The bus could not make it up to our house and would not for fear of safety to the other passenger students. Our nearest neighbor with any children our age was about three miles away.

Rodman's Gulf gas station, five miles down the dirt and gravel road from our home with its freezer full of popsicles, was our substitute for the Good Humor Truck that would never come again to our home. It was a difficult five miles to ride a bike, and though there were few, each car or truck that did pass us left us in a mile-long cloud of dust to tint our hair and clog our nostrils and lungs. This was not the paved sidewalk of Baldwin's Grand Avenue to the Caravel Ice Cream or Powers candy store.

We trekked the five miles often to escape Loretta. She never seemed to care that a twelve-year-old with his nine-year-old sister was gone miles away for most of the day. In fact, she gave us quarters for the popsicles as I no longer had any source of earning spending money. She viewed it as a way for us to spend our idle time and get us out of her hair. What she did with all the time she had alone is a mystery but based upon the monthly arguments whether the phone bill would be paid or not, one could assume she was on the phone long distance complaining about her new life in the hills to everyone back in Long Island.

There was forced labor weekly assigned to us by Harry to keep us out of the house and Loretta's hair. We raked rocks out of the clay dirt surrounding our home, eventually turning it into a lawn. After a half-day of that each day we'd spend four hours round trip going to and from the Village of Van Etten just to get an ice cream bar with the change Loretta flipped our way, sometimes twice a day in the summer months if Loretta was in one of her particularly sour moods.

Seventh and eighth grades were brutal. Trekking a mile down and then back up again on a mud-laden or snowy dirt road every day to a bus left our feet wet and either caked with mud or frozen. It was challenging to make friends and break into the already established clicks as a new kid in town and school. My Long Island accent gave me away for sure as the new kid on the block, and as was typical, the first kids to latch onto the new kid were the heads… referring to the underclass dogs of the school who smoked pot, took drugs, and engaged in sexual encounters of one sort or another. It hadn't been any different than in the fifth and sixth grade in Baldwin, except I had established friends to hop, skip, and jump from depending upon the behavior I was witnessing or experiencing. I had a false hope that it would be better in a rural town.

For all the help and work I had done at home, my dad bought me a 90 cc Honda motorcycle. It couldn't have been timelier as that Stingray I'd gotten in the third grade was worn out, and the seat and handlebar height adjustment had reached its max two years earlier.

The Honda enabled me to explore the hills as much as my dad would supply me with gas, and it allowed me to visit and befriend some of the local heads that lived within a good motorcycle ride during the summer. While I didn't have a license, I rode the dirt roads and veered off when the occasional car passed. They were the only friends I found, and I maintained them until I could meet others through team sports like basketball and track. I tried to participate in fitting in while also maintaining just enough distance not to be engulfed in some of the amoral and mischievous behaviors they'd pursue.

Life just really sucked, and it sucked, even more, the day I was riding my motorcycle through a fresh-cut hayfield when it caught fire. I didn't know what had happened, except that suddenly I looked down and my pants below my knees were on fire. I jammed the brakes and leaped off the motorcycle, dropping it onto a row of tethered hay. I slapped my hands on my pants to put out the flames and then kicked piles of hay back from my burning bike. As I watched the fire, I was terrified they'd spread to the grass. My heart was raging and beating through my chest! Black smoke billowed high into the sky from the rubber seats and tires burning. The smoke, the sweat, and the hay dust from kicking hay as far away from the bike as possible clouded my vision, and the air was so hot from the heat of the day and flames I felt like I was in hell. With the hay clear and slight burns to my hands, I watched as the fire grew less and less until there was nothing left to burn. The fire died out, and so did my heart.

I left the bike barely smoldering and walked several miles back to my house in melancholy and silence. I borrowed my dads' pickup truck and drove it through the back roads to the field where I could lift what was left of my bike into the pickup truck. I was fourteen but already had learned to drive a bulldozer, backhoe, tractor, pickup, and Willy's jeep in the span of the last two years living in upstate. I was a natural with wheels.

For such a short time, I had freedom with that bike exploring abandoned old horse-drawn buggy roads traversing over the hills and through the forests and on old logging trails and gas pipeline clearings. I'd often be gone for whole days just exploring the countryside and surrounding dirt roads, and even if gas were low, I'd find my way back to some waterfalls or cool spots in the forest I discovered and just hang.

Chapter Seven
Genesee Cream Ale

1971 – 1972
Playlist:
Hitchin' A Ride, Live Marit Wedvik
Cracklin' Rosie, Neil Diamond
Spirit in the Sky, Norman Greenbaum
Fire and Rain, James Taylor
American Pie, Don McLean
Day After Day, Badfinger

Aside from riding my Stingray back and forth to Rodman's Gulf station, I also spent time that first and second summer in upstate hanging out with a mixed bag of boys ages from the oldest 16, my age of 12, and down to eight. They lived just a half-mile in the opposite direction from Rodman's Gulf station, and that was the smoothest last half mile of our biking trek as it was a paved highway.

These kids and a group of other local kids loved to hang out at a swimming hole in Cayuga creek. It was a picturesque deep hole carved in a slight bend in the creek bound by two clay-covered banks where high or drunk teens sculpted all sorts of imagined or known sexual positions and depictions out of clay.

Some of them had the sculpting skills of Michael Angelo and created vivid and realistic clay models that made me feel like I'd sinned just by looking at them.

A short run and leap on a rope hanging from one side of the bank could land you across to the other side, where one could strategically land to slide down its slippery clay slope into the hole. A continuous flow of fresh cool water flushed you clean of your clay-claddened body and instantly replenished the hole with clean, clear water for the next jumper.

It was an idyllic landscape, a page out of a Huckle Berry Fin book, a Creekside oasis on a hot country summer day with the katydids chirping in the trees and enough humidity to hear the corn stalks in adjacent fields cracking. It could be a solitary and serene place, and then your time there would be interrupted by a raging freight train that would pass or teenage boys who hung out making out with their girlfriends, smoking dope and drinking whiskey.

In the fifth grade, my best friends in Baldwin started stealing whisky from their parent's liquor cabinets. I stayed clear of participating, worried that I'd already had enough troubles at home just trying to be a normal kid, and I wasn't begging for more with a risk of being caught drinking.

I thought leaving the city-influenced areas of Long Island and moving to a rural area would surround me with a higher quality set of friends. The fact was that drinking whiskey and beer was even more prevalent among rural kids with nothing else to do, particularly those not living on farms, than those in the city and suburbs. And when a new kid came into school, it was always the sordid element to be the first approach and offered their friendship, and with it came opportunities, such as cigarettes, drugs, alcohol, and sex.

I managed to stay away from that first summer of whiskey and the other elements, but in seventh grade, in a new school, the boy from New York City as my accent had identified me was soon surrounded by all of the kids known as the "heads" or the "bad elements". Most everyone already had their "groupies" of friends from elementary school. A hip kid from the city was undoubtedly faster and further along the narcotics trail than the local heads one would think and made me attractive to them, and the groupies of "cool" kids stayed clear!

After meeting some my age that lived closer to home, with no other options, the summer after seventh grade, I found myself hanging with a bunch from age 10 to 14 and camping out most of the summer. They introduced me to Jenny. No, not some local girl like my sixth-grade girlfriend; Jenny referred to Genesee Beer, a local upstate New York favorite produced near the Genesee River.

Genesee beer could be purchased in the off-sale bars of the Mchann and Van Etten Hotels, but not by us. We got it from the local cop's son, who got it from some eighteen-year-old (legal drinking age at the time), and in turn, sold cases of the stuff to us to which we'd stash a few yards off the road in a field until nightfall would come and we'd consume it. For whatever reason, Genesee Cream Ale was the favorite among the rascals I hung with, but if the hotels were sold out of it, a regular Jenny was sufficient.

At first, I took sips and managed to dump most of the can of beer out while no one was looking, just trying to fit in. But it wasn't long, and I got caught by one of the boys dumping my beer while taking a piss. At that moment of shame and denial, I had to prove I could down not just one, but two or three in front of the gang. Three full warm beers in my belly had me feeling its effects almost immediately, and it became easier to join in from then on. We drank copious amounts of it, getting smashed until we'd pass out.

Hanging with these hillbilly rascals was undoubtedly more fun than hanging around the house with Loretta, although it seemed to have a different set of potential consequences and risks.

My whole life seemed crazy; I hardly had any money to chip in for the beer but gave what little I had. I'd ask Loretta for a couple of bucks for hot dogs to contribute to the night of camping. Sometimes she'd give it to me, and sometimes she just gave me a package of hot dogs, which would be my contribution. The eldest of us had a job and often had enough money to supply the rest of us with beer.

We'd tell our parents we were camping on a hill behind my friend's house. Once it was dark, we retrieved and hauled our stashed cases of Genesee with us as we walked the endless country dirt roads. Drinking, singing to the stars, dreaming, and scheming about the girls in school we wanted to make out with, telling stupid stories and jokes, we all laughed our way into the wee hours of the morning at just about anything that was said under the influence of the booze. When we ran out of beer, we'd turn around and piss our way back to our campsite or old barn that we found to hang out.

I loved looking up into the stars as we walked the roads feeling the buzz of the beer, the dew of the night air, and feeling awe at them. They were brilliant, zillions and zillions of them shining the brightest in a clear non humid night.

The Milky Way was often so visible, and then a rumble in the distance would soon lead to a cloud of dust!

Sometimes a car or pickup truck might intrude on our marches, and when they did, we'd scatter into the roadside woods or field, ducking into the weeds out of site to let them pass. The dirt from Rumsey Hill would fill the air from the passing vehicle and usually left a cloud of dust hanging over us for at least the next mile of marching the rural dirt.

At times with the night air so hot and humid and all of us sweating from the beer-drinking, we sometimes couldn't hear a vehicle approaching above the incredible night sound of the tree frogs and crickets and had to scramble. Diving and leaping into the road ditch weeds, we'd duck low and watch as the beams of light from the headlights peered over the hill and approached. If we'd suddenly see some headlights, we'd all shout, "Car! Car! Car!" and leap from the road as our hearts would pound with mischievous adrenaline and alcohol flowing through our veins while our lungs breathed heavily with a frantic nervousness over getting caught. The smell of hay, or in the fall, a wet dew and Golden Rod would permeate our nostrils until the vehicle passed and cover our clothes with pollen and dust from leaping through it.

It was always an exhilarating feeling of escape and bravado when it happened. Knowing the driver and passengers in the passing car or pickup didn't notice us gave us all a sense of joy and escape that we'd gotten away with our mischief and dodged getting caught once again. Avoiding the cars didn't mean we dodged our nerves over the worry of being caught nor a tribesmen's nervous stomach invoked into vomiting. Of course, the Genesee volumes in our bellies helped a lot too. More than one of us had usually puked our guts out anyhow, and we longed for a spot to rest in our sleeping bags, so we'd return to our campsite for the evening.

Sometimes we'd find an abandoned barn to sleep in, which kept the morning dew off us, but mostly we slept in some field where we could build a campfire and keep the bugs away with it smoldering throughout the night. All of us would wake up hungover with our heads covered by our sleeping bags until the morning sun evaporated the dew off our bags and shoes.

Another favorite activity with the tribe was BB Gunfights. I didn't own a BB gun, so my friend Rogan lent me one of his. These were real BB guns, and you often had a big welt to prove it if you got shot by one. The only rule was that the shot had to be below the chest to ensure we didn't shoot our eyes out.

We hunted each other! Dashing into the woods, sneaking behind fences and around the barn, stalking each other like wild animals. It was a bit more realistic than the play army games I'd left in Long Island.

These summer nights and days were not just here and there. None of our parents would give us money for all the nights we wanted to camp out. And the constables' son wasn't always available either.

Rogan's dad had reserves if we couldn't get the beer from the constable's son, or we didn't have enough money for it! He made barrels of homemade wine every year from grapes he'd acquire from one of the many finger lake vineyards nearby. His boys would generously drain a gallon here, a gallon there, from one of his five or six 55-gallon barrels. So, when the Cream Ale wasn't affordable, potent grape juice was. We just stole it, and I have to include myself as I participated as the only skinny guy who could slip through the cellar window to fill a jug.

The wine lay a faster drunk in all of us than any Cream Ale. There were nights of us singing and dancing around the fire so intoxicated that I could hardly believe no one in the hills that surrounded us hadn't heard us and driven up the logging road leading to our favorite hillside to catch us. Some mornings when I woke up, I had no memory of when or how I got into my sleeping bag and fell asleep. I would wake up with such a pounding headache I thought my brain was dying, and it would last nearly two days.

By eighth grade, I was pretty much surrounded by some of the worst kids Spencer and Van Etten had to offer. I had two different groups of friends. Those down by the railroad tracks and the Cream Ale tribe. Near the tracks and stream I'd witnessed some make-out sessions and other sexual acts that, at the time, I was too immature to understand. It seemed the rail-road gang I hung with were always high on weed or something else and not cognizant of any of their surroundings or who was with or watching them. One of them taught me how to beat off when I wasn't even old enough to ejaculate. The alcohol, drugs, it all scared me to death.

I managed to hang with them all trying not to get involved beyond the alcohol. Through the year and into the following summer, I became a trusted member of the Cream Ale tribe. All of us less than 13 years old, my trust from them and my other group of friends was running thin. My ability to sidestep the pressure to participate in other high-inducing substances became increasingly noticeable and more challenging to remain a part of the group without experiencing it. I had to escape. I was trying desperately to make different friends in high school as I noticed a distinction in the type of kids that went out for sports versus those who didn't.

Those in sports were called the jocks, and those who werent' were generally referred to as the heads. The heads were the brave ones, taking no shit from the jocks or teachers, smoking the weed, getting drunk, getting sex, and always willing to pick a fight with a jock at any time. I was never sure if they were courageous or just crazy from the drug use, but they were a threatening bunch.

My science teacher, a minister, and a high school track coach, Donald Miller, pulled me aside and encouraged me to join basketball. I'll never know why he pulled me aside, but perhaps he saw me as the new kid sucked in by the heads and saw my efforts to seek other friendships. He brought me guidance and strongly encouraged me to join his track team in the spring. I followed Mr. Millers' advice and joined the basketball team. I sucked at basketball and hardly ever got to play except for the last few minutes of the game when the token third string I was on would be sent in to break enough of a slight sweat to deserve showering with the rest of the team.

There were games where I never needed a shower because I never got to play. Playing basketball or not as a teammate was a three-year humiliation event in front of jocks and the parents who came to the games. I took plenty of mockery as a benchwarmer and how much I sucked at the game. Through association on these teams, I slowly began to prove myself out to some of the better kids in the school and tried to earn their friendship, but it wasn't without a price.

Even though I sucked at everything in sports except some track events, I flourished at least in the benefit of escaping my home life. I indeed received a lot of bullying and chiding about being so tall and clumsy and not dropping the ball through a hoop, but my friends soon became the other third-string jocks who took the chiding and understood our positions and places in the pecking order.

Unfortunately, some of those third-string jocks got bullied so much they eventually found themselves as "quitters." That was the ultimate unforgiving and unforgettable jock sin to which you would be shunned and abandoned with the only option left to join the heads if you wanted any sort of friendship.

The major problem with any friends I made was that most of them were not within walking or biking distance to hang out and a ride from Loretta was out of the question. I was still stuck with my Cream Ale buddies in the summers until the oldest of our tribe got his license. We were both in the ninth grade, but he was a year older. Once he had a car and could freely roam the countryside, there was less interest in the Genesee camps and walks and more interest in cruising.

Our midnight walks became midnight cruises drinking and driving in the rural hills of Van Etten. To feed the habit and the gas tank, we were becoming thieves. The first time Rogan backed his car up to the town highway trucks parked miles and miles from town on a dirt road, my heart pounded insanely as I sat in the back seat with the others as he siphoned off gas from them into his gas tank. All I could think about was getting caught by some passing car that would surely see his car stand out against the construction orange highway trucks, and my living hell at home would turn into a blast furnace. I was scared to death to be in the car when that happened. I was scared to death at everything and repentant that I was even with the Cream Ale tribe.

"Isn't there some other way," I'd ask? "You got any money, Riess?" I'd be asked and I would fall silent as I had none. "Why don't we just go back and camp instead?" "If you want to go camp, go ahead? The rest of us are riding."

"Don't be a wimp, Riess," I'd hear from a clan member, "we won't get caught."

Ha, I thought to myself. *I'd be the first to be blamed.* They would blame the city kid as the bad influence on their innocent country boys. I'd be lynched as quickly as a black man in the early south, and I'd be the sacrificial lamb in this clan of boys who'd known each other since they were babies.

Stealing gas repeated itself two more times while I was a passenger partaking in the Cream Ale runs. I wasn't and didn't want to be a thief, and I felt shame in myself for just being a witness. After the third time, I never rode with Rogan again except to catch an occasional ride to school, and that ended quickly as the smell of cigarettes and early morning weed-filled his car to the point I'd get car sick, and you could smell it on my clothes. Humbly I refused the rides and got back on the bus the rest of the year.

Getting caught with Rogan in the act of stealing gas from a town truck, no matter how remote that was at two in the morning, five miles from town, on a rural road, simply wasn't a risk, no matter how small I could afford. I gave up all parts of the friendships that required gas, drugs, smoking, and alcohol.

Ninth grade was a lonely year. The one good friend I developed from the basketball team quit under the bullying pressure and gravitated toward the heads. Like me, he wasn't very good at the sport, and the jocks just bullied him out. It wasn't long before he smoked weed regularly and attended the abundant head parties. While I could have certainly made choices to participate further or more deeply, the ever threat from Loretta was a boy's home waiting for me near the Hudson River. Without friends, I would go it alone rather than risk getting caught and experiencing any more wrath from Loretta and her insanity at home. And Harry was finally living with us again full time, and he was watching me closely.

Chapter Eight
The Snow Storm

Our driveway 1972
Playlist:
Hitchin' A Ride, Live Marit Wedvik
Cracklin' Rosie, Neil Diamond
Spirit in the Sky, Norman Greenbaum
Fire and Rain, James Taylor
American Pie, Don McLean
Day After Day, Badfinger

Our first experience of living upstate in the winter saw snowfall after snowfall. My dad had purchased a 1965 Ford Comet for Loretta the previous summer, and that car was excellent in the snow; yet, Loretta would manage to land it into a snowbank or ditch, to which I would have to walk any remaining miles home to fetch a Willy's jeep or a tractor to pull her out of the ditch. She obsessed with Harry that she hated that car, and it wasn't any good in the snow.

I knew it was mostly her poor skills at driving through the deep ruts in our road.

The storms of the winter kept piling snow higher and higher. The banks on either side of our one-lane road were taller than the car's height, and I was becoming adept at using our tractor to plow out our driveway.

Having signed up for basketball in the seventh grade I had practice every night after and on some Saturdays games.

Loretta complained obsessively about picking me up from basketball practice or after Saturday games, so I often had to miss practice unless the weather was decent enough for her to drive. If she thought the weather would be bad, she would tell me to take the bus home or find another ride. Sometimes I simply walked the seven miles home from high school when hitchhiking efforts failed as the activity kept me absent from the house, and it was worth it, but bitter cold often left me out of that option.

One particularly snowy Saturday in February, Loretta drove me to school to catch an away basketball game bus. We didn't get very far. The roads were icy, and a frozen mud rut threw her out of control. As the Comet gained speed down the hill, it slid up the snowbank. The bumper and grill of the Comet flung snow across the hood and windshield, blinding us from what we might collide with ahead. The car bounced back off the snowbank and spun around several times until it rested against the opposite snowbank. We both looked at each other in shock. Loretta panicked, "I think we flipped over, she gasped!" it was the first real car accident I'd ever been in.

Our windshield and windows were covered with snow, but we sat upright. I tried to exit my door, but the snow had blocked my ability to open it and get out. The car was still running. Loretta turned on the wipers. We were now facing uphill, the direction from which we came. Loretta tried to move the car pressing the accelerator, it didn't move. I managed to crawl into the back seat and exit through the back door on the driver's side. I could see where we sped through the snowbank and landed on the other side of the road.

After several more attempts to get the car to move, she gave up. "The wheels aren't even spinning," I told her, and I began my trek home to fetch the tractor to pull her out of the snowbank.

I pulled Comet back up the hill and parked it in the south part of our yard. There was a bad leak of red oil in the snowbank where I retrieved Comet.

Upon returning home, Loretta immediately got on the phone with Harry and demanded a new car. She told him that we had flipped the car over in a snowbank, and it was no longer usable. Doubting her story, he asked to speak to me. "What happened, Curt?"

"We slid off the road," I responded. "We flipped over," Loretta shouted in the background. "Did you flip over," Harry asked? "I don't know," I responded. Though I knew we didn't flip over as there was no damage to the roof or body of the car, I didn't want to get crosswise with Loretta's story out of fear of reprisal.

"Did you try to move the car?" Harry asked.

"No, I didn't, but mom did, and when we got it on the road, the wheels wouldn't turn. I had to tow it home with the tractor. There was a lot of red oil from under the car in the snowbank where I pulled it out."

"The transmission lines!" Harry surmised. "That would mean the transmission is probably shot if you tried to run it without fluid," he again thought out loud. "Put your mother back on the phone," he demanded.

It was evident from overhearing Loretta's side of the conversation that Harry would simply find another car for Loretta and bring it up with him the following weekend. I was banned from any more basketball practices and games until she got another car. She didn't want me trekking the seven-mile walk in the middle of winter in case she had to go look for me and she didn't have a car.

While I explained the situation to my coaches, they understood, my teammates did not. They gave me a hard time for missing practices, knowing I was in school that week during the day, but absent after school because I needed the bus ride home. They chided me as a quitter, not knowing the issues or that we didn't have a car.

Harry brought Loretta another used Ford. When he looked over Comet, he saw no visible damage that reflected a roll-over. Loretta continued to insist, she had flipped over, as that is the story she sent back to Long Island. When he asked me again in front of Loretta whether we had flipped over or not, I simply said, "It is whatever she says it is."

Chapter Nine
Earning Comet

1973

Playlist:

Hold Your Head Up, Argent

Everything I Own, Bread

You Don't Mess Around With Jim, Jim Croce

Doctor My Eyes, Jackson Brown

Taxi, Harry Chapin

After Loretta plowed through the snowbank with the Comet, the car sat in our barn along with some old horse-drawn farm implements for almost three years. I used to sit in Comet as a twelve and thirteen-year-old, dreaming of driving and owning it.

It was May 6th, my fourteenth birthday. While sitting at the dinner table waiting for a birthday cake, I asked my dad, "Do you think I could have the Ford Comet to fix up?" He looked at me with his typical stern German look, and after a long pause, he said sternly… "no." After a few more seconds of silence, he said, "but you could earn it!"

"How can I earn it?" I eagerly asked. He looked at me sternly again and pointed out the window in the direction of the barn which Comet sat in; "tear down that barn," he said.

I would have to tear down that old wobbly barn that he had moved from across the road a few years back because Loretta complained it blocked her view of the valley below from her front picture window.

He had wrapped the exterior post and beam form with braided cables and put a car chassis under each main support beam to enable the structure to roll. In my tiny eyes at the time, it was a fantastic feat! With one of my older brothers behind the steering wheel of a Ford truck, the other behind a jeep, and my dad on a small bulldozer, they pulled that barn nearly 200 feet from its original location. In my eyes he accomplished what so few men could do!

I walked and stood in front of the colossal doorway that once upon a time opened to horse-drawn wagon loads of hay. Before mechanical hay balers, giant tongs fell from the sky of the haymow to capture the swaths pitched onto the wagons. They would be hand pulleyed up into the mow. The hand-hewn barn was typical sized in its day. It was 75 feet tall to the roof ridge, about 40 feet wide by 60 feet long.

The steel cables used to hold it together during the move still wrapped tightly around the structure like a Christmas bow holding the package together to keep it from falling apart. Relocating it was a pretty proud moment for my dad, mainly because it didn't collapse as he moved it. If I cut one of those cables, the whole thing would come precariously tumbling down. My dad knew this which is why he left all the cables wrapped around it for years, but wouldn't admit to his folly and mistake of moving it in the first place.

Sitting where it rested in the dirt, no longer with a rock foundation hastened the rotting of the bottom perimeter beams to which the entire upper structure rested. The balloon skeleton had become so weakened from the move that he never felt secure enough to jack up the frame and reintroduce cement pilings or footings. It was leaning badly as well.

I walked around that barn and surveyed each corner, wall, and cable. I looked at every joint and notch where wooden pegs held the beams together. I climbed its posts to the loft, looked up at the roof, and saw a million stars peeping through the old cedar shingles, stars made by the sun in broad daylight shining through the dark underside of the roof.

For a few self-doubting moments, there was self-pity as I leaned against a support beam well-worn and smoothed by some long-ago cows rubbing their necks. Did my dad want me to have this car? Was he expecting me to say forget it, I can't do it? Did he say sure, you can earn it thinking and betting I couldn't do it?

I crawled and climbed inside the structure, examining every crevasse and metal strap holding together the post and beam skeleton. I stared again at the millions of sunlight stars created from the rusted-out nail holes in the old cedar shake shingles. The beams were massive, most 14 x 14 inches, with lengths of 50 feet. The loft floor was made of planks some twenty inches wide by two to three inches thick, yet even they were rotting in places where the roof had leaked. I took mental pictures of the entire structure from corner to corner, roof ridge to ground, and exterior perimeter. I looked closely at the outer cross beams.

The craftsman who built this barn did a fine job, but they fixed the nail downward from their hammer blows on the siding. The structural beams rotted because the farmer didn't refresh the siding with paint to prevent the nails from rusting. A hundred years of rain and no paint to seal them from the elements rusted the nails. Rain followed the rusted nail deep into the core of the beam, where its moisture and mold quietly ate away its strength.

These rotted beams would have easily severed long ago in a storm, or a high wind had the cables not held in place. I had windstorms blowing about me as well, but in some way, I too had a cord wrapped around me, holding me together like the barn.

I often felt like that old barn looked, ready to crumble to the ground, but a cable of some sort was wrapped around me, holding me together for something better down the road.

I can do this, I thought. And if I could, I'd own that Comet and have a way of escape. I was only 14, but I had all the dumb kid confidence in the world that I could tear the thing down board by board. I ran back to the house and let my dad know I was up to the challenge.

"How soon can I begin?" I asked.

"As soon as you want." He said. "You can begin by pulling all the stuff out of that barn and emptying it."

"What do I do with all the wood?" I asked. "Stack what is salvageable into a pile and cut the rest up for firewood. After you have torn it down, we'll use the salvageable wood to build a smaller barn to house the cows across the road from where the barn came from," Harry instructed.

I was excited as hell! It was the best birthday present I'd ever received, even if I did have to work for it. I was so excited I could kiss the sky, and I soon would be walking the ridges of that roof, tearing the shingles and rafters away.

On the other hand, Loretta wasn't so excited over the idea. "Why can't you just give the damn car to him?" she demanded. "You gave your other son a car." An argument between them ensued immediately. "You'll do anything for your bastard kid from your first wife, but my kids get nothing. He'll get killed tearing that thing down; how is he going to lift any of those beams?" she asked.

"Settle down, I can do it. I want to do it!" I said. "Stop arguing over it; I can do it. I'll cut them to sizes I can handle with the chainsaw." I said.

I did not want to lose this opportunity.

"And I'll rig up a boom on the stake truck for him to use to help him lower the ones we want to save," said my dad. Loretta ranted on. She was obsessively anxious and against me getting up on the roof of that barn. "Loretta shut your God damn mouth," Harry retorted. I silently couldn't have agreed more and left the kitchen.

I couldn't wait another second. I immediately went out and began emptying what contents I could by hand. And since the grass was green and getting greener, I moved the cows back to the pasture across the road. They wouldn't need any shelter until next winter, and hopefully, I'd have this barn down. I'd build another smaller structure made for them before then with salvageable lumber.

By the last day of school before summer vacation, I had that barn emptied and was already pulling off siding where the cables didn't obstruct me from doing so. That summer, I worked from sunup to sundown every single day. Board by board, tearing that old barn apart, rafter and beam by rafter and beam, nail by nail until finally, I had a few scattered piles of boards, beams, and firewood. It took me six weeks resting only for water and meals. Besides the fact that I actually did this, what was amazing to me was how small the piles of siding, beams, and wood seemed when they were stacked up. Such a substantial massive monument could probably hold about 20 semi-trailers double-stacked side by side inside. And when you piled up all the skin and bones, they could easily all fit in a third of one semi-trailer. In reality, it was just a giant balloon, void and empty on the inside except for the air within.

It was interesting how the structure was so much larger than life until I dismantled it. For weeks, I pondered what I did and how I looked differently at that barn. I wondered whether I could apply this to myself in some way, make myself look larger? I thought about the bullies in school? Are they just big and hollow? The issues within our home, are they hollow? Are things a lot easier to do than one thinks? Dismantling that barn left me as a fourteen-year-old looking at the world a different way.

Six weeks into the summer, the barn was down, and I had six weeks left before school started again. I stayed clear of the Cream Ale tribe. I would give my dad more than he asked. Together we surveyed what was salvageable and laid out a plan to build a much smaller barn across the road for winter shelter for the cows. With help from my dad and some old steel roofing he purchased, we had constructed a lean-to structure that could house the cows we had and store enough hay for winter feeding by the end of that September.

Harry made good on his promise; the title to the Comet was signed over to me.

The first thing I bought for it was some gas and a battery. I could sit in the car periodically throughout the winter, dreaming of the day I could drive it, I could hear the engine running and listen to tunes on the radio. Even if it didn't budge an inch because the transmission was shot, I could turn the steering wheel and feel the whine of the power steering pump and knew soon, I'd be cruising in my Comet. Oh, Jimi Hendrix, excuse me while I kissed the sky.

Chapter Ten
Larison's Feed Mill

1974
Playlist:
Goodbye Yellow Brick Road, Elton John
Midnight Rider, Gregg Allman
Rhinestone Cowboy, Glen Campbell
Philadelphia, Freedom, Elton John

Sitting behind the wheel of that car all winter and listening to my favorite tunes motivated me. No matter what it took, I was determined to earn money to buy the transmission it needed and some paint, new tires, and a few other parts. I could hardly wait to turn 16 and get these wheels licensed and on the road.

Following an old farm trail through the forest and over the same hill where I burned up my motorcycle was the Larison farm. Sitting in that car with a "D" on the shifting column, which meant DRIVE, and the fact that it went nowhere when it was engaged, drove me crazy. The farmer also owned the local feed mill in our village. I had done some hay bale lifting and stacking for him since I was twelve in the summers, but I couldn't wait for the summer haying season to start.

I hiked over to Larison's Farm and asked Archie if I could work in his feed mill on weekends. "We're only open on Saturdays, but I can find you some things to do," he promised. That February, every Saturday morning, I hiked or snowmobiled through the woods and over the hill to Archie Larison's farm to hitch a ride with him in his Red and White Dodge Pickup down to the feed mill. All-day long, I either filled 100-pound feed sacks and stacked them or swept and vacuumed an endless supply of grain dust into a dumpster. Some days I went out into the frigid cold with a driver named Jerry Garland and a portable grain grinder to which I shoveled some farmer's ear corn from his bin into the hopper of a mobile truck grinder. It was hard work, but I never complained as all I saw through all this was a moving Comet.

It was perhaps the most strenuous year of work in my life between that barn and those feed sacks, but it was paying off in other ways than just funding a transmission. The guys in gym classes noticed my slowly developing physique of muscles and strength. I was ranking higher in the Dodge ball picks and pounding the opposing team as a force to be reckoned with. It was a physical outlet of the stress from home, and some of those poor guys had red welts from my dodgeball hits. The girls took more notice of me, too, during our shirtless lunchtime basketball games and rope climbs.

I was praying to the great Comet in the heavens that somehow, I could keep earning enough money and get the Ford Comet licensed for the road, but my weekly earnings were slow and meager. That summer, I baled hay, caught as much work in the mill as possible, and wanted to work there every day, but there wasn't enough work for me.

I even cleaned Archie's sister's chicken coops for a mere fifty cents an hour to take on any extra work opportunity. It took me five hours to clean three pens with a couple of feet of chicken crap and straw in them from years of buildup. Archie's manure spreader was parked outside the coops, where I tossed pitchfork after pitchfork of chicken crap into it. I got them done in half the time his sister and brother-in-law thought I would, so they paid me double, and I got five bucks for the whole job. It wasn't much, but every penny was counting.

No matter how hard I had to work for it, I was open to the opportunity to earn a buck. Finally, I had enough bucks to buy a used transmission out of a Ford Falcon that sat rusting away in a local junkyard. It cost me less than my first bike, twenty-five bucks, and I installed it into Comet. It wasn't too complicated to change the transmission out. Harry aided me with some instruction, and it took most of a day as I cautiously learned each step of the process.

After checking everything twice, all the transmission lines, mounting bolts, and filling up the transmission with fluid, I was ready to test it out. It had been an overcast day, and the sky was as gray as was Comet's color. I held my breath as I started up Comets engine. I got out of the front seat and immediately checked underneath the car to make sure none of the transmission lines nor the transmission were leaking fluid. It wasn't! Success! So far.

My abs ached from struggling with a transmission under a car all day, and now they ached with anxiety as I sat in the driver's seat staring at the shifting lever. I had no idea other than the junkyard owner's word that the used transmission I purchased would even work! I put the lever into the drive position. For a moment, the car held steady with no advance forward motion. Then, like a miracle, as the transmission filled its intricate cavities and endless micro tunnels in the valve body with hydraulic oil to power the drive system, Comet began to move forward. My heart was pounding, my palms sweaty. I took it slow, first around the circle driveway. Then a mile up the hill on our road to the end and back. There wasn't a slip, Comet was moving as she should. Tears began coming out of my eyes as my heart was filled with the elation of personal success in this endeavor rather than the endless days of self-pity for living under Loretta's roof.

My dad helped me paint the car silver a few weeks after the transmission changeout. It was sleek looking, and my dad did a great job. I found four chrome wheel rims with baby moon hubcaps at the junkyard where I bought the transmission. Twenty-five bucks purchased all four of them, and the tires had enough tread on them that they would pass the state safety inspection, so I'd be able to license the car next spring when I turned sixteen.

I installed an eight-track stereo player and managed to buy a few cassettes, and all that winter, I could play the Beach Boys, Eagles, Beatles, Jimi Hendrix,

Meatloaf, Bruce Springsteen, Queen, Johnny Cash, and a few other favorites. I loved all kinds of music but only had enough money for a few eight tracks, so over and over and over, those tracks would play. And I could at least drive the Comet up our dirt road and back or around the homestead and practice becoming one with my car.

Harry sternly warned me not to spend too much more of my hard work earnings on eight tracks in that I was required to buy my own automobile insurance. He had worked plenty hard in his life, inherited some, and while he let me earn that car, he also let me know that no accident on my part was going to jeopardize him losing everything he worked his life for. I had to have my own insurance policy in my own name for the car now registered in my name, and it was to be licensed in my own name. He made it very clear there would be no liability ties to him regarding that car.

I understood his message sincerely and continued to work hard and put my savings toward purchasing my first annual insurance policy the following spring when I would turn 16. It would cost me $250.00. That amount in itself seemed impossibly huge at the time, given my current wages, and there was little employment for me as winter set in, but I penciled in the amount I needed on a small piece of paper and put it in my wallet as a goal to reach. If I could just earn five bucks a week somehow, I could save enough for a down payment on insurance, license tabs, and I could get Comet on the road. It would be difficult to do on the wages, and so few hours I could get from the feed mill.

Chapter Eleven
May Day

May 1975
Playlist:
Rhinestone Cowboy, Glen Campbell
Philadelphia, Freedom, Elton John
One of These Nights, Eagles
Another Somebody Done Somebody, B.J. Thomas
That's the Way of the World, Earth, Wind and Fire
Killer Queen, Queen
Dancing In The Moonlight, King Harvest

My sixteenth birthday came the first week of May, and Comet was ready for the road, but I had no money to license and insure it. While I already had my learner's permit for six months, I had little practice on the road with either Loretta or Harry. I did have driver's education at school and simply practiced driving Comet up and down our dirt road with the bit of gas money I had. I was anxious to get my license to get another job and get my car on the road. It was three weeks since my birthday before Loretta would take me to the driver's testing station, and when she did, I failed it. I was so damn nervous and anxious. It wasn't that Loretta was with me; it was better than if my dad had brought me. She was actually consoling, telling me it took her several times. I was just a plain nervous wreck at 16 in more ways than one. Nothing in my world of being 16 made me a lot of peace and happiness.

Getting Comet road-worthy seemed like an enormous feat. From tearing the barn down, re-building another, cutting up the remaining wood into firewood, fixing ball joints, and replacing a transmission, just all of it, both exciting, stressful, and way more expensive than I had the money for. I wanted that license and the freedom of that car so badly I was in a mental state of absolute failure, self-imposed disgrace, and depression that I failed the driver's exam. It was the most self-tortuous longest three and a half weeks in my life, the time between the first failure and my second test, which I passed.

Though now licensed, rolling was another story. I still needed another $75.00 for the initial insurance premium and inspection fees. I'd exhausted all of any cash I'd earned using it for parts and buying some gas to just sit in the car and drive it up the road periodically. I exhausted my work opportunities at the feed mill too, probably being too efficient, and there really weren't many other employment opportunities in our small village for a young man. I had to find some employment, or I'd likely hang myself.

I borrowed Loretta's car and went looking for a job after school. The first place I went to was Ben's, Food Mart. It was a small grocery store where Ben, a butcher, ran the meat counter while his wife ran the rest of the shop. There wasn't any need for me. The next stop was Banfield's Hardware Store. Again, a local family-run operation which had more family members than work available for. I checked the Gulf gas station, the local dairy freeze, and exhausted the entire economic business community of my town… four businesses excluding the two bars. What else could I do?

There weren't any other farms around our hill area other than Larison's. There were a few farms I'd see along the bus ride to high school, and I thought to myself I could try there. A couple of classmates mentioned the local large chicken farms owned by the Palomaki families, but that work was seasonal. They hired high schoolers to help them pluck chickens from their cages when they sent them off to market. That would be too seasonal for me. I needed to have something steady. Plus, I could hardly stand the strong ammonia laded smell of the poultry operation every time we passed those barns in the bus.

Loretta was friendly enough to lend me her car and provide the gas while I looked for a job. It was heartbreakingly discouraging to have accomplished getting that Comet but finding no means to really use it.

Asking around in high school about opportunities, I quickly discovered that hardly anyone in our school had a job. There simply wasn't an economic base of any industry whatsoever, and most small businesses and farms had their own kids who supplied any extra labor for chores.

After a couple of weeks, I'd exhausted a five to a seven-mile radius, landing zero opportunities. I thought about a friend working in the next town over—Spencer. It seemed a bit far to go at the time, but maybe that's the direction I needed to head. Another friend suggested I try the Doc Mahlen dairy farm.

High school would be out for the summer in about three weeks, and I was determined to get myself on the road one way or another. So far, my unsuccessful job-seeking efforts had Loretta and Harry doubting I'd ever see Comet on the road. She was getting perturbed, too, in providing me the use of her car and gas money as dollars were always a tight commodity in our household, but I convinced her I would pay her back once I got a job.

And Harry, forget any more help from him. He wouldn't let me use his truck or provide any funds for job hunting. He was kind of funny after helping me get the car running. It was almost as if they helped me get the vehicle but weren't making it easy to have it. Frustrated and worn out, I planned to ask Loretta if I could borrow her car again for one more day. I would promised her I wouldn't be back until I found a job, and I would mean it. If I couldn't find one, I would abandon her car and find my own way in life. If I couldn't find a local job, I wasn't ever going back to that household. If I couldn't get Comet on the road and obtain some independence and freedom from living with Loretta 24-7, I simply wasn't coming back from that search. Sixteen years was enough for me in that household.

Early that morning, while feeding grain to our small herd of beef cows, I said goodbye to each one. I loved those animals. Between them and our dog, I had some consoling and comforting from the daily stress of the household. I let them each know I may not be back. I went and sat in the front seat of Comet. "God," I begged, "help me see my way to a job, help me to get this car rolling, help me, help me, help me," I prayed in earnest. I couldn't bear being at home any longer. Tears were streaming down my face as I prayed, tears of total self-pity, tears that wished things were different for me and everyone. None of us could do anything right, ever… and Loretta's seemingly worsening dramatic and swinging moods made an ever-tense environment. Since Harry retired and was now around all the time, his patience in everything had reached a hair-thin scale. To have to be at home one more summer and bear every day with her and Harry, their constant bickering and her erratically uncontrollable swings in emotions wasn't going to be an option. I'd rather hang myself…and sadly, I had considered it multiple times.

After the last senseless slap-happy beating with Loretta, I decided that I would run away. The only thing that had held me home was the promise of freedom through Comet. But the discouraging job hunt in our town so far had taken even that hope away from me. I was leaving, with or without Comet, one way or another.

I grabbed the small duffle bag of clothing and the few bucks of savings I had stashed in Comets back seat the night before and casually asked Loretta for the keys to her car because she was in one of her pleasant moods; she tossed them to me. "I'm not coming home until I get a job." She sensed something in my voice and stared at me but said nothing. If I couldn't find a job today, I wasn't coming back. I wouldn't steal her car; I didn't want to make anything worse for her. I'd leave it in a conspicuous place down in Sayre, Pennsylvania, where the police would find it once it was reported missing. *I'd hop a train to somewhere west, hopefully, Cleveland,* I thought, but it didn't matter. Anywhere but atop Rumsey Hill was going to be a better place.

I started that morning in earnest locally by walking into Doc Mahlen's barn while milking. He didn't need any help but suggested I head down the road to one of his neighbors. Down the road, I went. I stopped at the following four farms with dairy cows, each of them explaining they didn't need any help but encouraging me to try the next farm down the road. Ten miles seemed a long, long way to have to drive to a job for the minimum farm wage at the time. Especially when I had no money for gas and five of those ten miles was a dusty, rough gravel road. The last farmer I stopped at, I explained to him how many farms I'd been to and that they all have their own kids working with them, and maybe chasing work on dairies wasn't the direction I should continue. But the fact of the matter is there wasn't much else for employment. He said, try this guy down the road (heard that before). He's straight down route 34, about two to three miles on the curve. He's relatively new in the area, and I don't think he has any kids old enough to help. I believe his name is King. Once again, I said thank you. I was discouraged, but I wasn't giving up. Giving up meant I headed toward Sayre, PA, and I still had daylight hours ahead of me to search for something local.

Again, down the road, I went. Just past the last farm I visited was an Agway feed mill. Since I had experience in Larison's feed mill, I stopped in and inquired as to whether they needed an extra hand. A Mr. Smith worked there, and we chatted a bit about my search so far. He, too, recommended I try this King guy. He said, "King is a new customer of theirs, just moved to the farm he's on this past year, and that he was a very nice fella." He also thought that the only help he had was his aging dad. I got a little encouraged.

Agway was a feed mill with a small farm store that sold some hardware and farm hats and gloves. There was a stack of polka dot farm hats on a shelf, and I took to trying some of them on. As my favorite color had always been red, I purchased one of those hats for 50 cents. I thought it might make me stand out and look more like a farmer. Again, further down the road, I went. Every mile seemed like a hundred with the anxious alternative plans in my head. There were a couple of dairy farms along the way to the King Farm I was instructed to go to, and I almost stopped at each one, but having had two different people recommend I see this King farmer and particularly Mr. Smith's encouragement as he seemed to know Mr. King, I thought let me pass these two, and if there wasn't an opportunity at this King Dairy, I could circle back and visit them.

I'd left at seven o'clock that morning. It was about 5 pm as I left the Agway store. King's Dairy sat on a sharp curve on Route 34. The milk house was literally just far back enough from the highway to let a milk hauler pull up alongside it to collect the milk. I pulled in the driveway across the street where the farmhouse was, along with an old two-story chicken building. I knocked on the door, and a lady named Joyce appeared. "May I help you?" she asked, "Yes, my name is Curt, and I'm looking for farm work and wonder if you had any interest in hiring?"

"Well, I don't know," she replied but "go in the barn and ask my husband John. He is milking," she said. I crossed the street and entered through the barn door. I could hear a pitt-tish, pitt-tish sound coming from somewhere down the center aisle. As it was dark inside, I remember moving slowly to allow my eyes to adjust to the dim interior lighting. Walking down that center aisle, I found John King. He was kneeling between two cows massaging the cow's udder, stretching the milking machine sucking out the milk from the teats on the cow. Hi, "my name is Curt," as I introduced myself. "I'm looking for work. I've bailed hay, worked at a feed mill bagging and lifting hundred-pound sacks, know how to drive a tractor, clean pens, and am willing to do any sorts of labor." He continued to massage the cow's udder as he listened and then looked up at me. "You know how to milk?" he asked. I looked at the four-wheeled cart he had holding an extra milking machine and watched how he held pressure down on the device, stretching the cow's teats. "Yes! I have milked my neighbors' cows for him in his absence several times."

"How many cows did your neighbor have?" he asked.

"Two," I said. "I milked them by hand." He looked at me a little puzzled. "How many cows do you have here, Mr. King?" I asked.

"Sixty," he replied. "Well, I can see why you don't milk them all by hand!" I chatted enthusiastically. "I'm sure I could learn fast how to use those machines," I said as I saw a lack of confidence in his face. "Where do you live?" John quizzed. "In Van Etten," I told him. "How do you know how to drive a tractor?" he questioned. "We have a small herd of beef cows, and we have a couple of tractors for haying and plowing."

"I've done both!" I shared. "Do you have transportation?" he asked.

"Yes," I said. "I already own my own car."

"How many hours can you work?" he asked.

"I can work as many hours as you want me to. I'm done with school every day at 3:00 pm., and I'm willing to work Saturday and Sundays."

We chatted a bit more, and while we did, I watched what he did. To keep the conversation going, I asked again, "How many cows did you say you milk" I asked? "About 60 depending upon how many were dry," he responded. Dry?… I asked myself silently. I didn't know what he meant by that. I didn't want to admit to ignorance, but I also wanted him to know I wanted to and would be willing to learn. "What do you mean by dry?" I asked.

"It's when a cow doesn't give milk anymore," he said. "I put them in a dry feedlot until they give birth to another calf and then can give milk again," he said. And then he cocked his head. "Maybe you aren't as knowledgeable as some dairy farmer kid, but I like it that you have no issue with being honest about what you didn't know and that you are willing to learn."

As he took the machines off, I followed. He'd then dip each teat with an iodine cup, so at the next opportunity, I took the iodine cup, tapped the cow to the side of its stall, and dipped the teats on that cow when he was finished to show him I wasn't intimidated by these giant animals. "OK," John said. "I think I'm going to say yes, but let me talk to my wife and my dad and get back to you. I think this could work, my dad is getting on in years, and he is the only help I have besides my wife, Joyce. She is going to be having a baby, and maybe you could take over some of her chores. What is your phone number? I'll call you after I talk to them?" I told him my phone number, and it coincidentally happened that it was only one digit different than ours, and it was even closer than that in that it was sequential. The last four numbers of his were 6380, and ours was 6390! "Well, that's easy to remember." He said. "Thank you," I said. "I'll look forward to your call."

"I'll work really hard; I promise and will try never to disappoint you if you give me this opportunity. I'll stay and assist with some chores, sweep up, or anything else you would like me to do," I offered.

But he said, "I appreciate that, but no thanks."

"My dad will be here shortly to help me let the cows out when I'm done milking and sweeping up. I'll call you tonight or tomorrow." He said.

As I left the barn, I scoped out the farm carefully. The farm was a tidy and modern farm for its day. The barn was solid in appearance, with a round-arched silver metal roof. The farmhouse is stately, and all the buildings are painted white with green trim. Across the street was a cute but tiny home with another shed that appeared to house some equipment and tractors. *I could make this my home,* I thought to myself. *I could help this family, and hopefully, they could help me with an income to escape my own home.*

I felt so confident about my conversation with John King that I didn't stop at the two farms I'd passed on my way there, the Rhorda and Alves dairies. John's tone and the conversation went so well that I knew I had landed myself with at least a trial. While it wasn't immediately confirmed, the intuition God and his Holy Spirit planted in my soul was that I got the job and had to go back home and wait for a call. It was about 6:30 pm, and I immediately went home and told Loretta and Harry I'd landed a job, but the farmer just wanted to discuss it with his family and confirm. In a rare showing, Loretta expressed a little pride in this accomplishment… "see what you can do if you put your mind to it," she encouraged. Even I was so confident that I brought the duffle bag I had packed back into the house and shoved it into my closet.

Later that evening, John King called. "Hey Curt, I appreciate you coming to the farm today." He said. "I've never had farm help other than my dad, and I'd like to try this if you're still interested?"

"Oh yes, sir," I replied.

"Well, why don't you come for an hour or so after school is over, and we'll see what chores we can turn over to you?" he added. "Can you be here at four o'clock?" he asked.

"Yes, sir, I'll be there," I enthusiastically responded with "thank you, you won't be disappointed."

I borrowed Loretta's car to get to work for the first three weeks. After my first paycheck, I paid her back for all the gas I used and had barely enough to get Comet on the road. I first had to register the car with the state, get it inspected, and then get an insurance policy. All of it in my name and paid out of my wallet! I was sixteen!

I remember screwing the license plates on (which I still have to this day), placing the state inspection sticker on the windshield, walking around the whole car, and hoping that it would get me to the farm and back. So far, I'd only been driving it up the road a mile and back testing out the transmission, ball joints, and a few other parts for good working order.

The day after getting insurance on Comet, I parked it in the driveway closer to the house in preparation for the following day when I would drive it to school for the first time. What a morning it was! I walked around Comet as I had many times before in admiration and would do many more times in the future. She looked solid, dependable, and respectable with the paint job Harry helped me do. I opened the door and sat in the driver's seat. Scanning the dashboard, I inserted the key into the ignition and slowly started Comets engine. I listened to the engine purr. Then I opened my limited assortment of Eight Track Cassettes and inserted the Eagles. I adjusted the volume, rolled the window down slightly, and put Comet in reverse. It was all in slow motion, like I was in a movie. I couldn't believe I was going to back it out of the driveway and take it down the road versus hitching the railroad tracks I was scheming about just a few weeks before.

When I parked Comet in the school parking lot, it was surreal. Student parking for all but seniors was in the rear parking lot. And those very few lucky enough to drive had to enter the school through the cafeteria exit doors on the school's lower level. I can remember the smell of the first cutting of hay when I arrived at school and parked Comet. I remember the next smell was the chicken a la King; the school lunch ladies were already preparing for the first-period lunchtime. My homeroom was facing the front side of the school, so I could hardly wait for lunch, where I could look out the cafeteria windows to check Comet out.

After classes, I drove Comet to the King's farm for the first time and many more that followed, creating a routine of earnings and escape.

In May, it was a great day that I met John and Joyce King. The first few weeks working for them, I barely had enough money for gas to and from the farm after all the expense to get Comet licensed and insured, but the next paycheck, I opened a savings account in the local Tioga State Bank, made a deposit, drove to the Agway to thank Mr. Smith for his encouragement and advice and bought a second red and white polka dot. I wasn't stuffing or hiding cash in a drawer anymore. I was determined to build up savings and better prepare for the day I got kicked out again or had to leave. I was in the best spirits and mood I had ever been. I once again had a bank account in my own name and Comet; everything about Comet was in my name. The title, the registration, the plates, the insurance…I owned it. It would become a semi-living, semi-breathing, semi everything to me machine that I controlled and commanded.

Comet was like me and how I felt at the time. Broken but repairable.

Chapter Twelve
Good Vibrations

May 1975
Playlist:
Knowing Me, Knowing You, Abba
Walk This Way, Aerosmith
Fly Like An Eagle, Steve Miller Band
Good Vibrations, Beach Boys
God Only Knows, The Beach Boys

In 1966 the Beach Boys came out with their third US number-one hit titled "Good Vibrations." While in 1966, I was only seven years old singing along to those lyrics of love and hanging on, I was still singing them in 1975 at 16 nearly every time I went for a drive with Comet. "Good Vibrations" became the first million-selling single for the Beach Boys. And while they were making millions of dollars, I was dreaming that someday I'd make some too. With the wheel and Comet at my command, I grew confident that money was in my future one day.

Significant vibrations were happening to me. I'd been working at the King Dairy for almost six months, and by now, Comet was a familiar vehicle parked in the King family's driveway. My hours were 1-1/2 hours after school and half-day on Saturdays, about twelve hours a week. At farm wages, less than the minimum, I only earned enough for the gas I burned to and from the farm and home. But the vibrations between John and me were good. They were good with his dad and Joyce, and though I didn't exactly meet the definition of a qualified milker, I quickly learned and grasped the art. And it was art! Milking a cow with machines is more intricate and technical than simply putting the device on and taking it off. Milking had to be done correctly to avoid a cow getting mastitis. If the machine was left on too long, it could damage a cow's teat. Milk (and money) would be left in the udder if taken off too quickly. I learned a ton of knowledge in that first month too. Milking a cow helped facilitate the cow to continue to produce milk. And if a cow occasionally got mastitis from one teat being over-milked, I had to learn how to administer medicine if necessary, mark the cow and keep records to isolate the milk from that cow's quarter from getting into the mainstream milk tank. I quickly learned how to do other tasks besides the basics of feeding, sweeping up, and spreading manure.

John taught me how to clean hooves: another skilled craft! A confined dairy cow's feet had to be trimmed and manicured to enable the cow to maintain a healthy, steady balance. Otherwise, the hooves would grow so long and twisted it would impede their ability to walk correctly. John taught me the signs of sickness in a cow, what medicine to administer and how to administer a bolus (a giant cow pill) with a bolus gun. The gun was a very long-stemmed apparatus that you stuck the massive bolus of aspirin or antibiotic (the size of a small banana) in and held in one hand. At the same time, you grabbed the cow's head by its nostrils with your thumb and index finger, then with your other hand slipped the bolus chute down the cow's throat and shot the bolus into its esophagus with a push of your other index finger on the gun. I learned amazing things. One could control an entire cow or bull by squeezing your index finger and thumb into its nostrils and pressuring the middle. There was enough discomfort to the animal that it would do almost anything you wanted it to do. Without it, the bull might lead you! That's why bulls would get rings in their nostrils…tie a rope to it, and a wild bull would be as tame as you wanted it to be, and you could lead it anywhere.

I was learning fast too how to operate different equipment. I was proficient in a tractor and caught on quickly to using various pieces of farm equipment. Depending on the day and activity, it might include a mower-conditioner, a corn chopper, tether, hay rake, feeding cattle with self-unloading wagons, and I learned how to fix and repair all sorts of moving machine parts like blades, chains, tether tines, universal joints and more. John was big on preventive maintenance, but rocks in the field, inadvertent and inexperienced sharp turns on my part could all still create needed repairs. If I broke something, I fixed it on my own time and never added the time to my hours. Most of the days at the farm were great days. There were no laborious days too hard for me. These were all excellent vibrations toward adding my value and having me around that farm. I learned how to feed calves with and understand the importance of colostrum, teach a newborn how to suck milk from a pail instead of its mother's teat, how to keep records, milk cows in a sanitary way, sanitize equipment, and the milk house, and just about every farm task that had to be performed. John even taught me how to assist cows in calf deliveries. Hardly a job on that farm slipped by me.

The vibrations between this family and me were all good. All I needed to do was figure out how to make this work. John was impressed with my work ethic and how fast I learned and got things done. He hadn't quite factored me into his budget yet though. I had taken over most of his dad's chores in the barn and relieved him of those, but Joyce was still coming out and feeding calves and performing other duties. I wanted to make this work. For me, for them, but it wouldn't with the few hours I was given. Then one day at lunch, I just let them know what I was thinking.

"John and Joyce, I like working with you, but I have a problem." They both looked at me, a little puzzled. "The pay I'm getting barely covers my gas expense for travel to and from the farm," I stated. "I mean, I'm not unhappy with the pay level, and I'm not asking for a raise; in fact, I would work for less pay, say a quarter per hour less, if I could just help you more and get more hours," I told them. "I'd need about thirty hours per week to make this work for me, and right now, I'm only getting about 10-15."

I proposed to John that if he felt I was up to speed by now for milking on my own, he could spend more time on the tractor and in the field each day to accomplish more fieldwork. "I could come after school, take over Joyce's chores, take care of feeding the heifers, give the milking cows their grain and go directly to milking so you could manage more field time," I suggested. John liked that idea as he still had his dad busy emptying and driving wagons to and from the field during the day I was in school. If he could stay out an extra three hours, he could fill all the wagons with hay bales and leave them and empty them first thing after morning milking. "Come fall; you could get more corn chopped and plowing done with those extra fifteen hours a week."

I proposed that I spend three hours a day, from 3:30 to 6:30, after school and that I could accomplish all that I suggested within that time frame. Getting three hours a day would pay for the gas and repairs to and from my job for five days. Any hours I could get on Saturday would be a bonus, which would go to my savings. On Saturdays, I could clean calf pens and stalls, perform preventive maintenance, spread manure, trim hooves, or do any other activities that John would think of. I could work all day for fieldwork, haying, whatever he needed me to do in the summer.

John looked at me in that red and white polka dot hat I'd worn since I bought it in Agway, and he said, "OK, let's try it." Again, I said, "I'll take a quarter per hour less for more hours!"

"No, that's OK, Curt. Let's try your suggestion and see how it goes!" he gestured.

The first couple of weeks, John checked in on me midway through milking to ensure all was going well and on time. Over the next few weeks, I proved I could get all the chores assigned to be done efficiently and add the milking of all 60 cows in the same allotted time. I was fast, efficient, and moved between the cows like a snake, managing three machines and sometimes four. The fact that the cows weren't getting mastitis proved my work was quality and efficient.

It wasn't long before I showed John and Joyce enough responsibility to trust me with all tasks so he and his family could take a weekend off and leave the farm. Eventually, they took their first whole week of vacation since they were married.

The Kings became my new family. They prayed out loud and gave thanks at all mealtimes, and at their request, sometimes I did, too. I'd never prayed out loud at a dinner table before. I prayed to the other great Comet in the sky at their table, Jesus Christ. The King family was passionate about biblical study, readings, and lessons. They introduced conversations and prayers meant for me, with subtle and sublime teachings, were curious about girls I might be dating, and I put their minds at ease when I told them I was staying away until I was ready to get married. I loved these people.

They didn't have to bring some of these topics up. They didn't have to pray in the subtle ways they did at the dinner table for me. I grew to understand that though they were not my own family, they valued me, and they began to cherish me and my help as one of their own and didn't want me to mess anything up for myself. I also heard their private evening prayers when I wasn't around. I can't explain how, but they prayed for my well-being and safety when I was on the farm and away. I never shared with them how much trouble I endured at home. When the rain poured from Loretta's eyes and the wrath of her emotions soon after, I just lived the charade Loretta and my dad lived and let everything look normal so everyone would think we were "normal."

Life was better for me working with the Kings as I was hardly ever at home anymore. With my Comet, I was out earning money. And in those horrible times at home, I could now get in my car and drive myself away, turn on the music and the wipers and at least temporarily wisk the rain away.

I ensured I didn't mess anything up at the King Farm to jeopardize my employment with them. I grew fond of them and appreciated their connection with God. I loved this dairying work, cherished this family…and loved them. I could see myself having a family on a farm like theirs, living the way they did. It wasn't fancy, but it was everything I would have needed or desired, and I could see happiness in the daily lifestyle. It was stable, it was productive, it was loving, and while their children may or may not have been happy as farm children living with the confinement and slave-like schedule of two times a day milking that comes with the trade, it was the heaven I was seeking that Comet drove me to every day. Comet delivered two angels to me, John and Joyce King.

In the short time of getting to know them, this family showed a remarkable magnitude of giving that I'd not experienced before. Not just in thanks but in giving to their neighbors, church, and community. Several church members stopped by twice a week to dip into the milk house tank. Times were tough for these folks, and John let them have all the milk they needed for their large families.

I observed John and Joyce giving their church and community time, energy, and support in various ways. John donated gas for the church school bus each week. There was also work to do in the church, and John would hire me to help with remodeling projects. I had a hard time taking pay for this work and would not accept those hours of payment.

They checked in on their neighbors, like aging Mrs. Bowen, a former schoolteacher who had never married or had children. She lived alone and cared for her parents until they passed away, and now John and Joyce checked in and looked after her since she had no children of her own.

Ron, the guy who lived in the mother-in-law's apartment upstairs of the farmhouse, was given to in many ways, including free rent in his senior years when he could no longer work. There were other examples, equipment loans to another farmer when his equipment broke down and help to others in need that came in challenging or difficult situations. In my eyes, John was becoming a mountain of a guy, and in my later years, I would brand a food product line called John Mountain Organics. And his wife Joyce was a mountain of giving, approval, and support, like an older sister or a younger mother I never knew. I knew through Joyce that whatever I was to become and be in my future years, I needed a mate like her. Her cooking was fabulous, and while as a young man, I appreciated every pie she baked and every offer for seconds, it was the soul of this woman that I observed and admired. It was going to be a soul like hers that I was after.

John's mom and dad lived in the adjacent home on the farm. Every morning around 10:00, we both went to their house to have the mid-morning coffee break. John Sr. and Grandma King were terrific people, and you could see where John got most of his good nature and work ethic. Coffee breaks with his mom and dad were a habit before I arrived as a farmhand. I always dismissed myself before our ten-minute break ended so that John had private time with his parents. I was the newcomer to a coffee break with them, and while I was always invited, welcomed, and served a few cookies or a piece of pie, I respected that they deserved a few minutes alone as they'd had before I started working there. I was never asked to do this; it was just some intuitive consideration that was the proper thing. The more I worked with John and Joyce, the more consistent and constant contact I would have with my God, my Comet. I always talked to God while I was driving somewhere. My Comet was my mobile chapel, my very own space to speak out loud, sing out loud, and share my thoughts, troubles, and feelings. Being on the King Dairy, working closely with the land and the cows, and under the guidance of John and Joyce somehow developed in me that I could walk anywhere with God and communicate all day at any time, not just while I was driving or at the dinner table. Later in life, a pastor who would know me for at least ten years would tell me I was one of the very few people he knew who walked with the grace of God. And while I was generally a good kid in high school, I wasn't perfect then, and got into many mischiefs.

Chapter Thirteen
Give More Than You Take

Curt and two of the King's children.

July 1975
Playlist:
Emotion, Samantha Sang
Too Much Heaven, Bee Gees
Makin' It, David Naughton
My Life, Billy Joel

I was the first farmhand John and Joyce King ever employed. There was no time clock for me to punch in or out. I was told to report to Joyce when I arrive and leave to record my time. My new presence as a farmhand was a bit of a change for Joyce and, to some extent, a bit taxing. I'd only been working for a couple of months, and while relieving her and John's dad of some chores, reporting my daily time had created another task. When I arrived at the beginning and end of each day, I checked in to report my start and finish times of work. When I did, Joyce made a note of the exact time.

Monday: Arrival at 2:33 pm and finished at 6:13 pm.

Tuesday: Arrival at 2:45 pm, finished at 6:05 pm

Wednesday: Arrival at 2:58 pm, finished at 6:15 pm

Thursday: Arrival at 2:43 pm, ended at 6:00 pm

Friday: Arrival at 2:55 pm, ended at 6:20 pm

Saturday: Arrival at 6:30 am, finished at 6:34 pm.

The farm milk check came from the Crowley Creamery every two weeks, and I was paid at the same time the milk check came. As Joyce was preparing dinner and taking care of her children, I'd enter her office (the kitchen), and with dinner on the stove and children at her feet, calculating all those precise minutes was a bit frustrating.

I could tell Joyce didn't like her new role as a time clock and performing this task at the dinner hour. Additionally, though I wiped my feet rigorously, I'd enter her kitchen with mud or manure caked to my boots every evening after milking to report on my time of leave. Though my presence on the farm assisted in other ways, I created a new annoying task for Joyce though she never let on.

To try and solve the issue, I bought a simple four-column ledger.

At the start of a new two-week pay period, I reported first to Joyce but then recorded the date and the time of entry into the ledger using the barn clock. I did the same after finishing my chores at the end of the day, just before I reported to Joyce as directed.

At the end of this particular two-week period, she had her total. "OK, you had 36 hours and 44 minutes plus today's time of 8 hours and 42 minutes. That's a total of 45 hours and 26 minutes." She said.

"No," I said, "that is wrong." Joyce looked at me with surprise. Probably because I never challenged her before nor kept my own time. "Let me add it up again," Joyce suspiciously suggested. "No need, Joyce, I have it right here."

"Your total is about 3 hours more than mine!"

I presented to her my little green ledger. According to the barn clock, I showed the date, arrival, and departure times. "The difference between your time and mine, Joyce, is that each day I rounded all my time to the nearest half-hour only if I completed a full half-hour. If I serve any time less than a half-hour, I'll give you this time," I explained.

Generally, I was supposed to be at work by 3:00 pm every afternoon. If I arrived at 2:35 or 2:45, I recorded 3:00 and gave John and Joyce the extra fifteen minutes. We always tried to be done with milking and chores by 6:30. If I worked past 6:30 but not to 7:00, I recorded my time as ending at 6:30.

It was an honor system. "Would you trust me to record my hours in this manner?" I asked. "I promise I will give you more than I will take and more than you expect of me."

"Well, you don't have to do that!" Joyce insisted.

"But I want to!" I insisted. "I don't want to be a clock watcher, and I don't think you want to add up all the little minutes I arrive before or leave after the normal hours I'm supposed to work."

"But there are times when John will want you earlier or to stay later and finish up for him," she said.

"No problem," I said. "If I need to stay till seven so you guys can get to a church meeting or elsewhere, I'll just record the time if I stayed a full half-hour. This honor system will alleviate a lot of our time in tracking and counting minutes, reporting in, and keep me from having to enter your kitchen every evening."

Joyce was pleasantly surprised and said, "Well, let's try it."

I'd bet money that those first few weeks when my car arrived in the driveway and departed without me checking in, the time was noted to test my system and my honor. If it did happen, there was nothing wrong with that. Trust but verify is a good policy. And to that of checking my integrity, I would never object. I made sure I was always giving more than I took. I'd practiced this in every small job I had in my life so far, and now that I was working for a family who held these same values, I aimed to give them my very best and support their efforts to grow their family, along with aiding others.

The little green ledger and, more importantly, my ethic to give more than I took worked well for me at the King's Dairy, the Turner Farm in Horseheads, New York, and later in my college years at the Fisher Farm in Story City, Iowa. I always ensured I exceeded my employers' expectations, never once were my hours questioned by any of them, and I never had to punch a clock.

Giving more than one takes is a gigantic way to live. You'll receive trust, honor, and, more importantly, freedom from a punch clock, suspicion, someone looking over your shoulder, and worry-free from ever being fired or laid off. Who will fire or lay off an employee who gives more than they take?

Later in my life, the clock watchers made the layoff lists in my corporate career, even if they had more talent than others; if you only gave what you were paid to provide, you make the bottom third of the list. Offering more than you take in everything you do and, in every action, offers freedom and confidence in oneself and others in yourself. It's a way of life. It's a building of your soul, and while it is an age-old biblical concept, I learned it first from the cartoon character of my childhood called Casper The Friendly Ghost. John and Joyce were the first human beings I saw it in practice. The more you give, the more you are entrusted to multiply and deliver. I saw John and Joyce giving plenty.

John and Joyce seldom had a night out to themselves. Three children kept them home evenings. So, I offered to stay after a day's work and babysit occasionally. No charge. I didn't expect them to pay me the same wages as the hard farm labor required. They seldom took advantage of this, but I was there whenever there was an opportunity when they may have been required to attend an event without kids. They were great times to get to know the family's children more. I seldom saw them while working except in passing or during meals, and I loved holding them as babies. Though I had very far away thoughts of fatherhood at the time, it reminded me of the long-ago times as a kid of holding and rocking my nieces and nephew when they were babies.

I never recorded babysitting hours in the little green ledger.

Chapter Fourteen
Corn Stalk Alley

Fall 1975
Playlist:
Give A Little Bit, Supertramp
Night Moves, Bob Seger and Sam Morrison
409, The Beach Boys
Little Deuce Coupe, The Beach Boys
Blinded By The Light, Manfred Manns' Earth Band
California Girls, The Beach Boys

I'm not sure exactly why Huey and Dewy loved to chase us. They were Juniors when I was a freshman, and both were star football players, and Huey was also a star basketball player for our school team. Neither one of them owned a car, and seldom if ever, did I see them driving a car to school. However, they always seemed to be cruising on a Friday night in one of their parents' cars, usually Huey's dads' truck.

I was basically absent from home most evenings and the whole weekend. The freedom Comet afforded me at just 16 allowed me out of our house not just every night as I chose to be but especially Friday and Saturday nights. Those four or five of us in high school lucky enough to have a car usually found ourselves cruising the streets around Spencer to pick up our buddies and head to Ithaca or Sayre, Pennsylvania, for a Pudgies pizza. For whatever reason, their own nasty kicks, I guess, Huey and Dewy would always find me and tailgate my butt to the point of almost tapping bumpers. I would usually have to pull into someone's driveway and let them pass to relieve the stress of their antics and pressure. Soon again, they'd resurface from some side street, and the ritual would begin again until I hightailed it out of Spencer and headed to Ithaca.

They generally didn't follow me out of town. Huey's parents must have had a perimeter set like dogs in a yard. I knew a little of Huey's dad and saw him in action on Huey's older brother and younger brother at some basketball games. He was like a military sergeant, stern and fair, but cross him, and you would get the shit kicked out of you. I never understood exactly why I or my buddies deserved their bullying while in the Comet. In school, they never approached me or even mentioned or teased any of us about their antics. I figured they didn't want to take a chance that one of their coaches would get wind of their poor behavior. It was like some weird power play when they were behind the wheel of their parents' vehicle, or it was simply plain jealousy that they didn't have their own wheels, and as a freshman, I did. What I indeed had over them was freedom.

One late August evening, my friend Steve and I were cruising the streets of Spencer when Huey and Dewy roared up behind us. Steve slapped the dash; it's those idiots again. Let's shake 'em down this time, Riess! I was game. I threw myself into slap-and-spit mode and tried to lead them to the nearest gravel road. I'd done this several times before leaving them in the dust with my prowess in maneuvering and handling Comet at high speeds up and down dirt and winding roads. They always gave up, turning around and speeding to some other kid to harass.

But this night, they wouldn't bite. I'd lead them to a gravel road, and they just parked at the end of the road and waited for us to return. I must have worn them out too often, and they'd grown weary that Comet never let them win.

Comet was fast, but we couldn't outrun the cars they had. We could only outsmart them or outmaneuver them. I tried unsuccessfully to ditch them or lead them off to a gravel road, only to repeat the chase repeatedly. This night I had a problem, too; I only had a quarter tank of gas, and no gas stations were open past 11:00 in our towns. I would typically just head out of town past their doggie perimeter and head home at this hour, but I had Steve in the car and had to drop him off at his house in the village.

We were flying down one of the back roads with Huey and Dewy hot on our tails when Steve suddenly said, "Take the corn!"

"What?"

"Yeah, take the corn. This field is narrow, and behind it is alfalfa. You can cut through the corn and ride the edge of the alfalfa field to the other end of the road."

"Are you sure?"

"Take the corn," Steve shouted. "Any fences?" He shrugged his shoulder, smiled wide, and said, "Guess we'll find out!"

Huey and Dewey were stunned. I can still see them in the rearview mirror, stopped at the entrance of the corn tunnel we produced.

It worked! Husks flying, ears of corn slapping the Comet bumper, stalks collapsing beneath the Comet underbody, creating a loud and booming grinding. It was like a scene from the Dukes of Hazard TV series. Bouncing along the edge of the alfalfa field led us to a tractor path that brought us a quarter mile up from where we left the dumb ass duo. A sharp left and we headed back to Spencer to drop Steve off and me to head home. We never saw Huey and Dewy, so we assumed they were still waiting for us to come out the way we went. It was a fantastic ride, and we outsmarted those idiots. That positive traction rear end I had pulled from a Mustang and put into Comet made this machine act like a bulldozer when it came to snowstorms, the cornfield, and a few other fields and stream antics the Comet swam us through. Caliente…the Mexican word for "hot"… Comet was hot in more ways than I knew!

Several days passed from that chase, and Comet's hotness seemed to cool! In fact, Comet was losing power traversing those daily hills. I discovered a leaking fluid line to the transmission under the body. It probably got stressed from that Cornstalk escape! I checked the fluid level in the tranny dipstick, and it read empty. Though I filled it with new fluid and fixed the leak, the damage had already been done. Comet and I limped along for the next couple of weeks and stayed clear of any chases.

A visit to the local junkyard exposed a 1968 Ford Cougar 289 V-8 with the transmission attached. That would fit snugly into the front-end motor mounts of Comet. Out with the straight-six and in with the V-8 and the second transmission, I'd put into Comet. The change was swift, accomplished on a Sunday, and I was back on the road Monday morning to work. Ford Mercury made interchangeable parts for those years of their production on several models of cars. Comet could receive pieces from multiple Ford-produced Mustangs, Cougars, Fairlane's, and Falcons. Parts were aplenty, and I went through plenty with all the rough riding we did together.

Chapter Fifteen
Stevens Single Shot

Curt sits contemplating another of Loretta's moods after a day of work.
The French desk, which Loretta sat at each day, sits behind the chair
Curt is seated in.

February 1977
Playlist:
We Will Rock You, Queen
Telephone Line, Electric Light Orchestra
I Never Cry, Alice Cooper

When I was twelve, my dad gave me a Stevens Single Shot 12-gauge shotgun. At the time, it nearly knocked me to the ground when I fired it. It was too powerful, and the stock too long for a twelve-year-old's arms. Still, like everything he could barely afford for me, he could only afford it once, so he got me the adult size I would eventually grow into. My dad was never a warm, fuzzy guy, and Loretta always played him as the bad guy, but he did what he could.

At age 17, I'd finally grown into that gun though I'd awkwardly hunted deer and rabbits many a year with it before then.

It was the first Sunday in February, and I returned home from church and a coffee visit with Mr. Hansen. As was more the norm than not, I was the only one who had gone. My dad was out in his garage, as usual. The garage sat about 100 feet from our house.

My little sister must have irritated Loretta for something she didn't do when requested. I walked into the house, finding Loretta in a frenzy, yanking at her hair and slapping her through and through. Her fuse was short and explosive. As sweet and pleasant as Loretta could be one minute, some pent-up anxiety and anger she seemed to hold within could easily be set off, and we were the punching bags to relieve her stress the next minute.

I usually stayed out of the way and didn't interfere with these episodes involving my siblings. Particularly my little sister, because half the time, I thought she deserved what she got. Her mouthy responses, excessive lying, and denial about one ridiculous thing after another brought so much wrath to our household. Ice cream, for example, was a nightly treat. But if you ate it before, cleaned out the carton, and denied you did it, you'd be beaten for it. That's how scarce money was for the luxuries in our household. And my little sis would do it often and lie and blame me. It was one of many other antics she'd lie about, and disputing the blame simply wasn't worth an escalation of an argument into the frenzy I just walked into. So while I would deny her accusations, if Loretta or Harry thought I did it, I just took the blame and promised to bring home another from my paycheck.

Walking into the situation, I had no idea how it started, but Loretta was in a vicious mood. No matter how hard my little sis tried to retreat to her room and say she was sorry and begged Loretta to leave her alone, Loretta just kept at it, following her into her room and beating her to a pulp.

I heard my sister's screams and pleas to stop outside her door. Though she'd crossed me many times, the vicious attack I had walked into had already escalated beyond a normal lashing and slapping. I always felt no one deserved Loretta's wrath. I wanted to enter Comet, return to town, and leave the scene. But the door remained closed, and the screams and crying persisted. Against my regular act of flight from the household, I swung open my sister's bedroom door and saw her on her bed, trying to cover her head with a pillow. Pleading at the top of her lungs to leave her alone, she tried vainly to escape the pounding of Loretta's fists. As did the rest of us kids, Daffy knew better than to lift a finger back at her. If we did, Loretta got a kitchen tool of one sort and returned with the weapon lashing at us.

Loretta had within her grips Daffy's long brown hair swinging her head from one side to another, making her neck look like a rubber dummy trying to drag her head out from under the pillow. "Leave her alone," I shouted. "Get the hell out of here," Loretta called back. "No, you leave her alone, and I mean it. Now," I responded.

Daffy was a mouthy little bastard and a liar on many fronts as she was a product of the same, but she didn't deserve what I saw.

"Get your hands off her," I demanded in a loud stern shout, already shaking with nerves.

"I'll leave her alone," she shouted, "I'll leave her alone, and I'll take care of you too!" She left my sis and headed for me. "You want me to leave her alone; can you order me around?" Loretta began shoving me back into the hallway, swearing obscenities, smacking me left and right now, and backing me into my room. Instead of covering my head with my arms and allowing her to beat me as I'd done before, I put up my arms and, for the first time, began to push her back. I nervously laughed at her, swore at her, and told her: "You're crazy and should see a psychiatrist." I threatened her, "The next time this ever happens, I'm calling the cops." That threat took her already out-of-control frenzy to a new height.

Her mental instability, bordering on insanity, kicked in. "Really," she said, "well, you can get the hell out."

"Call the cops on me, and I'll kill you."

"You say, call the cops, you ungrateful little bastard; I'll call the cops on you!" Outraged and attacking, she slapped and clawed her fingers into my face.

I raised my voice in defense and told her, "You're freaking crazy." I was now holding her wrists from clawing at me. "Get off me, you bitch, or I'm gonna put your ass in jail."

"Oh, really, jail," she screamed. She left me in my room to grab a metal ladle from the kitchen, returned, and tried to smash my head with it. Holding her arm with the scoop, I grabbed it from her and threw it down the hallway. Grabbing her other arm, I forced her away. "You have mental problems. You should see a doctor." I pushed her back into the hallway and then locked my bedroom door.

That was it. I'd had it. I began packing my clothes into my duffle bag and gathering a few things. Loretta unlocked my door and came charging in again with another cooking utensil. "Where do you think you're going?" she demanded. "You just got done screaming at me to get the hell out, so I am anywhere but here," Suddenly, her position changed. "You're not going anywhere," and she began smacking me again with the utensil. Then she opened my bedroom window facing the garage and screamed for Harry. "Harry, your kid is beating me up! Harry, get in here, now."

I couldn't believe my ears; all I was doing was keeping her off me. "Harry," she screamed at the top of her lungs, "get in here now."

From my point of view, he couldn't get there fast enough to calm her down. If it weren't for him, all her kids would be dead. She'd certainly be in jail for abuse because she never knew how to stop once she started. Her rage fed itself, and if she didn't think she was inflicting enough pain to get through to you, she lay on more. He finally arrived and ordered Laurie off me. "What the hell is going on?" he asked.

I didn't say a word. Loretta did all the talking claiming that I attacked her. My dad knew better. And as usual, my sister never came to my aid. I couldn't blame her; she was scared to death for half her lifetime.

Loretta told him I was packing and leaving and would call the cops on her. My dad just looked at all this craziness and asked, "Where are you going."

"I don't know, but I can't stay here anymore. She's sick. She's insane. This is not normal behavior."

"I'm not sick, you ungrateful little bastard," Loretta lunged at me, with my dad pulling her back. "And you're not going anywhere," she demanded. "You get his keys, Harry; he's not going anywhere."

"Why?" I shouted, "Afraid I might tell the world how sick you are?"

Now I was infuriating my dad, and he began to do what he usually did, side with Loretta to keep some semblance of peace. He could never side with a kid; there would be hell to pay for weeks.

"Give me your keys, Curt. You're grounded for a week." Harry insisted. "No," I said sternly, "you're not grounding me. I have a job and responsibilities. I'm leaving this crazy hellhole. I don't need this kind of shit anymore; I'm done."

"Give me your keys, Curt; you're not going anywhere," he demanded again. He could see that I was hot, determined, and had reached the end of my rope.

"No," I said again, "it's my car. I paid for it, own it, and nothing stops me from leaving." I was sobbing through this debacle, and I could hear my sister crying.

"Oh, really," Harry said, "OK, we'll see about that."

Nothing had cooled down as yet. I was still frantically packing with tears streaming down my face. Loretta was screaming at me the whole time; my heart was pounding, and the insanity had reached an all-time high on my barometer of home life.

I heard my dad's bulldozer startup as I packed up my things. I looked out my window, and he was heading straight up the driveway toward my car. As his dozer had a bucket loader with groundbreaking teeth welded to the blade, I saw nothing but a Tyrannosaurus Rex heading toward my car as he raised the loader into the air with its teeth pointing downward, threatening he was going to drop that loader onto Comet. I couldn't believe it. The bastard was going to run over Comet and flatten it to pieces.

That 12-gauge Stevens was in my closet. I pulled it out, broke it open, and loaded it with a deer slug. I'll fix that bastard, I whispered to myself. I slipped additional shells into my pocket. Loretta was out of sight, and I didn't care where. I calmly walked out of the house to the side of my car, holding my rifle in plain sight but safely aimed at the ground. I wanted Harry to know I meant business as much as he did. My weapon was smaller, but it would do equal damage. The dozer was loud, and its cleat track noisily thumped toward Comet. Harry crawled his bulldozer closer and closer to the back of my car. As he raised his front-end loader with the threat that he would smash and flatten Comet, I raised my shotgun with a different threat.

I aimed that shotgun at the exposed radiator with the front loader bucket and blade in the air. I whispered, "You touch my car, and I'll blast your fucking engine apart so your beloved hunk of iron will never run either." Then loudly, I pleaded with him to stop, but he couldn't hear me. As he approached and saw me with the gun, he tried to make eye contact, but I had a steady aim at his radiator because it was going down before he dared touch Comet. I held my stance and adjusted my sight as he drove forward, staring back at me.

I heard Loretta scream through the back porch window behind me, "What the hell are you doing?" Holding steady with my aim as he crept closer when he was within thirty feet, I cocked the gun. Out of nowhere, Loretta came sweeping sideways and knocked the gun away. As she did, the gun went off.

"What are you doing?" she screamed, "what are you doing?"

I stood there in shock. *What had just happened,* I thought to myself. *What had just happened to me?*

Everything was now in slow motion in my head. Loretta was screaming in slow motion, struggling to take the rifle away from my grip. I turned toward my dad; he was slowly leaping off his dozer, heading toward me. I froze. I was in some sort of shock! My heart was racing, but everything in my vision and mind was processing in a frame-by-frame slow-motion picture like an actor in a movie and watching it unfold simultaneously.

My body and mind were frozen. Everything was visually in slow motion! I felt my dad rip my shotgun from my hands. I watched the butt of it heading toward my head in slow motion. Harry knocked me to the ground and began beating me with it. I saw darkness and lay limp as I felt my body battered by the butt of my gun as he swung it like a baseball bat, beating my back and arms as I pulled them over my head and tried to roll away.

Now Loretta was pulling him off me. As I came to and stumbled to get up, he knocked me to the ground, this time swinging the barrel end of the gun and hitting me in the stomach. I fell to the ground again. As Loretta pulled him off me and tried to wake him up to sanity, I managed to crawl through a split rail fence. Then I escaped like a man out of prison on foot down into the valley below.

My head was bleeding. My hair, face, and jacket were soaked in blood.

"God, what the hell is happening to me?" I prayed earnestly for an answer. I hiked to the falls below and washed my face and head with frozen hands. The water was open in spots and cold. Still, it felt holy, healing, and refreshing as I splashed and splashed it all over my head, watching it drip red onto the snow and disperse into the flowing water below. I wasn't sure what to do. I looked into the stream's open pockets of water gurgling down through the rocks and ice. I loved this place as I retreated to it many times when the rain and wrath poured from Loretta. The deep, almost rainforest ambiance and flowing water gave me peace. I followed this stream for miles once as it traversed down numerous cascading waterfalls of bedrock slate, ever-winding its way through the hills to the valley of Van Etten and Cayuta Creek.

I never aimed that gun at my dad, only his bulldozer. But, when Loretta swept the weapon away, and it went off, the trajectory of the barrel swayed past Harry. The discharged bullet could have easily killed him, it was a deer slug at close range, 30 feet, and it would have torn a hole through his chest and out his back.

Loretta was hyper-crazy, and she thought I was aiming for him, and that's the story she would have believed and told. Over and over, I hashed through my mind what could have happened. What would have happened had I killed my father?

My gut was empty, not just of food but of everything. I had no feelings. I was numb. I didn't even feel the pain of the welts all over my body anymore. There seemed to be no soul left in me. There was nothing.

I can't describe the coldness I felt. Not the air temperature but the coldness of the void I was experiencing in my mind and body.

I rehashed the scene: the frame-by-frame slow-motion picture and second-by-second audio play of Loretta screaming her crazy lungs out. The split-second by double picture frames of Harry leaping off the dozer, ripping the rifle from my hands and the gun's stock aimed for, and hitting my head; every blow as I lay on the ground felt like I was hit with a sledgehammer. My head felt as if all of my teeth had popped out.

"God, What if that bullet had hit my dad?" I would have immediately run to him and done whatever I could to help him. What would Loretta have done? She would probably run to me, drag me away from him, and go nuts. I always believed Loretta was partly insane based on her behavior, perhaps caused by the tragic loss of her first child. She would have gone over the edge if Harry were killed, and I went to jail. Over and over, I rehashed the scene and the imagined consequences had it gone the way of a bullet hitting my dad.

Listening to the stream gurgle as I pondered probable consequences, I knew I had to flow with it. I had to follow the water. Returning home was not an option.

What I didn't know was what Comet's fate was. All I knew was that If I went back up the hill and found my Comet crushed, I would be too, and the next slug would be mine, and there would be no miss.

I couldn't take it anymore. "I just can't take it," I sobbed until my gut ached from pouring every tear I had left into the stream below. If Comet was dead, I had more shells in my pocket; I'd need to find my gun.

I didn't care anymore. Not about home, Loretta, Harry, my sister, the world. I was empty.

Hours passed, and I was freezing. I prayed and prayed and prayed for something. As darkness came, I snuck up behind the field of our house, climbed one of the maple trees, and observed the homestead. Comet was still parked where I had parked her. There were no signs of damage from my vantage point, and the bulldozer was parked back in its usual place. Lights were on in the house; it was now about 6 pm. I'd been gone since about 1:00 this afternoon when all this transpired.

I still had my keys in my pocket. *Maybe I should make a run for the Comet, jump in, and drive off, never to return,* I thought.

After sitting on a branch in that tree for two hours, I slid to the ground. I was frozen.

In the darkness, I snuck back to Comet. I inspected all sides, and there was no sign of damage. Comet was left untouched, probably intentionally, because I would have no choice but to go. I was sure of it. Harry probably left the car intact as he would give me a directive to get out.

I stood by the driver's door for a few moments listening. I could hear Loretta and my dad talking at the kitchen table. They seemed calm. Though I just wanted to get in the car and leave, there was one thing I wanted to do more than anything else. No matter what happened, despite the beatings before, the defeat today, and the insanity that I lived with every day, I wanted to tell Harry I never aimed that shotgun at him. I wanted him to know that. For all the misery we suffered, even under him, I knew he was a victim as we were. He deserved to know that. I couldn't imagine his feelings having his son pushed to the point of potentially killing him. It was never my intention.

I decided to enter the house. It was a risk, but I wanted my dad to know the truth. He was generally a good guy, always caught in the middle. I often asked him why he stayed married to her. "I stayed for you kids," he told me. "I was married once before and lost my kids, and I didn't want to make the same mistake." It was true; I observed his efforts to have visitation time with his two daughters from his previous marriage, but ultimately, he failed.

When I opened the porch door and entered the kitchen, Loretta stood by the sink, and my dad sat at the table.

"I'm sorry," I said. "I'm so sorry. I want you to know I never aimed that gun at you." What tears I didn't think I had left began dripping from my chin. "I was going to stop you with a bullet hole through your dozer radiator."

They were both silent. Harry wouldn't look at me; he stared straight ahead. He never said a word. I repeated, "I'm sorry, I'm so sorry. Again, I want you to know I never aimed that gun at you." Again, "I was going to stop you with a bullet hole through your radiator."

The silence remained. Neither said a word. Harry just stared straight ahead, never looking at me. I was sure that once either of them, particularly this time Harry, opened their mouth, they would ask me to leave. As I stood in the kitchen covered in blood-stained clothes, the conversation void was never filled. It seemed forever before I broke the silence and told them, "I must go. I can't stay here anymore, I'm afraid," I said, "I'm afraid if I stay, one of us will get killed." Silence ensued.

"I need to get some of my clothes, or I'll have to explain how all this blood came about," I stated in a questioning tone. Silence remained.

I went to my room and grabbed the duffle bag I'd packed. I only filled it with the clothes I paid for and a few other things with my farm wages. For the last two years, I was told to buy my clothes with my own money, work boots and shoes, and just about anything else I needed, in addition to paying half my wages to them for room and board.

I didn't hear anything from my sister's room as I passed it, and I assumed she was asleep by now or just staying clear of any trouble. I walked back to the kitchen and said goodbye. The silence broke only from Loretta.

She asked me, "Where are you going?"

"I don't know," I said. My dad stared straight ahead, never made eye contact with me, and never said a word. It all felt horribly wrong, and I was sure he was also thinking about how he got into this mess.

I pondered what his thoughts were in his actions. "What was he thinking trying to take my car away or smash it? Was it just a threat that was taken too far?" Whatever his thoughts, his silence told me he was deeply hurt, and he understood how vital Comet was to me.

Before I closed the door, I said again, "Dad, I'm sorry again." I said nothing to Loretta, and I left.

I drove to my friend Steve's house and asked if I could get cleaned up again. His mom asked me what happened, and I told her, "I got kicked by one of the cows." My polka dot hat could conceal my head gash and cuts for the most part. But it was apparent from my jacket and clothes that something horrible had happened. "It looks like you got kicked by more than one cow Curt," her husband Dave questioned. Hesitantly I quietly responded, "Well, maybe a couple…maybe a little trouble at home,"

"Would it be OK if I stayed the night here?" I asked.

Mrs. Hansen nor her husband questioned me further. They invited me to "stay as long as you need to" and opened their home.

I slept on their couch for a few days but knew I could not stay at anyone's house long. No matter where I stayed, I'd bring trouble into their home. Loretta wouldn't stop at the phone; she'd be at the front door. I'd witnessed this before with my older siblings.

I went to school and went to work like any typical day. I was embarrassed that I had left home and was reduced to this. I, the high school student council president, was kicked out of his house, basically true, as I was sure I had no choice.

The charade story that I had tumbled with a bull served me well when I was questioned by one of my coaches and other teammates as the gunstock welts and bruises all over my body showed visibly in the locker room showers. Working on a farm made it believable, as well as the fact that we had a small herd of cows. My closest friends kept the secret. We all seemed to have them.

I stayed at Steve's that first week. When I told my best friends, Jack and Dave, that I had left home, they also talked to their parents and opened their homes to me. Their parents told me I was welcome and could stay as long as necessary. I shared with them that I very much appreciated this, but again, "If I come into your home, I'll bring trouble with it." There was no way around it. I stayed at each of their homes for a couple of nights. When I stayed with Jack and again explained why I couldn't stay with him or trouble would come to their house, Jack told me about a small cabin up the hill. His friend and neighbor Wayne had built it. It was a single-room cabin, about ten feet long by ten feet wide, with small bunk beds, a table and chair, and a wood stove. It didn't have running water, electricity, or a bathroom, but it could do. It had a small front porch with a couple of chairs to hang outdoors on a rainy day.

"You could stay there, Curt, and come to our house to use the shower, bathroom, get water, and what you need. And it's full of Playboy magazines," he laughed.

In his early twenties, his friend Wayne built the cabin on his parents' land. He lived with his parents in Michigan Hollow and cared for them. I went to Wayne and asked him If I could use his cabin for a few months. He said yes. I never told him what happened to me, but Jack gave him enough of the story. I offered to pay him rent, but he wouldn't take any payment. "I'm working on some stone walls, and I could use occasional help hauling stones if you have some time." I really would have preferred to pay Wayne a monthly rent, as I barely had any time left in a day between school and work, but "OK," I said, "If you tell me where you want them, I'll haul them."

Now having a semi-permanent residence at the cabin in the wood, I had plenty of time chopping wood to heat myself and contemplating how to survive and work through all this. One not-so-subtle realization came to me, and that was that I was on a new journey. I had closed the door on my life with Loretta mentally, physically, and dependently. In every aspect, I no longer needed nor desired that mother. My most profound sorrow was not for myself; it was for her. She did not know how to be an ordinary mom. She was mean-spirited, angry, manipulative, abusive, confusing, and hungry for much more than Harry could ever afford her.

As for me, I wasn't sure exactly where I was going, but I was flowing with the stream and trying to be as flexible as the water that flowed in it.

For the rest of my senior year, the King family watched me back out of their driveway and headed south toward Spencer, the usual way home to Van Etten, when in reality, I needed to go north the other way to my new cabin in the wood. This family highly regarded my work ethic, praised me, and prayed for me. I couldn't bring myself to have to explain my situation to them. No matter what I shared with them, especially the truth, I'd be guilty in some way by association with failing within the family. How could I explain the fact and the craziness of pulling out a shotgun? They'd think I was unstable and might fear having me any longer around their family.

So learning from Loretta, the master of charades, I backed out of the driveway as I had when I lived at home and headed toward Spencer, pretending to head home. A mile down the road, I could make a left-hand turn and take the long way to my cabin in the wood. I did this for several months to make everything appear as normal as possible to them. They had grown to respect me for my talent, labor, and love for their family. I didn't want them to see me differently than they had already known.

I kept my life as normal as possible, still going to St. Paul's Lutheran Church on Sundays, just as I always had, alone. Loretta had brought us to church until I got Comet, but after that, she stopped attending, and I continued on my own. My dad never went and didn't believe in God.

I'd gotten to know some older community businessmen and their families through the church. I respected them and saw them as model community members. My absence would surely spell something was up with them if I didn't attend, and they knew the Kings and might question them. I wanted to appear and remain as normal as possible; besides, I enjoyed their fellowship.

I didn't know if Loretta or Harry ever called the King family to tell them I wasn't living at home any longer, and I doubt they would. They wouldn't want to expose the whole story and shame of that day's activities nor what really happened in that house.

After the first month of my absence, Loretta sensed I was not coming back for good. She was sure I would have returned and shown up begging to come back after a week. She knew I liked and respected two church members, Ralph and Paul Efthimiou, as I often spoke fondly of them. Loretta telephoned Ralph. He was another local dairy farmer and partner to his brother in a gas station and heating oil business. She asked him to convince me to go home. She didn't know where I lived but knew he could find me working at Kings' Dairy. He came over to the Kings while I was milking one evening. He must have asked where I was or naturally knew where to find me as a farmer and walked into the barn and found me huddled with a milking machine stripping out an udder.

"Hi Ralph," I enthusiastically greeted him. "Surprised to see you here! Are you looking for John?"

He quickly got to the reason for his visit. "Curt, I came to say I think you should go home."

I was taken aback. I didn't think anyone except Steve, Dave, Jack, and their parents knew I was gone from home.

"Your mother called Curt and sent me here to ask you to go home." I sensed he was uncomfortable being dragged into this role by Loretta. I crouched down between two cows and adjusted a milking machine. A large gulp entered my throat. "She wants you to come home, Curt. She told me so."

I moved over to another cow and crouched down. I was trying immensely to act like nothing had happened, and I didn't know what Ralph was talking about. Still, the tears held back by a dam of emotions flooded my cheeks, and he looked at me sympathetically.

"I'm OK where I am, Ralph," as I slid between and hid between two cows. "I'm sure you're OK, Curt, but it's the best thing. You really should go home."

"I can't," I said as I stood up, taking off the machine on a cow and heading to another. "I just can't go back home, Ralph. It's not in anyone's best interests." That's all I could say. The gulp in my throat choked me, and the tears streamed down my face. Ralph continued to press me to go home. I nodded my head no and slid between two more cows. I didn't want to share any reason why; I didn't want to share any of what happened that day and why I couldn't return to that house. *Sharing any of it would condemn me,* I thought. I was sure Loretta just gave him a reason, such as his father, and he got into a spat. I'm sure she left herself and all the other details out.

I hoped Ralph would believe in me, in my decision that it suited me, and I wanted to tell him I'd be OK. Still, all I could do was wipe the tears from my face with my dirty shirt sleeves. He pleaded with me to reconsider going home one last time. He could tell my emotions welled up so much that I could no longer respond, so he stood staring at me silently. I continued my milking chores and would no longer give him eye contact or communication. After a long silence and slightly exasperated, he finally turned and walked away without saying goodbye.

Occasionally, one of Ralph's daughters Ali, who was in the same grade, would curiously ask how I was doing. I always liked and respected her. She was kind and one of the honor students in high school, and I'd tell her I was OK. She always smiled at me with a caring eye, and I told her all was well…it was.

I'm sure Ralph called Loretta and told her what transpired between us in the barn. I'm sure Loretta, no matter how vicious she was at times, also cried her heart out for me. It was how Loretta was, love you, condemn you, beat you up, and love you again. She was mentally ill in some way.

I never told anyone what happened that day as I was embarrassed and scared of my reputation's consequences. My closest friends knew that I had some falling out without any details. No coach or anyone else questioned my story other than the Hansens when I showed up at Steve's house, covered with bruises and a gash to the head.

Every week, I filled Comet with fuel at the ARCO station that Ralph and Paul owned. When either of them was at the cash register, they always said a big hello and asked how I was doing. "Everything OK, Curt?" they'd ask with concern and care on their upper lip. "Yup!" I let them know with an enthusiastic "OK!" They'd smile without worry. Despite the hardship of living independently, I continued my regular activities that they observed as expected. I went to church; gave from my pocket to the offering plate; I took communion with them, sang with them, sat with them, and they seemed to have faith that I was going to be all right, even though I could no longer show up in a suit and occasionally attended with some soiled clothes. I'm positive I received a prayer or two along with the handshake and the pat on the back from them as I continued to attend as best I could.

I had a church family in the Kings and a church family at St. Paul's. Many of the adults in the church seemed to take special care to greet me more frequently to chat and ask how I was doing than typical. Without saying so, they were all there for me if I needed them.

Chapter Sixteen
The Pope

February 1977

Playlist:

Knowing Me, Knowing You, ABBA

Go Your Own Way, Fleetwood Mac

Walk This Way, Aerosmith

Barracuda Heart, Little Queen

Fly Like an Eagle, Steve Miller Band

Hotel California, The Eagles

Some of my friends visited with the one and only school guidance counselor about going to college. No one had ever broached the subject with me about going to college, least of all my parents. My friend Jack told me he was going to college to manage hotels. My friend, the Duke, wanted to become a professor. Most of my classmates planned on driving cement trucks or practicing a trade like carpentry or had no plans.

I needed some time on my bridge. Having not traveled to and from home daily since I moved out, I'd spent less time going the route of Beckhorn Hollow, where I'd sit on a one-lane steel trestle bridge across Cayuta Creek. My favorite time at the bridge was dusk. Even as it got dark, I'd sit in the middle of that bridge with parking and dashboard lights on, along with one of my favorite tunes playing low and my door open, pouring all of my thoughts down through the grated deck into the flowing stream below. Some of those thoughts were happy, sorrowful, and many just plain self-pity. Listening to the water rushing down seemed to flush everything out of me and allow me a path to clear thinking.

On that bridge on a cold February night, staring down into that half-frozen stream, I decided I would go to college. I had some dreams at the time. I liked dairying at the King's farm and dreamed of being a dairy farmer. Why not attend college, learn more about business, and become a prominent farmer?

The sky above the trestles was loaded with stars. A gazillion of them always was in that part of the country when the sky was clear. They seemed limitless, and I felt the same way whenever I looked at them.

Cayuta Creek below was gurgling and churning in and out of the ice and snowbanks. Comet's engine was purring smoothly, putting out heat, unlike that old straight-six that never warmed up. The tune Paradise by the Dashboard Light was playing on my eight tracks. *Why not!* I thought. Why not go to college? Even the frozen water on the banks will eventually melt and flow away. Why should I confine myself to Van Etten? I needed to flow into the world somewhere, somehow. I could always come back if I wanted.

I made up my mind.

I was going to college.

Easier said than done. As student council president, I wasn't a dumb kid in high school; I had to maintain a certain grade point average to run for the position and maintain it after winning it. In ninth grade, I could follow the New York State Regents protocol of selected classes for college prep or go to a vo-tech school called BOCES for the afternoon and learn a trade. I followed the Regents prep course but wasn't as prepared as I should have been.

I wasn't the most academic in the mathematical or science areas either. My parents had no formal education past the eighth grade. They never spoke to me about going to college. And living under the duress of my home environment, I only had one thing in mind: surviving teenhood. I tried contacting the guidance counselor numerous times about applying to college. She kept putting me off and rescheduling. Most schoolkids referred to her as "The Pope." She was short and stocky, and she never seemed very helpful and had the reputation of telling most people they couldn't do what they wanted.

In an earlier aptitude and career test, she recommended I become a bartender. Or a mortician because I listened to people well and with empathy. That was my skill, she said.

When I finally got an appointment to see her and told her I wanted to go to college for dairy science, she looked at me without pity and said, "Why are you wasting my time? You will never go to a college because you will never get in." She must have pulled my file and reviewed my grades and classes before I got there. "Why not?" I asked.

"You won't," she jeered sternly and asked me not to waste her time.

Assuming she took the time to review my file, I asked her, "What college would let me in…for anything?"

She pulled out my records, reviewed my grades and courses, and repeated, "You will never get into a college." I glared into her eyes. She stared back.

I saw in her my mother telling me… "you won't amount to anything."

I glared back at her and politely told her, "I'm going to go to college," I stopped short of being rude and saying, "But not with any help from you." I never talked to her again and didn't waste her time.

I told my friend Jack about this. He was the one who first inspired me to look into college. I told him I wanted to go for Dairy Science, and the Pope said I'd never get in. "Don't listen to her; she's an asshole," he said. "Apply for hotel/motel management or food service. Colleges let anyone in for food service." He insisted.

"How do you know?" I asked.

He said, "Look, they let me in!"

"But you're a straight-A student, Jack!"

"That doesn't matter, listen, if they don't let you in for dairy science, then get in another way…through food service! Why don't you apply to Cobleskill? That's where I'm going?"

"Where is that?" I inquired.

"About two hours away near Albany. Go to Cobleskill with me," he encouraged.

The best thing the Pope did for me in the six years I was at Spencer-Van Etten High was to tell me I'd never get into college. The worst thing she did was exist in that role for as long as she did, hardly ever providing guidance to students like me and promoting the local vo-tech skills school for most Spencer-Van Etten High School boys.

I did precisely as Jack told me to do. I applied to two different Ag and Technical colleges within the State Universities of New York. I was accepted by both of them into their food service curricula. When I filled out applications, I also filled out the necessary forms for any government aid or scholarships available. Through an essay to the Statler Foundation, I won a scholarship worth $500.00 per semester for up to four years as long as I pursued my studies in food service. I also received some aid from the then Pell Grant system through the federal government. I qualified for some funds through a government-sponsored low-interest loan but was still short. Even with financial aid and my savings, I needed about $8,000.00 more to pay for room, board, and tuition for the next two years, and I wasn't getting any help from my parents.

There was no doubt that I would continue to work while in college. That was a given for me. Since I was eleven years old, I'd been working at some job or another, starting with a paper route, and not working never entered my mind. I was a white kid in America, always working, providing child labor like many of my brethren in Africa, China, Mexico, Vietnam, and many other countries. The U.S. wasn't much different for kids living below the middle class, no matter their skin color. Still, I was sure I was much better off than they were, as I grew up eating everything on my plate because of all the starving children I heard about in India.

But, $8000.00, holy crap. It took me almost three years to save the $2800.00 in my savings. Working full-time would take me at least two more years, and I would have to find a place to rent. I certainly wasn't going back home to pay the room and board fees my parents imposed upon me, and put up with Loretta. With college almost in my grasp, getting another $8000.00 seemed impossible. I can't stay in this one-room cabin on Michigan Hollow beyond this summer. Another winter here, and I'd surely freeze, never wake up or kill myself from depression. And I'd be stuck in Spencer and Van Etten while most of my closest friends went to college. I needed a way to figure out how to get a loan.

Having finally decided to go to college, I became a little depressed. Moving forward, the door was always half-open. I got approved for some aid through applications, but coming up with $8,000.00 on my own seemed like the door was finally shut.

Though it seemed like a dead end, I repeatedly told myself I'd find a way. Like driving Comet down some old dusty dirt roads only to find some dead-ends where some farmstead once stood, I'd back up, turn around, trace our trails backward and find another way out.

Chapter Seventeen
The Bermuda Triangle

March 1977

Playlist:

Say You Love Me, Fleetwood Mac

Take The Money And Run, Steve Miller

Baby, I Love Your Way, Peter Frampton

Walk Away from Love, David, Ruffin

You're My Best Friend, Queen

Got To Get You Into My Life, The Beatles

Devil Woman, Cliff Richard

There was another family I grew fond of. The Hansen family. Through my classmate and friend Lance, I knew his parents well. After my chores at the King Dairy and to extend my stay away from my household, I'd often visit, having several cups of coffee with my classmate's dad talking about the farm and my chores. As everyone referred to him, Lance's dad, Dave Sr., was a medium-built man accustomed to factory and farm work.

During the week, he worked the night shift at a factory called Morse Chain in Ithaca, and on weekends he hauled cattle from local farms to slaughterhouses with an adjoining neighbor. Dave loved the farm and talked with me about what I did daily at King Dairy. He loved every detail, no matter what it was, from fixing a universal joint to sanitizing the milk pipeline.

Week after week, year after year, it became a ritual that Dave and I would talk two or three times a week all evening after he woke up at about 5 pm. I would stop in after my chores were done at the King Dairy, and we'd share coffee and conversation until he had to leave for his job at Morse. We'd share ideas on how I fixed things, and he'd give me tips on tackling the fix the next time.

We talked a lot about my future farming dreams. He told me if I built such a farm, he'd come to work it with me. I was sincere back then in all of those dreams. Being a farmer is really what I wanted to do, and I wanted to be in the Spencer community to help it and families like Dave's thrive.

The Hansen household appeared economically worse off than my own and the average family of Spencer. The family dwelled in an old two-story white clapboard-sided village home in Spencer with poor insulation. Dave cut wood for heating. He had five boys, all of whom had to participate in the hauling, cutting, and splitting of wood to heat their home in the winter. A central wood furnace in the basement was the primary heat source, and a second wood-burning stove was in the kitchen.

The majority of the home seemed not to have heat. The central heater provided warmth to the living room; if enough, it might have made its way to the upper levels. In a few sleeping-over experiences, the upstairs bedrooms were like cold-air dormitories in fraternities. During winter, a bedsheet was hung between the kitchen and the living room to maintain heat in the kitchen.

The kitchen was the only comfortable room where everyone gathered. Many a Sunday morning, I would stop over for a cup of coffee with Dave before going to church, and Dave had just stoked up the wood stove to boil coffee and provide heat. We'd sit chatting with our coats on, seeing the vapor of our breath in the air as the kitchen slowly warmed.

Dave Sr. was an incredible influence on me. As a teenager, he was one of the few adults who would talk with me one-to-one and spend hours doing so. As I got to know his five sons, they'd come and go from the house, sit in on our conversations, and then go about their activities with their other friends. It wasn't unusual that Dave Sr. and I and his wife Carrie would often sit and chat about the world, future dreams, and everyday living.

I seldom ate at their household even though Carrie offered many times. What I saw they had was minimal, and they had a lot of hungry boys to feed. Out of care and concern, I would take some of the boys, particularly the younger ones, many a Friday night with proceeds from my paycheck to Pudgies Pizza in Ithaca. There I would purchase a large sheet of pizza with my farm wages, which would be wolfed down in minutes. It was my quiet way of helping out while at the same time giving myself another alternative to being home.

My dad allowed me to cut firewood and sell it briefly. I had to split the proceeds with him. I cut some firewood and delivered it with my dad's truck for free. When I gave a dump truckload to Hansen's house, I had to take money from my paycheck and pay my dad for half. It wasn't sustainable for me as it was a significant chunk of my meager farm wages.

Dave Sr. did various jobs to make an extra buck for his family. He even coon hunted (a term used for hunting raccoons) at night for their pelts to sell. Dave and I would often track till one or two in the morning on a weekend night, searching out raccoons for him to skin and sell the hides. We were constantly in freezing temperatures as we walked through forests with knee-high snow with flashlights flashing hollow trees in search of those creatures. In those days, a good pelt would bring 25 to 50 dollars. I'd have to work 12 hours to make $25, so it was good money for Dave. Sometimes, if I had enough energy after a long Saturday of work, I'd go into the woods alone, hunt the coons, and give the pelts to Dave to skin and collect the pelt money.

Dave loved all of my dreams. We'd rehearse over and over many times how to build out a great dairy. We'd talk about local land, location opportunities, and where in Spencer and I might get that dairy farm off to a start. I asked him once, "Dave, what do you think of a dairy farm where people could come and see the cows get milked, buy their bottled milk, and maybe have an ice cream shop where we could make creamy ice cream?" He loved these ideas! He saw different systems since he picked up cattle on weekends at various farms. He'd share the other milking systems he'd see on his cattle runs, and we talked about the differences between pipeline and the milking parlors he saw. He shared many different ideas on what to consider and how to make the best dairy farm from all his observations as he went from farm to farm on weekends. As he discovered my dreams, he began to have a keener eye for things at other farms that he could bring back to our coffee conversations. I grew very fond of Dave Sr. and the whole Hansen family. They were all good people and gave in more ways than most. On more than one occasion, before the morning of Christmas, Carrie picked up their Christmas tree and brought it to another family who could not afford one. Christmas ornaments, lights, and all. It was crazy kind, and she did it. Dave referred to me as his sixth son, and when I discovered college classes for farming, animal husbandry, and dairy cattle science, he quizzed me on what kind of classes existed for that. Having never had the opportunity for higher education, he had no idea classes for such stuff existed. Neither did I until I one day asked John King how he got into farming. He went to college for Animal Husbandry at the State University of New York in Delhi.

Ever enthralled with my enthusiasm and dreams, Dave sat down one Sunday morning with me and asked me if I'd yet made love to a girl. A little shocked, I was honest and admitted that I had not.

Dave got up, pulled the coffee pot off the stove, poured himself a warmup, and poured me another cup. "Curt, I'm sure you've seen some dirty magazines as a young man," he said. It was good I wasn't sipping coffee, as I would have choked and spit at him as I wasn't sure where this was leading to or where this was going. The fact that he brought up this subject was so out of character that I was shocked.

"You've seen pictures, right?" I acknowledged with a sheepish nod. "Well, Curt, that little triangular patch of hair between a girl's legs leads to a place most young men get lost in and don't know how to cope with or escape at your age. It's a mystery all boys want to explore, and once you're in, you're hooked." He took another sip of his coffee.

"Stay out, Curt; stay away until you're ready to marry and get that farm." Dave looked at me with some watery eyes. I could sense he was speaking from experience.

"Don't let that triangle detour your mind, drive, soul. It can capture everything you dream about and destroy it all." My knees began to shake with anxiousness. "I've never known anyone like you. You have great aspirations, Curt, more goals than anyone I've ever known, more goals than my boys or I ever had. I want you to succeed at them." Dave took another sip of his coffee.

"Stay away from the girls until you've acquired what you need to accomplish your dreams."

He must have seen the confused and awkward look on my face that we were even having this conversation. As he spoke, all I could think of was the Bermuda Triangle, a section of the Atlantic Ocean geographically located near Miami, Bermuda, and Cuba. People, planes, and ships have been lost in the Bermuda Triangle and have never escaped.

The whole conversation was so awkward that I was silent for what seemed like forever, though maybe it was just a few seconds. I gulped down a good sip of coffee, and to break the pause in silence, I joked and said, "Dave, so the patch is like the Bermuda Triangle!" Dave laughed and said, "Yes, you got it,

I like that," he said, "the Bermuda Triangle…It's the same, Curt. I don't want you to get lost. Stay out of the Bermuda Triangle!"

"Well, I have no girlfriend now."

"Yeah, I know," he said. "But you're up there in that cabin alone…I mean, don't get yourself in trouble!"

"Well, Dave, as you said, I will wait until I get married."

"Good choice," he said.

While it was one of the most awkward conversations, I'd not heard anything like that from my parents. In fact, on my sixteenth birthday, Loretta gave me a box of condoms as she was sure I'd follow in her footsteps of pre-marital teen sex. Rather than coach me to stay out or away, she equipped me to do so.

Dave cared for me deeply enough to have a father-and-son-like coaching conversation, and though I already subscribed to his advice, I would try hard to hear his words repeatedly in my head in future times of temptation.

Chapter Eighteen
Pressure Cooking

March 1977
No Playlist

Out of the clear blue and for unknown reasons, a sophomore kid named Robert and his buddy Don began taunting me into a fight on several occasions. As if I didn't have enough pressure, I had two guys begin to try and pick a fight with me nearly every day.

As president of the student council, I attracted a little teasing and bravado from jerks like these guys who knew that I could not succumb to a fight in my position.

Robert and Don's taunts, though, were becoming excessive. To the point that I met with Principal Raymond Starr and registered complaints. On several occasions for almost two months, I made sure Raymond Star understood from me that I would be forced to defend myself at some point as their bullying was becoming brazen. He indeed cautioned me and stressed avoidance, but I told him there would be a time when that would not be possible. "Do you want me to speak with them?" He asked.

"No," I said, "that would make things worse in more ways than one and invite others to do the same. I just want you to know how long this has been going on. I have reported this to you, and I'm trying to avoid them."

Avoiding them was impossible as they were both in my drafting class, and I endured their taunts in the hallways every day to and from the course. Some shoves and pushes became more emboldened. The more I tried to ignore them, the bolder they became. They made me look like a sissy sometimes, and my buddies would egg me on and tell me not to take any of their crap. "Don't take that crap kick the shit out of them," one of my buddies said.

"I can't; it wouldn't look good," I'd explain.

One afternoon I left the drafting class to get a drink of water. While I bent over at the water fountain, Don and Robert followed and surrounded me on both sides of the fountain. Don poked me in the back with something while I was drinking and said, "Riess, have you ever been stabbed to death before?"

I continued taking in water as I sized up the situation. I was so tired of these guys and pent up with anger and frustration, and though what follows is so unlike me, I seized the opportunity to set things straight with them. I released the fountain button while maintaining a posture to go back to drinking, and I looked up at Don and said, "since I am alive and living, I guess the answer to your dumb ass question is no, I have never been stabbed to death before," and I turned back to drinking. Robert looked on as Don poked my back again with something. Was it a knife, I wondered? I maintained my posture in drinking, looked up at Don, stared at his face, and then, with my eyes, directed my fist to come up swinging and bloodied his nose.

I hit him again before he knew what had happened. I managed to take him entirely by a nasty surprise, and blood was spewing everywhere. Suddenly, I felt a metal chair hit me over my back. I turned to see another chair swinging straight into my head as his cowardly buddy Robert used it as a weapon. As I moved to defend myself against Robert, Don got up from the floor, bleeding everywhere, and jumped me from behind. We both stumbled and scattered through the remaining desks and chairs, making a considerable commotion. Robert hit me again with another chair and knocked me to the floor, where I hit my head. I briefly blacked out and covered my head with my arms as I felt my face and head being kicked by Robert and Don's feet. I had flashbacks of being pummeled again by my shotgun.

The noise and commotion brought out our teacher Mr. Mack and my buddies in the class, who took after Don and Robert and beat them back.

All three of us were escorted to Principal Stars' office. Once there, Don and Robert were told to sit in another room, and I pointed at Mr. Star and said, "I told you so."

He asked, "what happened?"

"I was asked if I had ever been stabbed to death while bending over to get a drink of water while they poked something into my back. I took that as a threat and defended myself."

"What did they poke you in the back with?" He asked.

"I don't know; I didn't see it, but based on the threat, It could have been a knife!" He didn't respond or say a word.

I never found out if either of them genuinely had a knife. Still, since our teacher, Mr. Mack, had only seen the event from the standpoint that I was on the floor having my head kicked in…his story got him, and Robert suspended for two weeks and suspended from drafting class indefinitely. I was never questioned by Mr. Star nor anyone else about the matter again. For the rest of my senior year, I was without torment by anyone as news spread quickly that I was very capable of defending myself one on one.

Chapter Nineteen
Crushed

April 1977

Playlist:

She's Not There, Santana

I Want You to Want Me, Cheap Trick

Feels like the First Time, Foreigner

Cold as Ice, Foreigner

Go Your Own Way, Fleetwood Mac

I Go Crazy, Paul Davis

Fun, Fun, Fun, The Beach Boys

In high school, there was Madison. Since the eighth grade, I have had a crush on her. Finally, in my junior year, we went out for a ride a few times, I even went to church with her family, and one Sunday, she came to meet my family, and we began to turn all those years of crushes into a little more than a friendship. Madison was cute, seductive in her personality, and had a great figure. She had breasts that I'm not sure I would not have known what to do with had we ever made out and long, flowing blonde hair that draped about her neck and shoulders. She was from a solid religious Baptist family. I sure thought her least of all to have scruples that would ever veer from her religious upbringing, but late one evening from a night in Ithaca, as I would often do on my way home, I drove through Spencer Park.

I pulled up to a spot where I would park Comet under a huge maple tree during many a summer evening and coat her with a protective sheen of wax and chrome polish. When there wasn't someone around to socialize with, I did this to kill time before returning to my cabin in the wood. As I waxed and polished, I would hang there and think about life as I did on the Beckhorn Hollow Bridge. Comet and I would dream together of days long into the future.

And as I polished every nook and cranny of its front grill, I'd pray and gratefully whisper thank you, Comet, for all you do for me.

This particular evening, I recognized a car parked at the edge of the parking lot. It was Robert's. His mom's car that is. Though he hadn't bothered me since our fight, I still had enough pent-up anger to throw at him if he asked for it. I stared at the car for a few minutes with my lights off. In the faintness of the streetlights, I wondered what in the world would Robert's car be doing sitting here in Spencer Park at nearly midnight.

I started Comet up and steered head-on to the grill of his car. Once in position, I flipped on my headlights with the brights on.

The windows of Robert's car were slightly fogged, but not enough to not recognize Madison jumping up from the front seat, blouse undone with her tits hanging out, and the next head to emerge for sure was Robert!

I couldn't believe my eyes. And then the reason for the taunts all became clear. Madison must have been quietly dating him; now, she was making out with him. She was going down on a sophomore.

There they were, scurrying to button and zip up as I sat bumper to bumper with my headlights glaring straight at them. Blinded by Comets headlights, they thought I was the police. I wasn't expecting this, certainly not with Madison, and for the moment wished I'd never found out. Half angry as I had a crush on her but more disgusted, I held steady with the headlights and wrecked the hard-on he had for her.

After they scrambled to their passenger and driver positions, their faces blushed and full of embarrassment, I backed up and then slowly pulled forward to pass and reveal it was only Comet and me. Their faces went from shame to relief that I wasn't the local constable. Robert flipped me the finger. His finger meant nothing to me, but I was crushed. Madison had been teasing and flirting with me since eighth grade. If there were a girl in high school that I dreamed about or thought someday I'd slip my hand where it wasn't supposed to go, it was her. I couldn't believe what I stumbled upon.

I left Spencer Park and headed toward my home on Rumsey Hill. Comet took me to Beckhorn Hollow, crossing my bridge without stopping. I was bummed and had nothing left to pour into the creek tonight. We took it slow up Cooper Hill through the valley across from Harry and Loretta's house. It was the long way back to Jay Rumsey Hill and their home. I slowly drove past. There weren't any lights on. I wasn't living there; I just needed to see it. For most of my childhood, it was where I only knew the comfort of a bed and a decent meal and not much else, but it was still home.

Comet and I crept slowly up the washboard hills with the windows open wide, trying to catch the fresh country air and the noise of the crickets and tree frogs. We took the long way back to my cabin in the wood. I was emotionally exhausted; every damn week was always something, and I was spent again.

The following day, I woke up with anger. It was Sunday, and the cabin was cold. It was raining and chilly. I built a fire and traced all my disappointments in what was supposed to be the best year of my high school life, my senior year. I wallowed in self-pity. I was disgusted with myself, with everyone.

The next day at school, I looked for every opportunity to catch up with Madison. I could tell she was trying hard to avoid me. During lunch, I found her in the common area near the gymnasium and asked her, "How in the world could you lead me on all these years and then go make out with the *menace*?" as I angrily referred to him. She blushed and said, "Be quiet!" I pressed her again with the question, this time in an even louder whisper. That's when I first heard, "Curt, you are a great guy. I mean it. You are the kind of guy a girl wants to marry, but right now, I want to have some fun!"

"Fun," I huffed. "Fun! I'm not fun? We laugh together all the time," I charged.

She stiffened, her face red as a beet, slapped her books together, and told me to "Hush up." She was embarrassed and didn't want anyone to know about this. She walked away from our conversation, and I kept her secret to save her reputation and keep me from looking like an idiot for flirting with her all those years. I thought that was one more door to close and nail shut forever.

I was so damn perplexed at the time that I didn't know what else to do or how to respond to her comment. "Fun!" What the hell did that mean? Didn't we have fun hanging out? Going on drives with Comet? Hell, we laughed all the time in classes. Sometimes I got kicked out of history classes because she and I would start giggling and laughing to a disturbing level.

I had asked her to the school dances, but she was never allowed to go to the school proms or dances as her Baptist religious views forbade dancing. But she sure liked dancing in the front seat with Robert. She must have thought she was missing out on some unique exercise seeing the evidence of stretched round tummies growing in the high school halls. I had plenty of friends who subscribed to the wood shop motto of "Gluing is good, screwing is better, it spreads her thighs, opens her eyes, and gives her pussy some exercise." Three of my classmates were already high school fathers, one with his third baby on the way as he graduated.

Nearly a five-year crush gone up in a sweat, not mine, but hers… Puke!

I tried to convince myself that it didn't matter, but the heaviness in my heart from other matters, my family problems, living alone in the woods, and hiding that secret from everyone were overwhelming. I was sensing I was becoming somewhat fragile. I had to keep myself busy, or I'd fall into depression. I had to stay focused on the future. In retrospect, I thank God I never viewed Madison as willing to make out. I would have broken down. I would have shown her where I was living… in a cabin in the wood, and she would have had fun with me. I imagined the opportunity with that girl for a lot of years. That was the high school blonde I dreamed about. That was a girl I would have married someday had she waited. But she wanted to have fun… and with someone else!

I was simply the boy she might like to marry later on. I was so angry and insane over the episode I could think of a thousand names to call her through my lips. I held on to possibilities with her for so many years, if only in my thoughts, and she probably never knew the depth of it. She can thank or blame me; she never got to spread eagle that night in Spencer Park, or perhaps she did. I didn't want to think so. And as for Comet and me, it was just one of the longest and slowest night rides back to the cabin in the wood we had together. Downer drives were becoming the norm.

Chapter Twenty
Will Parker

William Mack and Curt Riess on stage in the Musical Oklahoma

April 1977
Playlist:
Oh, What A Beautiful Morning, West End Orchestra and Singers
Kansas City, West End Orchestra and Singers
I Can't Say No, West End Orchestra and Singers
The Farmer And The Cowman, West End Orchestra and Singers
All Er Nuthin, West End Orchestra and Singers
Oklahoma, West End Orchestra and Singers
Spring 1977

Living in my cabin in the wood was getting depressing. Since sixth grade, I had gone out for track each spring and ran various events, eventually settling on the high hurdles and high jump in high school. Loretta would ask me, "can you see yourself in the Olympics?"

"Not really," I'd respond, "I never get first place." For all of her instantaneous bouts of insanity inflicted upon us, she would occasionally encourage you and tell you that "you can be anything you want to be."

"Why not an Olympic athlete?" she'd inspire.

"Try your best," she'd encourage, "you can do anything you set your mind to." That was always the tormenting issue about Loretta. She could be as encouraging and motivating one day and tearing you in half the next. Even when I ran for student council president, she was optimistic and proud. Still, I no sooner won, and she'd use it against me in multiple demeaning ways claiming I was now on a pedestal, thinking I was better than she.

Our high school put on a musical every two years. I wanted to participate in a production of My Fair Lady and tried out for a few roles when it was put on but didn't earn any parts. Junior and Senior students got preference as it was their last chance to experience and perform. Deservingly, those students in the drama club who participated in the school play year in and year out (to which I had not done) received the best roles.

In my senior year, the school was auditioning for roles in the musical production of Oklahoma. I had a lot of idle time in that cabin in the evenings to memorize lines and practice if I could land a role. It was something different, and I thought it would help keep me from becoming stir-crazy. The one glitch about the play was that practice was simultaneous to track training. I thought long and hard about choosing one over the other. Track and running were a part of my life and I didn't want to disappoint coach Miller. I decided to audition for a role in the play, and if I got one, perhaps I could do both it and track.

I auditioned for any role I could get, and to my surprise, I landed one of the lead roles, the role of Will Parker. A character who courted a sweet little gal named Ado Annie. It was a significant commitment to make and take on, and there was that conflict in that track practice was at the same time as theater practice. I needed a change. I was tired of running in more ways than one. I needed some other refreshing stimulation to aid me through this senior year and exit from high school. I chose the play.

I rehearsed my dialogue and singing parts every night in the cabin or while alone with Comet. While there were other choruses as a cast member that I would sing in the production, there were two main scenes and songs in which Will Parker played pivotal roles. It kept me sane, and it kept me from self-pity. It also reinforced my sense of fearlessness and kept my confidence up.

In the first act, Will Parker returns from a trip to Kansas City and introduces the cast to a new dance called the two-step as he transfers news and updates on Kansas City through song lyrics. Ado Annie, Wills's girlfriend, sings a song entitled I Can't Say No, alluding to her shenanigans with boys and how she can't say no to a flirty fellow.

Will Parker sings All Er Nothing with Ado Annie in the second act. Through the song lyrics, he lets her know that he heard she was kicking up some capers while he was in Kansas City, Mo. He tells her he listened to some things that couldn't be printed in papers from fellas talking like they ought to know. Will's character was so fitting, almost spooky in that his character life was so much like my own experience in high school regarding girls. His girl Ado Annie was a bit easy with the boys. She lets him know she was faithful to him but only went as far as she could go for her! Yet he behaved, giving up all kinds of lousy guy habits to secure her love. Unknowingly at the time, his character experience would draw parallels in my future, trying to find the perfect girl that wasn't loose, discovering new cities, and more.

Participating in that production was one of the most satisfying experiences in my high school life. I was being coached on my singing voice and dancing, brought on some ad-lib lines I created, and dance moves that the directors incorporated into the play. One of my high school teachers, Mr. Schanbacher, taught me how to lasso with a lariat. I got to be a cowboy wearing his chaps and cowboy hat swirling his lariat rope on stage.

Practicing my lines, singing, and learning the lyrics to the songs while in the cabin in the wood brought me somewhere else rather than where I was. Especially the lyrics of Oh What A Beautiful Morning. It was so befitting of me working on a farm with cattle and appreciating every beautiful morning I worked there. I had made new friends in the drama teams, built up some esteem, and reinforced the confidences I'd always had despite the spite, hurt, and miserable home life I'd endured.

Playing the role of Will Parker also brought me more recognition within the local community. In the small towns I lived in, the high school musicals were attended well for entertainment. After the play, folks in town would greet me with a "hey Will" as a friendly gesture and compliment to the performance

they remembered. Little did I know at that time that in less than two years…
I'd be encouraged to go to the Midwest, Kansas City, and like him, I'd also be
tested with girls that went about as far as they could go.

Chapter Twenty-One
Tioga State Bank

May 1977
Playlist:
Out of My Dreams Ballet, Original 1955 Oklahoma Studio Orchestra
Oh, What A Beautiful Morning, Gordon Macrae, Darcy M. Proper
Finale: Oh, What A Beautiful Morning, Gordon Macrae, Shirley Jones

A few weeks after starting work at the King Dairy, I opened a savings account at the local Tioga State Bank. It was locally owned by the Fisher family and named for the landmass and region south of Spencer, which wrapped both sides of the great Susquehanna River. A large area of the country where settlers in the 1700s flocked to homestead land and make a living from farming.

It was a small country bank with a few offices in the small towns carved out from the great Tioga landmass. It had a rich history of serving the local area. It is still in existence today and still owned by the Fischer family, celebrating more than 150 years in business.

Looking ahead and knowing I would need more cash to get to college, one Friday night after depositing my paycheck, I asked if I could meet with a bank representative about inquiring for a college loan. I was told that I had to meet with Mr. Fischer and that I would have to make an appointment.

I made the appointment.

A few days later, I returned to the bank to sit across from the bank's owner. He asked me several questions about which schools I was applying to and which I had been accepted to. He explained some of the options that might be available to me. He said his bank offered both personal loans and some loans that the government could provide through his bank. While he explained these options to me, he curiously looked at me and my hat. "You're the boy who works at the King Dairy, correct?"

"Yes, sir, I am."

"Why aren't your parents here with you, helping you through this loan process?" he paused briefly, "you know I can't give you a loan without their signature as a co-signer?"

My heart dropped into my work boots, not into them, onto the ground below the sole. "Really?" I asked.

"Yes," Mr. Fischer said.

My heart was pounding with anxiety! I hesitated, not knowing how to answer. The anxiety welled up in my chest, my head, into my whole being as I sat there peering through the bill of my cap at my manure-laden boots. "But I don't live with my parents. I'm independent and live alone."

"You live alone? He questioned with a facial mixture of surprise and suspicion?"

"Yes," I answered.

"Where do you live?" he asked.

"Here in Spencer," I responded.

"And your parents won't cosign for you?"

"No, they would never cosign for me."

Mr. Fisher leaned back in his chair and sized me up. "How old are you, Curt?"

"Seventeen, but I'll soon be eighteen in a few weeks."

"Why is it that you don't live with your parents? Why wouldn't they cosign for you? Don't they want you to go to college?"

I took several deep breaths, dragged my sorry eyes up from my boots, and looked into Mr. Fishers' eyes…he had a poker look on his face, without emotion, void of a smile or any implication he might be judgmental. I was honest about my whole situation without too many details. I told him where I lived alone in the cabin in the woods. I left home many months ago and wanted to go to college. I told him my parents weren't even aware that I was applying. They would never cosign, not because they wouldn't want me to go to college, although neither of them ever encouraged or talked about it, but because they just don't understand these things.

All the while, he took notes on a notepad. He reviewed my bank account and noted that I was depositing a check every other Friday, like clockwork. Only occasionally was there a significant withdrawal, usually when Comet needed repairs. I deposited every dollar I had except for what I would spend on meals for the next week and gas and oil for Comet. He asked, "Do you have any other assets?"

"What?" I asked.

"Assets," he asked again. "Like any other bank accounts, car?"

"No, sir. You're the only bank I bank with. I do own my Comet, my car."

"Do you own it outright?"

"Yes, sir, it is registered in my name."

"How did you buy that car?" he asked. I told him how I earned it by tearing down a barn. I went to work and paid my insurance and all other repairs and maintenance expenses.

My hat identified me quickly when I walked in, as it had done so for years, and I always wore the same color, a red and white polka dot hat. In my records and savings account book, my history was right there before his eyes. He noted the steady growth and mentioned how often he'd seen me in his bank over the last few years.

Knowing I worked for the King family and who they were, he asked, "Do you think you could get the Kings to cosign a loan for you?"

I told Mr. Fischer, "I bet surely they would support me if I asked, but that was simply out of the question. I'm just a hired hand. I'm not a relative, and I would never do that. I can't do that," I told him. "I simply can't put them in a position to say no to me if they could not do so for any reason." My love had grown more for them than they probably realized. I respected them, but while it seemed to be a lifetime knowing them, it was only three out of my 18 years. "Mr. Fischer, there is no way I could remotely make them feel obliged to do such a thing."

Mr. Fisher looked directly into my eyes, hearing what I had to say. "They would be a reference, of course?" he asked.

"Of course," I said.

"Who else could be a reference?" I thought for a minute, "A couple of my teachers," I said, "Mr. And Mrs. Miller, Mrs. Schwartz…" and… I hesitated momentarily and thought about saying the following, and then it poured out… "You, Mr. Fischer… you just told me you noticed me many times over the years in your bank; in fact, whether you were here or not, I was here every paycheck day for the last two to three years, depositing into your bank. Here, you can see for yourself my record of savings. You are the best reference I have, Mr. Fischer! No one else could provide more evidence than you have here about me that I'm responsible and capable of saving and managing my money. I would have had even more money than this in your bank, but while living at home, I had to give up half for room and board."

Mr. Fisher was a sizable man compared to my lean frame. His poker face stiffened, and he leaned forward and placed his elbows on his desk. "So all this time, you were planning and saving this money for college?" he asked.

"No, sir, I wasn't. The college track had never entered my mind until recently, and I didn't do any planning for college until a few months ago. I was saving for something beyond college, and I'm still saving for it."

"Like what?" he quizzed.

"I'd like to farm someday, maybe like a big dairy farm or some business… I'm not sure yet."

"Well, what inspired you to want to go to college if you weren't saving for it?"

"My friends, sir. Some of my friends are going to college, and one encouraged me to get more skills to get where I want to go."

"Are you going to use your savings for school?"

"No, sir, I mean, yes, in a way. I plan to get a job, work while in college, and continue to grow these savings, to maintain them as a backup for emergencies, books, or other items I'm not sure about just yet."

Mr. Fisher looked the whole of me over one last time. I sat erect in his chair with my polka dot hat on, my brown curly hair protruding from beneath the sides, my well-worn jeans and dusty t-shirt from work, my work boots emitting the smell of manure, and my hands tightly clasped together. I stared intently into his eyes as he looked me over. And then he wrote down a few more notes. "What schools did you apply to again?"

"SUNY Cobleskill and SUNY Delhi," I enthusiastically responded.

"Did you get an acceptance letter from them?"

"Yes, sir, I did, from both!"

"Which one do you want to go to?"

"I haven't decided yet, but I will as soon as I get the loan."

Both schools had the same tuition, room, and board expenses. Comet and I had driven to both of them one Sunday to see what the campuses looked like. They were only a two-hour drive away from Spencer. I could have gone to either college, but I leaned toward Cobleskill because my friend Jack was going there.

"Mr. Fischer, one more thing." I ensured Mr. Fisher looked not just into my eyes but through them as a portal to see into my soul. I hoped that he might see beyond college, too, that maybe one day I'd be a more significant customer of his. I hoped he had some compassion and that while he got to use my money for a couple of years, he'd take a chance on me and let me use his money now. "Mr. Fischer, I promise to repay you every dime you can loan me. And I'll keep my savings here until I need them. I promise." He wrote a couple more notes on his pad and leaned back in his chair.

"Are you coming in this Friday to deposit your check?" No, sir, I said, the milk check comes every two weeks. My next payday is the following Friday, a week and a half from now. "Drop off a copy of your acceptance letters tomorrow and then stop and see me on your next paycheck deposit, and I'll let you know my decision." He directed.

Mr. Fisher wasn't much of a smiling guy during our meeting. He was a very serious, inquisitive banker trying to learn as much as possible about me. I'd seen him often as the bank president behind his desk, working and always looking down at papers on his desk. I never paid much attention to him, but now I wished I had. I wished I'd introduced myself to him long ago, but I was surviving with many issues. One thing was for sure, he had a poker face with me the entire time I was with him, and I couldn't read his thoughts. Whether he was satisfied with what I told him or dissatisfied. It didn't matter. I told him the truth, and I could offer no more.

The following week was among the longest weeks of my life. I had so many emotions going through my gut. My head was spinning with hope, doubt, and fear of failure all at the same time. The closer I got to the following Friday, the more I became anxious. It didn't help, too, that Oklahoma's production was in a few days for three nights. Mr. Fisher couldn't call me as I had no phone, and he knew that. He told me to see him the next time I deposited my paycheck without indicating what might happen.

I had the same feelings the whole week after performing in the play anticipating a meeting with Mr. Fisher for the second time. There were feelings of excitement, tense nervousness, joy, fear and doubt, and the satisfaction of a bow with audience applause or approving laughter that they were entertained. I wanted a bow out of Tioga State Bank with a loan in my hand.

Thursday before payday came. Comet and I went for a long ride in the evening. My soul was like a two-foot bungee cord stretched to a hundred feet…my stomach was the opposite, like a logging chain tied in a knot and weighing me down. My thoughts were flitting like a butterfly between failure and success. What happens if I don't get the loan? Even more fearful, what happens if I do get it? It seemed easier to process in my head to accept a no from Mr. Fisher and, in essence, fail. If he said yes, following through on this journey could be even more challenging than I could imagine. Except for the typical budget information the colleges had shared with me, I had little idea how much money I would need. Surely there were going to be expenses I didn't know about yet. It would all come from my pocket, some from Mr. Fisher's.

I drove to Ithaca to Pudgies. We were alone, me and Comet, just the two of us. I needed some pizza. I needed to hear and converse with my God alone in temple Comet. My emotions were a bust. Stuffed with pizza, we drove back to the cabin. It was a dark, moonless night. I looked up through the branches of the trees; the leaves were growing big enough to block the starry sky.

The following day, I woke up and sang the song from the play, Oh What A beautiful morning. It wasn't one of my lead songs as Will Parker, but I loved the inspiring ending of "Everything's going my way." I'd sing the whole song repeatedly as I spread manure or did other fieldwork. It was a cheerful song and helped me to think positively. But, in reality, I was nervous as hell the whole day. As much as I told myself everything was going my way, my stomach had an empty feeling, not one of hunger; I didn't feel hungry at all, but one of emptiness, expecting failure. While I told myself that if Tioga State Bank couldn't help me with a school loan, I'd find another way. I was on pins and needles and scared of the rejection I expected. I'd already had enough of this year—enough of living in the cabin, embarrassed and hiding that I was camped in the woods. I was tired of Campbell's Soups and Spaghetti-O's. I was up to my eyebrows with all the challenges. And if Tioga State Bank wasn't going to come through for me, I didn't know what bank I could try next.

Like most paydays, I handed Joyce the little green ledger when I arrived after school before setting out on my chores. She would take it, review the hours and tally everything up. She had studied and tallied the last two weeks and completed the day. When I was done with milking, I headed for the kitchen. Thank you as always, Joyce. I'll see you tomorrow morning.

I got into Comet. The keys were left in the ignition as usual, and I stared ahead at the shop. I looked in my rear-view mirror to see if John had yet come out of the barn. I'd left him in there finishing up sanitizing the milk house.

Usually, I was the last one out, but I told him I had to get to the bank before they closed tonight. John was always OK with the few excuses I had to give to leave early if I had to.

I never carried my keys or wallet for fear of losing them in the barn or field and always left the keys in the ignition if John might have to move the car by chance. My wallet was always in the front seat. I wondered momentarily if Mr. Fischer would trust me the way I trusted everyone else, the way I trusted Comet, the way my King family had always trusted me. He doesn't know me; he doesn't know how hard I work; he only sees the result in my savings. Was it enough? I wondered if he had called any of my teachers. I pondered if he called John or Joyce. They never said so. References were the only way for someone to evaluate me, and I never thought about references until Mr. Fisher asked for them.

I stared at the keys in the ignition switch. I was hesitant to start Comet up. I just didn't want to face a possible rejection. Mr. Fischer was adamant about me finding a co-signer for that loan. In a doubtful weird way, I was hoping when I turned the keys, Comet wouldn't start, that something had gone wrong, and I'd have an excuse not to hear Mr. Fisher deny me the loan. My self-esteem was at one of its lowest points. Coming off the ecstasy of performance-induced adrenalin from Musical Oklahoma this past weekend to where I was now was a steep decline. I was so soft and fearful of rejection.

John tapped my window. I missed him in my rear-view mirror, watching for his exit from the barn. "Everything OK, Curt?" He must have been a little mused that I was hurrying to get to the bank, yet I was still sitting there. I turned the ignition key to start Comet. "Yup, everything is fine. See you tomorrow."

Before heading to the bank, I scrubbed my boots to get as much manure and dirt off them as possible. Milking cows never left you clean and certainly not smelling fresh as a daisy.

Comet drove me to the bank, and I parked on the side of the building near the Big M Grocery store. I sat for a minute, silently prayed to my God, and asked him to lead. Lead me wherever I'm supposed to go.

Inside the bank, I deposited my check. The balance on my account was over $2800.00. (Though considered small today, not bad for a teenager in the 70s.) I asked to see Mr. Fischer and was told to sit and wait.

I could see he was with another person. His face was stern and never smiling.

It wasn't a long time, maybe twenty minutes or so, that I had to wait, but after this past week, it seemed like an eternity, and my knees bounced with nervous energy.

Mr. Fischer escorted his customer out, nodded to me, and said, come back.

He sat up straight as he cleared his throat, pulled out a file, and placed it on his desk. I began to panic on the inside. He opened the file and flipped through a few pages, again clearing his throat for a second time.

"Well," he said. "I can't give you the loan for $8,000.00 that you requested." I choked. My worst fear became a reality. My heart was already pounding, and I began to feel something in my chest I'd never felt before. He shuffled another paper from the file and laid it on the first. I was ready to burst with emotions, so I had to get out of there fast. I got up. Quaveringly I said, "I understand. Thank you for trying" I started to leave when he held up his hand. "Hold on; I can give you a loan up to $7,000.00 toward your college expenses." An intense heat swept through my body like a fever. I felt like I could feel every single vein in my arms, chest, and legs, my whole being swelling from a rapid heartbeat!

"The maximum I can loan you would be $7,000.00," he said. "I'm sure you can make up the other $1000.00 you'll need through work?" I froze in disbelief! He must have seen confusion all over my face. "Sit down," Mr. Fisher motioned. "Also, I want to be clear about the terms. Because it isn't a government loan, you must repay it within five years of graduation. Interest will accrue, but you won't have to make any payments until after you graduate." He laid out the interest amortization table and taught me how the balance would grow with interest applied. He explained what payments would be due after my two-year degree. He told me he expected to see my official enrollment documents and that the payments from this loan would be made directly to the college for tuition and expenses and not to me. "Are you acceptable with these terms?" He asked.

I couldn't believe what I had just heard…I was kinda in shock. "Yes," I said, "I, I, I, agree to all the terms!" My head was spinning.

"So, I don't need anyone to cosign with me?" I asked.

"Would anyone cosign for you?" he asked again.

"No," I responded.

"Then you don't need one for now."

I tipped the bill of my polka-dot hat up and stared at him. "Thank you, Mr. Fischer. Thank you so much. Thank you so much," I repeated three times.

"You told me you turn 18 soon, correct?" he asked.

"Yes, sir, actually, in another week."

"Well, that's good. You have to be 18 before we can sign the loan documents. I'll need a copy of your driver's license and official enrollment letter to prepare the loan documents."

"Yes, sir, here is a copy of my license." My hand shook as I tried to pull it from my wallet and hand it to him. He summoned someone over to make a copy.

"Now that you know you will have the loan, which school did you decide to attend?" he asked.

Just two weeks ago, he asked me that question, and I said I would decide as soon as I got a loan, so now I had it.

My inner thoughts welled up. I hadn't given much thought at all as to which college I'd choose. The past week and a half were a crazy ten days of wrecked nerves, doubtful fears, and performing in the musical. Mr. Fisher deserved an answer. I squeezed the bill of my hat in a V formation between my hands, paused momentarily, looked him in the eye, and with all the confidence in the world, put my hat on, stood erect, and said, "Cobleskill!" "Yup, Cobleskill!" I said again confidently.

Mr. Fisher gave me a rare half-smile and handed me my license back, "Good luck Curt," he said, "better get that official enrollment letter to me and your acceptance confirmation, oh and by the way, nice job as Will Parker."

"Thank you, Mr. Fischer… thank you…thank you so much again for everything."

I went next door to the Big M market and bought my usual quart of ice cream, a liter of pop, and a few candy bars.

Comet and I drove back to my cabin in the wood. I pulled Comet close to the porch, rolled down the windows, left the key on, popped in an eight-track of the Eagles, and turned the tunes up. I sat on the front porch chair and devoured my ice cream, drank my pop, and ate my candy bars. That was often dinner unless I went to Ithaca or opened up a cold can of soup.

This was one crazy senior year of high school, but I got into a college, and I just accomplished a loan for it. I pulled my hat off and stared at the inside cavity that was empty of my skull. *This is one lucky hat,* I thought. Aside from

Comet, my polka dot hat was a part of me as my arms, hands, and fingers. And it suddenly occurred to me that while the unique paint job on Comet was a marker that identified the car Curt Riess drove, no one else in Spencer wore the hat I wore, day in and day out. I was recognized everywhere simply by the hat. Even in Ithaca, walking down the common mall area, if someone from Spencer was there and saw the hat, they'd identify me and call me from afar.

That hat made Mr. Fischer take notice of me too. That or my smell, but the fact that he noticed me over the nearly three years of making my milk check deposits, I could only conclude that it was my hat. It stood out like a marker, a logo, a corporate identity, and a persona.

It was Friday night. I had to get up early and milk cows in the morning. And while I would generally pick up one of the Hansen boys or my friends and traverse up to Ithaca for a pizza, I just sat on the porch of my cabin and thought about the past few weeks. The play, the stage fright, the adrenaline that flowed once I was on, and my transformation from farm hand to Will Parker each of the performance nights. My soul felt frantic from all the nervousness that I might not get the loan. I'd been hanging on to the edge of my life with this loan. My anxiety over it gave me so much adrenaline and testosterone production that I poured it into all three nights of the Oklahoma Musical performance… Mr. Fisher was there…and took notice. I finally felt a calm, peaceful joy that I hadn't felt in a very long time. I whispered to my God and gave thanks for all. I was going to go to college in the fall. To Cobleskill. On my own. My friend Jack was right; the Pope was wrong. All I had to do was complete graduation in a few weeks, and then I could work full-time for John over the summer and put every penny I earned away. I was going to need it.

The following day was a beautiful morning, the one after that, and the one after that, and every morning till the day I left for Cobleskill, I would hum or sing the lyrics to Rogers and Hammerstein's "Oh, What A Beautiful Morning." Everything was finally going my way.

Chapter Twenty-Two
Prom

March 1977
Playlist:
Sex & Drugs & Rock & Roll, Ian Dury
Rockin' All Over The World, Status Quo
Rock And Roll Never Forgets, Bob Seger
We Will Rock You, Queen

The Senior prom was still ahead of me; a girl expected me to ask her to go. Not Madison, but another friend. We'd been friends most of our high school years and regularly hung out together in the library during one of our scheduled study breaks. Everyone who knew us patiently expected me to ask her to prom, and I was surprised that several of her friends were pressuring me and prying me to see when I would pop the question. I wasn't going to go to the prom and hadn't given any thought to asking anyone. Not because I wouldn't have wanted to ask her, she was a great gal, and not because I didn't like her. Though I was working and had some money in the bank, there was no room in my budget for a tux, renting a hotel room for the night as was the tradition, or budget for a corsage. I had little motivation to participate in prom with everything I had going on this past semester.

Like everyone, she had no idea I was living alone or of my enduring pressures. When one of her close friends finally asked me why I wasn't asking her to prom, I didn't handle it well. I was too embarrassed to share my budget woes and situation and said I'm not going. When pressured with questions about why I wasn't going I did the usual thing with adversity, I retreated into silence and avoidance. Thus, the typical table where a group of us usually sat in the library was absent of me for the remainder of the year. My stupidity took a toll on our friendship and lost was a daily laugh and interaction all over a misunderstanding of my silence and lack of truth on my part about the challenges and shame I felt living alone. Just days before the prom, one of my buddies asked me if I would ask her, and I said no. Perceiving how close we were as friends, he asked me, as a courtesy, if it was OK if he asked her, and of course, I said, "Yes, of course, she is a great gal; please ask her." She accepted his proposal and was delighted to have a date she thought might not have occurred.

I'd always had fun and enjoyed dancing with many girls at the school dances sponsored by the student council. They were held three times a year, and they insisted I attend as this was the last we'd all be at, and I should come. It was the first of many lasts for me. Some other girls and guys didn't have dates that convinced me I should go to the dance solo with them.

So, I went to prom wearing red Converse sneakers, jeans, and the best white shirt and tie I could garner from my closet back home. While most of the guys and girls were in rented tuxes and gowns, there were a few others that I fit in just fine, and we had a good time, albeit, at times, running into my buddy and the girl I wouldn't ask out was awkward. We just danced about each other and kept our distance. The damage of silence between her and me had already been done. I owed her an explanation and apology that I couldn't give at the time and never gave. I hope she reads this someday and accepts it when she does.

Our prom wasn't much different than a typical school dance. It was always held in the school cafeteria and had plenty of students with booze on the breath of those old enough to drink and plenty who weren't. There were about five chaperones; parents and teachers were required at these events, and we always had a live band. This night's prom was simply a declaration that those who could afford to rent suits, tuxes, and gowns did while the rest of us showed up in our best shirts and tie. Most of my classmates were already over the legal drinking age of 18 for months, and before the dance, they were loaded with alcohol. Everyone was having the time of their life! For a class of 92, probably 60 or so came to the prom. For most, it was an evening of drinking, getting high on weed, and dancing to the music.

Three girls I danced with most of the night also didn't have dates. We hung out as a clique and had a great time. After the dance, I was invited to bring all three girls I hung out with to one of the rented hotel rooms in Ithaca and party all night, but I passed on that and strayed to one of the other party scenes I was invited to. That scene on a country road on the edge of a cornfield was packed with a galvanized cattle trough of beer kegs, and a heavy whiff of weed hung in the air. It wasn't my scene. I saw trouble arriving at the party in several vehicles, so I returned to my cabin in the wood. I had to be up for milking and chores the following day, and staying clear of prom-night troubles was in my best interest. The moon was about half full as I drove through the woods toward the cabin. The leaves on the trees were almost mature enough to filter out the moon rays which hit the forest floor below. Despite my lack of full participation in the prom formal, I reflected on the evening and how much fun it was. It was the last dance as we knew dances in our teen lives, indeed the last dance in so many ways for many of us.

But I was still dancing in other ways. Besides needing to get a loan for college, once it settled in that I was going to go to college, Loretta asked me if she could throw me a small graduation party. While I was puzzlingly grateful, I declined. All I could think about was the constant charade this woman lived. I mean, I wasn't living at home, but she wanted to have some neighbors, my boss, and some friends over as if I never left home and we were some normal family.

She begged me again to allow her to give me a party. For her sake and for fear of reprisal, I went along with the idea and participated. Both Harry and Loretta attended the evening of my short graduation ceremony at SVE as if everything was normal. It was very awkward, I was only their second kid to graduate high school thus far, and she took some pictures to portray a typical family. At the graduation party, I showed up late to find mostly neighbors, my Great Aunt Rose from New Jersey, John and Joyce, and a few of Loretta's friends from the various part-time jobs she held over the years. As I sat on the deck outdoors among the guests feeling like a parade animal, there were so many moments I wanted to flee and leave. I was sick to my stomach whenever someone asked me how I was and about my future plans.

I had to tell them I was going to college for Foodservice as I was accepted, but I only used that curriculum to get in. Once enrolled, I planned to change to Animal Science, but how could I explain that deceit? I would have fled the scene without John and Joyce being there and my Great Aunt Rose. It seemed such a farce and a lie that all was well in our family. Another deep underlying force wanted me to come out and tell all and hurt Loretta. And while I was sharing that I was planning on going to college, I also wanted to add "no thanks to Loretta and Harry," but I didn't. That kind of person isn't me. I suppressed the pain felt deep within and mostly retreated to silence. I was happy to see that my Great Aunt Rose was there, not so much for me but for Loretta. She was the family matriarch on the Stellato side of the family and knew all about Loretta's miserable life more than any of us, and she always looked out to care for and check in with Loretta.

The coming summer would be one of my life's hottest, most extended, and most filled with anxiety summers. Living in the cabin daily with no running water or electricity and hanging out wherever I could kill time in the evening was exhilarating and excruciating, particularly during the hot evenings. While the cabin was shaded in the woods, it could get hot, and leaving a door open invited the mosquitos.

Mentally the most challenging was anticipating college and wondering precisely what it would be like. I awaited lots of information that my acceptance letter indicated would be forthcoming months before the fall semester. Every week I drove up Rumsey Hill to pick up my mail. All proof that Harry and Loretta saw that what I told them a month before was for real. With each letter I received, I opened a whole new world. Every envelope I opened held a new adventure for me. One letter would welcome me; the next would explain my room and board arrangements, how I would get my meals, and what dormitory and room I would be in. Then eventually, the bill would come and scare me by explaining what was due ten days before I started my first day. I was working as many hours as John and Joyce could afford me. I was high with emotion and anxious over everything.

As fall approached, I became very apprehensive. There was no doubt that I was moving forward and going to Cobleskill, but some utterly unexplainable emptiness within me made me feel incomplete. Perhaps it was my circumstance. Maybe it was that for most of the summer, many of my high school friends disappeared into permanent full-time jobs such as cement truck drivers, factory workers at Morse Chain or Ithaca Gun, and elsewhere. There was nothing to maintain steady contact, no daily classes, and no means of communication to get together. High school had been a social connection for us all. I was isolated in the cabin with no phone. The only way of getting in touch with some of my buddies was to drive to their house. With them living tens of miles apart in various directions, I couldn't afford to waste my gas on dropping in and finding them not home. We didn't have smartphones; we didn't have the internet; we didn't have social media; hell, I didn't have electricity.

I had more time to help Wayne move stones for his wall, so I killed evenings doing that for him in gratitude for using his cabin.

Chapter Twenty-Three
Leaving Spencer

Late August 1977
Playlist:
Help Me Rhonda, The Beach Boys
Love Hurts, Graham Parsons
On and On, Stephen Bishop
Some Times When We Touch, Dan Hill

As mid-August rolled around, colleges and universities had various start dates. The last week of August was the start date for new and returning students for Cobleskill. As I wound down my last two weeks working with the King family, I made some rounds to say goodbye. Some of my classmates and friends that planned for college I never saw again. We never said goodbye nor wished each other luck, and when I would inquire about them, I'd find out they had already left for college. The classmates who became full-time tradesmen or factory workers were already in the mode of living for the weekend and had found new associations through work. There was an absolute emptiness inside me. I was probably seen as a loser stuck wearing his polka dot hat in his high school farm job by most and not worthy of being wished well in anything. So, I said my goodbyes to those who meant the most to me. The King family, Mr. and Mrs. Hansen, My best friend, the Duke's mom and dad, Lou and Estell Ross, Wayne Meyer, Fred and Adele Garland, Paul and Ralph Efthimiou and their spouses, Glen and Doris Ahart, Mr. Frandsen, Mr. and Mrs. Donald Miller, Pastor Jack Bunde, Mr. Fisher, Mr. Smith at Agway, and a host of other just outstanding plain decent folk. The week before I left, I drove up Rumsey Hill to say goodbye to Harry, Loretta, and my little sis. Loretta cried and asked if she and Harry could accompany me and see me off to Cobleskill.

It's a three-hour drive, I explained; there is no need. While we reconciled all that spring and most of that summer, everything was still very awkward with Loretta and how she pretended nothing had happened, that nothing had ever happened between us or to us. She was still living the charade, still forcing me to dance.

"I don't think it's a good idea for you to come to Cobleskill," I insisted. The day I arrive, I'll have to spend moving in and carrying my stuff up to the dormitory. There is a host of activities I need to get settled into. Loretta wouldn't hear a word and used her tears to tug at me. She insisted that she and Harry follow me up in case Comet breaks down.

I tried most skillfully to convince her otherwise without making it look like the truth I was feeling in that I just wanted to get as far away from her as possible and would prefer she not know how to find me. But she persisted, and rather than make trouble or make her feel any the worse, I acquiesced and told them I'd be leaving the following Saturday morning.

My last goodbye was to my friend Dave, the Duke, who would remain living at home to attend Corning Community College and later move on to Cornell University and, of course, my King family. They were the last people I saw before leaving for Cobleskill, and I was filled with sadness and joy.

As I packed the rest of my small batch of belongings from the cabin in the wood, I took one last look at where I'd stayed for the latter part of my senior year, shut the door, and thought I'd like to build a log cabin in the wood someday. This one didn't have electricity, a kitchen, a bathroom, or running water, but it kept me dry and held enough heat from a wood stove to keep me from freezing. Most of all, it was a peaceful and serene abode during troubled waters in my life. A small creek gurgled at the bottom of the hill, and at night I could hear the frogs, crickets, katydids, owls, other critters, and a host of other natural music of nature that would surface in the night wood. I was never tired of that part of living there.

I stopped by Wayne Meyers and said goodbye, gave him the key to the padlock, and thanked him again for allowing me to live there. I carried stones for one of Wayne's earliest stonework walls as rent payment as he refused to take any money from me. His stone wall construction skills would surface later in his life in landscape books as some of the most pleasing stonework of art ever built, and eventually, his grounds would serve as a venue for events like weddings. The very first wedding was that of one of the King children, Steven King.

Loretta and Harry followed me to Cobleskill. Gees, I could never rid myself of the awful, awkward feelings I had to endure dancing around the constant charade she carried. I just wished they'd stayed home.

The day I was forced to leave home for good, I always felt I was on my own without needing parental supervision or advice. I didn't need any chaperones, certainly no help from Loretta. She acted as if she were the caring parent, the over-doting mother hen, sending me off to college even though she had nothing to do with it. On the contrary, she seemed to make everything as difficult as possible to alter my success at it.

Arriving and then moving into my dorm room, we spent some time together walking about the small campus and checking out the dining hall to have lunch. Loretta and Harry seemed to immerse themselves in a world they never knew. Like me, they'd never been to a college before, and I think they were primarily curious about where I was going, what I had gotten myself into, what the environment was like, and what I would experience. From the deer slug day to now seemed surreal but the incident was always fresh in my mind and not easily forgotten whenever I was around Loretta. I wondered how she could walk straight and tall and act as if her life was a charm and there was no malice or evil which I believed engulfed her. I looked at her often and thought she must be living in some other world in her mind as she acted as if everything was perfect at times.

I couldn't get rid of her fast enough. I was constantly tormented between hate and what I was taught in church and scolded many times by her; to honor thy mother and father regardless of her behavior. I granted them the time and opportunity they wanted to lounge around and partake of the college move-in day scene, but it was just bizarre. I felt so much angst for her and yet so much sorrow. She always wanted some extraordinary life she yearned for and claimed to have had before meeting my dad. I was polite and let her bask in her dream world. She had never dreamed of her son attending college, but she now lived it in real life.

When they finally left, I had to park Comet in the parking lot it was assigned to. My new roommate Abe arrived. He was a tall, good-looking Italian guy, thin like me, with a full head of brown hair like mine, only wavy rather than curly. I met his parents and many housemates I'd be living with the following year. As first-year students like me continued to move in, I wandered about campus. I explored the dairy barn and agricultural areas. Yes, I entered as a freshman in food service. Still, after one semester, I knew I'd transfer into the dairy science and animal husbandry majors. As my friend Jack advised, I had to get into college and prove myself. I was determined to do so.

141

Chapter Twenty-Four
Cobleskill

Cobleskill
September 1977 – May 1978
Playlist:
Help Me Rhonda, The Beach Boys
Love Hurts, Graham Parsons
On and On, Stephen Bishop
Some Times When We Touch, Dan Hill

My first year in college was a fantastic year of everything! I supported my room and board by milking cows at the campus dairy, working in the college cafeteria, and later for a small local construction company performing landscaping labor and other odd jobs in constructing garage decks and other structures.

My classes were going well, and I was pleased and content for the first time in 18 years. I enjoyed my lessons and did well enough to maintain my grades to stay in college. Though finances were tight, I always worked to keep a stash of cash to get the necessities I needed. I was free at last from Loretta. I had no phone and didn't write. I drove home for Thanksgiving and Christmas break to visit them. Other than that, I had little communication with her and Harry.

After my first semester of food service classes, I submitted a transfer request to the animal husbandry majors. It stunned some of the professors I was getting to know. They appreciated my hard work and effort and saw such a switch and difference in my major as irrational. They had me go through counseling and interviews with professors in the ag sciences sector to ensure I hadn't gone off the deep end somehow. The two worlds were far apart in culture, classes, and careers. What they did was look at the records. They didn't appreciate my background and that I had worked in agriculture on the farm. Undoubtedly, they viewed that experience as limited and with apprehension. They didn't understand how deeply immersed I was in King Dairy and its operations.

I lost one semester to the food service curriculum. Now I would have to make that semester up in agriculture, which meant I would carry 21, 22, and 23-semester credits of classes for the subsequent three semesters of the two-year program. My advisors were not happy about this and strongly encouraged me to reconsider. But I explained to them that I was paying for my college expenses… everything! And I only had enough loans and financial ability for two years. I had to get my degree done in those two years. I convinced them this was a career choice from the start and that though I enjoyed my food service classes, it wasn't in my heart. I was approved to move forward with the condition I would check in with my advisor three times a semester to see how I was doing.

There were so many experiences that were new in college. As my friend Jack was the one who encouraged me and led me toward attending Cobleskill, he had wanted to be roommates. I liked Jack, but he had a way about him that didn't make friends easily. I declined to be his roommate in favor of us both getting to know new people. I was afraid too of living in the shadow of Jack. He was the high school superstar athlete, and I surely thought he'd do the same in college. He had a girlfriend for most of his high school years, and we all became great friends, but Jack's first year at Cobleskill brought him new girlfriends and new adventures. It did for me as well.

Cobleskill was full of social activities, and Friday and Saturday nights were hell-bent drinking nights. It moderately started with lady's night on Wednesday at the Poolside Pub. The drinking age was 18, and most dormitory houses had parties with kegs of beer and alcohol every weekend. And after those parties, the downtown bars were open till 2:00 am.

It was the disco era, and dancing was all the rave. Yet, there were still complex rock groups and other genre bands like the boss Bruce Springsteen, Steely Dan, Earth, Wind and Fire, and others that developed my taste for various music styles. And there were many places to hang out and listen to music while having a beer.

Many students at Cobleskill came from downstate Manhattan and Long Island suburbs. Those weekend nights brought out a lot of fast Long Island girls. Under the guise of drunkenness and standing room only on crowded dance floors, girls were brave in frisking my jeans. I was always naïvely shocked that such behavior existed. I raised myself to stay true to my Christian values and not get into trouble. Our coaches always told us that the boy always got the girl in trouble; I wasn't so sure after just a few experiences at Cobleskill. I was behaving, but it seemed everyone around me wasn't. My hormones were constantly raging, but I pushed that testosterone into work and earning money as I had to.

A girl named Jan lived on the second floor across from our house. We met at their house party, and she loved playing with my polka-dot hat. She always jumped onto my lap, stole my hat, and wanted to wrestle. She'd take it off me, tease me, shove it behind her back or up her shirt enticing me to tackle her and grab it back.

Why do you wear that hat? She'd ask. Because… it's lucky…and I'm a farmer, I said! But you're in food service, she'd challenge; not for long, I'd retort. Jan was an equine major. I'd been to the horse barns with her several times as they were close to the parlor where I milked cows. There were a few uncomfortable moments when a stallion hung long and low as he peed, and she'd stare at its penis and then look my way to see my reaction. I always blushed a little and looked the other way. She joked one day that if I were half as big (as the stallion), she'd ride me too! I just blushed.

Jan was two-thirds my height, charming, and had a great figure and a tiny little butt that kept my eyes glued to as she'd swing a saddle over a horse. We had a lot of great fun together. We went for a few rides in Comet about the countryside, but Comet didn't impress her much. She loved to cuddle, and I so loved that. I don't know why, but I truly loved to be touched and cuddled up close. I didn't experience much of that as a youngster. It wasn't long before I began to feel more than just a cuddling feeling for her. She was so much fun! A sassy tom-boy kind of fun! For the first time, my emotions began to edge out and grow in some fondness that might have led toward love.

I began to want to spend more time with her, and when the sun went down every day after work, I wanted to be with her. I gave her my class ring and asked if she'd commit to being a steady girlfriend. She accepted, and after that, she frequented my room a lot. Many nights to the Vault (a Bar so named because it was once a bank and had an old Vault within); while dancing, she'd rub against my crotch in a manner that sent quivers up my spine. I was always the polite one and behaved like a gentleman.

One night, we returned to my room, and Jan was reasonably aggressive in a make-out session. Her breasts were bare and small as she was in size, and with my hand caressing the middle of her chest from her neck to her belt, I told her she had nothing to worry about from me in that I would never take this any further as I was saving sex for marriage. Looking into her eyes, I realized I had said the wrong thing. Her eyes and facial expression dispelled the quiet disappointment she would not verbally communicate out of shame. She had wanted me to take things to home base, and she lay motionless and was much less cuddly. It wasn't long after she buttoned her blouse and left my room, saying she had to get up early to head to the barns. My manhood suddenly felt like tomato soup with an egg dropped into it. I soon discovered I wouldn't be her stud that evening or any other evening.

The following day was a Saturday; her roommate knocked on my door and handed me my class ring and a message. The message was this; "Curt, Jan doesn't want to see you again. She doesn't want to be tied to one boyfriend. This hurts her to do this because you are such a nice guy Curt. But Jan wants to have fun! Curt, she said you're the guy she'd love to marry, but right now, she wants to have fun! She couldn't bear to come and say this herself, so she sent me."

I stood in my jeans, half-naked, without a shirt, socks, or shoes on as I had been lying on my bed studying. I was silent, as I didn't know what to say to her roommate. She opened her hand, and there was my high school ring, the only personal luxury I'd ever bought for myself. It was engraved with the emblem of Spencer-Van Etten High School with an emerald green stone with a bovine bull emblem underneath the stone to represent my zodiac sign of Taurus. I was dumbfounded and shocked, and my roommate saw the confusion and heartache on my face as I stood there frozen. She gently grabbed my hand, placed the ring in my palm, and folded my fingers around it. My roommate Abe heard the whole thing. I was so embarrassed, but he was cool about it.

Still frozen from shock in the doorway, he got up from his desk, tapped me on the shoulder to move out of the opening back into the room, and closed the door behind him as he left me some alone time. I was in awe at what I had just heard. Cute little Jan, she just wanted to get laid. What was wrong with me? Am I gay? Where were all the girls I learned about in Sunday School? Was I crazy? She was throwing herself at me for a good time, and I was too naïve and set in my morals and direction to realize it. I was stupidly confused and disappointed. I began to have real feelings for her, even talking about being a dairy farmer and possibly having horses on the farm one day. Though she did tell me once she would never marry a dairy farmer, I took it in stride, thinking I could one day sway her mind.

I lay on my bed, chin on my arms, wondering what happened to me. Abe came back into the room after about fifteen minutes. "You OK, Curt?" he asked. "Yeah," I responded. "I need to get some fresh air." I got dressed and walked over to the barns. I grabbed a pitchfork and a broom and swept hay and grain toward the cows, which they had pushed forward from foraging earlier. I loved cows. The barn and cows always gave me peace in high school. Their mammoth size and the fact that I knew how to handle them gave me comfort and confidence. Since I was twelve, from the beef cattle we had at home to John King's Dairy cows, they comforted my soul in times of trouble and disappointment. Now they were serving me in college as well. I left the barn and walked out to Comet in the parking lot. I sat in the driver's seat and started the engine.

"Cobleskill was the right place for me," I told Comet. "Or was it?" I asked.

"Of course it is," Comet bellowed back in the hum of her V-8. "Heck, pre-marital pregnancies and a life of hell are yours for the taking," Comet reminded me. I didn't know if these girls were on the pill, and I deliberately never carried condoms, so I wouldn't be ready when tempted. "Stay out of the Bermuda Triangle," I heard Comet reiterate. Jan wouldn't be the last of my disappointments or temptations.

Then one day, I met the Coby girls. They lived on the fifth floor of Davis Hall and often shouted down to those of us hanging out our den window. I could not have met a more diverse and sweeter threesome. Audrey, Lauren, and Vicky. We quickly became a groupie, heading downtown on weekend nights together, all of us hanging out and dancing together. We hung out many evenings talking about life, an imaginary world I created called Zobo, and just had simple fun. They were hugely instrumental in keeping me focused on schoolwork and helping me avoid the temptations that periodically came my way. We became such great friends that I didn't want to disappoint any of them by having a steady girlfriend or going astray with one. We were all just great friends, nothing more.

As a dairy club member responsible for overseeing some of the pregnant cows, I'd wake the Coby girls up in the middle of the night to see a calf give birth. They were in awe, having never seen such a sight. I once shocked them by sticking my hand and arm up a cow's vaginal canal to turn a calf's head and assist the delivery. They were in awe. Our times together on weekend nights kept me from traveling to Bermuda. We drank a little, danced a lot, and had even more often great conversations. We became close-knit friends and remain so today.

But another girl in their house had a crush on me. Her name was Sally. With a knockout body, she swooned all over me, barging in on the four of us at the dance parties. She had a triple-ten figure, and most guys would have given up everything for a night in bed with her. She had a body that made every guy's imagination desire to see it naked …just to see if it was real. She could and, at times, did make my hormones rage with her constant flirtations with me. I did, on occasion, speed up if I saw her walking ahead to follow her on her way back to her dorm, just staring at her figure. She was so hot.

I met her dad once as she introduced me as a friend. I'd only met one or two of the dads of the girls I went out with in high school. They were passive, but this guy, a very protective dad of his beautiful daughter, let me know he'd be the one to reckon with if I was ever caught screwing around with her. I told him there were no worries from my standpoint, but he made it clear to me anyway, which was oddly awkward as we weren't dating. I was walking back to the dorm when she casually introduced me to him. But I did have a second chance to think of him soon.

Our house was invited to Sally's house for a Sadie Hawkins party. They were trendy in college. A Sadie party was a great liberation for the girls as its rules permitted them to be assertive and dominant. It gave the not-so-pretty girls equality to all kinds of free liberties through party etiquette. The basic rules were that the girl was in control and asked the guys for favors and dances, and in return, they bought the guys the beers. Guys are not supposed to refuse a girl anything in agreeing to the terms of the invite.

It was a multi-keg party, and the girls would load the guys with beers, cheers, small favors, kisses, dancing, and sometimes make-out opportunities. A bunch of drunk guys was able and willing to do all kinds of stunts and grunts at the whim of the girls. Many of the guys would come home the following day from these parties with the panties from the girls they supposedly spent the night with. I figured they just found a way to steal a pair from some girl's drawer, just as the panty raid challenge strived for when guys would run through a girls' dorm and steal any they could find from an open dorm door.

The Coby girls and I danced on and off most of the night, having a great time together. Sally would barge in and grab my arm for a few dances and annoyingly consumed lots of time at the party with repeated requests to dance and hang drunkenly all over me. Under the rules, I couldn't refuse, and she seemed to be trying to let most of her housemates know I was off-limits to their demands. She had pounded down a few too many beers and shots when suddenly she disappeared from the party. I figured she might have had to use the bathroom or gotten sick since she appeared to have a lot of alcohol. I was quickly swept up to dance again with the Coby girls, and they kept me from having to give some of the other party favors asked from other girls.

About three or four dances and twenty minutes later, Sally's roommate approached me and said, "Hey Curt, Sally has a gift for you?"

"Where is she," I asked. "She's in our room. Come on, and I will let you in." Sally's roommate brought me to their room, unlocked the door, said, "Go on in; she is over there," and motioned me toward her bed.

I entered the dimly lit room, and her roommate locked the door behind her as she left. I walked over to Sally and whispered "hello" as she appeared to be sleeping. There was no response. Her blouse was unbuttoned and open from her neck to her belly button. She lay bare-breasted underneath it without a bra on. I sat on the edge of her bed, staring at what I had in front of me. "Sally, Sally," I whispered. "Are you awake!" She lay silent but moved, so the left side of her blouse opened fully to reveal the most beautiful breast I'd ever seen. "Sally," I whispered again, "Are you awake, are you OK?" She remained silent and seemed to be sort of almost faking being asleep.

This girl was so beautiful, and she lay lying with her left breast glimmering softly in the dim light. Her nipple was erect and pink, and I couldn't resist but to be the boy I was and stare. It looked delicious. I wanted to taste it with my tongue. My heart was pounding through my chest like the first time I shot a deer, and the rest of my body was throbbing with testosterone. The devil in my head said, "Take the gift." Did her roommate set this up, I wondered? Did Sally set this up? If I took advantage of this situation, would her roommate expose me to the other partygoers? My Coby girls lived in this house; what would they think?

"Sally," I asked again. "Are you OK?" I pressed my hand to her forehead and watched her for any movement. There was none. I moved my hand from her head to her left shoulder and gave her a slight shake watching her face and eyes for any movement. I gazed again upon her beautiful figure. I thought about Jan. I thought about Madison from high school. Should I move forward? Was she using the drunk excuse to cover the shame or embarrassment of being sexually assertive? Over and over in my head, the question of moving forward swirled in my half-ridden alcohol mind.

The alcohol she absorbed gave her the excuse to be naughty, permission to open up her heart and pants for a night, and then blame it for her actions the next day. My boyhood was fascinated with the opportunity to become a man right there and then! I pondered, where should I begin? Should I caress the underside of her beautiful breasts and slide my hand down the center of her belly toward her jeans, unbuckle them, grab the zipper tab, and slowly lower it to reveal whether her triangle had the same beautiful hair as she had on her head? Would I find lace panties? My jeans were getting tight as I thought through the possibilities.

"Sally," I whispered again, "Are you awake, are you OK?" She still lay silent, motionless. My body was raging with moral torture, my testosterone climbing with confusion, and then it happened.

I looked at her lips and breasts and took one last look at those jeans. The Bermuda Triangle was just a finger length below her belt if I wanted it, and I could shake her awake and see where a home run was possible. I paused. I thought of her dad, and he must have had reason to take the stance he did.

After an eternity of evaluation, I pulled her blouse over her breasts, pulled up her sheet and blanket, and covered her snugly. I tenderly kissed her forehead, said goodnight, and told her to sleep well. I left her room, assuming she was out for the rest of the party.

What I saw, I wanted. I wanted it so bad. I was a young man. Still, only 18, but 18 was old enough and much older than most of my high school buddies who'd entered the triangle long ago. But I was not going to take that gift from a passed-out girl. It was tempting. Had she awoken or initiated something like grabbing my hand or any part of me, my hormones would have engulfed me. I probably would have lunged into the triangle of lust that I could not afford to enter. I had to stay out of Bermuda lest I lose my dreams, values, and moral desire to save this part of intimacy for the girl I'd marry. I had to avoid

Bermuda for many economic risks and reasons too. My escape from everything I'd come from depended upon supporting myself and no one else until I accomplished the goals I'd written down.

Thirty minutes later, Sally emerged from her room. I wasn't surprised, and her actions toward me for the rest of the party strengthened my suspicion she might have been faking the sleep all along coyly, shyly inviting me to make love with her under the umbrella of alcohol as an excuse for her behavior. She avoided me the rest of the night, pretending or actually to be drunk, and I thought, *Sally, Jan, Madison, there is no difference among them.* Their hormones and desires are raging as much as guys are, as much as mine were. But they are weaker than me.

The following Monday, I ran into Sally in the dining hall. Knowing how frequently I visited the Coby girls on her floor, there would be no escape from awkwardness between us. She was bold and brave, and like the initiation she embarked upon at the party, Sally came up to me and said, "Curt, I'm sorry, I'm so embarrassed." I could see in her eyes and the blush of her skin that she was deeply embarrassed because I didn't follow her invitation to make out. She needed a way out. I cut her words off, took her hand, and said, "Hey, listen. Don't be embarrassed over anything." Deep down, there was a part of me with regret that I wanted that second chance if it could happen. "You have the most beautiful body I have ever seen I whispered," she blushed, "No, really, you do. I just…" I couldn't bring forth the words I wanted to say, but I said, "Hey, what happened, happened, right?"

"Probably too much alcohol, right?" She smiled at me with less of a blush and whispered, "Thank you," and as she pulled her hand from mine, she left me standing in the exit hall of the dining hall, stunned once again to hear, "Curt—You're the kind of guy every girl wants to marry!"

The hormones in the girls were raging just as much as the boys. There was another girl I became terrific friends with, just friends. We had become good friends and dancing partners at the Vault when the Coby girls weren't around. We became such good friends that thoughts developed in me that she and I might get through school and we could date and be a couple someday. She even had an interest in farming. We were about as close as friends could be without formally becoming committed to each other or experiencing other wants and desires as lovers or sexual partners. I was falling for Ruth as a friend, a deep friend.

Then one day near the end of the school year, one of my housemates came into the bathroom early in the morning while I was brushing my teeth and said, "Hey Curt, your friend Ruth…you should spend a night with her. I just came from her room, and man, does she know how to give a guy a blow job!"

"What?" "For real?" I asked him?

"Curt, man buddy, I'm not kidding." "She's wild and knows what she's doing" Ugg! My gut was filled with disgust. I finished my showering, dressed, and walked to the lot where Comet parked. Sitting and gripping the steering wheel, I asked Comet, what planet am I on? Every girl interested in me was more interested in sex than just me. Don't get me wrong; I was interested in sex, too, but an addiction to the Bermuda Triangle would kill my dreams. I just sat in Comet and revved the engine in prayer.

Spring semester was about to end, and before finals, there was one last hurrah down at the Stone Pony, another local bar in Cobleskill. Jan was there, and she still didn't have a boyfriend, and though she had passed on me over the year, we maintained some bar talk conversation and remained friends.

It was late, and we were both sitting at the bar when the closing song came on; "Happy Trails to you, until we meet again"… Jan asked, "Hey Curt would you walk me home?"

"Surely," I said. When we got to her dormitory, she stood on her toes and kissed my lips.

She gazed into my eyes and asked, "Would you come up and give me a back rub?"

"Sure," I said.

I honestly thought it was going to be as simple as that. When we got to her room, she undressed and took everything off except her panties. She stood bare-breasted facing me momentarily, smiled at me, and lay flat on her bed, breasts down. Am I the luckiest guy in the world? I wondered. "I'm ready," she said. The girl was naked, except for her bikini panties. I slid onto the bed, lay beside her, and scratched and rubbed her back. Once again, in the privacy of a dorm room lay a petite, nicely formed body that either trusted me to be the gentleman as I had been before, or she was trying to bust my balls and break my hormones and see if I would pull off those panties and mount her. For the fourth time, I stared at the slender form and hips of a beautiful girl who seemed silently begging me to take her panties off and fill her. Her room was hot.

I took my shirt off but kept my t-shirt on and lay my leg over hers as I caressed her back and occasionally slipped my fingers just beneath her panty line. She wasn't drunk; she was coherent and knew exactly what we were doing. Everything moving forward would be consensual, and it was up to me. She had done her part stripping down. She didn't show resistance of any sort. I massaged her back from her neck to just below her upper panty line, and she lay soothed, quiet, and fell asleep.

"Jan," I whispered, "are you sleeping?" She didn't answer. I asked again. Silence. I put my shirt on, pulled a sheet over her body, and said goodnight. She never uttered a word, and I left. Jan didn't win. She was trying to seduce me into a fun night, maybe testing me to see if I still had the same values I'd shared when we dated in our first semester. Once again, I left a beautiful young woman under a sheet without pursuing sexual liberties.

If I had taken liberty on any of these opportunities, it would have undoubtedly led to more occurrences with the girl. Or would it? While I saw Jan numerous times at bars and parties after that night, I never received another invitation to walk her home or scratch her back. She gave up on me. So far, I was winning. Or was I? My first year at Cobleskill unzipped a wave of sexual opportunities that perplexed me as much as they intrigued me. I lived with a handsome roommate named Abe, whom many thought might be queer. I wondered if my turning down some of the prospects that presented themselves thought me and Abe were queer together. I didn't care much what they thought, but they sure would have supposed so from their experience with me. I had been faithful to myself and my values despite the seductive temptations. I was in a world of desire and opportunity and soon back to how to survive the summer and earn some money toward the next semester at Cobleskill.

Chapter Twenty-Five
Baptism

A young man is baptized twice in his life, first by his God, and second by the lips of a beautiful girl.

-Curt Riess.

I returned to Spencer after my first two semesters at Cobleskill. I was 19 now but felt like I was a mature person of 25 or 30 from all the experiences the first year of a two-year tech college had afforded me.

I had wanted to stay through the summer working in Cobleskill, but I couldn't find any work. Employment opportunities were scarce. The economy of the seventies was hit badly nationwide, hitting rural areas of upstate New York even harder. President Carter's administration years brought gas shortages, double-digit inflation and interest rates, and unemployment.

I would have loved to work back on the King Dairy for the summer, but they had one of the Hansen boys I recommended after I left for college as a farm hand. I occasionally returned to help him when the King family went on a short weekend trip. Whenever they did, the farmhand called me to help him get through. He didn't have the capacity for such long days as I did, nor the common sense from familiarity I had earned about the farm operations over the years. I would return for a weekend here and there from college, and I was very willing to help ensure the King Farm was in good hands. I don't think they ever knew I did that for them.

I matured in many ways since taking on a job with the Kings and attending college; I was willing to drive a much longer distance to obtain my goals. Whereas a few years back, when I first landed the job at King's, traveling five to ten miles seemed like the limit. As in high school, there would be nothing in Spencer or Van Etten to find, so I looked beyond the outlying towns of Ithaca, Elmira, and Horseheads.

The area papers offered scant employment opportunities, and the few I applied for in factories wanted permanent employees. I answered a farmhand ad for a summer position at the Turner Dairy Farm in Horseheads. I was lucky enough to land the job on the spot during my in-person interview.

I lived at my best friend's house. The Duke and his parents had offered me a bed in their home for the summer. I planned to ask Wayne if I could stay in his cabin in the wood again, but they insisted I stay with them. I loved the Duke; he was like a brother. His dad was a character, like in a comic book, and between him and the Duke, we were always laughing at something and having a good time.

Loretta and Harry found it amazing that I independently made it through one year of college. Though they had offered me to go back and live with them for the summer, the single-shot Stevens event was still fresh in my mind. Now more than ever, I felt I had too much to risk if things went sour for me in that household.

Now that I was back in Spencer, I planned to visit the Kings once every two weeks to say hello and check in with them throughout the summer. They had been my guiding rock for the past few years and meant so much more to me than they ever knew. My friends who hadn't gone to college were entrenched in their local jobs and continued with the associations made at them. I reached out to my high school friends who went to college to hang with, but many had stayed through summer sessions at their school. However, Lindsey, a really good friend, came home from college, and we began to connect more often. I traveled back and forth daily to work from my friend Dukes' house through Van Etten to Horseheads right past her house.

So as not to become all-consuming and too much of a wall fly around my friend the Duke and his family, I tried to spend a lot of time visiting other friends after work and hanging out. I particularly enjoyed Lindsey's company and the occasional back hill ride we'd take together.

Pop King was still helping out on the farm but mainly stuck to tractor work these days, and as had been practiced before, he and his wife took to Florida for part of the winter in a camper they owned. It was late spring in May when they had just returned when John's dad had taken ill, and he was down and tired with flu-like symptoms that lasted for a week.

I milked mornings at Turners and was done at about 3:30 pm each afternoon unless we were doing some fieldwork. It was a Tuesday afternoon (May 31st, 1978), and after work, I stopped to say hello to the Kings. Joyce shared the sad news at the kitchen door that Pop King had passed away that morning.

I saw John in the field directly across the driveway, raking hay. He looked straight ahead to avoid visual contact with anyone passing by on the highway adjacent to the area. I could tell from a distance tears were pouring down his cheeks.

I told Joyce I would hang around with the farmhand and let John know he didn't need to come out of the field or house and that I was there to help. I did the pre-milking chores, milked the cows with the farmhand, performed the after-milking duties, and walked to Comet. I stood at the driver's door and asked Comet what to do. I glanced around the yard and at the field, just raked; I took in the smells of my farm family and wished I could have been there every day for them.

I never saw John again that afternoon. I wanted to shake his hand, hug him and tell him how sorry I was, but I knew he needed his time alone. They all did Grandma King, Joyce, and the family. I'd only known these people for four years now. While growing deeper and deeper in love with this family, I took precautions not to assume the same was happening to me.

After milking, I hopped in Comet, turned the radio off, rolled down the windows, drove to Spencer Park, and parked under the two large maple shade trees where I usually parked. There I sat in my car and prayed for Pop King. I prayed for John and Joyce, Grandma King, and their families. I prayed for the grace that I would use to benefit this family in their time of need now and any time they might need me.

While conversing with Comet, I applied a coat of wax and chrome polish. When I finished, I drove back to the King Farm to ensure everything looked OK. I didn't stop. I just passed by very slowly. There were a couple of cars in the driveway. Probably some family or neighbors or people from church. I was glad to see there were some people with them.

I called Turners and asked If I could skip the following milking day, explaining I needed to help another dairy farm friend. They understood completely.

The following day I arrived early to help John with milking. I made sure I came earlier than he usually got into the barn, so by the time he woke up and got his coffee, he would see the barn lights on, and I would be through the pre-milking chores. He came to the barn not surprised that I was there; he knew why I was there and simply said thank you.

"I'm sorry for the loss of your dad John." He simply nodded, holding back the tears still ready to emerge from his heart through his eyes. "I'll take care of milking and everything else, John. Go back to your family," I suggested.

"I'll be back later this afternoon," I said. John knew I had just started my job with the other farmer and insisted he stay and help milk, and he needed that normalcy. "We'll get through it faster, and then you could go to your other job," he told me. Nothing more was said between us. We just milked and listened to the swish and swash of the suction cups, and I left John to finish cleaning the milking machines as I headed to Horseheads.

This was the King family's first funeral, supporting them with my labor and farm-formed hands. Except for the companionship of the cows, I sensed that there could be a deep feeling of loneliness and self-pity that could set in each day of such sadness or crisis as one would feel enslaved to have to serve the milking chores no matter what the circumstances, a funeral, a school play, a kids baseball game, I was there for them to attend those events in high school. Still, there wouldn't always be a farmhand, I pondered.

In that contemplation, I prayed that John and Joyce would always have a dependable farmhand. For the first time, I had some second thoughts about my life's dream of farming, particularly dairy farming. Since the age of five, I had always wanted to be a farmer who could help feed all those starving children around the world I used to hear about when I didn't want to finish my meal. But now, in this devastating moment, there was no freedom from the required twice-a-day necessity of milking the cows. Perhaps my career thoughts were changing because of what I was learning at school, but the reality of dairying is that a barn is lonely in times of trouble. Even I had experienced the loneliness and stress of performing milking in my times of remorse and crises.

I had gotten to know most of the extended family, even in the short visits with Joyce's parents, Grandpa, and Grandma Vander Schaaf, who made me feel warm and welcome when they visited and treated me like a faraway grandson. They consistently expressed their appreciation of my work for John and Joyce. They shared the accolades John and Joyce spoke of me and how grateful they were for my presence and abilities. I heard more tributes through them second-hand than I ever did firsthand from John and Joyce. Still, I knew they silently expressed their appreciation for me. Other family funerals would follow, and all of those times, I was thankful for the opportunity to serve them and enable them to peacefully and confidently attend funerals and other events. At the same time, I took care of their most significant financial asset, livelihood, and farm.

Over those short years with my King family, I got to know them all, their children, the extended family of brothers, and other family members when they visited. The introductions given to me by John and Joyce made me feel like I was family.

And so, I slowly became.

The summer got hot in more ways than one! I often thought about the girls at Cobleskill this past year. Some of the girls from high school were back from college in town. I wondered what their first year of college experience was like. We'd go for an extended ride a few nights, but Comet kept me straight, whispering in my ears many a night of temptations, "Drive, boy, drive. Down the highway, down the highway, not down to the belly button. Put the pedal to the metal and ride fast! Stay off the lips and hips, and don't cross the yellow line, don't cross the yellow, don't cross the yellow! Ride fast, boy, and I'll take you where you want to go."

Comet hummed to me through motor and prayer. We were a boychine, a combination of speed, agility, metal, feelings, and soul. While some of my surrounding college mates popped speed, Comet was my speed when I needed to release tensions. We pushed more than 100 miles per hour down Route 34 and elsewhere. If Comet had a bigger engine, we'd have gone faster. I loved speed, testing the limits of Comet, road, and track. But the summer was getting hotter.

Though I never paid too much attention to my looks, my farm boy physique was admired by both girls and boys alike, as gym shower mates would attest to me in various challenges. I was tall, slender, and broad-shouldered. I had pecks that other guys wished they had, but nothing on me was bulked up from weight lifting. My muscles came naturally by splitting hundreds of cords of wood with an ax for my family and others, as well as the farm work I performed.

I knew I was attractive to some girls in high school, but I attributed that to my personality. In college, where not many knew me, it proved that my physique was the attraction! Girls had given me many opportunities to make them debutante of Comets back seat. My Levi's jeans were always tight in a sexy way, mainly because I was growing out of them and couldn't afford new ones, so I stretched their use. I bought some at second-hand stores in college, and it seemed that no matter what I wore, my crotch and butt were attractive targets to be groped by a passing girl in a standing-room-only crowded bar. It was an uncomfortable feeling even to know such behavior existed.

The summer continued to be a hot one. The King family took a brief vacation and left the farmhand to perform the work. Once again, I got a call from him. This time, however, it was a dire call. He was in pain and had an appendicitis attack. His dad rushed him to the hospital, and I took over the farm for the next four days; while he was recuperating, I ran their farm and put in minimal hours at the Turner Farm.

I had no phone number to call the Kings, nor did the Hansen boy. Mr. Hansen came to help me out in the mornings during milking. The Turners again understood the situation I shared with them, and I got to their farm by 9:00 for fieldwork, skipping milking. They had their nephew and son who could fill in. By the time the King family returned, the Hansen boy had healed enough to return. I never submitted any hours to them and made no fuss. I did what I thought was right for them and what was in my heart.

"Paradise by the Dashboard Light" is a song by Jim Steinman. It was first released when I graduated from high school. The song was released on the album Bat Out of Hell, with vocals by the American musician Meat Loaf alongside Ellen Foley. The song is most notable for its unique structure and length, spanning at least eight minutes of music. It is about the same time it takes for a typical male to thrust into a vagina and ejaculate.

The lyrics depict a boy and girl leading up to their first sexual act of love in the front seat of a car. The song can probably describe millions of first-time experiences for many American post-war boomer children making out in their daddy's car or pickup by the green dim of the dashboard light. It certainly was for most of my high school friends. And how ironic that at the end of the song, the male vocal sings about waiting for the future of time because if he has to spend another minute with the girl he screwed, life was too miserably long. Right on, Mr. Hansen!

I took the message in that song literally as a message in favor of abstinence and continuing to avoid the Bermuda Triangle. I saw my parents and others leading miserable lives together as husband and wife. I was not interested in that temporary paradise and then waiting for the end of time with that girl for the rest of my life.

I got to know Lindsey as the steady girlfriend of one of my best buddies from high school, and we became great friends through him. This summer, she grew into one of my best confidants. She was vital in encouraging me in eleventh grade, helping me win the position of student council president against the odds of a popular jock and other honor students running for office. In high school, I thought Jack and Lindsey would be together for life, but they had broken up and gone their separate ways mid-way through their first year at college. Jack found another girlfriend, Lindsey, another boyfriend. But this summer, Lindsey and I were in many deep conversations. We talked about life, the stars we gazed at in the evening, where they possibly came from, and what the future might hold for us years ahead, not necessarily together but separately as friends and adults. We talked a lot about our first year of college experiences and how demanding it was for each of us for many things, particularly about growing up. We just had a zillion conversational words about this and that and enjoyed each other's company.

I would invite Lindsey for occasional rides going for pizza or chasing a sunset on a gravel road. Once, we were coming around an "S" curve without any lights on, with only the moonlight to guide us. Lindsey got very nervous and asked me to turn the lights back on, and I would if I could. The fact of the matter was, there was a short somewhere in Comets wiring that I never could find, and every once in a while, the headlights would go off for some split seconds, five, sometimes ten. I never deliberately turned them off, as was thought. It was never long enough for me to worry, slow down, or stop. I would laugh at her concern, and just in time before she'd get mad, the lights would miraculously come back on. She thought I was doing it on purpose.

While I could have shown off my racing skills and thrown the car into a spin or skid, Comet and I never did that with Lindsey and only a few exceptional times with some of my buddies. I didn't want to scare or put them in danger and risk them never riding with Comet and me again. Still, the short in the headlights deterred Lindsy's desire for any evening rides. We had plenty of daytime opportunities.

Occasional rides with me were an escape from her home and ordinary circumstances. Comet carried us on back roads in conversational dimensions we never envisioned would have occurred between us. Within the four glass walls and behind that steering wheel, Comet was privy to the soul talk of two young teenage lives entwined by their individuality, secretive personal home life challenges, and newfound college experiences.

Throughout the summer, Lindsey and I visited almost every other night. We were never romantically involved and were just the best friends a boy and girl could be without going too far. And while Lindsey was a beautiful girl, I never felt attracted to her in any sexual way. What we had, our friendship, I valued too great to let any affectionate relationship interfere and cause the failure of our company.

Lindsey, indeed, was someone special, not just good-looking, but with personality plus a genuine soul of and to the world. She was like me in many ways and wanted more out of life. Lindsey was kind, had always been. She cared for her siblings and her family and quietly took gratitude every day that she could move forward and dream. She was the sunshine on a rainy day, no matter what. That summer, we'd become soulmates.

One evening on my way home from work, I stopped at her house, and a couple of high school classmates were visiting her. I was surprised to see them, and they were equally surprised to see me. Neither of them was a close friend of mine in high school. I didn't stay as long as I usually would as I did not want to intrude, and quite frankly, it was a little awkward, which worried me why it felt awkward as we were just friends.

Additional future visits when I dropped in to see Lindsey; those guys were there again. I had to admit I felt a little jealous for the first time. Lindsey was an inspiration to me, my soul mate in conversation. Though she and I never fully divulged our challenges in our home lives, we knew we were trying to escape something, whether it was economic circumstances or other.

The next time Lindsey and I were alone, leaning against Comet staring into the night sky and in a shallower conversation about our day, I did the unspeakable. I didn't want to lose my time and friendship if she became involved with one of these guys. I asked her if she was interested in a relationship with either of those guys. Lindsey was shocked and could read me like a book to see the jealousy and concern in my facial and verbal expressions. "Of course not," she said, and she turned in front of me and looked me in the eyes, put her hand on my shoulder, and said, "Listen, Mr. Riess, I have no interest in them, absolutely none." Facing me, she reached around my neck and pressed her lips to mine, holding me in a headlock to her lips. Lindsey was comfortable with this and probably thought not much of it; I was not. She had a boyfriend for years in high school and had more experience kissing than me. She sensed this, pulled me closer, and kissed me again, almost as proof and a message that if she were interested in anybody, it was me.

I didn't want this kind of relationship with her. I loved her as a friend, one that I needed and cherished. I wanted her as a friend, though, just as a friend— a friend for life.

Lindsey, oh my God, Lindsey, I thought; *I want nothing more.* I knew that a romantic relationship with her, in fact with anyone at this time, was impossible for me to bear out. As our tongues intertwined and her grip around my neck with her arms pulled me tight, I silently asked God to help me. I can't lose Lindsey as a friend. Then the seemingly unimaginable happened next. She leaned into me and pressed me against Comet's fender, and as we kissed, her right hand left my ribs, and she gently slid it down my jeans and traced every curve and wrinkle between my belly button and thigh.

She entirely took me off guard; even more, I was embarrassed at not knowing what to do next and froze. While most guys would've done anything to have this interaction and relationship with this girl, and I would do anything for Lindsey, I honestly had no intentions of advancing a romantic relationship with her. She was a beautiful girl, it was the least and last experience I wanted with Lindsey, but that brief make-out moment was about to change everything.

This first base action happened so fast and unexpectedly that I was in a state of "Oh my God, what happened," not a mood of joy. I didn't reciprocate, and I didn't put my hands anywhere! I didn't even have my arms or hands around her waist; they were pressed flat against Comet to keep me upright.

All the embracing and advances were hers. Lindsey was calm and sensed my surprise, resistance, and reluctance. Pulling her hand out of my pants and still hanging onto my belt, she looked at me and said, "Hmmph. I have to go in now," and kissed me goodnight.

I got into Comet, and we drove to my bridge on Beckhorn Hollow.

As Comet and I sat on the iron trestle bridge, I poured out my innermost feelings of confusion and anxiety to God. Comet, I'm so lost and confused. I had turned Comet's engine off but quickly started it again. I needed it back on to hear its hum amidst the creek's rushing waters. I needed to hear something other than my aching heartbeat and a head filled with panic. I needed to hear Comet's heart, the purr of its engine, the tapping of its valves, and its whirring fan belt for some normalcy. Lindsey had just broken a barrier to which I had mentally and physically built a wall, not just with her but with every girl because I had too much at stake…as in my whole life.

I was living on the edge financially, balancing between moving forward with success and leaving this area or falling backward into the abyss of the hills that Comet and I raced up and down and loved.

Most of my high school classmates suspected that she and Jack were sexually active throughout their relationship. God knows there were plenty who were. I asked Jack once in high school how far he'd gone with Lindsey, and he told me it was none of my business. I respected that for him and for protecting her. I wasn't naive, though. I couldn't believe that Lindsey was falling for me but instead had a physical need that she wanted me to fulfill, but I just couldn't swim down that stream. "Don't cross the yellow line," Comet whispered. "Let's go ride somewhere else," I'd hear. "Let's go up the hill, kick up some gravel. Ride fast, boy, ride fast, stay off the shoulders, lips, and hips," Comet murmured. "Don't cross the yellow line. Stay out of Bermuda!" I'd hear Mr. Hansen's advice echo in my mind.

Confused and somewhat embarrassed, I avoided stopping by Lindsey's for the next few days. I stopped by to see my King family and just get the soul fix that I needed periodically from them. I didn't have a phone she could call me; these weren't the days when cell phones existed. So, she called my friend Duke's house and left a message with his mom for me to stop by. My soul was still perplexed. I loved Lindsey for all she was and would do anything for her, but I wasn't sure what she wanted from me.

I stopped by her house the day after I got her message. As I pulled up to her home, I remembered that awkward feeling of "what will I say," and how will I act?

Seeing me arrive through a window, Lindsey bounded out of her house toward me. Before I was out of my car, Lindsey demanded, "Where have you been, Mr. Riess?"

"Oh, just about, working late the last few nights," I said. Lindsey acted as if absolutely nothing had happened. "Is everything alright with you, Mr. Riess?" she asked. "Yes, everything's great, Lindsey!"

"Want a glass of water?"

"Sure," I said. We greeted her mother. She had a great mom, a wonderful person from all appearances, happy and who always greeted you with a smile and a warm hello. Lindsey seemed to have a great relationship with her. For sure, nothing was too easy in their household. Money was not abundant, and her dad might have bounced around in his jobs. For years on end, ever since I met Lindsey's mom, as wonderful and upbeat as she was, something was amiss. I could never precisely pinpoint what my gut was trying to tell me about her family. I knew that perhaps, like many of my classmates in high school, they were a family in need, living in modest shelters with potentially hidden secrets not fully in public view, not unlike my own. I suspected we were all sternly taught, "What goes on in this house stays in this house."

It was a steamy humid evening during the first week of August, which meant a thunderstorm was imminent, and we were only a few weeks away from leaving to attend our second year at college. We were well past the summer solstice when it remained light past ten at night, and the days were already getting shorter for daylight. I asked Lindsey, "How about a ride to Pudgies for a pizza?"

"Sure," she enthusiastically responded. "Let me get my bag." Comet and I decided to take route 96 and go to the Pudgies in Horseheads rather than to Ithaca.

It was a longer drive than Ithaca, but we were less likely to run into people we knew, particularly any classmates and her old boyfriend. Lindsey and I enjoyed some Bee Jees music from an eight-track, and I never tired of her chatty, inquisitive questions of "What do you think of (this)" or "What do you think of (that)."

After ordering pizza, we had fantastic conversations while sipping cokes and munching on pizza. For nearly three hours, we sat and chatted about everything, often bringing laughter to each other. Lindsey sometimes stared long and deep into my own green eyes, but I never suspected anything of it. She always had that twinkle in her eye and a broad, beautiful smile that her personality-filled. We talked a lot that evening about going back to college. What might become of us after that?

"Are you going to college after this next year?" I asked. "Of course," she said. "I want a four-year degree." I hadn't given that any thought yet. Her answer and reply encouraged me because she was already looking forward to it. I was beginning to explore the possibility of going beyond the original two years of college I had planned. Still, I knew my realities and that two years were all I could afford.

Since Lindsey's advance on me a couple of weeks back, we had no intimacy, physical handholding, discussion, or mention of it. I felt we were back to where I wanted it to be. The deep and luscious non-intimate relationship we'd always embraced and held onto with each other.

We finished our pizza, got into Comet, and drove home. "Let's go to Ithaca, Lindsey suggested."

The road to Ithaca from Horseheads took us off course from our regular route back to Van Etten. The sultry and steamy evening turned into a downpour of rain. As my ever-present cheap windshield wipers couldn't keep up with the rain, there was an unlit wayside rest to which I pulled over and parked to wait out the downpour. The Bee Gees were blaring as loudly as the rain pounded the rooftop.

It happened so fast I hadn't even turned off the car's ignition. With the headlights and wipers still going, Lindsey leaned over, unbuckled my jeans, unzipped my fly, and baptized me with her lips. I looked down and saw her long, flowing, silky hair hiding the sensualness for which she'd initiated. I was helpless in avoidance, with nowhere to go. I couldn't think fast enough about anything from the disbelief that the action was happening. Nothing I could lament in our last three hours of conversation would have led to this other than my pulling over to wait out the downpour. But Lindsey obviously felt something different for me.

I turned the wipers and headlights off but left the parking lights on. The dim green dashboard stayed lit. I laid my right hand on her back, and my left hand stroked her hair. She quickly brought me to an erection, and I enjoyed this new sensation.

Though this is not where I wanted to be with Lindsey, I did nothing to stop her. If she wanted this, I could not withdraw without embarrassing her and risking our relationship. But it didn't stop there. Once I was rock hard, Lindsey rose, unbuttoned her blouse slid off her jeans, and slipped into Comet's back seat. I froze. She sat squarely in the middle, her knees raised, and heaven's gates opened. *Oh God,* I thought, *what do I do? Oh God, where do I go?*

If I reject Lindsey's overture and invite as I have all the other girls, Particularly Lindsey, I'll never see her again. She would feel embarrassed, and our friendship would be over. It happened to me before. I loved Lindsey and wanted her as a best friend but not a lover. I needed her friendship and wanted what we had for the rest of my life. I couldn't lose her. I couldn't just say no. And yet, if I said yes! Oh shit—my mind was racing at a million miles an hour, trying to come up with a solution in my split seconds.

Lindsey shook me from my thoughts, "Curt," Lindsey asked, "are you coming?"

"Curt, are you coming?" I heard her say faintly. She seemed experienced and maybe had done this before, and I was not.

I looked at Lindsey and slid over the front seat and onto the floor, straddling on my knees between her legs. My jeans were already unbuckled, with the fly already zipped down. I lowered my jeans and shorts and entered the Bermuda Triangle for the first time. Until now, I only heard the locker room descriptions of bravado and bragging about thrusting and pumping and a tight pussy. I was already so aroused I thrust into her only three or four times when suddenly I pulled out and ejaculated all over my underwear. Oh my God, it was wet and wild, but it wasn't tight like most boys in high school described it. It was moist, warm, pleasurable, and something I had never experienced before. Did I enter the gates of heaven—or did I enter the gates of hell?

What was I doing? My mind jerked from pleasure to responsibility, to embarrassment, to calamity.

I'd been baptized again, this time by a beautiful girl.

I couldn't afford this pleasure, and I had no protection in the form of condoms. I had no idea if Lindsey was on the pill, the risk, and opportunity I had avoided many times before.

"What's the matter, Curt?" she asked. I was embarrassed and couldn't enter her again, knowing that I had already ejaculated and there might be a risk of pregnancy. "Curt, what's the matter?" I couldn't utter a word, and I remained silent. "Curt!" Lindsey persisted.

I still didn't utter a word. I couldn't. My silence seemed like an eternity. I pulled up my underwear and pants and hopped in the front seat as Lindsey dressed. She remained in the back seat as I drove her home. We were both silent the whole way. I'm sure she took my silence as an insult and rejection when she might have cared enough about me to give herself and share her body. All of this was too risky! The whole experience seemed out of character for either of us.

When we arrived at her house, she left the back seat, slammed the back door, and never said a word. There was no interaction between us, and Comet was silent. It was as if Comet went dead quiet on the matter. The whole experience filled my head with fog and heartache. I returned to the Duke's house and lay awake all night rehearsing what had just happened to me and what might have provoked the experience or desire. Was I to blame?

I baled hay all day in the hot sun at Turners' farm the next day. I was in the wagon catching bales from the kicker and stacking them, occasionally not paying attention and getting sideswiped by one or two here and there. I couldn't take my mind off what had happened. I rehearsed our conversation before we pulled off the road. I pondered how many of our discussions and their content led to this. What did I do? What could I have said, if anything, to lead her on? I couldn't come up with any answers.

I needed to see Lindsey and make sure everything was all right. I had to explain my ineptness, say I was sorry, and try to clear up this whole gone crazy wild night. Or did I want to see Lindsey and get another chance at what she offered me? "Once a boy enters the Bermuda Triangle, he's hooked." Mr. Hansen was right. It was brief, but Lindsey set me wild for more. What would it be like, I thought, if a little more forethought was put into this exotic pleasure and I had a condom? While the whole experience was awkward and about as fast as a radio commercial, its effect on me was lasting. And it turned on a genetic switch that would not go away.

That day, I went to a drugstore. I walked up to the cooler, grabbed a liter of Coke and two Good Humor ice cream bars, mulled around other parts of the store, and then asked to purchase a condom at the checkout counter. In my teen days, condoms were behind the cashier counter, just like cigarettes, and one had to ask to purchase the brand one wanted. It was my first condom purchase, and had I not already been sweating from baling hay all day, I would have been sweating just asking for that condom.

I had to show my driver's license, which was embarrassing enough to declare that I was nineteen, and I was glad that I was in Horseheads, where no one knew me. Everyone in Spencer and Van Etten knew me, if not by my car, my polka dot hat.

I drove Comet down the highway and through the valley to Lindsey's house. I was going to smile wide, ask her if she wanted to go for a ride, and once she accepted, show her the condom and then take her to a swimming hole I knew of where I could shake off the dust and sweat and see if she'd go swimming with me—in more ways than one. I rehearsed everything I was going to say and how I would make it up to her, that I just wasn't prepared, but now I am.

When I arrived at her home, her mom greeted me warmly. She hollered up the stairs to announce that I was there, and there wasn't any response. Her mom called again, and I heard Lindsey tell her to tell me to leave and go away. Her mom looked at me, perplexed. She mouthed in silence to me, "What happened last night?" I just shrugged my shoulders. "Lindsey, Curt is standing here and can hear you." There was silence for about a minute. Just as I shrugged my shoulders again, saying I'd better go, Lindsey stormed down the stairs, grabbed my elbow, tugged me out the door, down the steps, and backed me up against Comet.

"You listen to me, Mr. Curt. I could have gotten pregnant last night. That was a big risk, and it's all your fault! What happened last night will never happen again," as she dug her index finger into my chest and pushed me with both arms against the side of Comet.

"But Lindsey"—I tried several times to get in a sentence as she ranted and said it was all my fault. I couldn't believe what I was hearing. She had to be embarrassed at her actions, and somehow, she was redeeming herself, trying to convince me that it was my fault. 'Lindsey, listen, calm down. Lindsey, I knew last night…well…I was hoping we could try it again!' I wanted her to know I was willing and accepted her forwardness. I tried to pass off my actions because I didn't have a condom. I reached for the condom to pull out of my pocket to convey to her by showing that we could try it the right way but fumbled, trying to get it out.

"My God, Curt, don't even hope to get a second chance?" she shrieked, "It's over, Mr. Curt, it's over. That was a big mistake last night!"

I totally agreed with her.

Now more embarrassed and confused than ever that I had even thought, remotely possibly felt that she and I might make real love instead of the flinging I experienced, my mind went blank. I was stunned and stood there dumbfounded as she unabashedly tried to shame me and continued to blame me, saying it was all my fault, and then suddenly, I felt a slap in the face. Lindsey's last words were, "I never want to see you again. You understand! Go away and don't ever come back."

I stood there in the twilight zone! I was still sweaty and dirty and couldn't believe what I'd heard. I threw the condom into the field across from her house. I got into Comet and left. The sweat from the heat and a hard day was still pouring down from my forehead, and once in the privacy of my car, tears of confusion mingled in with the sweat. Lindsey was the only friend I ever had to share my innermost thoughts. She'd become a soulmate, or so I thought.

I drove to my bridge but couldn't stay and sit still.

Comet and I rode some hills toward Newfield that weren't as familiar to me. We just wandered and wandered and wandered for hours into the evening as I pondered all that had happened this summer. I drove to Pudgies Pizza in Ithaca via back roads through Newfield and ordered spaghetti and a salad. What just happened to me is what I was trying to avoid the whole summer. I was just a few weeks from returning to Cobleskill and had already given my notice at the Turners' farm that I would be leaving shortly.

I stopped at Lindsey's house twice after she told me never to come again. She wouldn't see me. Her mom apologetically said, "She was sorry, but Lindsey won't come to see you." I had to see her. In less than a week, we'd both be back at college.

Without seeing Lindsey in the evenings, Comet and I wandered back hills I'd never been on between Van Etten and Watkins Glen and through Newfield. I was emotionally lost and tried to find peace among the beauty of new back roads, their creeks, curves, and tree canopies. On my last day at Turners Farm, just before heading back to Cobleskill, I stopped by Lindsey's house to see if she would just come out so I could say goodbye.

"I'm sorry, Curt," her mom said. "She left for college three days ago."

"Left?"

"Three days ago?" I asked.

Three days ago? Nothing? No goodbye? She honestly didn't want to see me! I thought.

I was hurt—more than hurt. I felt used. After all that we shared and talked about for days and days, hours and hours, the friends we were in high school and continued to be this summer? How could she leave me like this? Without saying goodbye? Without reaching out, just...well, just anything! Did she mean it? She never wanted to see me again? I couldn't believe it. I just couldn't believe it!

My stomach sank to my feet before her mom and then ached with cramps. Her mom heard my gasp and saw my body bend with the pang. "Again, I'm sorry, Curt." I nodded, turned away, and left. My throat had a deep gulp stuck in the middle, and I couldn't get a word out. I got in Comet and drove away. I went to the hills. I thought about the whole summer again. I re-hashed all that we talked about, all that we shared. After what happened between us, how could she just up and leave and not even leave me a note? "Was she so embarrassed she didn't ever want to see me again?" Tears rolled down my cheeks as Comet's wheels rode down the hills. The friendship I thought I had, that special close friendship that went awkward one night, just one night, seemed lost forever.

I deposited the last of my summer paychecks into Tioga State Bank the following week. I thanked the Duke and his parents for my stay in their home and drove back to Cobleskill.

I never saw Lindsey again.

Chapter Twenty-Six
Cobleskill Year Two

John and Joyce King attend my Cobleskill graduation.

September 1978 – May 1979
Playlist:
On Broadway, George Benson
Itsy Bitsy Teenie Weenie Yellow Polka Dot Bikini, Bryan Hyland
Stayin' Alive, Bee Gees
My Life, Billy Joel
Running on Empty, Jackson Browne
Two Out of Three Ain't Bad, Meat Loaf

My second year in college was even more amazing than my first, except for my roommates. Abe and I had been 100 percent compatible roommates. Still, we decided to accept some unknown assignments for the fall semester to branch out and meet new people. It was a massive mistake for us both. He was very unhappy with his roommate, and I landed two Long Island boys named

Atom and Neutron. They had been friends in high school and came to college together. They were stoned when I met them, and I think it was a week before they were straight enough to know I was their roommate. They weren't coy about leaving their drugs, mushrooms, speed, marijuana, and more exposed. There were more drugs than homework on their desks.

Abe and I were never in the habit of having our dorm door closed, but these guys would land me in trouble. The Resident Assistant made his rounds every day, casually popping into rooms with doors open for unofficial inspections. To avoid this random chance of him finding out our room was a stash of drugs, I quietly showed him our room while my roommates were in class. I told him I was filing a formal report that these were not my drugs. He wanted to know if I wanted to file a police report, and I said I'd leave that up to him as the RA! He didn't want to do that for many reasons I could agree with and understand. But I said, "For the record, I want you to note today's date that I shared this with you and that I don't approve."

My schedule was full. Cramming 23 credits of classes, extracurricular activities, and work had me flying higher than my roommates but on my own adrenaline and sugar. I used copious amounts of it in my morning coffee.

Another girl from Davis and I became great friends. She and I auditioned together for a college-sponsored talent show named Pearson Presents. With another friend from food service, we auditioned in another skit. And finally, as a solo act, I auditioned for yet another tiny routine. Most performances, songs, or shows had to be five minutes or less. A week later, the bill was up on what auditions were accepted. At dinner, Jane approached me and said, "Hey Curt, guess what?" I could see a gleam of excitement in her eye! "We're in," she exclaimed. "Pearsons Presents," I asked. "Yeah, can you believe it?"

"No, I can't; our skit is so simple."

"Well, our poker faces without a smile and dancing eyebrows to the song Itsy Bitsy Teeny Weenie Yellow Polka Dot Bikini must have won them over?" I could hardly believe it. "And that's not all," Jane went on. "Your solo act of you and your laughing machine is in too!"

"Serious," I asked.

"No joke, you're in." I put a small laughing machine in my jeans pocket. I ad-libbed some crazy dialogue of questions about college and faculty. For every answer to the questions, I'd press the mike against the button that activated the machine in my jeans, and it would bellow out hearty and contagious laughs for about ten seconds. "Curt, that polka dot hat of yours got a lot of attention in these auditions because you and Tim and your Hee Haw act also made the cut!"

I gasped again in disbelief. We auditioned for three acts because we thought we'd at least get one in and hadn't expected all of them. I had to see this for myself. We left our dinner and walked to Pearson Hall, where the acts that made the audition were listed. Sure enough, all three shows I had dreamed up had beat out plenty of others.

Weekends and some evenings of hard labor, reading and studying for my classwork, and three nights a week of practice for three weeks for the talent show left me little time to sit or drive with Comet. But, one Friday night, I sped home to Van Etten to collect some props for the talent show. A squeal came from the driver's side front wheel, and my dad said it sounded like a bearing was going. That Saturday morning, I visited the NAPA store in Spencer and picked up a set of new bearings. Harry instructed me to do it in his typical fashion, but he didn't perform any of the work. He warned me not to tighten the hubs down on the bearings and leave an eighth inch of open space to allow the bearings and spindle shaft to expand when they got hot. I performed the repair as he instructed, and by two in the afternoon, I sped back to Cobleskill, constantly pushing her to speeds beyond 100 mph. I had so much to do.

The talent show was a hit. Jane and I were a hit; Tim and I were a hit. My solo act was a hit. All three acts on the first night took the audience down, laughing to their knees. These skits were fit for the Saturday Night Live TV show! One could hear reviews about the campus as students shared some of the best talent in the show. "You gotta go see these two clowns and their dancing eyebrows…they just stand there in black pants and white t-shirts with their t-shirt sleeves rolled up and do absolutely nothing but dance their eyebrows to music." And other students could be heard, "you gotta go see this guy and his laughing machine, it's hilarious!"

The second night was the same, except it was a Saturday, and many faculty showed up. Our acts took the house down in roaring laughter again; however, some faculty were not impressed with the guy and his laughing machine and walked out of the show. Having received pressure from particular faculty who saw the act as crude satire, mainly because the laughing machine was in my pants pocket making it appear that it was my genitals laughing the third night, the director announced the act was cut. Many repeat attendees to the show booed and chanted, "Bring out the laughing guy, bring out the laughing guy!" The director apologized again and retorted, "We have many other great acts ahead. The show must go on." And we did.

The Hee Haw dance that Tim and I did with pitchforks had him chasing me during the finale and pretending to stick me in the butt with it, but on the third night, he stuck me for real! He landed two of the pitchfork tongs deep into my right cheek. When I screamed and turned to him on stage, holding my right cheek, and said, "You idiot, you stuck me with the fork." Stunned, he stopped in his tracks and did an about-face as I chased his full-rounded belly figure dressed in hayseed overhauls and a straw hat off the stage and through the audience seeking vengeance. That audience gave the hardiest roar as our acting turned to reality. The curtains closed as I chased Tim back onto the stage, ending my acting career at Cobleskill.

I soon learned a political lesson from a couple of my professors who had frowned upon the laughing machine act.

There was no mercy on my essay responses in quizzes or tests in those classes and no forgiveness or partial credit for any implied knowledge or answers. It was a different grading approach toward my work than I had experienced before.

I had little time or money for gas to drive Comet during the fall semester, but I'd at least go out once a week to start her up and make sure the battery got charged, especially as the cold weather set in. I occasionally slept in her as Atom and Neutron returned with girls and partied all night.

I hadn't driven Comet since I returned from Van Etten, but on Octoberfest weekend, guys from my house asked if I could bring them downtown to pick up some cases of beer for a party they were planning. As we drove downtown, I could feel a strong pull on the Comet steering wheel to the left, and I also heard some grinding which made me think a power steering pump was breaking down. Both symptoms were like what I had previously experienced with a failed power steering pump.

After the guys picked up their cases of beer and stashed them in the trunk, we headed back for the campus. At the five-way corner in the town center, Comet slumped and dropped the driver's side bumper to the ground as I pulled out to make a right turn. In horror, I watched as my left front tire and wheel rolled away through the intersection! I must have tightened that hub side too much when I replaced the bearings! The stress of the tight bearings had heated the spindle so hot they welded themselves together and snapped the spindle, which held the wheel on, clean from the knee action. Oh, Comet, thank you so much for this at 5 miles per hour versus the 90-plus miles per hour I raced back to campus the day I put the new bearings in a few weeks back.

The shock of what happened wore off quickly on my passengers, and they leaped to the trunk to grab their cases of beer. They ran off before a policeman showed up to direct traffic around me. I had to call a tow truck and have Comet towed back to the campus parking lot. There would be no roadside or field repairs this time.

As the fall semester progressed, so did the drug use of Atom and Neutron. Many weekend nights, they came home stoned out of their minds with girls eager to please. The lights went on as they popped their speed and lit up joints with the girls. Spinning a beer bottle, it didn't take long before they were all butt naked and involved in one sexual act or another as their drug-laden heads swirled in circles like bobble heads. They didn't care that I was there trying to get some sleep; in fact, they invited me to join in. After the first four incidences, the novelty of their porn show wore off, and it became evident this was heading toward routine. With my head under a pillow for more than an hour, hoping it would all go away, I'd eventually get up, open the window to air out the smoke, and retreat to Comet for the rest of the night's sleep, motor humming for heat in the colder nights.

I let the RA know about this repeatedly and exposed their drugs multiple times for the record. It would mean an immediate suspension from school if he filed a complaint, but for fear again that he'd explain, he wouldn't (one never knew what connection a kid might have to a specific New York family, so he was afraid to turn them in). He assured me that he'd have my back if they got caught.

Sleeping in Comet on cold nights with its front end sitting high on top of two tires to hold it up without a wheel wasn't fun.

A cold November weekend just before Thanksgiving, I found a used knee action for Comet from a local junkyard, removed the broken one, and installed the used one. Comet had sat useless this entire time, other than a place for me to sleep occasionally. I loved Comet. It had been my sanctuary for more than four years, but the stresses I endured with her became more significant and dangerous, and I was responsible for some of them. I was in a hurry at everything, and while I never cared in high school whether I crashed to my death, I was now naively putting myself in danger, trusting this rolling bucket of disrepair. Life was slowly becoming more worth living.

During the spring semester, I moved off campus into an apartment with three other roommates to rid myself of porn shows. My schedule and activity level was insane, but I still wanted to run the high hurdles and jump with the Coby Track Team. Running was always a stress reliever for me. Through the coach of the Cobleskill track team, I landed a job with his small construction company, Groski Construction. It was better hourly pay than any I had so far, reasonably flexible, and I could put in all the hours I wanted on weekends. Most of the work was landscaping labor, construction, backhoe operating, digging trenches, and foundation footings. It was a lesson that I didn't want to do this kind of work for the rest of my life, but with the better pay and the load of activity I was carrying, I didn't have to work as many hours during the week.

Because I changed majors, I had to make up a semester of classes and credits my first semester lost to the food service major. In my second semester, I carried 21 credits; this past fall, I took 22, and now this spring, it took 23 to graduate. I had no time to fool around and had to keep my nose in the books and my wallet filled to pay my rent and food. And still, another opportunity found its way into my schedule.

A professor approached me and asked me to chair the Spring Charity Event called the Cobleskill Carnival. It was incredibly flattering to be asked but also tremendous work! "Why me, Dr. Emanuel?"

"Curt, you're in my Beef Cattle Club, you're in the Dairy Science Club, you're carrying all those credits, you're working, you're on the track team. I see what you can do; you can do this."

"But Dr. Emanuel, I hardly have time to do what I do. I just can't," I insisted. "Curt, it's the busy people like you who get things done."

"All you have to do is lead. Get as many volunteers to assist you as you can. You've got guts!" he said, "I saw you in the talent show. People liked you. They will follow you."

"I don't know," I sighed.

"Curt, this is a big job; it's an honor and will look great on your resume when you go out into the world to seek a job." As I looked up at this middle-aged professor whose daily attire consisted of a string tie, jeans, cowboy boots, and a hat, he slapped me on the back. "You come to see me in my office on Thursday, and we'll get started." I didn't agree or disagree; I knew he would not take no for an answer. I had two classes with him, and I'd already experienced the unfair displeasure of two other professors because of the laughing machine act.

My final semester at Cobleskill with a 23-credit hour class load, chairing and coordinating the Spring Charity Carnival, a now steady girlfriend, and working 18-24 hard labor hours every weekend left little room for success at anything else. Once I knew I had some A's in classes and could figure out how to slack off on some and still come out with a passing C grade, that was the unfortunate course I had to take. I was working my tail end off. My girlfriend demanded more time and attention than I could afford to give her. Still, I enjoyed her company, and we shared more intimacy as stresses continued to build within me.

Three weeks before finals, I ran my last track race and took zero places in the hurdles and the high jump. I usually landed second or third place for the team. I was exhausted and glad to be done. Still working hauling railroad ties and building a retaining wall made from them, one week before finals, I fell to the ground and passed out on the job. I woke up 18 hours later in a campus infirmary bed. I had a high fever, and they diagnosed me with exhaustion and dehydration. I was mortified and embarrassed. Though I wanted to leave, the doctor instructed me to stay or suffer more severe health consequences. I took all my finals in that infirmary bed. Groups of my friends dropped in to say hello, and goodbye as the Juniors left as soon as they finished their finals. Most seniors like me stayed a few days after their finals to participate in the graduation ceremony.

A day before graduation, I was released just in time to say farewell to many great people I had surrounded myself with these past two years. I was surely going to miss my experience at Cobleskill. Aside from the work I had to do to support myself and keep myself fluid in my finances, I learned a lot, experienced more than I imagined, and met many great people.

Worn out, I participated in the Ceremonial Walk to receive my diploma. Loretta and Harry drove the 2-1/2-hour trip to see me walk as John and Joyce King did. They all seemed genuinely proud of me and happy to be there to cheer me on and be a part of my accomplishment. None of them had any idea of how much I worked through these two years and no idea I'd just come out of the infirmary.

As they quizzed me about my plans, I shared with them how a couple of my professors thought I should continue to a four-year school and how they encouraged me to get a bachelor's degree. For the first time in their lives, Loretta and Harry seemed to relish rather than resent the idea of me furthering my education. Perhaps it was because I did the first two years myself, and they could see they didn't have to ante up a dime. Maybe more, I shared with them that other professors encouraged me as they saw more in me than they ever did.

Harry seemed genuinely proud of me and basked in smiles of pride and pats on my shoulders. He made me feel good. Having John and Joyce there made me feel incredibly thankful. Their presence proved that I had become a small part of their family and lives. I had a two-year college diploma, but I was dead broke. Harry asked, "What are you going to do next?"

"I have to find a job; I'm all out of money from paying my college expenses."

"Well, you can come home and stay until you find one," he said. "And if you plan to go on to college again, you can stay rent-free."

"Thank you," I responded. "I will take you up on that. I only have another week left in my apartment here, and I've already looked here in the area, and there are no jobs." As much as I didn't want to return to that house, I had little choice.

Loretta eyed me and jested, "Wow, now, big college man!" I was never sure how to take her compliments; they were usually some form of sarcasm or criticism. I gave her the benefit of the doubt that she was in a good mood and meant a compliment. I was in a spirit of exhaustion. I could hardly wait for the event to be over to go back to my apartment and begin to pack up my things for the next chapter in my life. John King had offered me a job back on the farm.

Chapter Twenty-Seven
In the Middle

Fall 1979
Playlist:
I Can't Tell You Why, Eagles
My Life, Billy Joel
Sultans of Swing, Dire Straits
One of These Nights, Eagles
The Sad Café, Eagles
Strawberry Fields Forever, The Beatles
Hello, Goodbye, The Beatles
Who Are You, The Who

L.U.C.K. labor utilizing correct (Christ) knowledge.
Curt Riess

Graduating from Cobleskill carried three things forward for me. A school loan that had to be paid back, a yearning for more education, and an Associate in Applied Sciences degree which could land me some sort of job that paid more than farm work.

I took up John King's offer as he didn't have a hired hand when I graduated, and I was ready to milk cows and help him out if he was willing to provide me with forty to fifty hours a week. Farm wages were exempt from overtime pay, and I couldn't work part-time hours.

I worked for them because I loved them, and I'd dream someday of being able to help them somehow more, big dreams like one day I could buy him some new farm equipment or a new cab-over tractor.

Living back in Spencer after being gone for two years was lonely. My high school friends who did not attend college were employed in factories and other jobs. As before, in the past two summers, they established social circles with co-workers they met. Most who went to college had continued going into their third year, and hardly any of them were home for the summer.

My friend, the Duke, was around as he attended Corning Community College, but he'd changed somewhat. He was steadfastly focused on his long-term goal of getting into Cornell and his Ph.D. I applauded him, and though we occasionally hung out, he naturally developed other friends from Corning Community College and the K-mart store where he worked. He, too, probably viewed me as not moving forward and in the rut of my farmer dreams.

I was definitely in that dream rut. I loved this town, I loved this area, and I loved the King family. I developed an excellent local reputation as a dependable, hard worker among the elders. Comet and I were as solid a part of the landscape as the surrounding hills. Or not.

Comet and I rolled down Beckhorn Hollow to our bridge one sultry evening like we'd done many times in high school. As I watched the waters of Cayuta Creek flow, something was again gone in me. Something was lost inside me, inside my head, inside my soul. The bridge was solid as ever, though it always showed more signs of rusting, just like Comet. I thought about Lindsey, Jack, and many other classmates and where they might be. Some were in far-off places the military had taken them, and some were in colleges in other states. I had no idea where and at what schools they were, as we had not stayed in touch.

There wasn't one local classmate my age with whom I felt good socialization. I was caught somewhere in the middle. Just enough education to know things could be different and better and to be socially ignored by those who hadn't gone beyond a high school degree and didn't seem to want to bother with a college guy. And for those attending a four-year school, my two-year education wasn't considered enough.

I often eat dinner at home now. Unlike my years of high school, where I avoided any chance of being at home, it was a little more peaceful with my little sister gone from the house. My dad, the guy who always made me independent, who was always lecturing me about being safe with my car, who insisted on me having my insurance policy to protect his assets, the guy who nearly got shot by the craziness of that awful turning point in my life, the guy who had everything debt-free, did a fantastic thing one evening.

Sitting at the dinner table, asking me what I wanted to do and discussing my options, Harry said, "Whatever you decide, Curt, I'll help you. If you decide to farm, I'll borrow money and mortgage my home to help you get into dairy farming if that is what you want."

I couldn't believe it when he offered this help. In a rare moment, Loretta seemed very proud, not just of me but of my dad. He was not a generous man with the means for this kind of offering. He made you work for everything you wanted. For him to offer something like this was totally out of character to the man I knew and Loretta often described as Hitler. I don't think any other child of his ever received that kind of offer or confidence. I wondered what he was thinking, what his thoughts were. I easily could have been a dropout living alone in the wood. Still, against the odds, I stayed in high school and graduated from college. He did not. He knew I was a worker, working on the farm in high school, at home, and through school. Whatever his thoughts, they were never easily deciphered. Still, his offer was a vote of confidence from a dad to put his home and his whole life savings at risk for his son's future.

"Thank you, Dad, but I can't accept your offer."

"Why not?" he asked. "Don't you want to farm."

"Yes, I do, but," I said, "You know I went to school to become a farmer— it's what I wanted all of my life, but on that journey, I got an education, and I think I should get more! My professor told me to continue with college because he knew of my desire to go back and farm the way John King did… as a family farm; I had shared this with him. He told me it was a thing of the past. We studied the demography of farmers in the U.S., and the demographics were not on the side of the family farm to survive. He and other professors warned a whole class of dairy cattle science students sternly not to return and put their daddies into debt for those fancy blue Harvester Silos that so many farms were putting up.

"He spoke of giant dairy herds out west in California and south in Florida that were popping up with minimal capital structures or cost. Corporate farms of 1200 cows or more, and he predicted they'd one day be 12,000 cows with no end in sight of the onslaught that would come to family farm operations."

"They won't make it with debt," he insisted, "and few would survive without debt."

The deadly demographics of the aging dairy farmer across the great Midwest in states like Iowa, Minnesota, and Wisconsin were already into play.

Small dairies by the thousands with 50 cows or less died as the farmer died or retired. "None of their children returned to the farms; they worked in population centers like Chicago, Milwaukee, Minneapolis, Omaha, and Kansas City. That trend," he said, "will creep into the east coast soon. Go west, young man, go west," he told me. "If you want to be in agriculture, go west where the real agricultural revolution is already underway."

An even more frightening thought was Harry loaning me money. He'd lose everything if I failed because of my fault or because of the demographic predictions. That was a risk I could not bear. The offer, my dream, Harry's proposal; it was all too perfect and tempting, and I should take him up on the help if I was out to satisfy my desires. But I was always looking out for others. And to avoid failure of any sort, I was best to follow my head and the education I received, not my heart.

Harry looked at me with amazement. "Well," he said, "maybe that is what you should do. If you want to go to one of those colleges out west, I'll help you fix a new car. That Comet will never make it out there in one piece."

A sudden realization came upon me. I now understood the emptiness and lonesomeness I felt wasn't just a loss of friends. The sadness of reality was the loss of my dream! I went to college to learn how to be a great businessman at dairying. The irony of getting an education, it had warned me to leave the dream. And now, suddenly, another sadness entered my heart as Harry suggested I abandon Comet for the good of my future. I couldn't imagine any other car! It's odd and quite funny, but I never thought about owning any other vehicle except for one doubting frustrating weekend in college. Comet was my wheels, my home, my church, my sanctuary. We were intertwined. I was a boy, Comet a machine; we were one, boychine!

Harry just woke up my senses. I always surmised that someday Comet's life, and mine for that matter, might end together in some tragedy, especially in those darker days of my teens. Cobleskill gave me the feeling that there is something out there yet to find, something more in life to live for. Comet, the great Comet in the sky, also instilled in me there was something else to see. Harry reminded me about the wheel that fell off last fall and a few other dangerous parts I fabricated for it in high school.

Since that accident, I have considerably slowed my recklessness and speed. As much as I loved Comet, my dad was right; driving her was dangerous. He seemed to care about me now more than ever, and he reciprocated the care I had just given him by turning him down from investing in a risky future of dairy farming.

Listening in on all these conversations with Harry, Loretta supported moving on to more education, a stark contrast to just two years ago. Though she was controlling and wanted me to stay around the Spencer area, she self-sacrificially agreed with my dad on all fronts. She insisted he honor what he just offered regarding the car help.

That summer, John King had planned a new addition to his barn. He was adding space to enable him to raise more calves and add a manure pump and storage that would enable him to avoid spreading manure daily. It also would allow him to convert old calf-raising space into more tie stalls for more milk cows. John knew that I needed more money to pay down my school loans. Agricultural workers were exempt under state and federal law from paying overtime, but John gave me all the hours I wanted as long as I was willing to assist his block layer with work on the new barn addition. Since I had some experience with Groski's construction company in college and with my dad building his garage in high school, I told him I could do this in addition to the farm work instead of hiring someone else to help Ron. I put in plenty of hours.

The waters of Cayuta Creek always used to mesmerize me. But my visits to the bridge became less often after graduating from Cobleskill. Its flowing waters irritated me more than gave me peace, and they reminded me of what might be passing me. Every drop was on an onward journey to the Susquehanna River and the Chesapeake Bay, where I hadn't been yet. And it all started further upstream, somewhere else I hadn't been.

On the farm, day in and day out, John and I milked cows, mowed hay, baled hay, and put-up fodder, and then I worked extra hours on the addition. I enjoyed all of the work. But something deeper was tugging at me.

Ron, a carpenter and mason, lived in an apartment in the main farmhouse. John had been a very generous landlord letting this elderly bachelor work off much of his rent occasionally.

As we began work on the addition after laying the first three layers of the block, I questioned him about mixing the cement. "Hey Ron, this isn't mortar cement," I told him. Ron grumbled something I couldn't discern and told me to "shut up and mix another bag of cement."

At lunch one day, I brought this matter to John's attention, and he simply said Ron knows what he is doing and ignored my concern. So, day after day, we laid up more courses, and I would again mention to Ron that this wasn't the mortar cement brand or mix I used with the Groski construction company. He'd grunt and say, "Mix it up and bring me some block," This went on for several weeks as we would lay up to two to three layers per week in the evenings after he returned from his carpentry job. The wall was growing, and my frustration was that no one was listening to me.

Again, I brought the complaint to John and encouraged him to look into this. John had other things on his mind or didn't want to pay attention to the new graduate's knowledge. The wall was creeping higher; it was now two-thirds toward the finish line of its planned height, and from a visual standpoint, it looked good. But I was concerned it was weak.

Each time we worked on the wall, Ron directed me to clean all the tools and mixers and burn all the empty bags in a barrel, unfortunately hiding the evidence of the wrong cement brand.

When the co-op delivered yet another pallet of cement, I couldn't take it any longer. The next day during the coffee break after morning milking and chores, I said to John politely but insistently, "John, I've mentioned this several times, and you and Ron just don't seem to want to listen. I'm not mixing any more cement for Ron or hauling any more block unless you go out and look at the pallet of cement that just arrived!"

"It is NOT mortar mix." I insisted. "Even my dad says it's the wrong cement to use." John frowned, took his glasses off, cleaned them, and looked at me rather sternly for bothering him again with what he must have considered nonsense. "OK, Curt. OK," John responded. "I'll take a look."

Later that afternoon, when Ron returned from his other job, I began mixing up cement, and he started laying blocks again. Where was John, I thought! I was furious. The pre-milking break came, and I asked John one last time to come out and look at the bags of cement used for mortar. After the coffee break, he followed me to the construction site. He lifted an empty bag, and nowhere on the bag did it indicate it was mortar. "Say, Ron," John called, "Is this the right mortar to lay block?" Ron looked at me with disgust and came over to the pile of bags, looked puzzlingly at it, and said, "SHIT! Clean up my tools, dump that cement mixer, and wash it out." John walked away in one direction and Ron in another to his apartment.

The next day a pallet of new mortar arrived, and we laid up the remaining layers of the block for the next three weeks with the correct mortar. "What about the rest of the wall, I asked?" John answered, "When we finish laying up the rest of the wall, we'll fill the wall with cement and re-rod." I envisioned a cement truck backing up and filling the wall and soon realized that vision wouldn't happen.

After Ron laid the wall, I was back mixing regular cement for the next two weeks. I would pour the cement into two five-gallon buckets and carry one in each hand. I walked a hundred feet of wall on 12-inch planks filling the wall with a solid cement core, shoving a length of re-rod through the block every five feet.

It was grueling work, and while I never complained, I wasn't delighted. I viewed it as a wasteful pain in the neck of time and money, even if it wasn't my own, all because no one would listen to me. I was the one who suffered the labor of fixing it. And yet, it wasn't the labor that bothered me as much as the point that no one listened. I was still considered a high school kid. I could tell John was silently and equally as aggravated as I was with all of this extra labor and cost.

With the addition completed, fall filled the air with the smell of chopped corn silage. October came, and early one morning, while I was milking cows, John took a call in the barn and then hollered down to me that the call was for me. On the other end of the line was my dad Harry telling me he wanted me to go home and be with Loretta before he called to inform her that my older brother was killed in a car accident earlier this morning. I couldn't believe what I was hearing. It wasn't just the shock of my brother's death but the event that occurred earlier that morning, around 1:00 am. I slept across the hall from Loretta's bedroom. She woke at about 1:30 am screaming and sobbing. I opened her door and shouted, "Wake up."

She repeatedly cried in a low shriek, "Something terrible happened to Gary; he was killed."

"No, you're dreaming," I shouted. I kept trying to wake her up and tell her she was dreaming.

She sobbed profusely, repeating loudly and crying that "something bad happened to Gary."

"No," I tried to reassure her, "you're dreaming!"

Finally, she said, "If I'm dreaming, turn on the light," so I did. There she sat up in bed sobbing that Gary was dead.

I consoled her and said, "No such thing; it was all just a bad dream."

I don't know how she knew this, how the dream communication occurred, but she was right on at the hour of his death. It spooked me. And now I had to go home and be with her while my dad called her.

I explained to John that I had to go home and be with Loretta. I didn't tell him why. I could already see on his face that he knew from my dad's call.

I went home and sat in the kitchen till the phone rang, and I picked it up. My dad was on the other end and asked me to wake Loretta. I walked to her bedroom, and she was already awake. Her door was still open from the episode when I awoke her last night. I handed her the phone. She said nothing and started sobbing uncontrollably. I sat on the edge of her bed. I tried to hug her, but she pushed me away and asked me to leave her alone. It was a long day of silence and sobbing on her part. My dad was on Long Island. He had dinner with my brother the evening before his death, and Loretta already resented that. He was returning this morning.

When he returned seven hours later to be with Loretta, I returned to the farm that evening to assist with the milking chores. John asked how everything was, and I said OK, except my older brother had died in a car accident around 1:30 am. He knew I needed some normalcy, and work was my usual.

Loretta would go through the funeral as if she had lost her only child or husband and into the most profound depression and grief I'd ever known. Her words to Gary's first love and the mother of his two children were hurtful again, as they had been many times before. Not even a funeral was an exception for the reprieve of Loretta's scorn. Gary's former girlfriend and his children were hurt by Loretta so severely that she soon distanced herself and her two children to another state and left no forwarding address for anyone. It saddened me as I was close to those children, and it would be ten years before Loretta or I would see those kids again.

It was a chilly early November day, and John and his family left the farm for me to do afternoon chores. Before milking would begin, the heifers across the railroad tracks needed feed. The wagon had to be filled at the barn across Highway Route 34. As I rolled onto the highway, the John Deere 2510 stalled. Crap, I thought, the tractor was out of gas. I immediately hopped off the tractor, ran to the garage, grabbed a gas can, and tried the gas pump, which was off.

John forgot to turn on his secret switch. Several cars honked and slowed down at the tractor's obstruction of the highway. One of them was Ernie Smith, the neighboring dairy farmer. I wasn't supposed to know how to turn on the gas pump. John had maintained a "secret" switch to assure his mind that neither I nor any other high school worker after me might use his pump for our personal use. I couldn't waste time going downtown to the gas station and filling up gas cans. I had known about the secret switch for years. It was a charade I hated, but I pretended I didn't know where it was. I never used it; I would never steal.

I was tired of the years of charades Loretta put me through and aggravated that though I had just graduated from two years of college, both John and Ron still viewed me as a high schoolboy. I anxiously decided to turn on the secret switch and pumped the gas I needed into a five-gallon can. I didn't care. I knew this would expose the gas switch charade, and in a way, I felt freedom coming.

At Cobleskill, I had the space for two years to be myself, uninfluenced by anyone except those I allowed. People looked at who I was and what I did and valued me for it. No judgments or preconceptions followed me from high school to dampen any opportunity. People listened to what I had to say and followed me.

This incident was needed to end this charade once and for all. And more immediately necessary was that I got the tractor and wagon off the shoulder of the highway using a small can of gas and kept passersby out of danger. I then pulled up to the gas pump and filled the tank.

I stared at the meter ticking away, recording the gallons of gas pumped into the tractor. I knew that John would probably notice. Throughout the rest of that evening's chores and milking, I became irritated and angry. I fumed over every time he had to turn that switch on for me to use the gas pump, and how I felt guilty and frustrated that he trusted me with everything else on his farm, but not that. The more I thought about the charade I had to put on for that silly gas switch, the more I beat myself up for having seen him use it, for him not trusting me, and for withholding the truth of my knowledge of it for so long.

As Comet and I drove around the hills that evening, I felt anxious and troubled and knew this would not go well. "Comet, I know I have to tell him," and I rehearsed over and over how I would let him know what happened and that, in a way, I'd been dishonest in that I never fessed up that I knew! I whispered and rationalized back and forth as to who was the blame, "him or me!" I thought about how foolish he would feel having used the switch when I knew about it all along! "It's your fault," Comet kept telling me. Tell the truth, Comet urged. I pushed the pedal to the metal and spun her rear tires up the next hill and home.

The next day at lunch, my knee bounced under the table with nervous energy. John took to his daily paper as I waited for Joyce to dish up lunch, and she was serving a hot plate I loved. I began eating as he continued reading his newspaper and passively took a bite here and there. About halfway through my meal, John put his paper down and focused more on eating.

I cleared my throat; "John, I'm sorry, but I have something disappointing I need to tell you." As he kept eating, his eyes were now focused on me, "John, I just want you to know in case you hear from a neighbor that the 2510 tractor stalled on the highway on my way to the barn yesterday. It was out of gas." His facial expression immediately told me he remembered forgetting to turn on the gas pump like he usually did when he and his family left me to run the farm. The look on his face and his next question erased my rehearsed explanation which I planned to share. "How did you get gas?" he asked.

A colossal lump entered my throat as I gulped, "John, I'm sorry, I used," I swallowed again, "your secret switch."

His face darkened, and he paused with silence. Then with a firm tone, he asked, "How did you know about the secret switch?"

"John, I'm sorry; I saw you turn it on long ago… I've known about that switch since high school, but you didn't want me or anyone else to know about it, so I pretended I didn't know and just forgot about it until yesterday when I had to use it." His face flushed red with anger. "I never wanted anyone to know about that switch," he demanded.

"I know, John, and I never touched or used it until yesterday. And I never took any gas from you except that you occasionally gave me." His face turned from a deep red to purple. He was furious; even Joyce looked on with concern. "So, you knew about that switch all this time and never said anything to me?" Lunch went silent, and I nodded yes.

That half-question, half-statement was the ultimate condemnation I expected, and I was ashamed. The lump in my throat was now choking me, and my appetite ceased. I couldn't hold back the tears already primed to stream down my cheeks before lunch began. I would generally stay for seconds if they offered and a piece of Joyce's great pie, but I had to leave the kitchen. I looked at the half glass of milk I still had and my half-eaten plate and left the table for the barn.

I felt enormous humiliation. I was instantly demoted, not physically, not in pay, but mentally ashamed for withholding the truth. I lived with this lie for so many years and couldn't, wouldn't do it any longer.

It brought to light the entire charade I lived my senior year in the wood but had acted as if I lived at home. It shed light on my life of charades, pretending I had an everyday normal home life, ashamed ever to divulge the truth. It was wrong what I did. How often did John have to turn on the gas pump when I knew how? And I felt guilt every single time. They knew nothing of my high school home life, the charades Loretta forced upon me. They only knew that I had lived a charade on their farm. I just disappointed two of my most influential and essential people, and I was even more devastated than they were.

That evening Comet and I sped in the dark down Route 34 to Sayre, Pennsylvania. My gut ached, and tears continued to stream down my cheeks. I pushed her beyond 90, 100, 105, maybe 110 miles per hour as fast as her 289 eight-cylinder could go. When I got to Sayre, I pulled into the Pudgies Pizza restaurant, ordered an entire sheet of pizza and a couple of liters of pop, and then Comet and I drove the roads through the back hills of Lockwood and back to Van Etten.

We took it slow home. I felt like I'd thrown away my whole life with the Kings in one minute of truth-telling. And what they didn't know is that those few tears they saw shed down my cheeks were the start of much more. Twenty years of charades, living with Loretta, welled up and poured out of my eyes. Regrets, pain, covering for her and Harry as typical parents, and then there was the stupid switch. I never liked knowing where that damn switch was, and I tried to put it out of my mind so many times.

I wasn't going to live like that any longer, for no one, no more charades, no more, I was done. It was the last time.

"You're free now; Comet whispered," as she took me home through the hills slow like a snail while I gorged on the sheet pizza filling my belly with false comfort.

I was wondering if I was going to be fired the next day or not. My confidence in all other matters I served the Kings told me I didn't have to worry, but dishonesty, even just withholding knowledge as I did, was undoubtedly a sin.

And I had more trouble. Life at home was once again becoming unbearable. Since my brother's death, Loretta was in a mental illness with mood swings as wild as ever but with even greater despair. It was depressing. Gary's death brought some post-trauma and grief back from her past life. I knew she had lost her firstborn son to a tragic death falling off a roof at three or four. I thought her Olympic-sized grief had to be for more than my brother Gary, perhaps grieving all over again for her first son too.

I felt the same with the secret switch admission. It brought back all the charades I had endured all these years, and immense feelings of remorse welled in me. In a small way, I might have known a little, just a little, what Loretta might be going through.

Creeping along one-lane back roads, still stuffing myself with the comfort of pizza, I prayed to Comet: "Comet," I conceded, "I have to go. I have to move forward." Nothing seemed like it was before I graduated college. I was a different man. Going to Ithaca to the North Forty on a Friday or Saturday night wasn't the same fun. My girlfriend dumped me, and I was socially alone. My re-payment of my school loan to Tioga State Bank will start soon. I barely had enough money to maintain myself and felt hopeless. I wanted to go West to further my education as my professors coached me.

Driving the hills, I felt a turning point, a new reality in my life. "I wish I could take you with me, Comet. I wish we could roll down new roads together playing the Beach Boys, Eagles, and Beatles. We're one: Boychine. But we're both broken in lots of ways. Going west is a long haul, for you, for me!"

I turned off the music; Comet purred along the gravel roads. The silence was only broken in the cool night air by her valves tapping with each slight acceleration!

Comet, I prayed, "Bruce encouraged me to go and look at universities in the Midwest." Dairying was a goal forever for me as a boy, but getting an education and not following those in the know meant I was letting my heart rule my head. "Even though you cannot let it go from your heart, your education may show you another dream. Don't be afraid. Go learn some more," Comet whispered.

"Dr. Emmanuel suggested I continue in schools like the University of Madison, Kansas, Missouri, or Iowa State. He particularly recommended Iowa State." When I asked him why he said, "It fits you, Curt; ISU is Curt, it is a great school, and I see you there." He said nothing more, nothing less. He got to know me well in my two years in the classes, clubs, and the Coby Carnival I chaired for him. "I see you there too," Comet whispered.

"The trouble is, Comet, I'm out of money. I feel out of control again and don't know who I am. What am I doing back here in Spencer? I'm not going anywhere right now. Working back here for farm wages and your constant breakdowns aren't going to pay the bills. And what would I go back to college for?"

I prayed hard for answers, insights, and some guidance.

"I love you, Comet; you're my chapel for prayer, meditation, and a place for spilling my fears, tears, and emotions. But the days of you and me breaking down along a highway and being able to jimmy-rig parts and limp home just isn't going to cut the grade anymore. We are broke. You guzzle almost as much oil as gas, and your valves are tapping like a drummer."

Comet and I pulled alongside a stretch of road and parked near an open meadow. The meadow allowed me to peer into the dark sky above and see heaven full of stars. After extensive meditation, I prayed to the more extraordinary Comet in the sky. We sat for hours with the motor running, the heat on, and my window half down.

Comet finally whispered back. "Your free; create your luck. That is why you went to college. Go back to work, go back to school. Use the knowledge you've gained and apply it. To move forward, you may have to give up some of the things you love, the car, perhaps the Kings, but don't give up on me, use the strength of labor I endowed unto you, utilize the correct knowledge given to you and follow me…to Iowa."

Chapter Twenty-Eight
Boychine – Ode to Comet

Fall 1979
Playlist:
I Can't Tell You Why, Eagles
My Life, Billy Joel
Sultans of Swing, Dire Straits
One of These Nights, Eagles
The Sad Café, Eagles
Strawberry Fields Forever, The Beatles
Hello, Goodbye, The Beatles
Who Are You, The Who
Everything I Own, Bread

Every day of my life in Comet was a thrill. It is hard to describe when communicating with a machine and becoming entwined and part of it. Communication is not just with your soul; it starts with your thumb and index finger with the turn of a key, and then with your hands on the steering wheel, your toes communicate with the gas pedal simultaneously. Your eyes become the portal to where the machine goes, and your heart beats with every RPM.

Five miles of dirt road were in any direction I wanted to get to town. This way or that way, from Rumsey Hill to Wynkoop Creek or Cooper Hill to Beckhorn Hollow, there were hills to climb, curves to swerve into, and more off-the-beaten-path crossroads for narrower and riskier skill tests. Stop, start, spin, burn rubber, heck… spin the entire vehicle round and round as many times as I desired; I poured my teen and home life frustrations into spinning wheels. The Comet was solid, low, and balanced, and so was I…in more ways than the eyes of some saw in me. Though a few neighbors sometimes saw my antics as I passed and wondered just when they would pick me up out of a ditch, hardly anyone else ever saw my dirt track roadster skills. Almost all the time, I carefully ensured my antics never endangered anyone else, and I was horsing around on roads seldom traveled.

I created a reason to go to town every day, sometimes two or three times. And every day, the five miles of dirt to Wyn-coop Creek was a self-satisfying hair-raising dare of speed and dirt road handling skill, to the dismay of some neighbors residing on Rumsey Hill that had to suck up a cloud of dust as I sped by. Besides school and work, I went to church on Sundays and even took my little sister to drive her back home, about 18 miles round trip, so that I could turn around and head back to town again to meet up with a friend.

I loved to drive Comet. As navigator and captain at the wheel, I anticipated my routes, the dangerous curves, the sweeping hills, gravel edges, shoulders, banks, ditches, and hazards through which my feet, hands, and eyes would coordinate Comet. Comet and I had become one piece of engineering; a car made of steel with its heartbeat and circulatory system of engine coolant, oil, and lubricants guided by human flesh, brain, and soul. Understanding and visualizing the operation and feel of every mechanical inch of the vehicle and how it worked made me part machine. This is how it was with Comet…we became one, boychine.

Speeding down one of my favorite roads, I saw in my head how the engine's crankshaft pumped the pistons up and down to power the transmission. I saw the camshaft spinning valves up and down, tapping to let fuel and air in and exhaust out. The fan rotated to cool the engine, and the tranny fluid flowed through a series of small canals to power the drive shaft, which drove the gears in the rear end to power the wheels where I wanted them to go. And the steering wheel is connected to a valve body that directs the power steering this way or that. Those pistons beat faster than my heart, but both were in sync to power Comet precisely where I wanted it to go. We were terrific together, spinning wheels that hugged the bearings, steel on steel, miniature ball bearings bearing all the weight of that machine spinning in grease as fast as my brain sent signals to my foot through my nerves.

When I stepped on the gas pedal, I envisioned the cable pulling open the throttle and the jets in the carburetor flooding the manifold and the piston combustion chambers with a mixture of fuel and oxygen to provide the propulsive explosions for me to direct acceleration at every curve I knew. I knew just when and how much power to add to perfectly slide the rear end on the gravel edge and pilot Comet back to a straight position. I learned how to throw it into a spin to the left, pilot it back straight forward and throw it into a right spin for any number of times I desired and always come out of it clean. I don't know what I was practicing for, but Comet was my mechanical bull, and I was the cowboy. Only I controlled this engineering marvel's direction, speed, and sensations. Boychine!

One of my favorite routes to town was a crossroad from Rumsey Hill to Beckhorn Hollow. In my typical fashion, I'd race down Rumsey Hill and throw the Comet into a skid for a hundred feet before the right hairpin turns onto Morey Road and Albee Hill. Both Morey and Albee Hill roads were one-lane dirt roads with trees growing on the shoulders. There wasn't any room for most of these roads for another car to pass, much less an error. If you came across another vehicle, you would have to back up to a spot where a ditch carried rainwater runoff off the road and sit until the other car passed. The weird thing about these two roads was that I never really raced through them once I was on them. They were beautiful one-lane dirt roads covered with tree canopies. It was the kind of road you just savored and made sure your windows were rolled down so you could smell the damp mosses and ferns growing on the forest floors and hear the crickets or katydids. The slope down Albee Hill was cut sideways into the hill and afforded a view of the creek and valley below. I was an extraordinarily pent-up and frustrated teen from living with a bipolar mom, and the Morey-Albee Hill crossroad seemed to tame me down and give me some peace and solace. Once you reached Beckhorn Hollow, a hairpin turn was required and would land you on the one-lane steel truss bridge that crossed Cayuta Creek.

That bridge was beautiful. Sitting at an angle to Cayuta Creek with the mountain as a backdrop, it was a postcard bridge of yesteryear and a past automobile era…even then when I was sixteen. Painted silver like the Comet, we just camouflaged both souls of steel together when we merged, and from afar, one would never know we were there. Sometimes I'd park Comet right in the middle of the bridge, kick my door open and watch the flowing stream of water below through the metal grate that made up the road surface. I would make sanity dates with that bridge listening to the Beach Boys, Eagles, or Bruce Springsteen, just watching the water flow by. If I were there in the middle of the day, I could sit there for an hour or two before another car came and made it necessary for me to get off that bridge and let them pass.

Many a time, if I needed to slow down or mentally time out, the route to that bridge and the bridge itself was my transport to a more peaceful inner feeling. I often thought about how many horses and drivers, how many cars crossed that bridge, and how it carried them toward town for provisions; now, it was where I dropped my inner troubles down through the grate and into the water below. It was a bridge to freedom of sorts, but the absolute liberty in my life was Comet. Comet was taking me places I'd never been before and giving me experiences I'd never had before. Comet spun the wheels beneath me to financial freedom and independence.

Comet was the absolute bridge to my future. While I loved racing against the clock and testing Comet and my skills to the limit, Comet was delivering me into a future that I had barely just begun to discover and certainly did not comprehend fully at 16. And while I took Mr. Hansens's advice about avoiding the Bermuda Triangles, I loved listening to hits and tunes about love and the girl I would one day find. Cruising many nights with all the windows down, pouring out my anxieties and emotions, my eight-track or radio blaring, I owe Comet my life for where it took me and the path toward the girl I'd find nearly five years later.

Chapter Twenty-Nine
Yaphank

Fall 1979 – Spring 1980
Playlist:
Start Me Up, The Rolling Stones
The Great Gig In The Sky, Pink Floyd
Nebraska, Bruce Springsteen
I'm Goin' Down, Bruce Springsteen
Hey You, Pink Floyd
Walk This Way, Aerosmith
You Can't Always Get What You Want, The Rolling Stones

I took my dad up on his offer to help me fix up a car. At a junkyard in Horseheads, a brand new 1979 Dodge Ram Power Wagon pickup truck had rolled and was totaled by the owner's insurance company. It was the coolest-looking pickup truck on the market and only had 1500 miles. It had a roll bar that protected most of the car from severe damage, and I began to patch the truck up. Still dreaming of the future in farming, it was natural for me to look to a pickup truck as my next vehicle.

It was a huge mistake. I got it fixed road-worthy enough to pass the New York Vehicle inspections and license and insure it. Its full-time four-wheel-drive system and oversize wheels and tires with automatic transmission gave me about six miles per gallon. It was draining me financially.

I had parked Comet down by the cattle barn. My dad told me to sell it and get some money for it, but I couldn't do that. I still loved that car. I'd still go down to Comet in the barn, sit in the front seat, and think and commune with it and my God. As long as the engine ran, I could hear it whispering back.

Every day I drove the Ram, it had no thrill or love affair. And there was undoubtedly no racing around and spinning round and round on the dirt roads.

I never talked to the Ram, and my traverses through the hills dramatically diminished because of the fuel consumption. I'm sure many people along Rumsey Hill appreciated this new drive as it slowed me down.

I was applying for jobs posted on the Cobleskill job board. Most jobs were closer to New York City. After several interviews for one job, I landed an Assistant manager job at the Yaphank County Prison Farm in Yaphank, Long Island. It was difficult to tell John that I was leaving his employment, but in my gut, something between us at that time, over the secret switch, said it was time for me to move on.

Long Island was seven hours away from Van Etten. I had no place to live and called my Aunt Peggy to ask if I could rent a room at her home. She resided in Bayshore then, and one of my cousins was gone to college, so she had a bedroom open; of course, she said yes, but would not accept any rent.

The Ram was just too much truck to take on for me at that time in my life. My dad saw that too. He suggested we trade cars. He had just finished fixing up a Full Size 1977 Chevy Impala Station Wagon and was selling it. He said he'd swap me for the truck, and I took him up on the offer. Though it was a station wagon, it had quite a bit more zip than the Ram, rode like a Cadillac, and, most importantly, had much better fuel mileage. Plus, as I loved to explore here and there, it could occasionally serve as a house and bed with a sleeping bag.

The Impala took me to Long Island to start my Yaphank County Prison Farm job. After two weeks of orientation and training, I began managing staff who provided an activity for the prisoners. It was an awkward job among uniformed prisoners who were there to learn trade skills such as butchering, carpentry, and other trades. As a young "pretty boy," as some of the prisoners nicknamed me, they'd call out to me, whistle at my ass as I walked by, and make obscene gestures to me, inviting me to some party they were making up in their minds.

They were tough and rough, much older and burlier than I was. My boss trained and coached me to ignore their remarks and that we could do nothing about it. They had guards on standby at the trade stations they worked, so there was nothing to worry about, he said, but never less, I worried every day I was there that some knife-wielding prisoner learning meat cutting would pull me aside somewhere and try to rape me.

I landed another job as well. My older sister had a friend named Diane Russo, who owned several 7/11 Convenience stores. She was having trouble keeping staff at one of them on the midnight shift and just had her midnight person walk out on her. She asked If I could help and fill in while she looked for another person to fill the job. Thinking it would be temporary, I said yes.

While I never required much sleep as a kid and could perform the job, getting to and from Yaphank with the Long Island traffic was grueling. I liked the extra pay and could see how it could enhance and help me reach my goals more quickly. I had no friends, no social life, and I knew nobody except my cousin John and his mom, so I thought, *Why not take a second job?* I asked Diane if I could keep the job, and she let me have it.

I could earn another eight bucks an hour in addition to my $20,000.00 a year salary from the prison farm. So for nearly a year, my schedule was limited to working the Yaphank Prison Farm from 8 am to 5 pm. I would drive to Bayshore, nap at my Aunt Pegs' house from 6 to 10, then go to Wantagh and work the 7/11 store from 11 pm to 7 am. Then I took the Sunrise Highway to the east end of Long Island and back to Yaphank, and the drive was just about an hour with the traffic.

It was an insane and grueling 18-hour day of work and commuting every day for nine months. But I had my financial goal written down in my wallet and took it out every day to remind me what the benefit of this craziness would be. If I could sustain this, I could pay off my loan to Tioga State Bank and save enough spare funds to go to Iowa State University, which had accepted me into their Ag Journalism school. Choosing the Ag Journalism sector allowed most of my agricultural credits from Cobleskill to transfer in, reducing many classes I would have to retake.

I ate my dinner on the job at the 7/11 store every night at 11:30 pm. It usually consisted of frozen sandwiches or other junk food from Diane's store. From four to five am, the donut trucks delivered their goods, and coffee and donuts were my breakfast from 5 am until 7 am as I rang up customers coming in for theirs.

I soon learned why Diane couldn't keep anyone on the night shift at that store. By one in the morning, the crazies, as I called them, were all out in fine form, mostly high or drunk and coming into the store for food. Nearly all of them had remarks, threats, or slurred profanity directed at me, the cashier, as they tried to distract or scare me as they stole merchandise. I caught on quickly and charged them for what I saw them put down their pants or into their jackets, and they didn't know the difference. Many of them were neighborhood regulars. They thought they were getting away with something. Occasionally one of them would question why a pack of cigarettes cost so much more than they were used to paying. I'd ask them to take down their pants or open their jacket, and they'd see why. The glares I used to get from them told me they knew I'd outsmarted them.

Poor Diane was being bled to death by theft in this store. The worst cases were the teens who would come in groups. One or two would try to distract me with a small purchase while the other twelve filled their jackets and pants with stolen goods. There wasn't much I could do in those cases; they all walked or ran out as I shouted at them that I'd call the cops on them next time. And I did at first, but that was useless as the thieves were long gone by the time the police showed up. The cops did show up every morning though, around 2 am for their free donuts. Diane said it was OK and that they could have whatever was left over from the day before and free coffee. She viewed their routine as a good presence in the night.

The cashier counter looked as if a bat had beaten it, and it had. Under the counter was a small baseball bat. I was told if there was trouble or crazies I couldn't control, I should take the bat out and bang the counter with it as a threat. There were only a handful of times I had to use the bat and scream obscenities like "get the f…k out of my store" to chase out some pot-high or speed-high thieves.

The prison farm was a much calmer scene than the midnight train wreck of a population that visited the 7/11 from eleven to seven. I ate my lunch at noon at the Yaphank Prison Farm, which was usually a badly needed break. I had an hour as I took no other breaks in the day, and I usually wolfed down a hero I bought at a local deli and then stretched out and took a nap in my station wagon. I missed driving Comet, but the wagon had its benefits.

I maintained a pretty smooth and steady schedule for the first six months, but the stress from the evening shifts at the 7/11 store was beginning to wear on me. The worst pressure was when the staff person to start the 7 am shift was late, and then I had to race through traffic to get to my job at Yaphank by 8. Her name was Lulu. She was a small petite cute gal who continuously checked me out downtown and pinched my butt when we were behind the counter together. As we transitioned the shift changes, Diane, the store owner, would usually meet us at the store for the shift change to ring out and warn me about her telling me right in front of her to beware of her; she's just trying to get in your pants! Shocked that she would say that right in front of her, Lulu smiled and said, yup!

She constantly flirted with me, and I returned the same in fun. That kept her coming in on time so I wouldn't be late for my second job. Then one night, she showed up around midnight with a couple of beers and worked the night shift with me. As we chatted and kidded around, it became very apparent Diane was right. She was after only one thing, and it lay inside my pants. "Wanna have a little fun?" she asked.

"No," I replied, "not here in the store, thinking that would be the end."

"Of course not," she said, "let's go to your car." I hadn't kissed or been with a girl for almost a year. She grabbed my keys, left the store, and went and sat in the car. I stayed in the store until she suddenly started honking the horn and making a scene. This crazy girl, I mean, she was hot and out there honking the horn in the middle of the night like crazy! I yelled through the door, asking her to stop. She just smiled through the windshield and motioned me with a wave of her hand to come out.

I finally locked the store door, jumped in the front seat of my car, and asked her if she was crazy or something. "Something!" she said seductively. She slid into the back. "Come on back," she said.

"No," I said, "I don't have a condom." Hoping that would be the excuse to get out of this dilemma. "Let's go back into the store," I suggested. She was stripping. The parking lot lights were just bright enough that I could make out the Bermuda Triangle. I'd been here before… I knew better, I didn't want to be here, but I slid into the back, and she zipped down my pants, erected me, and slid on a condom. Unfulfilled and disappointed in my sixty-second performance that night, she soon turned her sights toward another guy within days, and she wasn't interested in me. But she would be late for her shift many times, which would cause me stress in more ways than the disappointing one-night stand with her.

One such occasion led me into an accident. I was on Sunrise Highway racing to Yaphank when I dozed off and suddenly smashed into another car's rear end. It was my fault. When I stopped and got out of my car, six Puerto Ricans got out of the car I'd hit. At first thought, I was ready to leap back into my car and lock myself in until a cop showed up. But, they seemed friendly enough, high, and as they surveyed the damage, pleaded with me for "No pigs, no pigs," They asked, "Everything is OK with us, no pigs," they didn't want to report the damage. The rear end of their car was smashed with heavy visible damage to their trunk and fenders from the solid bumper on my station wagon. I had damage; my grill was shattered, and my hood bent down. It was my fault, and I knew it. I said I was sorry, and one of the guys from the other car said, no problem and pleaded again, "no pigs, no pigs (cops), OK?"

I looked at the six of them, the broken plastic from my grill and their taillights, and said, "OK. But you better get your tail lights fixed soon if you don't want to attract cops."

"No problem," they said, and they quickly got into their car and sped off. I got into mine and did the same.

That was a scary day for me. I knew I was pushing things to the limit. My body, soul, and physical capacity were tested, and I lived on cold cuts and sugar.

When I returned to Bayshore at my aunt's house, she asked me, "What happened to your car?" I explained the whole story. "You're going to kill yourself, nephew," she said with love, "you can't keep up this schedule. You should give up one of your jobs." I thanked her for her passion and went back to work.

My goals where in my wallet, and nothing would keep me from achieving them. I already had enough money to pay down my student loan from Tioga State Bank, my first and most immediate goal.

I kept going and managed to get in my four hours of sleep a day and almost a fifth during lunchtime at the prison lunch break.

On another typical night at the 7/11 store, a gang of kids came in to steal. This same group had been back a few times. I took the bat from under the counter, beat it with it, and told them to get out immediately. They looked at me and asked what the f—k? And I told them, "You know what the f—k, get the f—k out of my store and don't come back," I smashed the bat into the counter three more times before I started to come out from the counter. They all fled, screaming obscenities at me, but I was in no mood for their shit, and I went and locked the front door for the next hour.

It was May and my 21st birthday. How many months I'd been employed at the 7/11 was a blur, but it seemed like a lifetime. The nightlife at this store was insane. I had become quite hardened, learned how to swear to speak their village language with the best of them, and my fingernails were bitten raw from my rattled nerves. I wasn't putting up with any bullshit from the drug-high clientele.

Then one night, three African American men entered the store at about 3 am. As they perused the store, one of them came up to the counter and asked for three packs of cigarettes as a diversion while the others were stuffing their jackets. When I refused to give the guy the cigarettes until they first paid for the stuff they were stealing, one of them shouted and threatened me. I shouted back and told them to get the f…k out of my store, and went for the baseball bat. As I bent down, he reached over the counter and grabbed as many packs of cigarettes as he could. When I came up with the bat, he shoved the merchandise racks on the counter at me and knocked them and me to the ground. They all fled.

That was it. I'd had enough. So far, I'd been lucky none of the thieves had a gun. Every week I shared with Diane the episodes of crap and how much she might be losing to theft. I told her I couldn't do it any longer and suggested she shut down the store during my shift. "Nothing good happens after midnight," I told her. She explained that she couldn't do that because of the franchise agreement rules. We concluded that from now on, we'd leave all the lights on in the store, but we'd lock the doors from 2:30 am to 4 am, and I'd mop the floors and stock the shelves with goods during that time. I did that regularly every night anyway when it was slow, but I'd specifically do it during these hours as a reason to lock the doors to the customers. This way, if, by chance, the franchise found out, it could serve as a legitimate reason for downtime. This was the norm for the remainder of my employment at Diane's store. There were still plenty of crazies before those hours, and then the worst came knocking at the door while it was locked, but I ignored them and went about my business.

The insanity of working these two jobs was catching up with me. I was becoming numb. My Aunt Peg was sensing it in me too. Except for my two years at Cobleskill, life has been one freaking hell. And now, every day, just flipping from one full-time job to another without sleep, I was living on the edge, but Iowa was my focus. Everything I was doing was to get me to Iowa. I didn't know what to expect when I got there, but my soul kept whispering that Bruce Emanuel was right. "Iowa, go west, young man, go west, young man." I can't explain it, but Comet or my soul kept whispering to me repeatedly when my head would fill with doubts, Iowa, Iowa. Could it be the Holy Spirit working on me? I know God had spoken to me through Comet many times. I don't know what it was, but I was told to go to Iowa, and thus I maintained the crazy but hopefully temporary life I had.

It was the beginning of June 1980 when my Aunt Peg told me my former boss, John King, had called, and he asked if I would call him back. He asked me if I was interested in returning to the farm as he'd like to have me back. I thanked him but declined. The pay here was so much better, despite the hours, and though I was working only four to six more hours a day than I worked on the farm, I was making almost triple the amount. The stresses were undoubtedly more significant with the midnight nuts at the 7/11 store and the commute to Yaphank, but to reach the goals in my pocket it was the only way for me.

A week later, I received a second message from my Aunt Peg that John had called again and asked me to return his call. I called him. "Curt," he said, "Your mom called me and told me you are working two jobs in Long Island. I know I can't pay you what you earn down there from two jobs, but I heard you were killing yourself with them. I could use your help if you're willing to return. My mom has been diagnosed with cancer and is dying, and I would like to have you back if you can help me."

My heart sank. I'd learned to appreciate John's mom through all the cookie and coffee breaks we had with her, and I knew how much John loved her. "How bad is her cancer John and how long does your mom have to live?"

Though he cleared his throat, his voice was still raspy, and he said, "I'm not sure, but maybe two to three months." I loved John, and my heart ached for him. I was mentally and physically worn out too. I thought through this quickly. Obviously, my aunt had called Loretta and ratted on my situation.

I'd reached the monetary goals on the paper in my wallet and would sacrifice nearly two-thirds of my current pay to return to John's farm. The voice inside me was telling me I should do so. The fact that Loretta was interfering again was admirable showing she cared but it was also concerning to me. I'd have to go back and live with Harry and Loretta temporarily again on the farm salary. John asked again if I would consider coming back. He must have sensed my silence as my mind raced through all these thoughts.

My aunt Peggy coached and scolded me to give up these jobs all too often as she saw me come home each day for three to four hours to shower and nap.

"John, I'd have to give my employers at least two to three weeks' notice, and I could be there by the end of June. Thank you, Curt; it'll be nice to have you back. See you soon."

"See you soon, John. Hi to Joyce and your mom."

Chapter Thirty
Sixty Seconds

1978 – 1980
Playlist:
Honky Tonk Women, The Rolling Stones
Roxanne, The Police
Highway to Hell, AC/DC
Smoke on the Water, Deep Purple
Imagine, John Lennon
I'd Do Anything for Love, Meat Loaf
Paradise by the Dashboard Light, Meat Loaf

Escalation, escalation, ejaculation! I'd had two one-night stands, a total of sixty whole seconds of ejaculation! What a waste! Until this point in my life, I was led into a trap of physical exchanges that went far enough that hormones and embarrassment wouldn't allow a detour or retreating path. I avoided close relationships with girls and wasn't like my college housemates cruising for the one nightstand. I was trying to stay focused on a life beyond those five minutes. "Don't get lost in the Bermuda Triangle," I'd repeatedly heard. "Stick to your goals, find the love of your life." I tried to stay on the high road. I was often obsessed with staying focused and passing up and avoiding opportunities, but it wasn't easy. "Get some Playboy books, jack off, do anything to avoid the trap," a little voice said. To keep me from going insane, I poured myself into work using my testosterone, working long hours performing difficult labor.

But the Bermuda Triangle won me over in sixty seconds, engulfed my senses, and captured my whole being. That resulted in a short-lived few months with Carrie, who turned into a steady girlfriend. Her looks teased, and her advances and retreats enticing my desire for that patch of the sea did begin to drive me crazy and play with my mind. I wanted to be around her, not because

I loved her. Sure, she was fun to hang out with and cute, but love…well, I wasn't exactly sure how or what that felt like with a girl. I wanted that opportunity to feel her body and penetrate the moist warm miracle inside, which finally happened between us in my last semester of college at Cobleskill. I was her first, and with a two-night sixty second exception, she was mine.

Sure, I wanted to find a girl to love. Someone that I could wrap my arms around, gaze into her eyes, talk about dreams, and caress every curve and hair on her body, not just because she might be beautiful but because of what she wanted out of life. I wanted a partner with goals of her own, one that would share the adventure and appreciate the miracles in life like a newborn calf, frogs, plants, and growing things. I wanted to sit across the dinner table and have an intelligent conversation about our day's work and experiences. I needed someone who would be openly honest and willing to be vulnerable with me. I would try to share my vulnerability with her, and as hard as I tried to have those discussions, Carrie wasn't the girl.

I had no role models of such a girl or woman in my own family, and the typical role models I did know outside my family were all subservient to their husbands. Even though that is an admirable pursuit, I wanted someone aspiring to be something beyond a homemaker. I needed someone to dream with who was supportive and endearing of me, and would appreciate the same of me toward her, toward our lifelong future together. I had no issues with equality. I grew up in the feminist movement years. And yet, I met so few girls seriously seeking a career at college. Most were seeking sex and husbands.

I could never love a woman like Loretta, and certainly no one as sassy and snotty as my little sis. As I studied courses in college, I also studied the girls I met. There were some very charming girls at Cobleskill and some very sexy, lustful opportunities, but something was always missing. What was missing in each, I never entirely understood or knew. Perhaps it was simply that thing they call love. I wasn't sure and couldn't understand or know at the time. I was too young, trapped with hormones but not love. There wasn't much that I loved in my life up to that time. But I felt a more profound calling that there was a suitable mate somewhere out there. Someone to have an exciting life with! I prayed to the great Comet above to lead me to her. I prayed that God would lead me to a girl I could love once I got to Iowa State University, which would be in just a couple of months. And I prayed for Loretta as she was still mourning over my brother's death almost a year ago and driving us all nuts with her ceaseless despair, sobbing, and sorrow. One could only have so much compassion, not understanding how much she suffered in grief and from the past.

I needed a girlfriend, a confident, someone to love more than ever. I needed a best friend. I was alone. I was 21 and driven, but what I needed now in my life was a soul mate. Forget the past. I was dreaming about a future life, a good life far from the crazy relatives I had, far from Loretta, far from everything and everyone that grabbed at me in New York.

Chapter Thirty-One
Get Out of Spencer

Summer 1980

Playlist: None

"I am a success today because I had a friend who believed in me, and I didn't have the heart to let him down..."

Abraham Lincoln.

I was raking hay one hot August afternoon when my friend Jack pulled alongside the road and waved me over. I pulled the tractor over to the edge of the highway.

After obtaining his two-year degree from Cobleskill, Jack was fortunate to move directly to a four-year school. While I worked for a year to repay my loans at Tioga State Bank to borrow again, he just completed his third year of college.

Jack rolled down the passenger window as I stepped up the bank to his mother's car. Jack asked, "Curt, how the heck are you?"

"Doing well, Jack," I answered.

"Why are you still raking hay on Kings farm?" he asked in a somewhat condescending and disappointed tone. "Don't you want more than this?" I nodded my head with a frown on my face. "Get out of Spencer, Curt. Go back to school. There is nothing here for you." His personality was akin to bragging, and he espoused how great his last college year was and how much of a world he'd discovered outside of Spencer. While we were friends in high school, he made no effort at Cobleskill when we were attending there together or after that to maintain our friendship. Frankly, I hadn't seen or heard from him since we both graduated from Cobleskill, and I was surprised he stopped to say hello. He was generally condescending when he spoke to someone, and I wanted to respond to him and tell him I was raking hay for the same reason he was still driving his mom's car. Affordability! But, I gave him the benefit of the doubt and believed he meant well. I looked at Jack with a long hard stare as he was still rambling about his third year of college experiences. Listening to him through the window, I should have told him that I had just returned from working two jobs in Long Island and saved for a year to go back to college and that I was only home temporarily on the Kings farm. But I didn't.

Sweat was pouring down my face. I rolled up my t-shirt from my belt to wipe the sweat from it. "Thanks for stopping, Jack. Your college year and experiences sound great—I'd better return to work. Get out of Spencer, Curt!" he again shouted as he rolled up the passenger window as I turned away, and he drove off.

Why didn't I tell him I planned to attend Iowa State University? I pondered? Why didn't I say to him that I had just returned from working for a year at a county farm from 8 am to 5 pm and then another job at a Seven-Eleven Store from Eleven at night until seven in the morning to pay off my school loans so that I could borrow again to go Iowa State University? And that I was leaving Spencer for the Great Mid-West. As the tractor wheels spun and the tines of the hay rake neatly positioned hay for bailing, I thought again, *Why didn't I tell him that I was going, that I was delaying my entry for one more semester to help my King family.*

Why was I so afraid to tell him? Would my endeavors have seemed a little far-fetched going to an out-of-state school with triple the tuition cost of an in-state school! I mean, him finding out that not only was I leaving Spencer, but I was leaving the state and traveling to a part of the country he probably hadn't even imagined existed? Was I afraid he'd question my judgment and try to talk me out of it and into something he chose as he'd done before? I felt troubled. I headed to the barn to begin milking chores.

As I milked each cow toward the finish line, I quizzed my soul repeatedly about why I was afraid to tell a guy who cared enough to guide me in high school toward college, who, though he made no substantial effort to maintain our friendship, did make an effort to stop, say hello and sarcastically advise me to get out of Spencer.

I hauled the milk machines to the milk house to wash and sanitize at the finish line. I scraped the barn floor clean of manure and threw lime down to absorb and neutralize the smells and urine. By then, most of the cattle had finished their grain and mineral feeding, and I untied them and shooed them out the door and back to pasture. Then I fumigated the barn to rid it of flies.

As I closed the barn door and shut off the lights, dim sunlight filtered through the large exhaust fan to cast shadows through the fog of the pesticide in the air. I was afraid. I was scared to death and was worried I'd fail. While I was confident, I was not secure enough.

It was an enormously big undertaking for me to go in my direction. Perhaps enormous isn't a big enough description of the challenge facing me ahead. I was going somewhere I'd never been, traveling more than a thousand miles to a town and school I'd never been to. My savings were meager in comparison to the costs I'd face for the tuition and expenses I was about to incur; I had few clothes, hardly anything to my name, and I had no real friends left in town to cling to or share what I was doing as they were all in college, no girlfriend that captured my heart and to share my dreams with, and no Comet to chat with on a daily drive. My now newer car was just a utility. Having nothing and no one did give me one thing. Freedom! Freedom for a chance. I felt I had nothing to lose.

I was scared to death, though, to share my plans with anybody. I think primarily because they might question my sensibility and endeavor and try to talk me out of it. But mostly, I was scared of failing. If I did, no one would know that I had even tried. It seemed better to try and then let people know I succeeded if I did. I feared the shame of failure should it not have worked out. I hadn't even shared this plan yet with the King family. My seemingly self-absorbed hopeless situation, lack of funds, and fear gave me a feeling that odds of me failing were 99%. All I had was that pervasive suggestion from Dr. Emanuel reinforced by my Comet that I should go west.

Chapter Thirty-Two
The King Offer

Ariel view of King Dairy

Fall 1980
Playlist:
It's Still Rock and Roll to Me, Billy Joel
Upside Down, Diana Ross
Another One Bites The Dust, Queen
I Can't Go for That, Daryl Hall and John Oates
Jack and Diane, John Mellencamp
Up Where We Belong, Joe Cocker, Jennifer Warnes
Hard To Say I'm Sorry, Chicago
Leaving On A Jet Plane, John Denver

I was back on the farm for almost two months. I was scheduled to go to Iowa State University to start my first quarter semester the second week of August. I phoned the admissions office at ISU and explained why I could not attend the first semester as I was helping out a friend whose mom was dying of cancer.

On the other end of the phone, the admissions counselor told me the next quarter would start the first week of December and that I could enroll then. They couldn't guarantee me a room, and she suggested I search for off-campus housing before I came, as there was a student housing shortage.

I still haven't told anyone about my acceptance and plan to attend ISU. I prayed earnestly every day, questioning whether that course was right. And constantly, some little whisper in my soul repeated, Iowa, Iowa, Iowa, go west, young man.

September soon came, and fall was in the air, and we vigorously chopped corn for silage and filled the silos. I loved the fresh smell of chopped corn or hay and its slightly fermented odor almost as much as a freshly cut hay field. John took frequent breaks to visit his mom, first at home and then in October at the hospital.

By mid-October, we had nearly all the silos filled with haylage or corn silage. The remaining corn would be field dried for as long possible before we'd pick it for storage as ear corn.

Grandma King passed away. The entire King family would be gone for her funeral and visitations with relatives the following week. It would be the last time I ran the farm enterprise by myself, performing all chores from 5 am to finish by 6:30 pm. It was a peaceful and pleasantly different world than the last nine months of working in the Long Island hellholes. Worlds apart! The farm with its bellowing cows, your hands dirty with soil, and the smells of crops seemed to let you breathe God in the air all day long. You saw things grow. In contrast, Long Island was dirty, Sunrise Highway was littered with signs and artificial stimulus, crowds were everywhere, and many common courtesies found in our idyllic small town were nonexistent. I did enjoy being back in Spencer and back in this more tranquil and peaceful environment.

After the funeral, John sat me down for a longer-than-usual lunch. He thanked me for my help during his absences in caring for his mother. He then proposed that he was willing to help me start farming. "Curt, I'd like you to stay with me; if you do, perhaps it would lead to a partnership." I was stunned. I was so amazed that I didn't say a word…or even ask him how that might happen. My right knee was bouncing off the floor with nervous energy. He explained how I would build up a herd of my own; "You could earn part of your wages in calves and raise them using feed from the farm. As they matured into milking cows, you would receive payment from your own milk until you built up a large enough herd to move to another farm, or we see other possibilities here!"

I was stunned and speechless. It was a generous offer and it threw my mind into a whirlwind of thoughts that a sweat broke out on my forehead! They still had no idea of my plans to attend Iowa State. Indeed, this was an essential topic of discussion between John and Joyce. It wasn't something they just talked up in a day; these were plans they had pondered together and thought about for a while. Offering me this kind of arrangement meant a very long-term commitment, perhaps lifelong, and not one that would be easy for us to abandon if anything went sour. Our relationship had always been great except for the secret switch day, and I never took the Kings for granted. Receiving calves as part of my pay and raising them until they could start milking meant at least two years before I would begin to see any milk production checks. And how many calves could I build up in a year? My thoughts were faster than Comet, and I ever sped. This was all opportunity, but so was ISU. I was drumming up a response in my head.

"Thank you both, I'm honored to receive this offer, but may I think about it for a week and let you know?" My head was anxious, and I hadn't seen this coming. This was a huge confidence gesture for me as a person. My work ethic, care, and attention to his business as if it were my own gave them the confidence to make this offer, but it surprised me. While it was perhaps the seeds of my dream of farming, I had Iowa State in my head, and the sweat I broke out was becoming profuse. I left the lunch table feeling horrible rather than joyful. Had this offer been almost a year ago, before I went to Long Island, before I applied and was accepted into ISU, I would have taken it instantly as a sign from God that my dream would be realized, and indeed I was meant to milk cows.

I went home and told Loretta and Harry about the offer. Harry reiterated his offer to help if I thought I wanted this. Only then did I share with them that I had been accepted to Iowa State University and planned to leave right after Thanksgiving. "Iowa," …Loretta gasped. "Yes," I explained that I had delayed my entry in September to help the King family and that the next semester began the first week of December. The look on Loretta's face was of devastation. She had known I'd discussed the possibility of ISU before with them, but perhaps never thought I was serious or that I would actually be accepted. It was almost as if I had died like my older brother and had done this deliberately to hurt her.

She began sobbing uncontrollably. There weren't any congratulatory comments, no positive kudos, just bewilderment from her as if I'd done something wrong. My dad suggested I carefully consider the King's offer in that perhaps I'd pass a once-in-a-lifetime opportunity.

As they stared at me in bewilderment, I was not sure either of them knew precisely where ISU was located. I didn't either! I knew I would find it in a town called Ames, and I knew I was going. My decision to tell John that I would decline his offer was heartbreakingly difficult…for both me informing him and for him hearing so.

Loretta retreated to her bedroom. Harry reiterated that I think it through. A young man rarely gets an offer like that from a non-family member. Harry told me about a friend from high school who wanted to start a junkyard with him. His mom discouraged him, and he regretted not doing it. His friend made millions in the scrap business and would later supply him with cars to fix up and sell.

The big issue was Loretta. I wasn't sure I could ever have any peace living near her. The further the distance from her, from most of this family, seemed the best for me.

The following week my stomach churned as I thought through and through and processed whether I was doing the right thing now in going to Iowa. *Why go to Iowa,* I thought? The answer to my childhood dream was on John and Joyce's farm. I could take all my savings from the last year and a half, forgo getting into more tuition debt again, put it toward purchasing heifer calves, and accelerate building up my herd. Though we didn't talk about it, I'm sure there was the possibility that I could rent and live in Grandma King's home now that she had passed. It was a tiny home located right on the farm grounds, and it would get me out of Loretta's household. But the words kept coming up from somewhere in my gut all week as I rehashed the possibility Iowa, Iowa, Iowa; a voice in my soul kept whispering, Iowa, Iowa, Iowa. Though I already knew in my bones I should go, I kept trying to talk myself into staying. Parked in the barn, I went and started Comet up and listened to her engine. As I always have done in my life, I turned to prayer, and sitting in the chapel of Comet, I heard the offer from Johns' lips again, but the message was different; *"if he has that confidence in you, imagine what you could do with more education stay the course"* and over and over I heard Comet whispering: *"Iowa, Iowa, Iowa follow me to Iowa."*

"I've never been there, never been to Ames; I don't know what to expect; I don't have any housing there," I made excuses in my head. "Why am I going now that I have this offer?" Over and over, I debated the pros and cons in my head. But *"Iowa, Iowa, Iowa"* kept coming from deep in my soul.

Christ has always been in my heart; I would not have survived this long without him. God knows how much I wanted to be a farmer most of my life, but the offer coming from John wasn't from God. He was leading me elsewhere. It had to be the Holy Spirit guiding me away from what I thought I wanted and dreamed about since age five. The direction from the great Comet in the sky whispered into my soul: *"Iowa, Iowa, Iowa."*

I went for a drive. Driving the back roads wasn't the same. I wasn't in Comet racing like a bat out of hell. I wasn't as carefree, taking sharp curves at speeds that would throw me into a tailspin or flip me over. It could be because the car I now had wasn't as capable and responsive. Perhaps I'd grown up. I didn't care whether I lived or not for many years, but now I cared about myself because others saw more in me than just the Boychine I'd always been. Indeed, I was a hard-laboring kid, but my professors at Cobleskill saw in me much more than I saw in myself.

John's offer should have seemed significant to me. I should have felt the same bigness and excitement as working myself into Cobleskill through applications and getting my loan, but I didn't.

I went to college to train in animal husbandry as a dairy farmer. Yet my professors told me to do anything but that.

Before attending church I looked long and hard at myself in the bathroom mirror Sunday morning. I owned nothing. Just a car, some clothes, and the textbooks I bought and kept from Cobleskill, which I thought would be lifetime references for when I farmed. My bank account had grown, but it was still reasonably meager. I owned a fully paid loan document from Tioga State Bank, which was worth displaying on a wall more than my diploma. It proved I knew how to use capital and provided an excellent credit record to borrow again at ISU. I was proud of that more than anything and still grateful for Mr. Fisher's confidence in me.

I thought hard about the sincerity and seriousness of this offer and that John and Joyce had to be talking about this for weeks, maybe months together, but I didn't see any confirmations coming back from the mirror that I should do this.

I went to church by myself, as I had done for years. I missed it while working the two jobs on Long Island. My schedule there, working seven days a week and catching up on sleep with the rest of the weekend, left little time for church attendance. I enjoyed St. Paul's Lutheran Church and the congregational families. Sunday's sermon was the standard fare and didn't enlighten me or help me sort through my decisions. I was hoping that by going to church, I might receive some enlightened message that would lead me to decide to stay. The service was like the mirror earlier, and I left there with nothing.

I tried in vain to see a sign that I should stay. It was an offer from John and Joyce's hearts. They still know nothing of the home life I had endured all these years, and Loretta continued to dive deeper and deeper into grief over my brother's death. My heart was broken for her, but there was nothing anyone could do. There was something she was hiding deep inside her, something bigger than all of us, and she was never going to let anyone in to help her. In one way, I'd become just like her, hiding everything and not letting anyone in to help.

And now my own heart was breaking on how to tell John I would decline his offer.

Mondays always seemed to be the fresh start to a new week on the farm as we discussed the week and weather ahead and planned based upon the forecast. At noon, I came from the field and went in for Joyce's lunch as usual. I never had to bring lunch. Joyce always welcomed me to have lunch with them. I never appreciated it more than when I lived in the cabin in the wood during high school; it was my best meal of the week during the school year, working on Saturdays and the day during the summer.

John was anxiously waiting to hear from me, and I dreaded the follow-up question he'd soon ask. I had no nerve to bring the subject up. The lunches this past week had been quieter between us after the offer, and we never spoke of it. John caught up on the local paper at lunchtime, which passed quicker for him, but last week's lunchtimes seemed unusually long for me.

And then it happened. Joyce served up a piece of her apple pie and a fresh cup of coffee, and John put his paper down. A week had passed since he shared his proposition with me on Friday.

"Curt, have you given any thought to our offer?" he asked.

He then took a fork full of pie. I looked at Joyce, who stood by her kitchen sink, and my stomach dropped to my knees. My wrists felt weak, and my heart began to beat fast. I finished the bite of pie in my mouth and chewed it into applesauce, buying some time before I could swallow it.

I sat the cup down, looked over at John, slid my hands above my knees, and squeezed them hard.

I looked down at my cup of coffee, and quietly and humbly said, "Thank you, John, thank you both, but I'll leave you and the farm in a few more weeks." They both stared at me with disbelief that they were hearing this.

I hadn't shared that I had delayed my entry in September to stay and help them. "Last spring, I was accepted to Iowa State University, in Ames, Iowa. I've been working toward this endeavor for a whole year. *I'm sorry,* I thought this through—I'm so grateful—I'm sure you are disappointed. I was going to give you both notice in another week, but now seems the appropriate time to let you know that my last day will be the day before Thanksgiving as I have to head for Iowa the day after."

John sat somewhat stunned and glared with disbelief and disappointment about what he had just heard from me. Now it was his turn to look down at his coffee cup and say nothing for a long pause. He took off his glasses to clean them, and I could see his eyes welled up with the fresh sorrow still evident from his mom's death. John and I were like a hand and a glove; we fit together. We could make great partners for sure. I looked at Joyce, and somehow, I think she knew this wasn't meant to be. She looked upon John and me with silence.

My secrecy of my Iowa State plans and my sudden announcement, not just a decline but also that I was leaving, surprised them. John's stature portrayed he was painfully disappointed. After his long silence, he choked up. He said to me, "Curt, I don't think you'll ever be a farmer. This is a great opportunity," he paused, "and if you turn it down, I just don't think you'll ever be a farmer."

He said nothing more. He used his handkerchief to wipe the corners of his eyes where small tears couldn't be held back. I looked again at Joyce with silence. He didn't congratulate me on my acceptance to Iowa State; his thoughts were elsewhere, and this news emotionally hurt him. This was a big deal in his life to make this offer, and somehow, I understood this was life-altering for us both. He had just lost his mom, and now was now losing me again.

For only the second time in my years of trying to enrich the lives of those at the King Farm through my service, I couldn't finish Joyce's pie. I excused myself, thanked Joyce as always for lunch, and returned to one of the silos where I'd left a fully loaded wagon of fresh-chopped corn silage that had to be emptied into the silo loader. Tears ran down my cheeks as I started the tractor and slipped the power take-off shafts into gear. I stared at the silage unloading from the John Deere wagon, dispersing and swirling around in the hopper before entering the blower, which shot it some 80 feet straight up a six-inch tube into the silo. My tears dripped into the swirl of the silage. I had to use my hat to wipe my cheeks. As I did so, I looked straight up into the sky to see where those tears and silage blended nearly a hundred feet above.

"You'll never be a farmer," he said sternly. He was probably right! His words hurt. He was hurting internally, and those words came out due to his emotional disappointment. Perhaps, knowing how difficult it was for him to get into farming at my age, it was a truth that he saw, a prophecy. My desire to be a farmer since age five, my life's dream, had just been given to me, and I turned it down.

As I stared at the top of the silo and heard the rush of silage blowing up the tube, for a split second, a tiny split second, a revelation came that perhaps that is why Loretta is the way she is. Maybe she is constantly in pain internally and taking it out on others. When you are hurt, your words are not always controllable.

I never saw John again the rest of that day. It was typical for that time of the year for him to remain in the field working while I took care of the feeding and milking chores. As I was milking, I saw his tractor lights pass by the glass block windows as he parked the chopper and filled wagon near the silo. He went in and never stopped in the barn to say goodnight. I finished the milking chores that evening. I was sad. I thought about their close friends, Glenn and Doris Ahart, another dairy farm family. I wondered if he or Joyce shared with Glen and Doris his plans to make the offer to me. And if so, he'd have to relive the disappointment again to tell them I turned it down. Joyce's parents too. If they had told them, I'm sure they also would be disappointed that I'd turned them down. I thought about the conversation that John and Joyce would have that evening. Devout in their faith, I'm sure Joyce would console John and tell him it wasn't meant to be and they should pray over the next steps in their life, and I hoped they prayed for God to lead me.

November passed quickly. On Thanksgiving Eve, I wished them a Happy Thanksgiving and said my goodbyes to the King family children and John and Joyce. I collected my last and final paycheck. There was no goodbye bonus, and I didn't expect one. John and Joyce had been there at my graduation from high school and my graduation from Cobleskill. I know from all their actions they cared for and loved me. Joyce had a card she handed me with my paycheck congratulating me and wishing me good luck. They asked me to come back and see them as I bid them a final farewell and Happy Thanksgiving again. I will, I said, I surely will. And in gratuitous thoughts, I silently said to myself, someday, I'll help you again. Something inside me told me the offer from John was never coming again and that I'd never return to that farm permanently. Still I hoped that one day I could help them again whether they needed it or not.

Harry seemed to understand everything I was trying to do. He seemed to understand I had to escape, get away, and go. Loretta did not, and my planned departure to Iowa brought on even more loss and a wave of more profound anger at me and grief that would last for years to come.

As usual for the holiday, Loretta made a nice Thanksgiving dinner. I watched the Macy's parade and the then traditional rerun of the Nutcracker play. I paid particular attention to the national weather on the evening news. Iowa appeared frigid, but the country I would pass through looked free and clear of bad weather. The evening news showcased information about then-president Jimmy Carter and his Thanksgiving in the White House, and further west than Iowa in Reno, Nevada, news about some nut case who had run down many people on a sidewalk with her Lincoln killing several of them. I packed my clothes into a few paper bags and loaded them into the car. I knew I would have to find employment, so all my work clothes and overalls were included. As I didn't own a winter coat, just layers of t-shirts, flannel wear, and a hoodie underneath farm overalls to stay warm for work, Loretta gave me an old woolen winter coat that was my dad's. On Friday, November 28, 1980, I left for Ames at five in the morning.

Chapter Thirty-Three
Iowa

Curt and Darcy dance the night away in spring of 1981 for a good cause.

December 1980
Playlist:
Sad Eyes, Robert John
Makin' It, David Naughton
I Was Made For Lovin' You, Kiss
Boy From New York City, Manhattan Transfer
You Take My Breath Away, Rex Smith
Somewhere In The Night, Barry Manilow
Dancin' Shoes, Nigel Olsson
We've Got Tonight, Bob Seger
Never Let Her Slip Away, Andrew Gold

It was almost Christmas. I would pick up my paying passengers to New York in four days and drive twelve hundred miles back to Van Etten to spend

Christmas with Harry and Loretta. Short visits back home went OK. Loretta still wasn't easy, but there was less likely to be an insane episode of abuse knowing that I wasn't home long. Besides, I had nowhere else to go, and the university closed the dorms during recess. I returned to Van Etten, driving a grueling 24 hours from Ames through blizzard conditions in Indiana and Ohio. Some sections of Ohio's interstate I-80 were shut down, forcing me onto parallel emergency routes and making the trip even more arduous.

I was at Iowa State for five weeks before returning for the Christmas Holiday, but it seemed like a year as those short five weeks were full of new potential. I've met many great people and learned of their backgrounds and where they grew up, mostly from small rural towns like mine and some from massive corporate farm structures, just as my professors had shared with me. My experience in the classes I have so far is exhilarating. Journalism was the right choice for me. My mind is rechallenged, and my brain is like an endlessly absorbent sponge. I am pumped with a new adventure, excitement, and a new life.

Just a few days at home to share my new experiences was tolerable. Harry and Loretta seemed glad to see me, but the morning cries from Loretta at her desk hadn't ceased. My five weeks in a new world were so differently refreshing and stimulating that I had an expectation that I'd return to Van Etten, and somehow it too would have changed. So much was so different for me in such a short time that I had a euphoric expectation that the changes I'd seen through my eyes and felt in my soul would be beamed to Van Etten! Of course, it didn't.

Snow drifts engulfed Comet on all sides where she sat as the north side of the small barn I'd built had no doors. I kicked the snow away with my feet and shoveled it with my hands. I opened the driver's door just enough to squeeze in and sit. Comet looked comforting as she always had. What a dashboard! I gripped the steering wheel, and images of my dirt road racing adventures and back hill journeys ran quivers through my veins.

So much had changed for me since I last drove her. I turned the key and started its engine.

Comet, the roads are straight as a ruler. The land is flat, and when I drove there, I first saw that it was nothing but a giant mud field for a thousand miles. Comet, you'd laugh! I had to pay a toll, not once but twice, to see it. Once I left the New York and Pennsylvania borders, it wasn't exciting a drive as you could imagine from your perspective. There are no twists, curves, hills, or mountains, and the only challenge I had, which I know you would have enjoyed, was the snow-covered interstate highways I maneuvered through on the way home.

The drive is simple, straight, and would have been gentle on your old parts, but if we'd broken down Comet, I might have had to leave you where you lay. I'm tight on cash and haven't been there long enough to find a job.

But Comet, oh Comet—I've got a different set of mountains to climb, a different set of curves to be challenged on. I love my classes so far. Journalism was the right choice for me. I can see the possibility of a job as a journalist in the future. While it's too early, I may have found something I can be as passionate about as I am about farming. There are various kinds of journalism, print, broadcast, advertising, and marketing. I'm taking introductory classes in them all, and I'm excited about them all. However, I'm told at some point, I'll have to choose a specialty in one to take advanced classes. I'm excited to get back and continue.

Comet, it's a big sky country with plenty of time to think and pray, and I can't wait to see what those huge fields produce. I'm told they are mostly full of corn and beans, and there are jobs for bean walkers and de-tasslers in the summer. I'm not exactly sure what either of those jobs is yet.

I was shivering. Comet always took a while to warm up and provide heat in the winter. *Comet, Iowa State University, is a beautiful campus even in winter.*

Arriving for the second quarter semester, I went early to find a room to rent because I had lost my guarantee of a dormitory room. Coming early to look for a room was fruitless. When I got there, I found a payphone and dialed number after number from local bulletin boards loaded with room-mate wanted ads. Standing at the payphones in frigid temperatures shoving in dimes, produced only cold fingers and a cold ear as I dialed number after number, trying to reach anyone with a room listed for rent. They had all gone home for the week between quarters, so no one answered my calls. After the first day of dismal success, I called home to let my dad know I had arrived.

Loretta opened an ISU letter stating I had received a dorm room assignment in the Fairchild House of Roberts Hall.

Boy, that was great news. Before the dormitory opened, I had four days to scope the campus and surrounding areas. So Comet, I did what we always did... I drove.

I drove west past ISU for two days, as far as possible then turned around for the two-day journey back. It was pretty cold in my sleeping bag at night, but the station wagon I traded that Dodge Truck for was a dry and airtight home when needed.

The drive took me beyond South Dakota and into Wyoming. What wonderful scenery. Still, the roads are straight as an arrow, but the landscape changes—fewer fields of tillage and more open pasture, prairie, and other interesting geographical topography. I saw landforms called the badlands that I'd only seen in some of the National Geographic magazines I used to get. It looked like something in a wild west movie. Oh, and Comet, the stars atop this hill in New York are as bright as possible, but nothing beats the stars in a Dakota sky. From the eastern horizon to the western horizon, as far as the eye can absorb the earth's curvature, the Dakota Skies are filled with zillions of stars. The skies are as dark as can be without humidity and light pollution.

Comet was just beginning to warm up and defrost the windshield. I loved the purr of Comets 289 V-8, and the Thrush muffler I installed a year before I parked her gave her a muscle car sound.

As a four-door compact sedan, Comet would hardly be considered a muscle car in my youth. I held a different view as beauty is in the beholder's eye, and hot wheels always make a car. Comet had highly polished baby moon rims and caps. I spit-shined and waxed them so many times I probably began to rub the chrome off.

The trek out west was an adventure Comet, boring probably for you without the hills and curves, but I love the wide-open spaces and seeing beyond the next hill. I wish you were physically able to be with me, but I couldn't risk a breakdown and the expense that would follow. My dad says I should consider selling you, but you have too many parts that I made and jimmy-rigged to keep us going. As much as I needed the money for college, I'd never forgive myself if anyone got hurt driving you. So, until that day when I might afford the proper repairs, we'll sit together from time to time.

IOWA…Comet, Iowa… Dr. Emmanuel was right. Iowa is a place for me. Although I know none of their real names, I've met some fantastic housemates. They all have nicknames. Like the kid from Connecticut, his name is…well…Connecticut! Then there are Yogi and Boo Boo (who resemble the characters in personality), Stony Jeff, Tyke, Whack-off, and others. I was indoctrinated into the house as New York. Not many know my real name, and it doesn't matter. I'm welcomed as a family member in the dorm house and easily fit in.

Choosing journalism was the right thing for me. I love the classes, and I'm honing a hobby I've enjoyed for many years into possible work life. Maybe I might write for Hoards Dairyman magazine one day instead of farming. Maybe never! Oh, and Comet, Iowa, may be suitable for me in another way! I met a girl. She is different. You'll never see her in your back seat!

I revved Comets 289 V-8 with a few pushes to the gas pedal. The fan belt squealed a little with each rev, probably a little loose from sitting for the past year.

Comet, our Fairchild House in Roberts Hall, has a regular seating table every morning and evening in the dining hall of the Oak-Elm residence. Our table area was next to another, where the girls from the Freeman dormitory house of Busse usually sat. Amazingly, the whole student body of diners instinctively respects the seating locales where each hall and house gather for lunch or dinner with other house members.

Every evening I'd sit on the side of the table that allowed me to scope out who was coming down the stairs into the cafeteria. And each evening at about the same time… I would be halfway through my meal…and see an adorable girl descending those stairs. She'd go through the food line, exit just in front of our table, and then pass us to sit with her housemates.

Comet, I don't think I ate more than three meals in that cafeteria when I spotted this girl. She was stunning and petite, and some inner soul magnetic attraction made me feel instantly connected. I hadn't spoken to her, but Comet, meal after meal, night after night, I watched for and stared at this girl coming down the stairs. Beneath my breath, I'd whisper to her… I want to get to know you; for you to discover that my own eyes are green like a traffic light, green for you as in let's go. As I stared at her eyes and followed them to the table she ate at, for the first time, I felt that this was the girl I'd someday marry.

I'd occasionally catch a direct glance back with her eyes, which sparkled blue! Everything perfectly matched on her. The contour of her shape, lips, almond-shaped eyes and cheekbones. I'd seen many beautiful girls, but something injected into my soul made me see no flaw in her and that she was a match to me. She was beautiful, and she moved in a sporty fashion. She didn't wiggle; she didn't waggle. Blue Eyes moved keenly, swiftly, confidently, and with ease.

Night after night, I studied her timetable for appearing in the Oak-Elm cafeteria. I positioned myself to see her prance down the stairs to the café. It wasn't long, and Blue Eyes began to stare back... short, shy glimpses at first, and then as time went on more prolonged glances, but then always turning shy and away as if she wasn't interested. When she finally caught on that I watched her every move and curve; she passed our table looking straight ahead, pretending she didn't observe or know of my interest.

I scanned for Blue Eyes at every dinner meal, and each time I saw her, I knew with certainty in my mind that I would marry this girl, a certainty for which I cannot explain. Perhaps it was the way she moved so confidently, the way she interacted with her housemates, her stature, the giggles I heard as she passed by with her friends; my certainty was something I couldn't explain, and though I hadn't even talked to her, a voice inside me was telling me this will be the girl I will marry. I didn't know her name or where she lived, although her seating group in the cafeteria began to give me clues. When I mentally whispered to her, I called her Blue Eyes!

Sometimes, though I was finished with my dinner, if I could, I'd wait until she was finished with hers and then follow her to the tray depository to get close and try to bump into her. I'd follow her up the stairs and trail her back to her dorm. She almost always entered the Freeman Hall kitty-corner across from our hall of Roberts.

Comet, Iowa State, is the birthplace of the Greek Housing system. The dormitory houses are organized with rules, rituals, and many planned social gatherings like a Fraternity or Sorority. It is a great social system, albeit not following the laws of the house is already getting me into trouble.

I lived under insane rules most of my life, and some of the regulations in Fairchild House seemed just meant for guys like me to break them. I lack freedom in the mandatory requirements to attend numerous house meetings of topical nonsense.

Nonetheless, as the new kid on the block, I was assigned to a task force to visit our sister's house of Busse and invite them to a Sadie Hawkins party we were hosting. This party had been planned long before I arrived in Fairchild. Still, I was quickly nominated and assigned several party tasks, including a role with the invite squad to present the formal invitation.

Comet, our delegation of six, arrived at the house of the Busse Babes on a pre-planned scheduled date and time during one of their house meetings. One of our housemates made the arrangements. We waited outside their den while their house meeting was convened, and we were summoned in. Comet! Comet! I couldn't believe who I saw.

There she was, Comet, the Blue Eyes girl I'd been staring down since the second day I arrived. As our delegation performed, that cute petite blonde sat in the front row. I couldn't take my eyes off her. She, too took extended glimpses, sizing me up as I stood in green work pants that used to be my dad's, red Converse sneakers, a flannel shirt, and my red and white polka-dotted cap. I'm sure I looked like a hick farm kid just off the hay wagon to her. I wasn't expecting to see her. It was a sealed fate that I was led there.

Why she wasted her time looking me over the way I was dressed was beyond me, except that those mental whispers I'd been sending her must have worked. These are the days of the Yuppie dress code. I am economically far away from any affordable yuppie or prep wear. There she sat, front row with another cute blonde. They inquisitively sized me up as I delivered my part of the skit. Blue Eyes leaned over and whispered something to the other blonde. She shrugged her shoulders, and both sets of eyes returned to me. I stared back intently as I convened my speech and hoped they might view my apparel as part of the skit, although it was pretty much my norm. Those girls looked cute and hot looking in their skinny-ass jeans and prep school blouses. But, that Blue Eyes—her eyes and mine connected 70 percent of the time during my delivery? Even her friend seemed to notice.

Sure Comet, there were plenty of stares and eye connections with many girls at Cobleskill, but these connections between her and I were electric. I remember the one steady girl I dated at Cobleskill telling me after the first time I asked her out how long she'd been staring at me, hoping I'd notice her. I was oblivious, unsure of what eventually led me to stare back and take an interest, but I did. Maybe her silent whispers made our connection as I was now sending to this girl.

As I wrapped things up as the chosen voice for our house, I glanced about the room making eye contact with as many of the girls as possible. Still, I could not help streaming back to the one pivoting set of eyes glued to me.

Comet, I've experienced some fantastic confirmations over the past few short weeks at ISU, which assure me I've made the right choice in going there. But for now, I must to continue with my story of Blue Eyes. I became relentless after her house visit and continued to stare down that cute blonde with hopes she'd see the green light in my eyes, which summoned her to come forward; let's go.

The Sadie Hawkins party was held, and here I am, Comet, just a few days later, telling you about that night. That crazy insane and never-to-be-forgotten night!

The party had a few themes, one of which was a marriage chapel and another a jail. These two are significant for the following reasons regarding that cute blonde. The newbies of us housemates were assigned roles during the party. I was given three half-hour periods in the marriage chapel as Rabbi Riess, along with Morgan the Monk and Patrick the Priest. We each had to perform marriage ceremonies for those girls who paid a guy to go through a mock marriage. The chapel could hold at least ten couples, and the presiding minister could perform about three ten-minute ceremonies from a script in that half-hour. The vows were pre-scripted, and all attending couples had to repeat the vows after the minister. The vows were not fundamental but intended to warm up the girls to have fun with the guys and get a kiss! Such vows as I shall keep you by my side, worship you with my body, dance with you, hold you till the hours of dawn, spend most of my Fairchild bucks on you, keep you out of prison...or lock you up if you're a bad boy and others were recited in each ceremony. Communion was included! These vows favored our female guests as they were the only ones allocated Fairchild dollars. The chapel was a colossal hit, and couples packed in every ten minutes. A lot of Busse Babes were married to Fairchild Boys that evening.

Throughout the early part of the party, I kept looking for Blue Eyes, wondering if she would show up. It was my second turn to minister in the Chapel, and there was no sign of her yet. I performed my duties diligently and married another 30 or 40 couples. The Chapel remained a colossal hit, and couples were flocking to it. Mainly because the word spread about the requirement to bring a drink for communion and the ceremonial marriage consummation of "and now you may kiss the bride." The boys—and girls loved that! Pay a guy to get married, and you get kissed. What kind of kiss you got depended on the chemistry or how much you might have had for communion and little as to how cute you were. No matter how pretty or ugly you might have been, you got kissed by a Fairchild boy if you paid to get married. Those were the house party rules, and there were consequences to a housemate if one was found out to have broken those rules. The Rabbi, Priest, and Monk were supposed to rat on anyone not following the rules. But in my Chapel, immediately after I pronounced the couple married and the groom may kiss the bride, I shut the lights off, waited about 30 seconds, and never saw anybody not kiss a girl. The last thing I wanted to be as a new guy in the house was a rat. If a girl didn't get kissed, I didn't see it. I can tell you, though, that even after 30 seconds or so, when I turned the lights back on, there were a lot of locked lips!

I served my second half-hour of stuffy fun in the chapel and was relieved by the Monk. As I left the chapel in my Rabbi attire, looking down the hall in the direction I had to head, there she was. Blue Eyes was getting her hand stamped and collecting her Fairchild bucks at the entry door. I didn't want to make a second wrong first impression dressed as a Rabbi, so I swiftly passed her by and headed toward my room to change. She glanced at me as I passed her only a shoulder-length away and knew who I was. When I came out absent of my Rabbi Robe, Blue Eyes was still standing at the check-in point and glancing down the hall toward my room, almost as if waiting for me to return. Kitty-corner, the check-in desk was the mock jail, so the door bouncer could monitor both.

The jail was another party feature where one could lock up a couple or anyone for ten minutes per payment for any reason.

Trying to be cool and acting like I hadn't noticed her, I walked past her when I felt a grab on the elbow, and she said to the jailer, "Hey, put this guy in jail."

"Put this guy in jail" were the first direct words I heard from this girl. Little did she know then that my interest in her was already locked up by sight, mind, and soul.

Into the jail I went.

Comet, honestly, I didn't know what to say. I was stupendously shocked while at the same time exhilarated at her overture. It was the second sign I received that this girl was interested in getting to know me. Once before, one of her friends, Linda Lackerman, passed by our dining room table and shouted, "Oh look, Darcy, there's that boy from Fairchild you were asking about." Why she was asking about me, I'm not sure. Still, perhaps it was my stares that occasionally turned to glares, maybe it was those whispers I'd blow into the air at her to marry me...or I'd like to get to know you, but just as I had my sights set on her, obviously so she had some of hers set on me. And while the first clue was a happenstance tease from her friend in the cafeteria, the grab on my elbow and a paid Fairchild buck to put me in jail was solid.

She lingered about the jail cell door chatting to others and gave me no reason for my crime, nor did the jailer who asked her what offense I committed. She continued conversing with a friend she came with as I sat on the jail bench. I was the first and only person in the evening thus far put in jail. I sat there contemplating what my next move should be. I came to my senses and asked the jailer to lock her up with me, except I had no money, so the jailer looked at her friend and said, hey, she put him in jail for no offense, why don't you pay to have her jailed with him? Done deal, she said, and her girlfriend anted up a Fairchild buck.

Blue Eyes came in and sat on the bench, and I introduced myself. "Hi, my name is Curt."

"Hello, glad to meet you, Curt."

"What is your name?" I asked. She told me her name, which I wasn't sure I heard correctly. So I asked her what her name was again, "Did you say, Marcy?"

"No," she said, "Darcy!"

"Marcy," I asked again.

"No," she repeated, "Darcy!"

"Darcy! Not Marcy, but Darcy? D like in, duh... Darcy," I asked again. She looked at me with amazement, and suddenly I realized I had inserted not just my big toe but my entire foot into my mouth.

I shook my head over my stupidity, "I'm sorry, what kind of name is Darcy?" I asked, "I'd never heard that name before." It sounded so foreign, sort of oriental, to me. Oriental, it certainly wasn't. She said she wasn't sure, but she thought it was French. "Are you French?" I asked.

"No," she said.

"Darcy, humph, that's a different name, but I like it, I said!" Score Comet, I mean score zero. I couldn't believe how awkwardly nervous I was and what I had just said. I felt like such a loser.

A little more chitchat between us ensued. I tried desperately not to shove my whole leg into my mouth, but I eventually did. After learning my name, she asked why my housemates called me New York. "I'm from New York," I told her. "Everyone here seems to get a new house name, and that's what they gave me." I asked her where she was from. She said, "Minnesota."

I asked, "Where is that?"

She looked at me astonishingly and probably wondered just how dumb a guy could get. "It's the next state north of here," she said as she looked at me as if I had just got off a boat from some foreign country.

"Time's up; you're free to go!" Oh God, the jailer just saved me. I only had one more leg left to insert into my stupid mouth. Could I have been any dumber than dumb? I hadn't had anything to drink yet, but I hoped she thought so as some reason for my total fumbling nervous boyhood insaneness. I thought I'd blown any chance of getting to know her further.

"Well, nice to meet you, Darcy; I'll see you around the party."

"Not so fast," Darcy said, "how about a dance? I'm paying."

"OK," I said with a big smile and asked, "How about a beer first? You have the bucks!" She obliged.

I fumbled for sure; I did try to make light of it again as we got our beers and told her again how much I loved that interesting name of Darcy. There was still enough intrigue to overcome the awkward conversation since she asked me to dance. We danced, and we danced, and we danced. After about ten songs, the music stopped for a pause, and I said, well, thanks, Darcy, and she thanked me. We both just stood there staring at each other, not knowing what the next move or conversation should be or whether we should keep dancing, so I asked her to buy me another beer.

Blue Eyes and I intermittently danced or sat talking for the next couple of hours. We never left each other's side. Now more relaxed, I had hoped that she might have seen that my earlier attempts at the small talk were just plain boy meets girl nervousness, which I had never experienced before with any other girl, perhaps because there was already a thumping heart and whim of desire to meet this girl that I'd never had before with any other.

Over a couple of more beers, I learned her Grandpa Henry had just recently died, and she spoke a great deal about him and what a wonderful man he had been throughout his life. She told me some stories of him and stories of her dad and his hunting. How both her mom and her dad loved Henry so much and that she would miss him very much. I didn't reciprocate with stories of my parents.

We learned that we were both Lutherans, me a Lutheran boy from New York, the Big Apple, and she a Lutheran girl from Minneapolis, the Mini Apple. Small talk informed us that we went to the same Lutheran church on campus. I learned that she wanted to be a commercial designer, and she learned I wanted to milk cows, but I was in journalism to learn more about my hobby and have a backup plan in case farming wasn't going to work out. We couldn't have been more opposite at the time in our career choices and our clothing attire, she in her Calvin Klein designer jeans and blouse, and me in my thrift store jeans and my dad's old General Welding Supply work shirts.

We talked about so many things for two people meeting each other for the first time. It was effortless for me to pour out so much to her and her to me. She found my own initiatives rather remarkable and courageous in that I grew up a poor boy from a rural county putting himself through school and that I had delayed coming to Iowa State for a year and a half and why.

She was amazed that I dared to strike out on my own and the fact that I'd never visited Iowa or Iowa State University before I came for classes. I never shared anything negative about my past troubles or family issues—only my dreams and why I was at ISU.

She told me a lot about her family, mom, dad, a cabinet maker, and florist business her grandpa and her uncles operated. Comet, I felt a closeness and easiness to this girl like I'd never experienced before. In our first evening together, we learned more about each other than I'd ever learned about any other girl, even most high school girls I'd known for years. We only chatted for about three or four hours, and I felt like I'd been with this girl for most of my life, or at least was meant to be with this girl.

New York, New York, you're up, shouted the Priest. It was my round three at being Rabbi Riess in the chapel.

I explained my assigned role to Darcy and asked her if she'd like to come and help me marry a bunch of people. The sparkle in her eyes said yes before her lips did. That will be hilarious, she said. I must get my Rabbi Robe on. Wait here, and I'll be right back, I said.

I couldn't have put the Rabbi Gear on fast enough. I was so ecstatic that I was talking to the girl I had stared down for a month in the cafeteria. As I ran down the hallway and turned the corner, I grabbed Darcy's hand and said, let's go. Into the chapel, we went.

By now, the chapel was filled to the brim with couples anxious for the ceremony. Word had spread throughout the evening how fun these mock marriage vows were, and a closet of a room that could hold five to ten couples comfortably now packed twenty to thirty couples like sardines. After performing the marriage vows and pronouncing to all that you may kiss the bride, I looked at Darcy, and she at me. We smiled, shrugged our shoulders, and both waited for the kissing to conclude. I never turned the lights off. I just wanted to share the moment with Darcy, and I wanted to see her face, look into her eyes, and dare to see if she'd let me kiss her. I married the next group, and again, after announcing you may kiss the bride, I stared at Darcy and gazed into her eyes.

I thought about all the other girls, Comet, that have come and gone before. All the girls I liked said they "just wanted to have fun" and then rejected me for not advancing toward their desires, but they'd be back later because I was the marrying type. I wasn't sure if I was facing the same situation. I wasn't sure whether I wanted this time to pass me by or if she did want to have fun. At the same time, this was a girl I felt I'd like to marry, and I didn't want to lose any respect at our first chance meeting.

I was performing my role as Rabbi Riess for the last time that evening. As I led the ceremony, Darcy looked at me with amazement at how I could command the audience and lead them to a frenzy and a passionate finish. In my last ceremony, I gazed into her eyes and asked if she would marry me. She nodded yes. I saw all the stars in the Dakota night sky reflecting at me through her eyes.

And now you may kiss the bride, I pronounced and shut the lights off this time.

In those 30 seconds of darkness, my heart pounded wildly. I'm going to take the chance, I thought. I reached for Darcy's head and pulled it toward my lips. She accepted the kiss and reciprocated. That was the first time I ever kissed a girl the first night I met her. But Comet, it felt so right. I felt like I'd known her all my life after our conversations.

The kiss ended between Darcy and me, and I flipped the lights on. There we were; me with a long gaze from an east coast boy into the eyes of this beautiful Midwest gal. She gave me a gentle approval and said, we're married! How about a drink and then some more dancing, Darcy? That sounds like fun, she said.

The word "fun" struck me slightly, but I ignored it.

The Sadie's Hawkins party went on to the wee hours of the morning. The rest of Darcy's Fairchild dollars were spent buying us drinks, mostly beer. We danced the night away, and as Darcy seemed to take ownership of me, I never received an offer or payment from any other girl to dance. That suited me fine. There was no one else at the party, for that matter, no one else I'd seen or met at ISU in my short few weeks that I even considered a possible date or girl of interest.

Comet, Emmanuel was right. Iowa State fits me. It was fate that I met Darcy and the test to know this wasn't over yet. I'd had plenty of drinks as the beer from the kegs flowed, and at about three in the morning, as the party began to fade, I invited Darcy to my room to see my fish. My roommate had a tank full of exotic fish, and I lay claim to two, an Angelfish and a blue-striped Guppy.

Now there's a pickup line Darcy gasped and rolled her eyes about! No, for real, come see my fish, I persuaded her. My roommate still had a hometown sweetheart in high school and went home nearly every weekend to see her. He never stayed for any social events, and I always had my dorm room to myself on the weekends.

Darcy reluctantly entered my room, and explored the fish tank for a few minutes. I showed her my Angelfish and the blue-striped Guppy. We sat on the couch beneath our lofted bunks above and chatted more. Half stupid from the beer, our chatting slowly turned to me trying to consummate our recent marriage. I thought I could somehow "respectfully" make out with her and see where it went. I didn't push aggressively, I was just testing waters, like a nibble on the neck, a drop of my hand over her shoulder landing next to her then tiny breasts.

I wasn't planning to misinterpret all the signs this evening about a girl who wanted to have fun like in the past, but that is precisely the stupid thing I did.

Darcy kept my hands in all the right places. Kissing was acceptable, but anything further wasn't swimming forward. After a few more retested advances, I wore out that welcome, and Darcy politely said it was time for her to go home.

Oh, Comet, I prayed. I hope I didn't blow it. I wished I didn't make a complete ass out of myself. How do I make amends now, I thought? How could I tell her I wasn't that kind of guy and did want to be respectful? She'd never believe that now. As we wrapped up our time on the couch, I offered to walk her back to her dorm room.

On the short walk back, I let her know that I enjoyed getting to know her that evening and enjoyed the dancing. Once in front of her door, I threw out a chance date.

Say, what would you say to a first date together? What did you have in mind? She asked. Well, you and I go to the same church. Are you going to make it in the next few hours? I never miss, she responded. OK, how about we go to church together in the morning? She looked at me a little wily and asked, unconvinced if I would make it? I assured her I would.

I am going to the eight o'clock service, what time do you go? I asked. Eleven o'clock, she said. How about the eight, I asked? No, she said, that's in only five hours. I go to the eleven. OK, I said. Eleven it is. I was not going to contest. She'd already given me forgiveness for too many blunders.

Goodnight, she said as she unlocked her door; she smiled back and asked again, unconvinced because of my intoxication: You'll come and get me for church? You bet, I responded. See you later this morning.

I walked the short distance toward my dorm. I leaned against the light post midway between our dorms and deeply breathed in the cool night air. I thought about the whole evening and how I inserted my foot in my mouth several times, and unintentionally insulted her, asking if she was sure her name was Darcy and not Marcy! I mean, I was a total idiot. I just hoped maybe she'd thought I'd been drinking, and I'd heard it wrong! She hadn't, and I hadn't. I thought about her tug on my arm, having never spoken to me, and paying her first five Fairchild bucks to put me in jail. That was a great sign of interest.

I thought about our dancing, mainly the first two or three, and how I politely thanked her and was willing to move on, not expecting to dance the rest of the evening together. Still, she just hung with me, grabbed my arm, and with the most beautiful smile and starry blue eyes, asked where are you going?

I have a lot more money to pay for dances as she held out her wad of Fairchild bucks. I know I reciprocated kindly and with a reassuring smile despite the nervousness.

I tried looking up at the stars, but the light from the post clouded my view. Alcohol also clouded my perspective and mind, but nothing was confusing my emotions, my elated rocky mountain-high feelings that I'd just spent the best six hours of my life with a girl who felt so right.

I etched the night in my mind and leaped back to my dorm room. I never went to sleep. I didn't want to miss walking Darcy to church.

Later that morning, I took one of the longest showers soaking my head in hot water, literally sitting on the shower floor. I had a slight hangover. I loved the dorm showers because they were an endless hot water spigot.

Cleaned up and in the only suit I owned, at about 10:30, I arrived at Darcy's dorm room to walk her to church. I knocked on her door, and she quickly swept me in and shut her door gave me a stern look, pulled her shirt aside, lifted her collar, and scolded me, saying, look what you did to my neck. Don't you ever do that again to me! Ever! she dictated in a stern warning!

I apparently left her a little hickey. I was dressed in my pale blue disco-era leisure suit, ready to escort her to church, and I found myself in yet another extremely awkward moment… I didn't know what to say. I smiled with a blush at first, but from her nonverbal's, I quickly removed the smirk off my face as she was dead serious and upset about it.

I told her I was sorry, really sorry. She didn't respond.

I stood inside her room, embarrassed and wanting to crawl into a hole. An awkward silence seemed to last an eternity as she fussed with her hair at the mirror and ignored me. I wasn't sure if we were still walking to church together or even if I was welcomed. As she continued to fuss with a mirror and ignore me as if I wasn't there, I turned to open the door and leave. I thought she was just being polite by not asking me to leave. Just as I passed through the door, she said, I'm done. I just need to get my coat on.

Boy, did I read this girl wrong? She was having respect for herself even though, while at a party, she could let her hair down, as they say. Respectful consideration is what she wanted, and though she didn't quite realize it yet, it is precisely the kind of girl I was seeking. Though I was embarrassed, I was pleased with her stance.

I gave her my worst first impression the first night of our meeting, acting out how all the other girls before her wanted me to. Girls want to have fun, Comet, and so does this one, but clean fun. Respectable fun. I found a solid person of character in my Midwest gal.

The walk to church was awkward as it was cold, and we didn't say much. I felt a little bit of a cool shoulder from her for sure. As we sat next to each other in the pew, I looked up at the myriad of stained glass throughout the church. I glanced at Darcy during prayer to see how nasty the hickey was, but she had her collar tightly hiding it. Her hands were clasped, her eyes were closed, her lips softly reciting the Lord's prayer. I kissed those lips last night, but I knew that chance wasn't coming again for quite a while. Alcohol gives us a little excuse to misbehave, but last night would not be the norm with Darcy.

I prayed, Comet. I prayed that if it was meant to be, let me stand at the altar one day with this girl beside me. Let me stand with her and color her world. I felt sure she could also color mine. Don't let the hickey be the first impression I asked. Give me a chance to show her and prove who I really am. She said yes when I asked her to marry me last night; give me a second chance to ask her again.

I walked Darcy home along with one of her housemates. There wasn't any hand-holding. The cold shoulder was still pretty icy. Maybe she thought the whole evening wasn't as fun as I did. As we approached my dormitory, I offered to walk her the next twenty yards to her dorm even as it remained awkward with her housemate along. I'm good, she said, thanks for going to church with me. You bet, Darcy, thanks. See you later, and she waved goodbye. See you later, I said.

There was little gas left in the Comets tank. *Comet, Thanks for being my sanctuary during many times of despair and trouble.*

I turned off the ignition feeling the key between my thumb and index finger for the last time. Everything shut down, including the Beach Boys playing on the eight-track. Then the heater fan slowly rotated from a whir to a dead stillness. I caressed the steering wheel with my fingers. I didn't realize that that would be the last time Comet's engine ever ran again.

Comet's battery would die, and the remaining gas would evaporate from its tank. Comet would never go down a road again, though I would sit in the driver's seat in the coming months and years and converse with my God in its sanctuary.

Stored in a barn in upstate New York, rust would eat at her bones, forcing her unibody frame beyond repair and use.

In the heartland, I'd found a new sanctuary, a new listener to share and converse my dreams with, another Comet to journey down my road in life. Darcy.

Chapter Thirty-Four
The Hallway Kiss

January – May 1981
Playlist:
Dance The Night Away, Van Halen
Night Fever, Bee Gees
He's the Greatest Dancer, Sister Sledge
Love Is the Answer, England Dan, John Ford Coley
Chuck E's in Love, Rickie Lee Jones
(Our Love) Don't Throw It All Away, Andy Gibb
I Want You to Want Me, Cheap Trick
Just When I Needed You Most, Randy Van Warmer
Master Blaster, Stevie Wonder
Three Times A Lady, Commodores
Don't Cry Out Loud, Melissa Manchester
What a Fool Believes, The Doobie Brothers
You Don't Bring Me Flowers, Barbara Streisand

Love Don't Live Here Anymore, Rose Royce
If I Can't Have You, Yvonne Elliman
It's A Heartache, Bonnie Tyler
Hands Up, Ottawan

Journalism breathed a new life into me at ISU! And so did Darcy. I could hardly get enough time with either of them. I was now torn about whether it should be a backup to farming or a full-time career! I did well and impressed one particular professor, Dr. Boyd, with my farm knowledge and class skills. He encouraged me to apply for a farm broadcast internship at WMT Radio and Television Station in Cedar Rapids.

I won the internship with a scholarship to help pay for school but with a catch. I don't get any money until I finish the training, so I would have to stretch my remaining savings through the summer.

Finals were over at ISU, and I had a week before starting with WMT. I sped a quick 1200-mile trip to see my parents and John and Joyce. It was that or sleep in my car for a week as I had done other times during a short ISU recess or holiday that I could not travel back to New York. So much has happened to me in the last six months. It was like a movie, surreal in many aspects. I needed that long road trip to and from New York to think things through.

Arriving home, the dandelions were in full bloom throughout the yard. I used to love mowing the lawn. Making it neatly trimmed made you feel perfect when you were done. It was therapeutic for Loretta, too, as she loved riding her lawnmower. Walking around a neatly trimmed lawn and her flower gardens gave her temporary reprieves of peace. It did for me too.

I walked across the road and down the hill where Comet was stored. One of the rear tires had gone flat. I could never afford new tires, so I always bought retreads. I'd put them on the front wheels until they were bald and dangerous and then transfer them to the back wheels wearing them fully out. They often developed small air leaks, and I constantly replenished them at least every month until they required air every week, too often more than one tire.

As I stood looking at her and contemplating my short cash summer ahead of me, I heard my dad's previous words; "why don't you sell that car? You need the money for college!"

I couldn't.

I walked around Comet, looking at its lines, flipped the spring-hinged Granada hood ornament I had added to give it style, and meandered down the old logging road into the valley below. It was great to smell the forest where I'd cut so many trees, huge Beech and maple, of which I sliced and split their trunks and branches into firewood. I hiked further down the valley to the slate falls descended from Darling Creek, birthed on my dad's property. It was still flushing from snowmelt trapped in the pockets of clay soils typical of this area. I once followed the creek by foot to where it emptied into Cayuta Creek, not far from the steel trestle bridge on Beckhorn Hollow.

I walked back up the steep part of the hill that I had sled down many times when I was twelve or thirteen using an old car hood. My shoes were caked with clay from the soft fields, and when I reached Comet's parking spot, I hopped into the driver's seat.

"How's the girl?" Comet whispered.

Did Comet whisper, *"how's the girl?"* Its engine wasn't running! It was my imagination, and it always had been!

"Darcy...Comet, you're asking about Darcy?" I didn't get a response. I never did! What I heard over the troubling years of my teens was what I wanted to hear, perhaps with some exceptions at times, from the Holy Spirit. I used to hear Comet speak through the muffler, the valves tapping, engines hum, or the brakes or fan belt squeal. I'd listen to imagined affirmations. How she talked all depended upon how I hit the gas pedal! But in reality, Comet was just a sanctuary in many times of conflict and trouble. Still, how could I ever sell her? Comet was a most sacred place, a protected place where I could shut everything and everyone out and commune with the real Comet; my God. Comet enveloped me like a cocoon as we sped through the mountains of my youth, but God carried Comet with me in it to avoid the cocoon becoming a casket. He had to; I survived too many close encounters with death.

At ISU, I landed employment at a large hog farm twenty miles north of ISU in Story City. It was called Hawkeye Hogs and owned by Bob and Nieda Fisher. They ran a farrow to finish farming operation of about 10,000 and more hogs annually. They are beautiful people and reminded me of John and Joyce.

The farm employed about fifteen to twenty full-time employees and several ISU students. They came during their flexible hours and performed various jobs and chores. So far, I have had a lousy assignment there. Unfortunately for Fishers and the hogs, his operation spread a swine disease like a pandemic. Every day my job was to sort through the feeder pens and pull out dead hogs. Some were so bloated from a day of rotting in the hot sun that as I pulled them from the cells to lift them in the tractor bucket, they would burst from the gas within their bellies and spill their intestines out.

Often, they would be half-eaten by the other hogs. It was disgusting work, but the pay was good, and Mr. Fisher was very good in allowing me to come and do the job around my class schedule. I had to commit to being there daily to do this chore nearly every day, I filled a ten-ton dump truck full of dead hogs and hog parts; guts, intestines, leg parts, hollowed-out carcasses, and boy did I smell at the end of my day. And yet, amazingly, I still love my bacon and eggs for breakfast!

My house brothers hated the smell when I came home. No matter how much I wrapped my boots and work clothes in double plastic garbage bags, they stank like death and pig shit. I stored them in the community bathroom as my roommate was never too happy with me. I had to scrub my hair and body with laundry detergent to try and rid myself of the smell. To find my car in the sea of student parking, all I had to do was look for the vehicle that looked like it was moving by itself as it was covered with flies.

Whether Comet ever really talked to me or not, I sat in its sanctuary again, communing with God over troubles. This time my trouble was Darcy. *"She's confusing,"* I uttered. *"She is fantastic in so many ways, and getting to know her has been wonderful. We have discussed each of our life goals early in our relationship."* I have never opened up on so many issues and conversed like that with anyone before. Not to the depth I've done with her.

"We've had a lot of fun together too. I'd take her on what I joked and called fun five-dollar dates. Yep, five bucks, and she didn't seem to mind—at least I thought!" Darcy knows I'm putting myself through school. She knows I work a lot, and I try not to take her out in the Chevy so the smell of hogs doesn't turn her off.

After a few of those five-dollar dates, I did take her out for dinner. It cost me a fortune! It was funny, though! There we sat in an Italian restaurant. We both ordered spaghetti and when the plates came, they were huge and piled high with spaghetti and meatballs! I couldn't believe how much they served up, and had I known, I would have suggested we split one. For sure, I thought she would never eat all of hers.

I'm usually a speedy eater, but I wanted to enjoy this dinner with her and extend the time we had to get to know each other better. We each had a glass of wine, some bread, and these two massive plates of spaghetti! As we began our dinner, I did most of the chatting, and she did most of the eating. I could not believe how fast this skinny blue-eyed little blonde wolfed down that plate of pasta. I watched her in amazement. I still had over half my plate full when she finished hers.

You know how I calculate Comet; I gave up my last girlfriend because she ordered two Big Macs at McDonald's. All I could think about was how many hours I had to shovel manure out of calf pens to feed that girl.

And Darcy, I mean, where did she put it all? She was so thin and petite!

So our future was back to five-dollar dates, big spender, eh? I tried to make them fun. I didn't have much of a budget for dating, but I wanted to continue to get to know this girl. As we began to date regularly, usually on a Friday night, Darcy and I would find a bar with ten-cent draws (beers) during happy hour. We'd go to the dollar movie theater and see a movie, then split a Big Mac or some other midnight snacking food and still maybe have enough for another beer at a bar. It was fun; we always had a great time with many laughs over how much we had left to spend, mostly a few dimes or cents toward the next date, but she was so great about it.

We also grew fond of this bar called the Fox. It has live bands that play jazz which Darcy loves, and which I've learned to appreciate through her. It is a quieter place where we can sit and chat, and we've done much of that. We could get our favorite cheap glass of wine (Mateus) and make it a nice evening for a little more than five bucks, sometimes ten! But she was so worth it. I mean, I couldn't last forever with this girl on just five-dollar dates! The Fox became our go-to place. A place where we quietly shared a lot more intimacy in our conversations and even began to dive into each other's dreams more deeply. Darcy and I shared much in the first four months we knew each other. I even shared my reservations about turning down John Kings' offer to start farming and doubts about returning to Iowa State because I missed them and the dairy. Darcy seemed to understand and encourage me in whatever direction I chose to take. She'd ask me if I thought I could find happiness in another career. "Of course," I'd tell her, "that's why I'm here at ISU, to study journalism."

A lump in my throat welled up. God, did I want to rehash the massive disappointment in her! I choked it in and thought carefully through the event again.

I had to travel to Cedar Rapids to interview for the internship at WMT. I saw Darcy the Friday night before I left, and she was genuinely excited and wished me great luck. On the third weekend in March, I left early Saturday morning to arrive for a 2:00 afternoon interview. I drove the State Highway 20 east straight through the middle of Iowa to get there. They provided me a hotel for the night to stay over as I had a second interview with another station staff member Sunday morning. Two farm broadcasters interviewed me. Jerry Passer and Rich Balvanz. I met and chatted with a third named Chuck Shaleen the next day as he was reporting on some event in the field on Saturday.

I returned home late Sunday afternoon, and my friend Kevin inquired immediately how the interview went. I shared how confident I was about the whole experience, and he was excited. "Sounds like you're going to get it, Curt," he encouraged enthusiastically. "Yeah, I think so, I'm a little nervous about not making any money through the summer, but I think I'll be OK."

"Have you told Darcy yet?" he asked. "No, I haven't." I wasn't in any hurry to share this news with anyone until I knew for sure and hadn't even thought about sharing it with Darcy. Still, Kevin was very anxious for us to share this news with her, which I thought odd. He liked me a lot as a friend and, at times, seemed a little jealous of my relationship with Darcy and the growing amount of time I spent with her and less with him. He was anxious for us to see her. He was so pushy for me to see Darcy that, for a brief instinctive moment, his anxiousness was suspect. Still, as fast as the moment entered my mind, it left.

He once made an envious comment when she and I began dating, stating, "Look, here he comes from New York, and he starts dating Darcy!" After dating Darcy more regularly, most of my housemates treated me indifferently. It was all subtle, but the comments came just the same. I didn't know why I'd receive some sly remarks about going out with her until one day, Kevin informed me that she had dated another brother from Fairchild House, and she dropped him. Many of them viewed Darcy as a prize but viewed me negatively for dating a girl who broke up with one of the brothers they loved. The more Darcy and I looked like a couple, the more I found myself defending her.

Eventually, I'd learn I was breaking some unspoken loyal order rule where a brother doesn't interfere with another brother's relationship. Except I had no idea until after dating Darcy for a couple of months that she had dated a brother, and besides, she wasn't his girl anymore when I met her!

Kevin often commented when I turned him down for a night on the town with Darcy instead, "Oh, going out with Darcy again—you'll see, someday, you'll see!" I didn't exactly know what he was referring to, and when asked, he wouldn't elaborate.

Keven rushed me out the door to visit Darcy. Chatting as we crossed the square, we entered the east end of the stairs in Busse Hall and trekked down to the first floor. We moved to head down the hall toward Darcy's room when suddenly Kevin spotted Darcy and another guy emerging from the stairs at that end of the hall. Kevin put his hand over my mouth and pulled me into a doorway. "Shhh!" he motioned me to be quiet. Then he pointed down the hall. Darcy stood in front of her dorm door, holding hands with another guy conversing. She was not inviting him into her room as they would have already gone in. They continued chatting for a couple of minutes, which seemed like an eternity, as we stood silent, trying not to be seen as we watched.

Kevin still had a firm grip on my shoulder; my eyes were wide with shock, disappointment, and then embarrassment. I turned my head and looked down at my shoes as I just couldn't bear to see the relationship I thought that we had evaporated! Then, …my worst nightmare happened; we watched as they embraced and kissed each other.

Kevin stared at me with his eyebrows raised and a facial expression already saying, "I told you so." I felt trapped in the doorway. I was less than 150 feet from Darcy and her new guy! I didn't want to be there. I wished we'd never come, but how could we leave? Darcy would surely see us emerge from the doorway.

Oh God, we were in such an awkward situation. I looked back up at Darcy; the kiss ended, and so did the embrace. The boy turned and left, and Darcy went into her room. I turned to Kevin with the heaviest silence of pain and angst on my face and in my heart I think I'd ever experienced other than the day I almost killed my dad. He stared at me until we retreated up the hallway and stairs; my legs were trembling with weakness.

"What a bitch she is, Curt. I told you so."

"Kevin, shut up."

"Curt, she was probably making out with that guy the whole weekend you were gone."

"Kevin shut up, just shut up! Darcy doesn't make out with guys; she doesn't even make out with me!"

The moment was horrible. I had no words to convey my emotions. My stomach ached, and my mind was spinning out of control. What I saw took me backward, so far backward, with pain; I felt I was living again in high school, rejected and manipulated. I've been here way too many times before. I didn't need it from this girl. I just wanted to be alone. My mind was flashing 100,000 thoughts per second. My worse speculations began to arise. Could she be two-timing on me? Was she using me? Using me for dating fun! It didn't make sense; it just didn't make sense; we were exploring each other too deeply as a couple. Something was amiss! It had to be!

My ground-up heart sank more profoundly than I could have imagined. The pain I was feeling proved I had fallen for Darcy, and I was scared I let myself think too much about this girl. I shouldn't have. I couldn't believe that after all the fun dates and evenings of conversation we had, she would do this to me; it just didn't make sense. She seemed genuinely interested in everything about me, the potential of "us"! But damn it—I saw it with my own eyes, so close I could almost taste the kiss!

I returned to my room and shut my door on Kevin to escape him. He must have seen Darcy sometime during the day or weekend with the guy. His odd rush for us to see her was a deliberate chance to see if we catch her with him, and by such iconic odds, it worked in his favor if that was his motive. I was angry with him too.

I was so embarrassed at how foolish I looked. I was sure this story would spread from Kevin to other house brothers within minutes. I was so, so low. My allergies kicked in hard as tears began to well up in my eyes, and a stuffy nose made it hard for me to breathe. I put on shorts and my Converse sneakers and jogged to relieve my allergies. I never had allergies in New York; I acquired them when I came to Iowa. Once I crossed the Mississippi River, I entered an atmosphere where I was stuffy and plugged fifty percent of the time.

Jogging relieved me from the allergies, and I was hoping for relief in other ways this night. I jogged to the barns and walked among the cows, where I usually could find solace and peace. They were resting and chewing their cud.

There was no peace; I couldn't get the image of the hallway kiss out of my head. I had to keep running and jogged back toward the main campus through fraternity row and past Friley Hall to the library. I ran as fast as I could, blowing off steam and trying to bury what I'd seen, even more, bury what I was feeling. I was so damn, damn angry, not just at Darcy and Kevin, but at me, for allowing myself to begin to love. I've never loved anybody other than the Kings in my life. Why did I let myself start to love her?

I jogged to the golf course past the equine stables and then across the campus back toward the Maple Willow Larch dorms and the parking lot, where I found my car. Sweat poured from my body, and I choked back tears as my heart raced! With rage, I pounded the hood of my car. Everything was suddenly empty in me—again.

To say I was devastated was just too simple. I had fallen for the girl, which seemed to trouble me most. I thought about this over and over as I ran. The deeper the devastation set into my soul, the angrier I got for allowing myself to begin to love her—anyone, for that matter!

I was raised by a woman who hated her husband, who was often wicked and did deliberate acts like this to hurt my dad. She seemed to hate everything in her life. She was the primary female role model I had growing up. Her misery and example kept me distant and distrustful of most female relationships. I repeatedly asked myself why I let my guard down. Why had I put my trust in Darcy?

I raced again, sprinting back to my dorm room, panting and sweating. It was more like a five-mile sprint than a jog, and it did nothing to relieve my pain.

I was still terribly tormented and soulfully troubled. My roommate Mark was back from his weekend at home. I still needed time alone. I got the keys to my car and drove into the countryside, where I sat on the side of a dirt road staring into the abyss of dark black Iowa fields.

I closed my eyes and threw in some cassette tapes. I tried to imagine my rides with Comet, the happy ones through the hills of Chemung and Tioga counties. The only ones that came to mind were those near misses as I played chicken with a tree at the edge of a dirt road, not caring, even wishing I would hit it head-on and everything would be over. I felt the same way again, but there weren't any trees here, just fields and fields of black topsoil, void of any growth this time of year, a dark sea of emptiness. And I was dark and empty, just like them!

As I sat and stared into the darkness, I became exhausted with self-pity. Loretta often wrote me letters and used her pen like a knife, yielding jabs and cuts to my inner soul; this was just, if not even more, painful. My mind rewound the other thoughts I had this weekend that troubled me. I was riding on edge with nerves from the interview, worrying about how I'd make it financially through the summer should I get the internship, and then worrying about what I'd do for work if I didn't! At every turn for the good in my life these past few months, the hallway kiss vanished them. They all disappeared from my mind. The self-pity falls just kept flowing.

After staring into the darkness for hours, I drove back to Ames. I had to walk past Busse Hall from the parking lot. I saw the light on in Darcy's room. I was calm, still very angry, but calm. It was late now, but she was always up late at her drafting desk. I went to the stairs leading up to her dorm and decided to stop, pretend as if I knew nothing had happened and just see what was up. I only got up three steps when something tugged hard at my brain, and I thought about the hallway kiss again. Did I want to knock on her door and possibly find someone again? I couldn't bear it. I just couldn't—not at the moment. And even if there weren't anyone, she surely would see that I was distraught from the past three hours, eyes red from sobbing and rubbing them. And what would I say?

In every relationship, there is a point when you either know you are moving forward or not. This was not a forward-moving experience. I became terrified to see Darcy. I was fearful of a truth I didn't want to believe: she misled me; she kissed another guy as she did me on our dates. A horrible realization set in that there was nothing special about me to her. Nothing. It had all been in my head. I backed down the stairs with my eyes glued to her window, turned away, and walked back to my dorm room, and I silently wept myself to sleep.

The next day I awoke wondering if the day before had all been a nightmare. Kevin soon reminded me it wasn't. I began looking backward into the history of our relationship, beginning to see the signs I hadn't seen before. Just before I left for Cedar Rapids, I asked Darcy when her birthday was, and she told me it had just passed a few days ago. That should have been a clue to me that we weren't as close as I might have thought in that she never mentioned her birthday to me. Or worse, I surmised, perhaps she had that other date to take her out, and that's why she didn't mention it.

Sometimes when I visited Darcy, there were substantial floral arrangements with Sunflowers, all kinds of daisies and other bouquets adorning her room. I had assumed she got them from her relatives operating the greenhouses or they were her roommates. But the last time I brought her spring campus tulips from one of my jogs, there were a beautiful dozen red roses and a guy visiting her roommate. I was a little embarrassed, so I said to Darcy, well, they're not quite the bouquet your roommate got there, but they're ISU grown with a wide grin! Her roommate Diane nearly swallowed her cigarette! Coughing and choking, she got up from the room, left, and never returned. After chatting with Darcy in front of the other guy in the room whom I thought was Diane's friend, he said awkwardly, "Well, I better be going."

His awkwardness made me feel sorry that Diane so rudely left him, and I told to Darcy, "That was pretty weird for Diane to leave a guy who came to see her and brought her roses." Darcy paused, looked at me dumbfoundedly, and said, "Yeah, well, she doesn't like the guy anyway," I later found out how blindly ignorant I was. The guy in the room who awkwardly left brought Darcy the giant bouquet of red roses! It was around the time of her birthday. No wonder Diane choked on her cigarette and never came back. What a blind fool I'd been.

And then there was Valentine's Day before that; it was early in our relationship, but I asked her to dinner, and she said yes, but she had a previous commitment at 5:00. She'd be available at 7! "Seven it is," I agreed. I thought her commitment was a school function, but I now doubted it. It might have been the other guy who had asked her out first. That day again, her room was adorned with dozens of roses.

There were other stupid times like this when I went to Darcy's room, and Diane sat there snickering away, knowing full well the other guy in the room was there seeing Darcy. I never had a clue, but it all became a little more apparent after seeing Darcy kissing that guy in the hallway that she had a lot of suitors! I had a lot of competition in which I was naively blind.

"God, she is a beautiful girl, full of personality, fun-loving, sexy, and with a smile that brightens a room when she steps in. She's a prize! Blue Eyes is a prize! Who was I to think she would only be interested in me and me? What girl would want a would-be dairy farmer who smelled like a pig and could only afford snapped Tulips and Daffodils from campus flower beds versus $30 bouquets?"

My self-esteem barometer was negative 1000! I was a financial world away from all the yuppie wear that adorned the guys I saw visiting her room. I wore a stupid polka dot hat, Levis, and drove a Chevy station wagon.

Why would I think that something special was happening between us? She is probably just another girl who wants to have fun, and I tried slamming her into that category in the back of my head. But that just didn't seem to make sense, or maybe I didn't want it; to make sense.

Her roommate went home for the weekend once and Darcy invited me to stay over after our date. She said, "You can stay here if you like." How would I refuse that? She pulled pillows and a blanket from her bed and made a comfy place on the rug on the floor. She stripped down to just her panties and a long t-shirt, and I undressed down to my shorts. We snuggled under a blanket with my arm around her. I pressed her close to my chest and tucked up against her. I didn't dare to go any further as I never carried a condom to avoid being tempted. Nothing happened that night; there was no back rub, no intimate contact, or even a good night kiss. It was apparent that cuddling together was all that would happen with Darcy. She made no overtures, no advances. I remember asking her that night if she had done this with all of her boyfriends as she caught me a little surprised at the invitation, and she said no, but I trust you. And there I lay with natural hormones erecting the tower of love, and she conveniently or deliberately fell sound asleep. I found something special in that, signifying that she trusted me and we were becoming a couple. I had many invitations to go further with other girls. Still, with Darcy, I found respect in her willingness to lay nearly naked with me and trust me not to advance. "Or is that what she wanted?" And once again, I wasn't acting upon the invitation.

"God, you know we went to church every Sunday since we met, except the Sunday I was in Cedar Rapids. It was easy for me to think something was growing between us! I mean, come on…give me a break! All those dates and times together? The Fox Lounge dancing and conversations. We were together most Friday and Saturday nights!"

After seeing Darcy in that hallway, I wanted it to be a dream; I wanted to wake up to know it was just a horrible nightmare! But it wasn't. For days I kept trying to rationalize the action. Maybe she was holding her options open, perhaps as simple as that? Even so, it didn't feel right.

I seldom, if ever, called home to complain about anything. But a few days after the hallway kiss, I did. I told my dad of the allergies I always immediately felt crossing the Mississippi into the West. I told him they seemed to worsen as spring progressed, and I wasn't sure I should return to ISU the following fall. He encouraged me to give it time, "give it a full year; always give everything a full year," he advised. "Get through four seasons and give whatever you're dealing with a full year before you make any major decisions," he reiterated. He sensed ISU was a good place for me even though he'd never been there. He might have felt that I lost something too in that conversation and tried to get me over the hump.

Two weeks had passed after the kiss, and I managed not to see even a glimpse of Darcy. I deliberately took alternative routes to and from classes to avoid bumping into her enroute to one of hers. I didn't want to run into her by chance, and I didn't want to see her. I was putting her out of my head. I'd never let anyone into my soul like I did Darcy. Now I just wanted to divorce everything about her from my brain, heart, and emotions.

I was trying to stay focused on reviewing and studying for finals that were coming and shut her out of my life; it wasn't easy. Again and again, over and over, I had to tell myself to stay focused on my goals. That constant little voice inside me always said, don't let anything or anyone interfere with your goals, except I had put Darcy down as one of them.

I had them neatly typed in my wallet on a four-inch square of paper. It was shaped like a pyramid with the most crucial goal on top. All the other plans supported the top destination. I never shared them with anybody lest they laugh or try to tell me they weren't achievable. At the top of my list was 40, representing the forty million dollars I wanted to earn by age forty. I was determined never to be as poor as my family and as I am now. Farming was on my goal sheet under that. I looked at agriculture from a different perspective; I was going to have a large grocery store with ice cream production on the farm where people could see the cows milked in a parlor with milk being pasteurized, bottled, and creamed before their eyes and lots of other ideas to make those millions on that farm. I had the goals of a bachelor's and master's degree to support my efforts toward the top of my pyramid. Every day, I took them out and read them ten times, implanting them into my subconscious. And then there was the girl at the bottom of the list, the one I prayed for, someone who would eventually share and support my dreams, and I keep and support hers. I had scribbled Darcy's name in that spot. It was probably the most important goal because I had never experienced real love, but it was placed at the bottom. And while I asked to be led to someone special in my prayers, that goal was intangible. It wasn't something I could turn into a number and achieve, so I left that one up to God at the bottom of the pyramid.

That two weeks' absence from Darcy and working to block her out of my consciousness seemed like forever but it was beginning to work. I ensured I went for dinner when I knew she would not be there. I knew her schedule well, and I didn't want to see the living cause of my pain! Midway through the third week of absence between us, I was studying in my room when a knock on the door came. My roommate Mark opened the door, and I heard Darcy's voice ask, "Is Curt here?" He looked over his shoulder at me with a frown; and he left the room without saying a word. Darcy walked in. I did not get up from my desk, which looked out the window the opposite way.

"Hey, where have you been?" Darcy asked. "Around," I responded rather coolly leaning over my chair to face her. "What have you been doing? Why haven't you been over to see me?"

"Just working," I shrugged. "Just working."

"Everything OK?" she asked.

"Yes," I said. Darcy obviously could sense I wasn't the person I was two and a half weeks ago.

"Well…what happened?"

"What do you mean?" I asked, almost with a snap and a rise in my tone as I thought she was referring to my deliberate distancing of herself.

"What happened with the scholarship thing, the WMT scholarship?" she asked. "How did it go when you went to Cedar Rapids? You never came over to tell me?"

Oh my God, I rose from my chair—I furiously, silently thought about how I wanted to tell her that I did come over to tell her. I wanted to test her by asking her a few questions and see how she'd responded that I'd seen her kissing some other boyfriend. At that moment, the angst I felt wanted to burst out of me, but I quickly tucked the emotions down deep as I learned to do in life. I suppressed them and buried them; it wasn't worth the pain that would rise. I was done with her. Besides, I convinced myself I had no right to know.

There was no use. I couldn't afford to wrap my head around this mess, and she had no knowledge or sense of what I saw or how I had felt for the last couple of weeks.

"Ooooh, WMT?" I sighed, quickly calmed my inner anxiety, and brought my tone back to normal, but it was too late; she sensed something and looked at me a little funny. "It went well," I said. "I haven't heard, but they were positive and encouraging." I paused momentarily as I silently wished she'd just go away. Her stance and blue eyes were searching for more of an answer, though. "I should hear by the end of this week, actually... through my professor," I said. "That's great; I'm sure you'll get it," she insisted.

"I hope so; if not, I'll find something else to do."

"You'll get it, Curt. I know you will."

Her sense of my quick rise from my chair and my mood of strong aloofness and unwillingness to strike up any conversation beyond her questions finally had its effect. "Well, it looks like you're busy; come by and see me later tonight when you can, OK? And make sure you call me as soon as you hear something. We'll celebrate!"

"Thanks," I said.

"See you later," Darcy asked.

Yeah, right, see you later, like a lot later, I sarcastically thought to myself. I said nothing as she left and I continued to avoid her.

Darcy returned nearly every day to my room to visit for the next two weeks. Our previous four months' roles were reversed. I made no effort to stop by her room, no jogging, no flowers. I just stayed focused on my studies. We made small talk when she stopped by, and she made it hard to resist genuine efforts to engage me in discussions about the coming summer and what might be in store for her and me. I tried to avoid any more in-depth subjects as we'd had before and steer the topic away to just how her day was and how her design projects were going. She sensed my continued aloofness and that I wasn't dropping by her dorm room to see her or asking her out for any dates, now nearly five weeks after the hallway kiss.

She caught glimpses of how difficult it was to put myself through school during our relationship. She probably chalked up my behavior to those stresses. As a nonresident, it cost me triple the tuition of an Iowa resident. She knew this too as a nonresident, except her parents were paying the bills. She also heard of my offer from the Kings, how important the goal of farming was to me, and my second-guessing as to whether it was the right thing that I turned them down. She had doubts about whether I would return to Iowa State the following fall and wanted to know if I was and whether I planned to live back in Fairchild again. She wanted the phone number to my parent's house if I should go back to New York, though she had no doubts about me getting that WMT scholarship, and she assured me of that time and time again.

One evening, I was walking back from the cafeteria when Darcy's friend Janice and I bumped into one another as she sat on the steps to her dormitory. Janice was a farm girl from Council Bluffs, a city in the southwest part of Iowa, settled on the Missouri River.

"Hey, let's walk," she asked.

"Sure," I responded. Janice asked me if there was anything wrong. "No, there's nothing wrong," I replied with surprise.

"Well, where have you been? I mean, we don't see you visiting Darcy anymore."

"Oh, I've been working many hours and just busy lately."

Janice could tell from my nonverbal's and quivers I was lying. "You know Darcy's a pretty hot babe," she said in jest, "and she likes you a lot," she coached.

I paused in surprise that the conversation turned so quickly to Darcy and responded with a crossed tone mixed with optimism and sarcasm. "Really?" I gasped half sarcastically; and I quickly caught myself remaining calm as the hallway kiss welled up inside me.

"She's a nice girl," I said, "but I'm not sure she's the right girl for me."

Janice threw her arms back in her Iowa farm girl ways and gasped, "whattaya mean? You two are perfect for each other!" That wasn't a surprise for me to hear because I thought so too, but if we were becoming so perfect for each other, why was she still out-kissing other guys? That damn hallway scene played fresh repeatedly in my head as we talked. My brain was in all directions over the issue, and though she was talking, I didn't hear much of what Janice said.

I searched deep inside as to whether I should share what I saw with Janice. Did she have a boyfriend at home who was visiting for the weekend? I wondered how many others there were while I was courting her.

Janice remained in control of the conversation, grabbing my arm and forcing me to look at her and pay attention to what she had to say, "listen, maybe there is something between you two that didn't go well, or perhaps she pissed you off in some way, she is a pretty strong personality, it happens, but I'm telling you to give it another try. Give it a second chance. She likes you more than you know." Janice and I approached the steps to her dorm. We sat down on them, having completed the circular walk around the Richardson Courtyard. We chatted a bit more, and I pondered whether I should mention seeing her kissing another guy. I wanted to bring it up as maybe some explanation could set me free of the disappointment and distrust I now harbored. Perhaps it was just her old boyfriend from home for a visit, I'd rationalize. Except she did tell me she wasn't dating anyone when we first met and that she had just broken up with a guy. Maybe it was just one of those guys who took her on a date before me. After all, she did not invite him in as she had always done with me…but then again, maybe he stayed with her the whole weekend, and perhaps he was leaving as it was a Sunday night? So many possible scenarios had gone through my crazy head in the past few weeks, and maybe sharing this with Janice would yield an answer and relief. It was aggravatingly apparent that I still adored Darcy deeply, even as I hurt over the kiss.

I couldn't look directly at Janice as she looked at me. I'm sure I portrayed bewildered looks as these thoughts raced through my mind. "Curt, Curt," she shook me orally, "is there anything you want to share with me?" I was still deliberating in my mind.

Maybe there was a scenario I didn't want to know about, and finding out would make me feel like a fool again. Indeed, if I spilled my observation and feelings to Janice, she would share this with Darcy. How would that look? I pressed my gut for answers. I would undoubtedly look jealous, and I wasn't about to give any girl that controlling advantage over me. Worse, I might look controlling, and maybe I cared too much for a girl who never took our dating relationships seriously. Saying anything, I concluded—would make me look like a fool. I would surely lose with any divulgence.

Janice was still looking at me with the question written on her face. "Anything?" She asked again!

"No, Janice, nothing."

"Well, give it another try, Curt. Give her another try. I wouldn't be here talking with you if—" and she caught herself not finishing that sentence.

"Thanks, J," I said.

"Goodnight Curt…another try," she insisted as she went up the stairs to her dorm door.

It never dawned on me that Darcy might have put Janice up to doing some soliciting from me to dig into my thoughts at the time; maybe not. Friends just sometimes sense something, like Kevin. The semester was drawing fast toward a close. Considering Janice's advice, Darcy appeared the following Friday afternoon before I could make the next move, asking me if I wanted to go to the union and have a beer?

After hanging out on the veranda for several hours, we walked to the central campus. The Memorial Union always had live music and ten-cent draws every Friday afternoon. The pub was called The Maintenance Shop, and boy, did I need some maintenance! As we walked and discussed the summer ahead, Darcy stopped me on the lawn in front of the Campanile, turned me toward her, and looked into my eyes.

"Curt, on occasions when we'd be together, and I'd say I love you, you told me you won't use the word love until one day you mean it. Curt, I care for you. I hope you come back to Iowa State; I hope one day you'll be able to tell me you love me when you mean it," and she kissed me.

This was just over a month and a half after the Cedar Rapids weekend.

I looked into her beautiful eyes as they stirred with an oceanic blue. Darcy always had difficulty making direct eye contact except when she was mad or had something heartfelt to say, and she was staring straight into my eyes, trying to peer into my soul.

I wanted to bring up the kiss. But I couldn't. Darcy was telling me right now that she cared enough to move forward in a relationship, but my underlying trust had been severed severely. This was the closest overture to a commitment between us, and she initiated it, yet it wasn't a solid commitment. I had no right to bring up that kiss and maybe no right to pass judgment either. We were still in the dating stage of becoming, but we hadn't yet…become!

I didn't know what to say to her in response. I had surmised she had a boyfriend at home, and the weekend I was in Cedar Rapids was the perfect time for her to have him visit, knowing I would be gone. The boyfriend at home, or whoever he is, was still a troubling image in the background of my emotions. I needed to change the subject away from us becoming anything…I wasn't ready. I detoured the conversation by sharing with Darcy that Dr. Boyd informed me I won the scholarship a few days ago!

"You did!" she gasped. "Why didn't you tell me? You did it! I told you you'd win it!" She embraced me and shook me more excitedly than I was about it. "That's fantastic; when do you start?"

"Right after finals. They arranged for me to rent a room in an apartment at the Kirkwood Community College Campus for the summer. I've already accepted the terms and conditions of the internship and scholarship."

"Well, why didn't you tell me?" She demanded again.

"I wanted to, Darcy, I wanted to, but I just…"

"Just what? I don't know, Darcy, I guess I just wasn't that sure you…"

"Sure, I what? Curt?"

"Nothing," I said. "It will be a great experience for me."

"Yes, it will," Darcy said with enthusiasm.

"I'll be in Iowa for the summer and returning to ISU next fall."

Darcy gave me a big hug.

"And what about you, Darcy? Any final decisions for you this summer?"

"I'm going back home to work at my grandpa's flower shop and earn some money to take you out on a five-dollar date!" We both laughed and began to walk back to her dormitory.

"I'm going to miss him… my grandpa. I wish you could have known him. He would have liked you. You and he are alike and would have gotten along well."

I thought to myself for a moment as we walked. I think I just heard a new version, but a more pleasantly assuring way of saying, Curt, you're the kind of guy a girl wants to marry someday.

"I'm sure I would have liked him too."

"You would have Curt, and he would have loved all of your attributes, just like I do."

That was certainly a reassuring comment from Darcy.

I may have read too much into this hallway kiss? We had fun on our dates and got into so many deep discussions, which made my heart pound with amazement at how well we connected. We had a mutual appreciation of our dreams and desires! While I perceived that we were steady daters, we were only four months into our relationship. We had no formal commitment between us. She might have a boyfriend at home, keeping him on a leash until someone better comes along. Could I be that someone? But, is that fair, Comet?

Is that fair to me? Is that fair to him? There was undoubtedly a positive in that she came around showing continued interest as I distanced myself.

And although some little voice deep inside me kept telling me, this is the girl, this is the girl. I should marry… and the Campanile kiss and conversation seemed 100 percent sincere. No matter what she said, the helplessness and disappointment I felt seeing her with another guy set me back. As history repeats itself. I once again erected a wall around my heart. It would take a while to dismantle it…because of the hallway kiss, the unknown guy, and the distrust.

Chapter Thirty-Five
WMT Radio and TV

My roommate and I and a puppet named Fred.

May – August 1981
Playlist:
Endless Love, Lionel Richie
Kiss on My List, Daryl Hall and John Oates
I Love a Rainy Night, Eddie Rabbit
Keep on Loving You, REO Speedwagon
The Tide Is High, Blondie
Slow Hand, The Pointer Sisters
Woman, John Lennon
Every Woman in the World, Air Supply
The Break Up Song, The Greg Kihn Band
Somebody's Knockin, Terri Gibbs
Stop Draggin' My Heart Around, Stevie Nicks
Take It On the Run, REO Speedwagon
I Can't Stand It, Eric Clapton

I started my internship at WMT. The farm directors wasted no time creating assignments, and I reported the morning futures market opens over the air on the radio. Occasionally I also got a chance to fill in on the noon farm news broadcast when one of the farm broadcasters had to be absent. It was an exciting opportunity to experience and work in broadcast journalism. My life at just 22 years old was full of disappointments and surprises. The surprises had been mostly since entering college from professors who saw something in me that I didn't see in myself. They pushed me toward journeys I'd never considered. Again, at WMT, it was my journalism ethics professor, Dr. Dale Boyd, who strongly suggested and pushed and supported me with a letter of recommendation to attain this experience.

Jerry Passer, Rich Balvanz, and Chuck Shaleen were the farm broadcasters who oversaw my activities. Jerry was the senior and chief farm broadcaster. Most of my summer would relieve them from covering county fairs and minor outstate farm news events.

It was a fantastic time to be in Iowa, and my residence at Kirkwood Community College brought forward two Iowa beauties to fall in love with. The sweet smell of sin was always so tempting on many a hot Iowa summer night. But Darcy was hauntingly always on my mind.

Since her affirmation under the Campanile, before we left ISU, that she cared deeply for me, I was again encouraged that there was more to our relationship than I had thought. I regretted that we now had to be separated so soon after. When my mind had time to be idle, I retraced all our fun times together, still trying to put that troubling hallway kiss out of my mind. I tried calling her often as she had encouraged me, but she was never home. When I called, and her mom would answer, she'd tell me she was at work or out with friends. When her dad would answer the phone, he'd be more specific and let me know she was out with Tim and John! I had to make a significant effort to drive to a pay phone to call her, and each long-distance call was expensive, so it became a little despairing to try so often and never seem to reach her. And who were Tim and John?

It was an eight-hour drive to see Darcy, but it was out of reach on my tight budget and no income. A call would suffice, but it would always take several times a week to try and catch her. When I finally got a hold of her, she seemed content to tell me how she was living her summer to the fullest and having fun back home, sharing her escapades with some friends. She seldom mentioned hanging with her girlfriends, whom she referenced and shared much with me at Iowa State. One evening, I got enough courage to ask her who Tim and John were. She told me she hung around with some guys from high school who lived in her neighborhood. They'd water ski nearly every evening as Darcy and one of the guys lived on the same lake. If they weren't out water skiing, they were out golfing.

I tried to reach her many times, and sensed reluctance in her mom's voice to tell me again that I missed her in favor of her being out with these two guys. As a father, her dad's tone gleamed to say I was yet probably one of many a suitor.

Sensing the disappointment in my trying to reach her daughter because she was always out having a great time with Tim and John, in her sweet way, her mom Betty began to remind me that "they were just friends, you know."

I wasn't so sure. The hallway kiss was less than two months ago, and distrust was still fresh in my psyche. Could either of these two guys have been that guy, I wondered? Though Darcy and I were becoming closer friends these past five months, there was never any formal commitment between us that we'd be faithful friends and not date anyone else. I thought our relationship had been crossing a line and getting strong enough to imply it. Still the hallway kiss struck that implication down. I fell in love with Darcy because she was a strong independent young personality. I was not and would not be assertive in implying ownership in our relationship, fearing she would back off. I should have shared more directly that I was falling for her. But I didn't. I was hoping my actions of care and interest spoke louder than words. It's the way I have always been. For all of Loretta's contradictory behavior to her preaching, she too always said, "Actions speak louder than words." And her actions, the poorest of them, indeed spoke volumes.

Those rare times I could finally reach Darcy on the phone, I'd hear about her job at her Grandpa Bachman's floral shop. At least she was sharing with me, but our conversations never got very deep on the phone, like when we were at college. Perhaps she might be losing interest now that we were absent. And now that she knew I knew about them, she freely talked about Tim and John and her daily activities with them. She seemed to speak a lot more fondly about the one who lived on the lake in ways that made me unsure that he possibly could be more than just a friend; perhaps the boy I saw her kissing that weekend. While I politely listened and kept putting quarters, adding up to dollars into the pay phone, I was annoyed hearing how much fun she was having with them and paying to listen to it. I also wondered why she would share her escapades with them with me. I didn't share how much fun I had with the two girls from Kirkwood on a nightly basis or our excursions to the Coralville Reservoir to go swim. I would never want her to think anything existed nor impart a chance of jealousy. I didn't get it, but I listened as that seemed to be what most of her fun was centered around. It seemed like a high school game of planting seeds of jealousy, but that didn't fit her personality. If she wanted to play that kind of game, she would have never concealed that all those flowers I'd see in her room over the months we were dating that were really for her and not her roommate. The jealousy game didn't seem like something the Darcy I was dating would do; in fact, the opposite. My psychic was still so troubled over the hallway kiss, but as time went on and I became more and more consumed with my work, I spent less time dwelling on it.

After the first month of our absence and calling three or four times a week to catch her home, I stopped calling so often and reduced my calls to once every other week. If she wasn't there, I left a message that I would try again at a particular time. She would try to be there for the call if she cared enough. Sometimes she was, sometimes she wasn't. When we did touch base, she was always interested in my experiences and where I was at the moment, as I often traveled to events for the station.

She always encouraged me in my experiences, but something seemed indifferent like I might have been an annoyance almost. Perhaps I just conjured up all this in my head, but the absence of growth in our relationship due to the distance was absolute. She sounded like she had so much carefree fun. I was a little jealous, not that I wasn't having fun, I was too, but working my way through college was such a financial stress that was ever-present and even more so this summer as there was no pay during this internship. The scholarship was paid to the university after my summer. In that aspect, I was envious of most ISU students. I was the among the small faction of students self-funding my education. It was tough to comprehend that 90 percent or more of the ISU student population had parents, including Darcy, who could afford to give them a free ride in college. That was a middle to upper-class concept and privilege I was not privy to.

My work with WMT took me crisscrossing Iowa to every corner of the state. My role as a Jr. Broadcaster was to cover the county fair beats, report with stories about 4-H, farmer interest groups, and new machinery technologies, and serve as one of the guest judges for the County Pork and Dairy Queen contests. I'm not talking about livestock contests between cows and pigs. Here in Iowa, they had beauty and talent contests for the beautiful young women who, if they won, would be named Miss (County Name) Pork Queen and Miss (County Name)Dairy Queen. Those contests were usually sponsored by the Iowa Pork and Dairy Associations, and what a hoot!

I'd pinch myself whenever I was asked to be a judge, a boy from New York City acting as a judge for the Pork Queens. Wow! I loved the job and saw adorable farm girls parading across the stages, showing off their talents and figures! While they had music skills, brains, honors from high school, stories of their families and community, and how big their dads' farms were I judged their lips, hips, and other curves.

They got my vote if they had anything close to the hourglass shape, spoke intelligently, had a big smile, and had a fun personality. Hearing about their dad's large farming operations had me fantasizing that if they were only a few years older and out of high school, I'd be interested in getting to know them. The problem with judging the queens was that I wasn't much older than they were, and the testosterone within me was still raging like a stallion. This work at WMT wasn't physical enough to work off the testosterone like farm work, and there were girls back at Kirkwood that knew it. They were as forward, presumptuous, and seductive as the girls back in Cobleskill. The east coast girls and the Midwest farmers' daughters all had the same hormones, and wanted fun.

I had an interesting night the second week I was at Kirkwood. I told the WMT staff about it. My apartment was on the first floor of a two-story quad. My bedroom window was at ground level. It was about 11 pm, and I was lying in bed thinking about the travel I had to embark on the following day. It was a hot Cedar Rapids evening. The apartment didn't have air conditioning, so the window above my bed was wide open. I heard a girl talking just outside my window. Jim, she called. I didn't answer because I wasn't Jim. Then she pulled off my bedroom screen and slipped in and down onto my bed. It was pitch black, and she mumbled something as she straddled on top of me and whispered, "Jim, wake up." My heart pounded with nervous shock, and I gulped out my name wasn't Jim. She froze in the dark at the sound of my voice. "Jim?" she asked, "Is this you?"

"No," I said, "I'm Curt."

She screamed and jumped off my bed. As I stood up, she also stumbled to the light switch and turned it on. She looked at me, standing in my underwear, screamed again, and left through the apartment's front door.

She didn't know Jim was gone, and I had rented his room. She had just returned to her apartment for summer classes from home on break.

After that night, we met again and laughed about it. "I was so embarrassed," she laughed. I told her, "No harm was done, although it shocked the nervous system!" I learned that Jim was not her boyfriend but "just a great friend." A friend with "benefits."

She was straightforward to get to know me, and from that point on, she'd been hot to get to know me in more ways the whole summer. She was lean with a great figure and was fun to hang around with, spending many evenings sipping a beer or a glass of wine and sharing with her where I'd just returned from, why I chose one Pork Queen contestant over another, and sharing some of the news I was broadcasting. I kept her laughing and living vicariously through the antics I was privileged to partake in through my storytelling.

I met a lot of wonderful Iowans through the internship work. I had to visit many small towns that didn't host a county fair but boasted some world-renowned claim, like having the biggest ball of baling twine in the world, the largest strawberry at Strawberry Point, or some other fun and forgivable weird hoax. It gave each community something to laugh at themselves about, kept a smile on everyone's face each time they saw their large ball of twine or giant strawberry, and helped create a summer festival around its theme. These towns were remote and wanted a place on the world map to be recognized.

There were some genuine notables like Adair, their town's claim to fame is that the infamous Jesse James bank robbers pulled off the first successful train robbery of his career just outside their village.

And there is West Branch, a town close to Cedar Rapids where U.S. President Herbert Hoover was born. Clear Lake, north of Ames by about 50 miles, is home to the famous Surf Ballroom, where musicians and singers Buddy Holly, Ritchie Valens, and the Big Bopper performed for the final time before a plane crash killed them all on their way to Minneapolis for their next venue. *Someday I'm going to take Darcy to the Surf,* I thought. It's a classic Icon where the heart of Iowa and Rock and Roll meets.

Undoubtedly the most famous town in Iowa is Winterset, where actor John Wayne, a big-screen Western legend, was born. His birthplace and a museum dedicated to him reside there. The museum is the only one dedicated to the Western star.

Pella is another great town, settled in the 1800s by Dutch Colonists; Pella features a windmill and is just a lovely small rural American town steeped in German-Dutch heritage and the birthplace of the famous lawman Wyatt ERP.

Iowans are proud of anything that will put their small town on a map. The Ax Murder House is a house in Villisca where eight people were murdered in the spring of 1912. Josiah Moore's entire family of six and two guests were all killed. The murders were never solved. You can stay in the house overnight as a guest and hear their ghosts.

Who would care much about a bank robbery except the town of Stuart, Iowa, where the infamous 1930s-era couple Bonnie and Clyde robbed the First National Bank in April 1934? That robbery puts Stuart on the map. History records they were killed by police in Louisiana a month later.

However, my favorite Iowa couple comes from near the Cedar Rapids area, and I dub their portrait the American equivalent of the Mona Lisa. It's a superb piece of art. Titled American Gothic it is like a fire, you can stare at it endlessly and wonder what these two people were about, what were their thoughts as they stood for the pose, and what toil and labor each endured through life. I wondered what kind of kids they produced and what kind of family structure existed within their household. You can look into their eyes, think of a million questions to ask them, see the soul of our country, and know a little about how we've evolved as Americans. Anamosa is where an American Artist we know as Grant Wood was born. I love Grant Wood's art. He depicts Iowa, Iowans, and the Midwest as it was in his youthful days, as it still is and could be seen in many of my travels. Hundreds of years from now, I believe it will hang in a museum behind a guarded glass frame with value and protection, just like the Mona Lisa in the Louvre in France.

My least favorite place in Iowa is Amana, which Iowa claims to fame for the Amana Colonies and their backward acrimonious religious way of living. Amana is just south of the Cedar Rapids area. I was assigned a feature news item to report. I got behind the scenes and into some of their homes. For all the Amana Colonies' glorification, I saw unfortunate situations.

I met with several farm families, and found it common to meet numerous mentally disabled children and adults present in each. I'm unsure if the closed society and in-breeding caused these abnormalities or they were simply by chance. But there appeared to be both depression and suppression in these households. Suppression of children and women was evident in how they were treated and talked at, not to. And throughout the community, immense secrecy and shyness seemed to be a pattern to hide things from outsiders and keep them out of their world. It was disturbing to know and see.

The use of religious preference to maintain a backward style of living and tax-exempt status didn't sit right with me. I saw modern farm machinery with rubber tires removed and replaced with steel wheels to abide by their religious views. What the heck! These people were living in hypocrisy. They weren't like the purists, still using a real horse for power in their fields for plowing and harvesting. I'm sure their way of living had many exciting and positive virtues of simplicity to praise. I am no perfect human being to judge, but at what price was there to the children born and raised within that environment?

The outside world was kept a secret from them. I viewed them as a cult! I had a hard time doing the feature I was assigned, which was to praising one farmer for his efforts at manure gasification. But I had to be the journalist I was being trained to be and not allow my judgments and interpretations to interfere with factual news reporting. The gasification project was a minuscule achievement compared to the hypocrisy I witnessed. I wanted to do an investigative report on why I saw so many of their citizens mentally disabled. But that wasn't my assignment.

Still, Iowa is a great state. While it is the most developed state in the union, as farmland is considered developed, and Iowa has plenty of it, what is most beautiful about Iowa is its people. And this boy from New York City has fallen in love with them.

Iowa is a place I could have lived as a youth. Comet and I could have raced from the Illinois border to Nebraska in a straight line and never had to take our foot off the accelerator unless, of course, we got caught by the police, which by the way, have awarded me plenty of their speed achievement certificates.

The Fairfax Hay Days was a typical event I was assigned to cover. Located just outside Cedar Rapids, it is a rural village with over 600 residents. The hay days were a popular event for many from Cedar Rapids. What I liked about this town was the steel trestle bridge. It reminded me of the many chats with

Comet on our own Beckhorn Hollow. I had several assignments, covered the machinery hill and agronomy areas, and reported on the most powerful and latest soil technologies emerging through satellite imagery and tracking. I judged the Pork Queen contest and voted for a great-looking girl, but she lost. After looking at the scoring sheets, the rest of the judges picked another girl. It appeared like a rigged pick for a prominent local farmer.

Fairfax Hay Days had an idyllic Independence Day celebration with turtle races, big wheel races for the tots, hay bale tosses for the men, which I participated in as a WMT representative, miniature rodeo bronco rides, and roping for elementary kids using sheep; showing pigs and cattle, and all the fanfare of a small Iowa farming village.

There was a huge street dance with hundreds of farm kids and adults, young and old. My Kirkwood friends and some staff from WMT came down, and we drank a lot of beer and danced. I never had to buy a beer or a brat as they were always purchased for me by farmers and others who saw me as a WMT celebrity. I kept up with the best of them in the bale toss and helped my team win a tug-of-war contest. It was so much fun and right up my alley as a farm kid, and I was having a blast.

My news reporting on the Fairfax Hey Days was a fun entertainment feature that ran more than two minutes, an enormous allotment of time in the broadcast arena on radio, and was aired early Monday morning. It highlighted the emblematic annual celebration of Independence Day in small towns across Iowa. As a feature piece, I was allowed some creativity as long as it surrounded fact-based reporting.

July 4 was more than halfway through my internship already. The summer went much faster as I focused more on my experience with WMT than on Darcy. Though I wanted to see her, I had zero income and barely scraped by. Luckily most of the weeks I was on assignment, I could turn in expenses for my lunch and dinner as I traveled. I ate more Iowa Pork Chops, brats, and fried fair food working at WMT than my entire life. McDonald's was my second kitchen, and my meals back at the apartment mainly were Cheerios and enough chocolate milk that I should have had my own cow and Hershey's factory.

Once again, because the money I'd earn from the scholarship would be paid at the end of the internship, going to Minneapolis was simply financially out of the question; besides, I was never invited by her, which was another thing that seemed odd to me. Hopefully, it was because she knew it was a hardship for me to come. Still, maybe it was because we hadn't traveled far enough in our relationship to spend a weekend together. Or…still, maybe she had that boyfriend at home. Whatever the reason, none of them felt good.

July 4 through the first week of August flew by in a blink. It was my privilege to experience the WMT crew. The farm broadcasters were leaders in their field, and Jerry Passer was a countrywide respected icon. He held stature within his field. WMT was considered the premier farm station throughout Iowa and neighboring states, and their farmers listened if the radio waves were within their reach. These guys were the Gods of the Farm news. WMT hired only the best.

Rich was always steady and unwavering. Jerry too, but Jerry, as good as he was, had a way about him that was kind of cocky, kind of showy, and good at self-promoting. He was good at and loved what he did and would let it be slyly known at times. In Iowa, the guy was "The Farm Broadcaster."

Chuck was a youngster in the field, trying his best and suited due to his good looks and personality for the TV side of the news.

My experience with WMT was terrific. It was a vast maturing and practical experience. Rich Balvanz and Jerry Passer met with me on my last day as an intern. Chuck Shaleen was gone on an assignment. We discussed my summer and reviewed some of my material. Rich was such a gentleman and gently critiqued my work with suggestions for improvements and helped steer me toward understanding what the audience wanted to hear. I debated with them that while the audience wanted to hear specific facts and daily reports like the futures markets in corn, beans, and pork bellies, they should also hear good and bad news about policy that affects them. They agreed that national or state policy news against farming should be aired and was aired so the farming community and their constituents could amass and try to alter policy in their favor. Our styles differed! I shared disappointment that some of my material was edited out because of listener complaints who disagreed with the facts.

At times listeners would call the station on some of my news reports with vehement disagreement. My news reporting wasn't editorial; it was fact-based and mostly pulled off the AP Wire Service, yet it was edited to satisfy some of the big advertisers on the station. Companies like Monsanto paid these guys' salaries and made the station profits. There would be no news about their product contaminating drinking water wells or Environmental Protection Agency findings. WMT was the "farmers" station and reported what the farmers "wanted" to hear and worse what its "advertisers" wanted to hear. It discouraged me. I told them that only what an audience wanted to hear went 100 percent against my journalism ethics class with Dr. Boyd at ISU. As a journalist, I'd been taught to report good or bad, liked or not, but factual news.

As my summer progressed and my material became closely watched and edited after a few airings brought controversy, I reluctantly succumbed to the mandates. I decided to air a piece of news from the AP Wire Service that farmers would love to hear. It was backed with USDA statistics about how farm incomes have risen in the past couple of years, particularly in the heartland. I wrote a positive news story and aired it live at the noon broadcast from a county fair I covered. It'd be great for farmers to hear some positive factual news and know their incomes are finally going up after years and years of suppression.

The station's response from the audience was overwhelmingly adverse, complaining that my news piece couldn't be accurate because farmers haven't seen proof of income rises in their pockets. Farmwives and farmers across Iowa called to let the station know this kid from ISU didn't know what he was talking about. The economy in 1981 was challenging, and Iowa farmers didn't want that kind of news on the airwaves, or it might jeopardize the farm subsidies they received from the government. After that last piece, WMT's general manager warned Jerry Passer he'd better review and edit every article I was writing and reporting in the future. No more live reports came from me without turning in my stories for review. He edited them heavily down to nothingness at times. My future reporting became feature news assignments rather than news.

I reviewed this experience with Jerry in that it was a huge disappointment to see that censorship in journalism existed at the micro-level of our nation. It was all about money, ad money for the stations, and farmer support. I understood their livelihoods depended upon it, but my professors at ISU, Dr. Boyd and others, taught us pure journalism. The kind that the Des Moines Register wins Pulitzer Prize awards for. Isn't that the whole point of freedom of the press? Freedom to tell the truth? To report the facts, and let people become educated enough about them to intelligently discuss and debate?

That part of my internship experience was frustrating to me. I could only imagine how, if the dollars at a small regional station like WMT were so crucial as to suppress the facts and provide censorship, what might it be like at ABC, NBC, or CBS world news?

As we concluded our discussions together, Jerry said, "Curt, I don't think you'll ever be a farm broadcaster."

"Really, why?" I asked.

"I don't know, Curt, but I just don't think you have it to be a farm broadcaster."

"You're probably right. Especially if it means I have to succumb to only those news stories that paint the picture of a farmer as a poor, abused, unappreciated member of our society to protect the billions of tax subsidies they receive, well then, that's not the career for me."

The most significant takeaway from that internship was that it taught me how a broadcast piece 30 seconds long could only portray a part of a story, precisely 30 seconds of it or less… whatever part you wanted it to show. There was little room for full disclosure and explanation in any broadcast reporting. It was impossible to share all of the facts to a story, and very easy to put a slant on it one way or another if the reporter wished.

We concluded our session, and he explained that a $2,500.00 check would be sent to Iowa State University to help pay my following semester's tuition expenses. I thanked them all for the opportunity and experience they provided, and I headed to New York for a visit home before returning to ISU.

On the long drive back to New York, I pondered the conversations in my exit interview with WMT. Jerry Passer said he didn't think I'd ever be a farm broadcaster. While it was a little unnerving to hear another person in my life telling me what I wouldn't be, I couldn't see myself talking about pork bellies and cattle futures for the rest of my life either. I also couldn't see myself working on the road all the time and reporting news, perhaps in the evenings when I might have a family I wanted to be home for in the future. I was grateful for the experience and Jerry's forthrightness. I knew it wasn't meant to hurt me, but I felt slightly disappointed; who wouldn't? While he couldn't identify what he saw me doing, his comments and assessment were clear about what he saw me not doing. So far in my career choices, I was finding out what I wouldn't be. Weirdly it was progress! I steadily discovered what I didn't want and moved and adapted toward what I liked.

There was one thing I knew for sure I liked and wanted, despite many misgivings and unknowns about her, I knew I wanted a second chance with

Darcy. When one of the Kirkwood girls seduced me after returning from an afternoon of swimming at the Coralville Reservoir, I slipped into submission only to stop the action while it was still lukewarm in its tracks, explaining to her that I loved another girl and was saving myself for her.

From New York, I talked with Darcy on the phone, and she told me her dad would be driving her down to ISU using his Ford van. I asked what color it was as I'd look out for it and help her move in. "It's brown; that would be great!" she said. I'll see you in a couple of days.

Chapter Thirty-Six
Second Chance

Darcy walks past the ISU Campanile on a return trip in 2020.

August 1981
Playlist:
Running on Empty, Jackson Brown
Falling, Lenny LeBlanc

Back at ISU, I unloaded my bags of clothes into the same dorm room I had the year before. I went to Darcy's room, but she hadn't arrived yet. I couldn't wait to see her. I spent most of the day helping first-year students and others from my house move in. Eventually, I saw the light brown Ford van from the fire escape stairs at the end of our hall, which we regularly used to enter and exit. I watched the van pull around the square; it had Minnesota license plates on it and stopped near the doors of Freeman Hall. I hadn't met Darcy's parents yet, so I had no idea what they looked like. From the driver's seat emerged a short blond man with curly hair. He moved to the back of the van and opened the doors. As he began to pull bags out of the truck, there she was. Darcy emerged from the side door and picked up some bags. I leaped down the fire escape and rushed over.

Hi Darcy, I greeted her and welcomed her enthusiastically. Hi Curt! I didn't warmly approach her as her parents were there, but she approached me and hugged me. Her dad eyed me the whole time. Curt, this is my Dad. "Nice to meet you, Mr. Hoff," and this is my mom, "Hello Curt, I'm Betty; it's nice to meet you in person rather than just on the phone," she said with a warm smile.

"Nice to meet you both. Can I lend a hand?" I offered, "Sure," said Mr. Hoff, "help me grab this desk out of here."

"Sure thing. And call me Bob." he insisted. As Bob and I unloaded and carried the heavier items into Darcy's dorm room, he pulled out his tools and assembled her bed loft. Betty and Darcy moved the lighter things in, like her clothes, food, and other small accessories, and I assisted with those as well.

It didn't take us long to unload, and then I asked if I could be of any more assistance; since it mainly was organizing and packing clothes into drawers and closets, I left them and returned to assist other house members moving in. Though brief, it was nice to meet Darcy's parents; they seemed very nice.

Around noon, Darcy came over and asked if I would join her and her parents for lunch. She told me her dad would like to buy me lunch for the help I gave them. I told her I appreciated that, but it wasn't necessary, and I'd pass. Darcy said they were going to Hickory Farm Park, a local restaurant famous for its barbecue, one that I was seldom able to afford. Darcy nudged me with her eyes and said, "Come on, I'd like you to meet my parents again." I accepted, and she took my hand and walked me back to the van. Suddenly, some of my insecure feelings about us all summer, the distance in our relationship, the hallway kiss, and the unknowns, had lifted like a weight off my shoulder. *Yes!* I thought to myself, *a second chance at this relationship.* Indeed, there was something real there after all.

Bob's work van had no rear seating, we both hopped through the side door and sat on a blanket dusty with sawdust. Her mom Betty turned and made some small talk as Bob drove us to the edge of town to Hickory Farm Park. It was only the fourth set of parents I'd met from girls I had dated. Darcy's dad had such tight curly blonde hair for a man in his early 50s, and her mom had short blonde hair. Darcy told me he'd gotten a perm! I'd never met a man before who'd gotten a perm! It seemed an oddity to me. At the restaurant they were both delightful and encouraged me to order what I wanted.

At first introduction, Bob's unusually curly hair made me think he was an artist or musician. I had curly hair too, but his curls were long-stranded and tight…the kind you get from a perm. I quickly learned he was a cabinet maker and had a shop with several guys working for him. Betty worked in the credit department of a family business called Bachman's. They asked me where I grew up and what my parents did, and I was pretty short, tight-lipped, and quiet. Partly because I didn't want to share much about them and partly because I was still a New Yorker, and culturally New Yorkers don't ask many personal questions about each other. There are reasons for it, many family business reasons, and those questions about one's occupation seemed a little too nosy. I tried to get them to ask about my summer at Cedar Rapids instead. Still they were curious and persistent about the family questions parents like to ask their daughter's new suitor.

Lunch was delicious, the best meal I'd had all summer except for some Iowa Pork Chops, and I offered to pay my way. Bob and Betty insisted on picking up the lunch tab. They indicated they were heading back to Minnesota after lunch, and I learned it was about a three-hour ride. At least now I knew where Minnesota was!

After lunch, they dropped us off at Richardson Court Association in front of Freeman Hall; Darcy's parents exited the van and embraced her warmly and long as they said goodbye. It positively struck me. I wasn't sure why, but it seemed like a genuine, long embrace of love that I hadn't seen or experienced in a long while. Darcy then turned to me and said, "Thanks for all you've done to help," and kissed me on the cheek. I'm sure Darcy's parents took that kiss as a sure sign their daughter was interested in the boy from New York.

I shook their hands and thanked them for lunch again, they thanked me for the help I gave them, and they drove away. As they exited the RCA court, we waved goodbye again. "I have a lot of unpacking yet to do, but how about a walk around campus after dinner," she asked. "Sure thing. Is there anything else I can help you with?"

"Nope, I just need to organize some more clothes and stuff; come and get me around seven, OK?" I smiled and said, "great, I'll see you then."

It was already three in the afternoon. I'd helped many of my dorm mates move their bunks and beds in with the adrenaline of anticipating seeing Darcy. I was in a different mood now—one of peace, content, and hope.

The campus dairy barns were a couple of miles to the other side of town, just past the Towers dormitories. While Darcy continued to organize, I walked up to the dairy barns. In the barns, I always found comfort. I discovered them during my first week at Iowa State as I immediately looked for work. As I walked, I rehashed my tormented summer's thoughts about Darcy, my insecurity, and my doubts there might be anything between us.

None of the cows were in the barn. They were all grazing in the field. I walked in front of the stalls with my hand extended, lightly tapping each post as I passed. The smell of cows was refreshing; it reminded me of my most peaceful home; though I never slept in the barn at the King Dairy, it was still home. The home of sanity! And when I needed that inner peace and comfort at ISU, I'd come to the dairy barns and find it there too.

I arrived at Darcy's room at seven and not a minute late. It was a beautiful August evening; her roommate had arrived and was unpacking. She didn't live far from Ames and only traveled from Des Moines. She was wise to avoid all the moves in the rush of lined-up students and their dads' pickup trucks.

Darcy and I walked across campus to Dugan's Deli and got a Big Mother sandwich, one of our favorites. As we sat in Dugans eating our sandwiches, I began sharing more of my summer experiences with Darcy. I'd already heard plenty about hers on the phone calls between us, and it was my turn to pour out the many adventures I was lucky to partake in.

As I made her laugh about judging the dairy and pork queens, she joked that there were a few new queens in her dormitory this semester but, as always, followed up on one of her witty thoughts with a sincere "I'm just kidding." Darcy loved everyone and appreciated everybody. Nearly two and a half hours had passed, and I had Darcy laughing and admiring what I had done during most of the summer. She told me she had a great summer, but nothing like mine. Her activity mainly centered around playing golf on the weekends and waterskiing with the neighborhood guys after work hours. And for some reason, she went out of her way to finally tell me who they were, that they were just friends and nothing more.

We finished our pops and walked back across campus, following a path toward Fridley Hall and the pond where Lance and Elaine, the ISU swans, resided. I was so happy to see her, and she seemed excited to see me back at ISU. I was looking toward falling for her again, giving myself that second chance. As we walked, I continued to share more of my experiences.

Chapter Thirty-Seven
Clues

The children of Brookwood Hall
Loretta is pictured first from the left in the second row from the top.

Fall 1981
Playlist:
I've Never Been To Me, Charlene
Being With You, Smokey Robinson
Woman, John Lennon
Every Little Thing She Does is Magic, The Police
Can You Feel It, The Jacksons
Happy Xmas, John Lennon
Good Thing Going, Sugar Minott
Step By Step, Eddie Rabbit
Memory, Andrew Webber Lloyd, Elane Paige

It was our junior year, and Darcy and I settled into our classes quickly. She had some essential design labs where she spent hours and hours in the design studio working on solo and group-related projects. I was busy too with my classes and back at the Hawkeye hog farm in-between classes and weekends trying to nourish my bank account and pay my bills. Since high school, I have had a small piece of paper in my wallet with my goals written on it. Every day I took them out and read them to myself and in my prayers. The paper was a simple four-inch by two-inch which I folded into a triangle much like a paper football. Depending on the year's goals (or years), I would list one in each triangle. Each had a task or plan that I had to accomplish to attain the ultimate goal, which I placed at the top of the list.

In high school, my goals changed often. Sometimes from month to month, depending on my need and what my home life was developing into. But since attending Cobleskill, I listed my longest-term goals on top and short-term tasks and goals to get there beneath. My ultimate goal at the top was the number 40, representing forty million bucks by forty years of age. The remaining goals were steps I thought I would need to achieve the main goal, like the letters BS for a bachelor's degree in one and the Letters DF for a dairy farm in the other and others like a certain number of dollars in the bank each month to get through school or books, and each triangle had a dollar number equivalent to the goal and a date to attain it. On the reverse side, I would place short notes that reinforced in my mind what I had to do to accomplish them. The triangle reminded me constantly of my triune God. I never felt alone.

It was hard to put in a full day at Hawkeye Hogs farm. I wasn't meeting my short-term financial goals because of my class schedule, so I asked Bob if he had any flexible work that I could perform which didn't require me to be onsite for standard hours for such tasks as castrating piglets and caring for the sows in the farrowing house. It was a massive operation, and I saw plenty of opportunities to work on various tasks with flexible hours.

I'd only worked for Bob for one semester, but he found me worthy enough to hire me back, and after my suggestions, he offered me two flexible tasks. The first was if I could be on the farm site anytime during the day and on Saturdays before the co-op closed in Randal, I was to take a tandem wheeled grain wagon to the elevator, fill it with corn, return to the farm and empty it into the grain elevator on the farm. He told me I could do that all day on Saturdays, and if I had two to four hours a day during the week, that would be my job for the semester. I could perform the task anytime the co-op hours were open, and I should continue to do it until he told me to stop. So that is what I did. It was about an hour and fifteen minutes round trip for each wagon load of corn. Three days a week, I was able to make three to four round trips, and on Saturdays, I could perform seven or eight if I arrived on the farm at 6 am and got the first load from the elevator by 6:45 am.

It was a mundane job, but the giant dual-wheeled John Deer Tractor with a heated cab made fall and winter work comfortable. I continued to haul load after load until the spring semester when my schedule changed, and Bob assigned me other tasks in the blocks of hours I could work.

Darcy and I saw each other almost every day, not for long periods, but just for short visits before or after dinner and sometimes to study. We never ate dinner together in the dorm cafeteria. It was still a ritual that you had dinner with your housemates.

We established a steady weekend dating ritual of going to the Fox Lounge. There was always some dorm party to go to, and she still seemed to require some girl time with her friends at the guy's houses they were invited to. I had to accept that whether I liked it or not. I understood social pressure as our house was always asked to go somewhere. I was a little older at 22, and those dorm parties were waning for me. I participated, but none of them or any other party did I find anyone I was interested in. While I would dance with some girls, hang with my buddies and have a few beers, not the prettiest girl on the dance floor could keep me staring. My eyes were for Darcy only. She captivated my being.

As the semester continued, Darcy and I grew into ever deeper conversations about each other's dreams for the future. She was solid on her dreams as a commercial interior designer, as I once and still considered my dreams of owning a super large dairy farm one day. As we talked and explored each other's possibilities, we found each other bending our potential careers to adjust to the other in a theoretical chance that we might have a future together.

As our love grew, so did my bank account. I'd occasionally surprise Darcy with dinner at Aunt Maude's on Main Street, an upscale restaurant for my budget. Dinner there was always special and romantic as the tables were draped with white linens and lit with candles.

She expressed her love for me in those conversations saying she would sacrifice some of her dreams to be together. The more we discussed our potential future careers. I learned how strongly she desired to be in the design field, and the more I doubted that she'd ever be able to accomplish her dreams with me on a farm. As we talked about the possibility of me farming and being in a rural area, I'd tell her I wasn't sure she'd be able to achieve her dream. She was always emphatic that she'd find a way to fulfill it and convinced both our dreams could be achieved.

I couldn't see Darcy being happy in a rural community. Divorce, I thought, would be imminent. It was not an option for me. I came from parents and siblings who divorced for one reason or another. I couldn't see Darcy being happy on a farm.

I wanted her to achieve her dreams and knew we would have to live near some significant metropolitan city for her to accomplish them. So, as I took new journalism classes in advertising and public relations, I also began exploring career choices in those fields. While I deeply loved farming, I was willing to examine corporate experiences. Growing up I hadn't been exposed to white-collar professionals besides seeing our high school principal, his secretaries, and the Pope behind their desks.

Our fall semester was closing in fast. Thanksgiving break separated us for a week, and before I left again for New York for Christmas break, I wrapped her dorm door in Christmas paper. I left her twelve notes giving clues as to where and how we'd spend the twelve days of Christmas together before we each went home. Each day I had a small gift for her, which I sat with her as she opened, and a clue about where we'd spend just an hour together around the campus community. Just a break, I convinced her. Most of my gifts were small and inexpensive, with a message of appreciation or humor to make her laugh. I always loved to make her laugh.

On the twelfth day, I gave her a small stone heart. It was a paperweight. It was a subliminal message that I had solid thoughts and feelings for her. I had written her a note in the Christmas Card I gave her, expressing my feelings and telling her I loved her in print for the first time. She smiled and assured me she knew I loved her already from my many actions. She told me she loved me too. We kissed, and then I asked her to dance. We were at the Fox Lounge.

A week later, we each went home for our Christmas break. Back in Spencer, I made the rounds to see Mr. Hansen and his family, the King family, the Duke, his mom, and dad, and I went down to the barn and sat in my car. I whispered my prayers in Comets sanctuary and prayed for the new year to be as successful as the last. As I always had, no matter how miserable she made my life, I prayed for Loretta too. She seemed unimaginably depressed and sorrowful. While there were no crazy episodes while I was home, her heart was obviously enormously heavy and broken. She was still deeply grieving over the loss of my brother Gary now more than a year after his death.

As usual, I'd find her sobbing at her desk every morning. I tried to talk with her about some of the letters she wrote me in college. They were hurtful and troubling. There seemed to be hints about her secretive past with her mourning and grieving for more than just my brother Gary, perhaps also her first son Robert. But she wouldn't go into any conversations about the past. It was more apparent than ever that the past held something very dark and emotionally troubling which wore on her. When she wasn't around, I'd glance down at her desk and see what she might have been reading or writing to gather some clues. She kept a journal though I never dared to look at it lest I be caught. Her first son Robert and the three baby pictures she always kept in the upper left corner under the glass top were still there. But she added another photo to the grouping now. She added Gary. Robert and Gary were deceased; I wondered about the three babies she always claimed were some friend's kids. There had to be more to know about those kids in that grouping than she told us. Could there be some connection with those kids that created the angst, misery, sorrow, depression, and dysfunction in Loretta's life, just as the pictures of her two dead sons had? Christmas holidays were always an exceedingly sorrowful time for her.

Chapter Thirty-Eight
The Forty-Million-Dollar Girl

Fall 1981
Playlist:
I Can't Go for That, Daryl Hall and John Oates
Waiting for a Girl Like You, Foreigner
Jealous Guy, Roxy Music Street Life
Under Pressure, Queen
Lately, Stevie Wonder
Souvenir, Orchestral Maneuvers In The Dark
How 'Bout Us, Champaign
Keep On Loving You, REO Speedwagon
Really Want to Know You, Gary Wright
No Woman, No cry, Bab Marley and The Wailers
Watching The Wheels, John Lennon
Cool Love, Pablo Cruise

I Made It Through the Rain, Barry Manilow
While You See A Chance, Steve Winwood
Ain't Even Done With The Night, John Mellencamp
Stop Draggin My Heart Around, Stevie Nicks
Time, Alan Parsons Band
Take It On The Run, REO Speedwagon
The One That You Love, Air Supply
Love On The Rocks, Neil Diamond
Hold On Tight, Electric Light Orchestra
Hard To Say I'm Sorry, Chicago

Finished with my Christmas break in New York, I picked up my ride-paying passengers and headed back to Iowa State. I was only gone for two weeks and was missing a girl in a way I'd never felt. She was something new and different than the rest. I missed our daily chat, dropping in on her for a few minutes to say hi. I missed our Friday and Saturday nights out.

ISU was switching over from the quarter system to semesters. Many classes I scheduled to take took on new names, number designations, and a lot more material crammed into one category to discover. Darcy was like that; there was a lot packed into that tiny package, so much to find and uncover.

January and February were slothful months for me. Work on the hog farm was frigidly cold, and I was now spending most days outside of classes spreading manure on the frozen cornfields. Tank after tank after tank, I'd fill from the pits beneath the hog barns where their feces fell through slotted floors. The smell was heavy with ammonia, and whereas in the fall or early spring, we would inject the manure into the soil, with the ground frozen now it could only be spread on top.

February 14th was my second Valentine's Day with Darcy. I decorated her door with giant hearts and balloons and planned a special evening with her.

I relived last year's Valentine's Day for a moment. We had only known each other for a few months, and she had many cards and flowers in her room. From whom, and for whom I wasn't sure at the time. They could have been hers; some could have been her roommates. I asked her for a Valentine's date dinner, and she accepted but only for a late-night dinner. She was awkwardly honest that she had a previously scheduled event at 5 pm and wouldn't be available until seven or 7:30. At the time, I thought she had a lab or some other school commitment. She said she was sorry at the time but couldn't break the engagement. Her honesty about the event kept me from popping over unexpectantly, as I had been doing more often.

Thinking her engagement was a school function; I was thrilled she accepted my invitation and glad to have her for the rest of the evening. As any Valentine's Day date conversation might be a little awkward, ours was for sure, and she didn't eat much of her dinner. That raised suspicions that her previous engagement might have been a dinner date. Darcy always chowed down her dinner on a date as she hated the dorm food. I asked her how her prior engagement had gone, and she looked suspiciously at me as if I knew something. Darcy came clean with a few more details and explained that a guy friend had asked her out for dinner before me. She was kind enough to tell me that had she known I would ask her out, she wouldn't have accepted the other guys' proposal but couldn't cancel. I tried not to look disappointed as it was an awkward, nervous admission for her as much as it was for me hearing it.

I quickly rehashed what I had heard from Darcy that day. Someone else in her previous or maybe current boyfriend life at the time, maybe in retrospect, the Hallway Kisser preceded me in asking her out as she said, and she accepted, not knowing I would ask her out.

It was gratifying that she was honest at the time, and the term "guy friend" sounded much better than the term "boyfriend." I didn't inquire with any more of the questions in my head like was he a guy friend here at ISU or a boyfriend from home who traveled three hours to see her. We had no commitments to each other then, and while I was certainly curious, I just moved on to enjoy the date with her. But that hallway kiss had me rehashing that first Valentine's Day date last year too.

This Valentine's Day was different. Her room wasn't full of flowers as in the past, and the only Valentine's card she received from any boy was from me. At least I thought so as this year the only visible one in her room was from me. It was a Sunday, and as had become a weekly Sunday morning routine, I walked with her to church.

The pastor's message focused on the love between a man and a woman, husband and wife. He spoke of the most romantic book in the bible, The Book of Solomon. King Solomon was a busy King, he had 700 royal wives and 300 concubines, and his claim to fame is that he wrote a song of love that focused on only "one" true love. Scholars think he wrote the song about his first wife.

While he had sexual privileges with all these women, his song extolled the virtues of his love and affection for one true love. The pastor's message echoed how having one strong true love could be lifelong and enduring even for King Solomon with all his privileges.

After the sermon, there was always a quiet prayer time, and I reached over and held Darcy's hand as we silently prayed. I prayed and asked my God to have Darcy as my wife, my one true enduring love, and asked how to go about it. Darcy and I were seeing each other regularly.

I made a reservation at Aunt Maude's restaurant for this year's dinner early evening, bought her some roses and a bottle of Mateus that we could drink after dinner, and gave her a heart-shaped box of chocolates. She appreciated the chocolates but told me in a friendly way that in the future, please don't spend my hard-earned money on chocolates as she doesn't like them. Again, an honest girl, but more importantly, I latched on to a critical set of words that held promise for me "in the future."

For the second time on a card, I wrote the words I love you, and I told her so. Darcy gleamed at me with her smile and eyes and told me she loved me too. She appreciated me decking out her door and told me how sweet it was. At dinner, we made a lot of small talk about this and that, and Darcy focused and expressed how busy she was with all of her projects and needed to get back to one after dinner.

The semester so far was one giant adjustment for me. I enjoyed my new classes in advertising and marketing, but everything seemed long and not moving fast enough. It could be the change to semesters from quarters. It may be something else? Darcy was ever-present at her design studios working on projects, and I was restless in that our time together seemed a bit short, even for Valentine's day.

A couple of weeks after, and as usual, I would drop by her dorm room to say hello. This time, however, out of the clear blue sky, she snapped at me and told me she needed a little space. I was caught surprised! She needed a little time for herself, she insisted.

Taken aback, I assumed I might have been overbearing, but how I pondered. I put in nearly 65 hours a week between working and my classes. I was as busy as she and just as stressed, but I'd never orally brushed her off the way she just did to me. A year ago, I could have done so with the Hallway

Kisser. Though I did brush her off with my absence of visits, she never heard a word about it from my lips.

I offered a self-sentenced verdict that I had been visiting too much. Maybe Darcy just wanted to see me on weekends? Or perhaps she didn't want to see me at all. "OK," I said. "well, I enjoyed my time with you, and I guess I just wanted a little more time. It's Friday night, and I was coming over to see if you wanted to go to the Fox or get a pizza from the pit or something… but I'll back off."

She sighed. "You know I just need a little time, OK? And tonight, I'm going to a party in Willow with the girls. I need a little time."

I thought to myself, *Bull-crap.* It was time to grow up and out of the dorm parties. I simply wanted more time with a girl I fell in love with, and she was now sending mixed signals. I felt played.

My heart sank to my knees. I wasn't sure what "a little more time" really meant. Did Darcy need time to rethink our relationship? What exactly, or whom did she need a little time away from me for? I was finally sharing in small and more direct ways that I loved her; maybe that sharing scared her off. I wondered why she needed to go to a dorm party. It was a living, breathing dancing catalog of mate selection! After all, that's how she met me!

I just stood there and gazed at her with astonishment at what she just said, and I'm sure disappointment was smitten all over my embarrassed face. I didn't ask her to explain. That's the way it was with me, always. My subconscious wouldn't allow me to question; I sucked it up, buried it, and moved on.

In my childhood, anytime I asked for an explanation on a matter in the home, I was told it was none of my business. And if I pushed for one, I'd be admonished, condemned, and sentenced to the streets. We kids learned to avoid the smell of trouble and disappointment that was ever present and common in our house. If we didn't, we'd get shut down.

In our relationship, I'd discovered Darcy to be a strong personality. Her directness in this matter left me wondering if she was breaking up our relationship or just needed a little space, as she said. Something was fundamentally changing inside me in that, for once, I wanted to demand an explanation! I felt a little outraged but pushed it down in silence as usual.

This time I almost burst and wanted a definition of what she meant by a little more time as she just left me hanging without an explanation other than that she wanted to go to a dorm party instead of out with me.

To hell with it, I thought! I didn't bother to ask or inquire any further for fear of an argument or, even worse, fear of more rejection. We'd never fought, never. It was a Friday night, and while I was looking forward to hanging with her, perhaps going to the Fox, she wasn't and had other plans. She needed some time without me around. How long, one night? Ten nights? Eternity? I didn't deserve this ambiguity.

I had a colossal gulp in my throat as I stood before her. I said nothing more and walked away. I'd learned from childhood to move away from confrontation. It never seemed to solve anything when two people angrily confronted each other in anger. In our house, it always exploded into insanity.

Walking away and burying it was one thing, but this time there was something very different about my feelings of rejection. I was invested in Darcy. She had entered my soul. Her ambiguity of "time" wasn't fair.

I couldn't see where or how I had failed or offended Darcy as I traced through our relationship thus far. I put myself on trial and questioned myself to see what I'd done wrong. Maybe I just needed to stay away as I'd done before. I'd stay away until she came back if she came back. But this was different; it was a direct pushback aimed at me.

I still wanted answers. Then I got a hair-brained idea that I would go to the same party. If I found her with a guy, I'd confront her dishonesty, and that would be it. I'd move on for good. I got immature in my thoughts; if she were dancing and hanging on a guy all evening, I'd let her know with my presence and do the same. I was feeling insane. I hung out on the fire escape for about an hour. It was an early spring night; I could see my breath as I exhaled. I saw Darcy and a few of her housemates begin walking toward the Maple Willow Larch residences. I knew Darcy by her light tan ski jacket, draping just above her waist. I loved that jacket because it exposed her cute figure and her "epic butt" as her best friend Janice called it. I waited till they were a block away, and then I followed. I stayed about 30 to 50 yards back and pulled my sweatshirt hoody over my head. I could hear the girls laughing. Darcy participated as I heard her teasing the other girls. How could she be so go-lucky and happy, I wondered after dropping me to my knees an hour or so ago? It agitated me even more.

They all entered the Maple Willow Larch dormitory. The co-ed houses were separated by the bathrooms and elevators in the middle of the floor. They were the only ones on campus and new that semester. Along with the semester transition, ISU was adapting to changing times, experimenting with co-ed houses.

I managed to roam around the party, staying obscure from any of the Bussee Babes. I also avoided chatting with girls so I could easily escape to the other half of the floor if I might be vulnerable to being spotted. Recognizing my immaturity at this but wanting assurances I wouldn't find her with a guy, the last thing I'd want Darcy to know was that I was spying on her. Especially after she just lectured me on giving her some space and time.

As the party ensued, a guy appeared to be asking Darcy to dance on several occasions, but she gestured a refusal. One brought her a beer, but I never saw her take a sip. Darcy was always cautious at parties we attended and never drank a drink she'd left alone nor one that someone else had gotten for her unless it was from me. She heard guys sometimes slip date rape drugs in the drinks they'd buy for girls. Her housemates took up the guys' requests and danced. Why wasn't she dancing, I wondered. She loved to dance. She just hung out with a couple of the girls and chatted most of the time they were there. Darcy and two other girls didn't stay more than an hour, and they left. I thought they would go to another party, probably a frat party, so I followed them again. They went home!

There was nothing. No boyfriend, no other guy, she didn't even dance with any of them.

I felt guilty for spying, but I couldn't remain ignorant this time if there was another guy. I had been through that torture of temporary insanity and depression before over the Hallway Kisser. While I had never mentioned a word to her about it, this time would be different if I discovered another relationship, even if it were just "a guy friend."

Our relationship had evolved into much more than just dating. As couple, we'd come a long way and I let her into my soul. If a guy was involved, I wanted to know positively.

I didn't see Darcy for a couple of days until she came to my room the following Wednesday night. My door was open, and as she walked into my room, she jokingly said, "When I said I needed a little space, I didn't mean that you shouldn't come and visit me! Silly boy!"

I was still in a sulky mood, and I just shook my head and said, "I was just giving you what you want."

She grabbed my shoulders, leaned over, and said, "Curt, I love you. I'm sorry for the other day. Let's discuss this and plan our weekly time together this weekend. I'm just under a lot of pressure with these projects. We'll go out and plan it, OK?"

I nodded yes and asked, "When, Friday or Saturday night?"

She looked at me and said, "Friday… and Saturday after studies!"

I didn't see Darcy for the rest of the week. I stayed away. When Friday came, she invited me to go to the design center and study as she worked on her drafting. We usually always studied till about nine o'clock before going out on the weekends. I appreciated her invitation and joined her at the design center, but I could tell that would never work for her or me. She was doing something with her hands, able to stand at the drafting table while I had to sit and read and work on problems. I could never sit still studying for more than a half-hour without getting up and moving around or try another location. And my movement in the design studio wouldn't only bother her but other design and architect majors working there too. Ten o'clock came, and we packed it up to head out to the Fox Lounge.

We talked through the necessity of time for her to complete her projects. Darcy explained the kind of pressure she's had and that if she got these projects right and perfect with A grades, she could use them in her portfolio to share in job interviews after college. She also explained that one of her professors, kindly referred to by many design students as the "witch," loaded project upon project on her students and expected perfection in an unreasonable amount of time. She was teaching them real work-life expectations.

Darcy's drafting and design boards would be displayed at the end of the semester before everyone, including professors and students, to be viewed and judged. This event was a big deal to Darcy, and I now understood more about her anxiety. I had a new empathy for her, and I was also relieved, so relieved to know that I hadn't done anything wrong.

As her boyfriend, I was a certain number of minutes within each of her days, but I wasn't everything. "Darcy, I've fallen in love with you, I said. I just wanted some more time in our relationship." She understood. She had a look on her face that said she was exploring where she could give me more time. As a rarity in our relationship, I pressed her a little more. "I also didn't understand the trade for time with me for a dorm party?" I asked. "Oh, I'm done with the dorm parties," she explained. "It was just about having some time with my girlfriends." She told me about the party she (and I) went to at Willow and that it wasn't the same for her anymore. She found them boring. "I'm looking forward to moving off campus next year." she said. I agreed with saying, "Me too." We both had plans to move off-campus in our senior year.

I asked her to dance. We held our bodies close, and I felt the genuine closeness of the girl I'd come to know and the apologetic comfort of her embrace. I asked Darcy if she wouldn't mind if we picked up a pizza and a bottle of Lancers, our other favorite cheap college wine, and returned to my dorm room. She liked that idea.

Back at the dorm, I turned off all the lights except those in the fish tank. We sat on the couch, chowing down a Pizza Pit pizza, and continued our discussions about the value of time and the short-term goals she had to accomplish, and I admitted I had nothing like the pressures she was under.

My most significant pressure was escaping my housemates, destined to haze me. I apologized if I took up too much of her time. She told me I didn't and again apologized for her actions last weekend. I asked her how I could help, how I could support her. She just asked for my understanding.

My roommate was again back in his hometown, seeing his girlfriend, and I had the room myself. After we'd finished our pizza and felt the effects of the bottle of wine, I stripped down to my underwear and invited Darcy up on my bunk. As we lay kissing and making out, I slipped off her tight jeans and unbuttoned her blouse; I lay on top of her and periodically tried to penetrate through my underwear and her panties gently. I still did not carry condoms as I was never active, and Darcy and I had never reached this passion this far into a make-out session. As I caressed her body, my hormones raged with a desire for satisfaction with the sexual sensations I was feeling. I wasn't thinking about right or wrong. I wasn't thinking about anything; I was feeling an urge for Darcy. As our petting intensified, my physical body took complete control of my mind, and I managed to slip past the rim of my underwear and past the side of her panties to penetrate her with two or three thrusts.

Staring at each other with raging emotions but also realizing we'd just passed a boundary, we both froze for a second and then she quickly slid upward to withdraw from me. We had never gone that far together before. She gasped and whispered, "Curt, I love you, but I have to get up early in the morning."

"OK, I understand I said." I lay in bed as I watched her dress. She was still in her panties and blouse, but I could see her beauty in the dim light from the fish tank. I had invited Darcy to stay over before, but she'd never let anyone see her coming from a guy's room or dorm in the morning. That wasn't a reputation she ever wanted. "I love you, Darcy," I said as she finished putting on her coat.

"I love you too, Curt. I'll see you tomorrow. Goodnight."

"Do you want me to walk you back?" I asked. I was still erect, and she probably knew it.

"No, you stay in bed; I'm fine. It's just across the street."

She stepped up on the couch, gave me a goodnight kiss, and said, "I'll see you tomorrow." I lay in bed for the next hour, wondering what she was thinking about now in her bed. Was she cool with this? She seemed to be. Would anything change in our relationship? I was hoping that it did, and made it stronger between us. All that counted for the moment was that I knew she loved me, and I loved this girl. I'd always known she was the one I would marry. Despite episodes of doubt, insecurity, and confusion, I always felt God led me to this girl for marriage. In my prayers, I asked God repeatedly how I obtain this girl's love in marriage.

The following day when I awoke, I showered, dressed, and went to the cafeteria for some oatmeal and coffee. As I ate, I opened my wallet and pulled out my goals sheet to view them and plant them into my subconscious. I pulled a pen from my pocket, scratched out the 40 million dollars from the top triangle, and put Darcy's name there instead; then I neatly folded it, tucked it into my wallet, and went to work.

Chapter Thirty-Nine
The Birthday Commitment

March 11, 1982
Playlist:
Lost In Love, Air Supply
Ride Like the Wind, Christopher Cross
With You I'm Born Again, Billy Preston
Listen to Your Heart, Roxette
Longer, Dan Fogelberg
Annie's Song, John Denver
Yes, I'm Ready, Teri DeSario
Wonderful Tonight, Eric Clapton
Get Closer, Seals, and Crofts
Take It to the Limit, Eagles
Cool Night, Paul Davis
Special Lady, Ray, Goodman and Brown
I Wanna Be Your Lover, Prince
Shining Star, The Manhattans
Peaceful Easy Feeling, Eagles

Darcy's 21st birthday was my second chance to celebrate a birthday with her. This time I asked Darcy what she would like to do for her birthday, and she just asked for a quiet evening with me at the Fox Lounge. Her birthday was on a Thursday, and she reminded me that she had a lot of work on some of her class projects and needed to work on them all the next day, Friday, and the weekend. She didn't want to be up too late.

I had bought her a herringbone gold bracelet with a single diamond mounted on the chain. It was only about 100 bucks then, but that was a fortune for me. I also bought a bottle of her favorite perfume, a pair of her favorite

Calvin Klein jeans, and a light plaid blouse. I wrapped them all and put them in a duffel bag and a bottle of Lancers and Mateus, our two favorite wines. I purchased some cheese, grapes, and crackers. I bought her four cards because they all expressed my thoughts. I wrote something in each of them, sharing my feelings about her, gratitude, appreciation, and love for her. In each card, I told her how much I'd fallen in love with her and expressed that how much I'd learn to love her in many ways.

I also bought two good-sized candles and…a couple of condoms! I packed them with matches and two wine glasses, along with everything else, into the duffle bag. I was determined to assure Darcy that I loved her and wanted her in my life, even though marriage wasn't an option right now. I let her to know I would worship her with my soul and my body. I wanted that communion with her to solidify our love and relationship if she would also.

I did plan a lovely quiet evening as she requested, but not at the Fox Lounge. As my roommate was still in my dorm room on a Thursday night, I anxiously rented perhaps the cheapest motel room in town at the Ames Motor Lodge, and I made a dinner reservation at Aunt Maude's.

Before I picked up Darcy for dinner, I drove to the motel room, put the flowers I bought for her on a table, and set up the bottles of wine along with the glasses, cheese and crackers, and grapes. I put the gifts I bought her on the bed, except for the perfume and cards I took to the restaurant in a small bag.

I picked Darcy up at five, and we went to dinner. We had a glass of wine with our meals at dinner, and I handed each one of the cards separately to her as we chatted. As she read them and what I had to say in each, I saw a smile come across her face. I handed her the wrapped present containing the perfume bottle with the last card, trying to imply that it was the only gift I had for her. She unwrapped it sprayed it on her wrists, and thanked me. Then she read the last card, to which I saw a slight tear come to the corner of her eye. She thanked me again, and I toasted to her, and she reciprocated with a toast to us both.

At dinner, I brought up some of our past conversations and some ambiguity and anxiousness I had had about them at the time.

I told Darcy how much I appreciated her willingness to give and take in her career choices and try to achieve both of our careers. I told her I was willing to try other jobs and put off my farming career, hoping we'd find a life together where we could both achieve our dreams, perhaps close to a metropolitan area where rural farming areas were within driving distance. I let her know that the night we made out and loved, however brief and quick, was a communion and commitment moment for me with her. She agreed it was a special moment for her as well. We finished our dinner, and as we drove down the main street back toward Lincoln Way, I turned left where I would usually turn right. "Where are we going," she asked. "Darcy, I have a few more gifts for you," and I pulled immediately to our right into the motel. The look on her face was definitely with surprise. "Come on," I said, "I know you said you didn't want to be out late, and we don't have to stay, but I have something in the room for you." She looked at me slyly and asked if I had a fish tank in there.

I wanted to consummate our relationship with lovemaking, and I wanted to know if she did too. I didn't want any more doubts, and I didn't want her to have any. The Ames Motor Inn was a remnant motel of the 1950s at the time, but there were only two or three other options in town in 1982, and I couldn't afford them.

I opened the door, and there was a queen bed, a couple of chairs, and a coffee table where I placed the flowers, bottles of wine, candles, and snacks. Darcy looked at me with appreciation and, of course, surprise. Whatever thoughts she had about going back to her room to do some drafting seemed to dissipate. "You're crazy," she said smilingly with appreciation. "You did all this for me? On your tight budget?" That was always something I appreciated about Darcy. She understood my situation and never hinted or had any expectations that I could shower her with flowers or gifts beyond my means. She always appreciated my borrowed tulips from the campus beds versus bouquets from florists.

I had preheated the room, and it was warm. "Come sit here on the bed with me." I lit the candles, poured a glass of wine, and toasted again to her 21st birthday. I placed into her lap my next present, the plaid blouse.

"You are crazy," she said again.

"Yes, I'm crazy over you!"

She loved it. It was a small petite plaid pattern of light tans, light browns, and cream colors. Then I handed her the Calvin Klein jeans, and when she opened them, she said again, "Curt, you're crazy. These are so expensive!"

"Yeah," I joked, "I had no idea how much of a fortune your mother spends on you for those jeans!"

She laughed and appreciatively acknowledged, "Yes… I know." I wasn't sure how many pairs she had, but she wore a couple of them repeatedly, so I thought this would be an appropriate gift.

"I guessed at the size," I said.

She was pleased to have another pair and said, "They're perfect." We sipped wine and ate some cheese and crackers, and reminisced over some of the funniest and crazy dates we had.

Darcy got up, poured us both another glass of wine, and moved to lie on the bed. I pulled the plate of cheese and grapes and spread it between us as we faced each other. As we lay on the bed conversing and snacking, we gently held and caressed each other's hands. When we exhausted our conversation around the day's activities, and there was a pause, I squeezed her hand more firmly and said, "I just want you to know that I love you truly. I meant what I wrote in the cards; I've fallen in love with you. I've discovered a person I want to grow with, and I appreciate and love you, Darcy."

I got up from the bed, pulled out a small box from the bag I had brought, the last birthday present I had for her, and handed it to her. "This isn't much, but it's all I can afford right now," and I gave her the small box containing the bracelet.

She opened it to find a matching gold herringbone bracelet to her necklace. She smiled, leaned over, and kissed me. "Thank you, Curt, this is so thoughtful. It goes great with my necklace."

"Well, the diamond looked a little bigger when I bought it, but it got lost in the mount," I sheepishly said.

"I love it, Curt, thank you."

I poured each of us the remaining wine from the bottle of Mateus. She put the bracelet on and admired it on her wrist. "Why don't you try the jeans and the blouse to ensure they fit?" I suggested light-heartedly. "See if they all go together?" She looked at me rather slyly, took a couple more sips of wine, and said, OK! It wasn't the first time she had undressed before me.

The jeans fit her perfectly. As she slipped on her blouse and buttoned it up, she went to the mirror and admired the clothes and the bracelet looking at it on her wrist through the mirror. I downed my glass of wine and then got up from the bed, and now opened the Lancers bottle of wine and poured myself another glass. Darcy finished hers and said, "I'll take one of those too." I brought her glass, and as I handed it to her, she put it down on the dresser and put her arms around me. She looked into my eyes and said, "Thank you so much; you always seem to make things special; this has been the best birthday." She looked at her bracelet again, "You shouldn't have; I mean, I know how hard you work, so I appreciate your thoughtfulness, so thank you."

We embraced in another kiss, and I placed my glass on the dresser and told her, "You look great in your new blouse and jeans, although you have always looked great!" I said. With another long kiss, I slowly began to unbutton her new blouse. With her blouse open, I reached around her back, unsnapped her bra, and slipped the straps off her shoulders. We both stepped to the bed and turned the remaining light off, leaving only the candles burning. I slipped my shirt off, and we lay on the bed, caressing each other and kissing. I reached down to her jeans, unbuttoned them, and zipped her fly down. I scratched and caressed her stomach from her belly button down to the area just above her vagina, the Bermuda Triangle; then, I slipped off her jeans and panties. I dropped mine off and pulled a condom from my pant pocket so she could see it. I made sure she saw it.

Darcy and I had never wholly made love to each other before. She'd withdrawn in previous attempts, and I knew if she didn't want to go any further this time, she would say so, but she said nothing. I rolled the condom on, and we made love for the first time together. She was 21, and I was 23.

We slept together that night, embraced in each other's arms. We shared our most intimate act of affection. For myself, I was sure now that she was committed to me. I knew her well and knew that going as far as we did was a sure sign that she trusted me and wanted to make a life with me, and she gave me perhaps what she gave no other.

If I had any doubts about our relationship before this night, they were gone completely. Did I fall more in love with her? No, because I was already totally in love. Did she feel more in love with me? I never asked, but I would say the intercourse only occurred because there was already true love between us and an unsaid commitment and implication that she was mine and I was hers exclusively. Sharing our bodies was born from the love that had deeply grown. After nearly two years of dating, the act of intercourse did consummate our relationship in a much deeper feeling of commitment toward eventual marriage. I know we both felt so.

As previously shared, Darcy would never be caught sleeping over in my room, fearing not just a reputation but perhaps allowing herself to be seen committed. Darcy's roommate and close personal friends knew I was taking her out for dinner but, unknown to me; they expected her back as they had some plans of their own to celebrate with her. They waited up late for her return. Of course, she never did. And word spread early and quickly that morning on her dorm floor that she didn't come home.

The following day when I returned to my room at about 8:30, my roommate was up and relatively disgruntled. He usually slept in late as he didn't have early classes. I was always courteous to be quiet as I grabbed my dop kit and clothes and headed down the hall to the shared bathrooms and showers. I asked him why he was up, and he grunted and said, "Could you please tell Darcy's crazy girlfriend not to come over here and perform like she's Julie Andrews?" I had no idea what he was talking about! Still sitting in his underwear on the couch, he explained that one of her friends had come over pounding on the door, singing, "Darcy, Darcy my sunshine, Good morning, Good morning to you, wake up Sunshine. I have a gift for you! It's a bright new day, and you're 21. Good morning, Good morning to you. Wake up, Sunshine; I have a gift for you!"

"It went something like that", he said. "And she just kept at it over and over until I got up, opened the door, put my hand up against the door frame, and asked her if she needed any help. She screamed and ran out the exit!"

I laughed and laughed, visualizing Mark with his ruffled hair standing in the doorway, asking her if he could help her.

Later, when I shared this with Darcy, she confirmed the story and told me it was one of her best friends Linda Lackerman. Knowing Linda's personality, we laughed, even more, visualizing the scene. She was a devout Catholic girl curiously observing some of the looser college activities and indeed wanted to catch Darcy in the act, but to her surprise, we weren't in my dorm room.

Darcy told me that when my roommate opened the door and told her Darcy and I weren't there, she called every hotel and motel in town, trying to find and wake us up. Lackerman, as Linda was lovingly referred to, was the girl who, in the first few weeks of myself scoping Darcy out in the Oak Elm Hall dining room, loudly proclaimed as she and Darcy walked by the table where I sat. "Oh look, Darcy, there's that cute boy from Fairchild, New York; yes, I think they call him New York!" She was always up to some antic, and we all grew to love her for them.

Ironically, she was from an Iowa river town along the Mississippi south of Dubuque named Clinton, actually called "New York" when it was first settled.

Linda and many others from both our houses knew from that night on we were in some way a more committed couple. When Darcy was spoken of in many conversations, the name Curt often followed: Darcy and Curt. We'd become one.

Chapter Forty
Red Badge

Dead Week 1982
The Roberts dorm and Fairchild house where Curt resided at ISU.

Playlist:
Baker Street, Gerry Rafferty
Listen to the Music, The Doobie Brothers
Born To Run, Bruce Springsteen

Dead Week at ISU was where every activity, noise, and college antics subsided. Frat, Sorority, and House parties were not permitted, and quiet and calm were the rule of law for the study week before finals. The dead week was sanctified and reliable. Everything ceased, pranks, noise, everything except the focus on studying for finals and completing lab exercises.

I made it to dead week with a clear head on where Darcy and I stood with each other. I also made it escaping the Fairchild mob numerous times from capturing and hazing me over the Red Badge sanctions levied against me. I felt secure as the quiet week was so honored by everyone and every house.

I was betrayed. On the third day of the week, with my door wide open as I studied for one of my finals, a mob of about 25 Fairchild house members silently crept down the hallway and rushed into my room. As I kicked and fought with three or four of them, knocking stuff all over the room, they dragged me out into the hallway, where more brothers joined in, trying to hold me down to strip me of my clothes. Shouting at them that it was the dead week and they were violating university rules, my hair was grabbed, and duct tape was quickly wound around my head and over my mouth. They didn't care about a quiet week this year! Wrestling and bouncing from one wall to the other and being dragged down the hall on the carpet left me with rug burns all over my arms and upper torso as they managed to pull my shirt off. Kicking and punching my way off them, they smashed my face sideways onto the wall and tried to duct tape my wrists. Then they went after my pants and pulled them off; I wiggled my wrists out from the duct tape and resumed my fight to freedom. Now naked except for my fruit of the looms, my resistance continued acquiring carpet burns bouncing from wall to floor and back again. Punching and wildly swinging my arms, one of the guys hollered for a coat hanger. The next thing I knew, my wrists were wired behind my back with a coat hanger and duct tape on top, binding them together. My ankles were next.

I was read the stupid accusations of my sins against the Red Badge Laws, and a couple of them spat on me for spilling some blood from their noses and lips as I fought for my freedom from their capture. Ten to fifteen of them finally subdue me and reduce me to a bloody mess lying on the floor, gagged and hog-tied with coat hangers. After a half-hour laying in the hallway for everyone passing by to see, the mob returned with a bed bag. I knew what that meant, having observed past offenders. I was lifted to a standing position, and the bed bag was tossed over me but I was spared being doused with any baby powder or other essential oils as no one wanted to spend any time cleaning it up during the dead week.

The mob carried me to Bussee Hall and dumped me in front of Darcy's door. She wasn't home. She was at the design center, cramming on a project. I lay there for about 15 minutes until I heard a girl say, what's that? The girl got some other girls and the Resident Assistant, and they opened the bag to reveal me. I was stained with blood from the cuts on my wrists, and the bleeding rug burns from my shoulders, arms, and torso. The bed bag showed evidence of it too.

The girls stripped me of my bag. Feeling pity for my bleeding and blood-stained body, they had mercy on me and started to cut the duct tape off my wrists with scissors. They were trying to set my hands free so I could take care of the rest, but I squirmed and mumbled for them not to do so as they were cutting into my wrists, not realizing I was wired with coat hangers. Finally, one of them said, let's get the duct tape off his mouth, and I agreed by shaking my head yes. They slid the scissor between my cheek and the duct tape, made a cut, and then peeled back the duct tape to my hairline. Once they got the duct tape off my mouth, I thanked them and explained that my wrists and ankles was wired with clothes hangers beneath the duct tape.

They wanted to call the campus police, but that would have meant a punitive sanction against the house and assault charges to members I would have to identify. I asked them not to do so. It was another half hour before one of the girls returned from her boyfriend with a wire cutter which they used to cut my wrists free. I could then free my ankles and rid myself of the rest of the duct tape wrapped around my neck and mouth.

The Resident Assistant told me if I washed the blood off me, she'd give me some pajamas I could wear back to my dormitory as I stood there in my underwear. I took a shower in the girl's bathroom, thanked everyone for their kindness, and returned to Fairchild's house.

Back in Fairchild everyone was studying and acting as if nothing had happened. The rest of the week, not one person acknowledged what had happened nor said a word to me about it. They got what they wanted, almost. They delivered me to Darcy in hopes she'd see me in a weak, humiliated, and disgraced moment, but thankfully she wasn't there.

I wasn't a boxer or an outwardly tough guy, but every bone in my body was wrapped with solid muscle mass from the hard labor I had performed all my life. Each Fairchild guy saw from the fight I gave them a subdued rage in me was always willing to come to the surface in times like this. They all knew now that I could take any of them down individually. They all continued pretending as if nothing had happened, and whenever they walked past me, it was quick and with their eyes down to the floor. No one spoke to me about the incident for the rest of the remaining two weeks of the semester. It was as if the incident had never happened, and I left it that way. I was moving off campus next year and would be rid of them. I focused on studying.

Chapter Forty-One
Fifty Rejections

Summer 1982
Playlist:
Short People, Randy Newman
Just the Way You Are, Billy Joel
Emotion, Samantha Sang
Lay Down Sally, Eric Clapton
Dust In The Wind, Kansas
The Closer I Get To You, Roberta Flack
This Time I'm In It For Love, Player
Grease, Franki Valli

I mailed out fifty resumes and requests to the top advertising and public relations agencies across the United States. Each letter was meticulously typed on a typewriter tailoring my interest and appeal to the agency's specific area of expertise, inquiring whether they had any summer employment or summer internship opportunities.

I received 50 rejections.

I did, however, get an offer from one giant hog farm to which I did not send a letter; Bob Fishers, of course, based solely on my existing work experience with him. He offered me full-time work if I could stay. I could have rented a room easily, and I would've been closer to Darcy to shoot up Interstate 35 to see her in Minneapolis once in a while. But looking ahead and knowing my plans and goals, including Darcy, I knew this would be my last summer back in Spencer and Van Etten. Next fall would be my last semester at ISU, and I'd be interviewing for a job in some corporate or advertising position.

The farming dream and goal weren't completely gone, but I temporarily sacrificed it because I loved Darcy. I reasoned that getting a job closer to the

Minneapolis metropolitan area would provide a temporary experience and transition to earn and save for that farm goal of mine. It allowed lots of opportunities for Darcy to have her career too. That was how I saw us in another year when she would graduate. So getting back to Van Etten and Spencer, seeing my dad and friends, and trying to comfort Loretta with me visiting home seemed the right thing to do.

The letters I received from Loretta this past year were painful to read, as always. I knew she was using letters and her journal to express the complicated emotions that troubled her. It was therapy for her, but it was emotionally painful for me. I got letters that told me the only child she truly loved was her son Gary and that he was the only child who truly understood her. She plainly stated she loved none of her other children. And her relentless letters of condemnation of my father and my other siblings, nearly always longing and wishing for my brother Gary to be alive, told me she was still grieving. It was already apparent, but she had to dig her pain into your soul through her pen.

With her letters and their contents embedded in my mind and against my benefit, I returned one last summer back to upstate New York to try and help relieve some of her grief and pain. I knew I'd face a problem finding decent work that paid well. While my pay at Fishers wasn't great, I could have all the hours I wanted to work. The upstate area was economically depressed. The whole economy was still reeling from the Carter years, which caused rampant annual inflation culminating in double digits in 1979 and 1980. Inflation had never hit this high in our country's history except in 1946, when hundreds of thousands of soldiers returned home from world war II and drove up demand for many goods and services. First-ever lines were three blocks long and longer at gas stations throughout our nation because of fuel shortages.

1980 brought America a new president named Ronald Regan with the hope of improvement, but his administration's policies were too new to be effective immediately. There was a lot of coverage of his election and other stories we journalism students were assigned to review and analyze from different newspapers and media sources. The goal was to study the various Journalistic styles of reporting the same stories in different media. These assignments developed a more profound interest in national and world affairs for me. And while a reader could get the whole story and details on most notable news subjects from a daily paper like the Des Moines Register, it was challenging to accurately tell the highlights of a report in a 30-second broadcast.

The southern tier of New York wasn't exempt from the national economic hardships, and wages were low, with a high unemployment rate of nearly 11%. Scanning help wanted ads for work was disappointing. There were hardly any job listings in local newspapers like The Elmira Star-Gazette. And the ones that were listed were for a full-time permanent position for which I had no qualifications.

I visited Turner Farm and asked if they would hire me again, but they could only give me part-time hours. Then I came across an ad for a permanent full-time third-shift night watchman at the Cotton Hanlon Lumber Mill in Cayuta, New York. Cayuta was a 15-mile drive from Harry and Lorretta's house. It was an easy beautiful drive through a valley with several meandering creeks occasionally reaching the two-lane highway. In my interview, I was honest that I would only be temporary, and the interviewer understood and said, well, it's a simple job, and he needed me immediately. If I could start tomorrow, I'd get the job.

Once again, I found myself with two jobs, one working an eleven to seven shift but only working from eight am to noon at the Turner Farm. It was much more manageable than my two full-time jobs on Long Island, but not nearly the pay.

At the mill, my job was to make hourly rounds at various mill points to make security checks, check on temperature gauges, and record my readings. Each station had a time clock I had to punch, so there was no sloughing off on the job, not that I would have anyway. It was simple and easy work, and I exerted very little labor. All I had to do was walk around the yards at night, checking on the kiln and boiler temperatures. I had numbers to call if they reached certain high levels, but on my watches I never had an issue. The biggest security threat I encountered and dealt with was tapping on fogged windshields of teenagers making out and asking them to leave the premises.

It was a pretty mundane and boring summer. Hardly any of my classmates were back in Spencer. Many had graduated and moved into careers in towns far from Spencer. I was a good year and a half behind them. And those that were still there had established friends. The only guy I saw periodically was the Duke.

My dad was looking for another wreck at the junkyard in Horseheads to fix up for himself and sell. He continued to do this work to supplement his retirement pension. He noticed a small Chevrolet Chevette, which he thought might be a more economical car to own and operate versus the station wagon I was still driving. It was used with only 3000 miles, but it was damaged from a head-on collision. He told me that he thought I could sell the wagon, buy this car and still come out with cash. He would help me repair it, as I knew nothing about stretching frames and bodywork. I followed his advice, and he bought the car. I'd pay him back as soon as I sold the wagon. For the rest of the summer, I filled my afternoon with a nap and spent the evening hours till I went to work fixing that car up. After we stretched the unibody frame to get the accordion wrinkles out of it, we bought new fenders and a hood, and my dad's bodywork skills made that car look brand new. It was a much smaller car, and I couldn't pack all my belongings to return to the apartment I would move into this fall, so I installed a hitch on the Chevette to haul a small utility trailer.

I bought a utility trailer frame and built my deck on it. I made it the size of a kitchen table. I then created the four sides and attached them with hinges to fold them flat in storage. I made sure they did not exceed the perimeter of the deck. We needed a kitchen table in the apartment, and I had nowhere to store the trailer once I got it there. The apartment lease I signed explicitly said we were not allowed to keep anything other than our car on the property. I could disconnect the hitch from the frame and store that in my closet. The trailer we could haul up the stairs and position in the kitchen and stack cement blocks underneath to act as legs in the four corners to hold the table up. It was genius, and when my roommates eventually saw it, they were glad we didn't have to foot any funds for a kitchen table. We threw a large tablecloth on top of it, and the only part of the trailer that one could see was about 6 inches of the wheels sticking out from beneath the tablecloth. It made for an interesting conversation piece!

With the Chevette now completed, my dad asked me to sell the station wagon to get his money back and buy another car for himself to fix up. He suggested I put the car on a used car consignment lot in Elmira, where he sold the cars, he fixed up, so I did.

Darcy was flying out to see her older sister Debbie and spend a week with them. Debbie lived in Honesdale, Pennsylvania, about an hour and a half drive from Van Etten. I was excited about her coming. I planned to pick her up early Saturday morning, drive her back to Van Etten to meet my parents for the first time, stay overnight, and show her around my hometown where I grew up. Of course, I'd introduce her to the Kings and a few other families I'd cherished. I didn't work the weekends at Cotton Hanlon or Turner's dairy farm. If the opportunity had existed, I would have, but Cotton Hanlon wouldn't let me work overtime, and Turners already had enough help and couldn't afford me any more hours.

My summer phone calls to Darcy were once a week, and I ensured that I reimbursed Loretta for those calls. The last thing I wanted to hear was an argument over a phone bill.

Catching up with Darcy each week, I'd continue to hear about the neighborhood boy adventures she was on. Now, I fully understood the relationship from our conversations and looked forward to meeting them someday. Darcy said they didn't get together as often as before as they both had jobs, and "times were changing," as she'd say. When I'd ask how the times are changing, she'd say, "oh, I don't know, they're working, I'm busy working, and I'm not as interested in hanging out with them."

I still hadn't been up to Minnesota or Darcy's home, but I was looking forward to having her see the area where I lived. I always cherished the hills and valleys of this area that I drove, and I still saw it as beautiful and wanted to share it with her. Strangely, I wanted to show her my first car too. Comet! As awful as it looked now, dusty and dirty and stored in the barn, I wanted her to see it. It wasn't impressive, but I wanted to tell her about it and my adventures driving it.

The weekend arrived for me to pick up Darcy, and though I had to work all night Friday, as soon as I got off work Saturday morning, I drove home, took a shower, and drove the Chevette to Honesdale.

Darcy's sister looked like an older version of her and a younger version of her mother. She was a pretty and petite woman. Darcy had a pleasant time with them, and her sister teased her by saying, "Boy, is she anxious to see you!" I smiled big, and Darcy rolled her eyes at her sister and threw her bag and suitcase in the back seat as she shouted goodbye. Debbie laughed in a teasing way as she hollered goodbye.

Darcy was impressed with the new car. It was small, but the interior was brand new and reasonably spacious. It was the same red color outside and inside as the Chevy station wagon. It was like I shrunk the car, she joked, as it was a four-door with a hatchback! We rolled the windows down as we drove the curvy road from Honesdale back toward Interstate 81 and north toward Binghamton.

Darcy shared about her week with her sister. She told me about a trip to New York City she enjoyed with Deb and Phil. She told me about the expensive restaurant where Phil met Horst, his best friend. "Horst," I stated, "now that's an even more interesting name than Darcy!" I joked.

"Yeah," she said, "it's different, and so is he. His full name is Horst Rechelbacher. He is a famous hairstylist. He's planning to start a new cosmetics company."

"Wow, an entrepreneurial guy; I'd like to meet him someday." (Little did I imagine then that I would meet Horst, founder of Aveda products, and work nearly 30 years later to help him formulate edible cosmetics using various floral honey varieties just two years before his death.)

"I mean, how do you start a cosmetics company?" I asked.

Darcy shared kind of a funny story in that when they met Horst at the restaurant, her brother-in-law Phil saw the prices on the menu, and he told Horst, "Horst, I can't afford this."

Horst waved his hand and said, "Don't worry, I invited you."

Darcy shared some of the menu items and their costs, as she was impressed at the prices too. "I was with Phil; I surely couldn't afford those meals either," she said. Darcy had a great time shopping with her sister Debbie and shared that they had bought some new clothes. I complimented Darcy on her new blouse and told her she looked great and that I was so happy to see her.

Once past Binghamton, we veered west on NY Hwy 17 to the Owego exit. From there, we drove the two-lane roads back to Spencer. My first stop with Darcy was at the Kings. It was lunchtime, and I introduced Darcy to the family.

She said, "I've heard a lot about you, and Curt thinks very fondly of you." We sat for a while, but since it was a Saturday and I only had two days with her, we hurried along to the next stop, and I introduced her to Mom and Pop Hansen. Again, stately but warm in stature, Darcy impressed me with her friendly and cordial presence during introductions. It was a side of Darcy I'd not seen as yet, and I admired her poise and position. I was always learning something new about Darcy that compounded my admiration and love for her.

As we went through the towns of Spencer and Van Etten, I gave her the "please don't blink" tour of both villages. Spencer is a four-corner town with the ARCO gas station on one corner, Tioga State Bank and The Big M food store on the next, the Napa parts Store on the third corner, and a tiny Ford car dealer and garage on the last. That was it. Three churches were scattered on the way in and out of the four corners which had the only functioning traffic light, a red blinker, for twenty miles in any direction.

Through Van Etten, I showed her Larison's Feed Mill, where I worked as a kid, the two bars opposite each other on corners, and Ben's Food Mart. That was it. "Please don't blink again," I kidded.

From Van Etten, I took her up Beckhorn Hollow and across the steel trestle bridge over Cayuta Creek. Little did she know how many nights I visited that bridge, dropped tears through the grate into the waters below, and tried to imagine some future ahead. I wanted to take her to see my cabin in the wood, but I didn't want to open those chapters of my life and explain why I had to leave home.

I was praying that Loretta would behave this weekend. My being home this summer had little positive effect on her mental well-being. Her grief was still enormous. Nothing I could suggest to her was of any use or comfort. I planned to introduce her and then whisk her away with plans to show her around and where I worked to stay away as much as possible. After meeting Loretta and Harry, the Duke's house, Ithaca, and dancing at the North Forty were the immediate plans.

Beckhorn Hollow would turn into Cooper Hill Road as we drove up the hills. Our neighbors, Bill and Helen Garland, lived across the valley from us. I had hiked across the valley to see them often throughout my teen years. I stopped to introduce Darcy and see how they were getting along. They were aging on in their years. The visit was brief, but they were so appreciative that I stopped to say hi. I drove about 50 yards from their house as we left home and parked on the side of the road. I pointed to the hill behind the valley farm they owned and said to Darcy, "There is where I live." She looked puzzled as she strained to look for a house in the valley below but saw just an old sheep shed. I told her to look up on top of the hill. Once you found it, you could make out the house's roofline in a clearing. "That's where we're going, but we have just a few more miles to get there."

Darcy was a gem in meeting my dad and Loretta. And they were both gracious to meet Darcy as well. Loretta was excellent and in good spirits welcoming her, though I could tell she was eyeing Darcy and conjuring up some inner thoughts almost immediately. Maybe it was that Darcy had my heart; I wasn't sure. But then she said, "You're so beautiful, Darcy; you remind me of when I was young."

"People used to tell me I looked like Elisabeth Taylor in my young years, and I see some of her in you too." *Wow! A compliment,* I thought, but then again, this was always Loretta to people on the outside. Her friends and acquaintances loved her. And then it hit me that in seeing Darcy, she might have just been reminded about herself, her youth somehow, and it brought her some joy. She remained pleasant and kind and showed Darcy her home and my sister's old room, where she could stay when we returned later that night.

I took Darcy into our basement and showed her the room I'd built in high school. It was pretty decent and paneled, but certainly not perfect. She scoped out the rest of the basement and noticed the other half of the dirt floor was still not cemented. She never said anything, but I could tell she was discovering through my surroundings, through the people I'd introduced her to, that I didn't come from a lot of money or a community like hers. I explained that my dad built this home and owed no debt. He always saved till he had enough cash to pay for the next step toward construction and completion, and he was saving for the next half of the cement floor.

She got a tour of my dad's crazy garage that he and I built from cement blocks salvaged from the four-story chicken barn we tore down.

I shared how my dad and I tore down this four-story chicken barn. One of my high school buddies, Jerry Thornton, knew that I tore down our barn the summer before and told with me that his folks were looking for someone to tear one of several of their old chicken barns down. I suggested to my dad that we could do it together and earn money. After all, I was experienced! So, we did the following summer; I was fifteen. While my dad made most of the money, he paid me, and I used it to repair the Comet. After removing the roof, we chopped it down with sledgehammers block by block. Often hitting the blocks, large chunks of the wall would collapse to the ground below and smash into bits and pieces because of the weakened cracks throughout the structure. We spent a good part of that summer together working away, eventually removing the third and second-story floors and continuing to break the building to the ground down to the first level. He used his bulldozer to bury all the debris on sight next to where the barn once stood. I built a lot of muscle in my biceps and torso swinging that sledgehammer, carrying lumber and block. My friend Jerry was always a good guy, a defender of those bullied (including me) by bigger guys who were often two or three years older and more developed than the rest of us because they were left back several times because of poor grades. Two years ahead of me, I modeled after him and took over his role, after he graduated.

I showed Darcy around our property, and of course, I took her down to the old cattle barn I built, which housed Comet. It wasn't much of a barn using the salvaged timbers from the one I tore down. She asked me again, "So you built that barn?" I proudly said, "Yes," but I could tell she was not too impressed. She never made any judgments, but she'd look curiously. I showed her my Comet, which didn't impress her much, though she appreciated that I had a car at such a young age. She had shared with me that her first car was a rusty green Volkswagen Beetle, and the back floor rusted through where one could see the road below. She could relate to me having an old car.

It was a sunny warm day as I toured Darcy down one of the old horse and buggy roads leading to an abandoned farm from the early 1900s. Midway to the farmstead, I stopped at the edge of a beautiful meadow. I was prepared and had a condom in my pocket, and we made love next to a young emerging forest of Maples.

After dinner with Loretta and Harry, we left for the Duke's house and then up to Ithaca to tour Cornell University by car, stop at my favorite bagel shop at the edge of campus, have dinner at McDonald's, and then to the North Forty for dancing.

We danced the evening away until midnight before we returned home. It was a fabulous day for me to see Darcy again.

Sunday morning came too fast. I wanted her to meet some of the folks I cherished at St. Paul's Lutheran, so we packed her things and planned an early departure to attend church. And I still wanted to show her where I worked at Cotton Hanlon. She said goodbye to Harry and Loretta and thanked them for their hospitality. She left them a small hostess appreciation gift she had brought for them.

What a class act, I thought about Darcy. On our way to Cotton Hanlon, we grabbed breakfast at a tiny Cafe called Beaches along Route 224. After a drive-thru tour of the Cotton Hanlon grounds, log lots and buildings, we turned around, drove back to Spencer, and attended church. Darcy and I held hands as we prayed, and I prayed that she was praying we'd one day become husband and wife. In the course of our many conversations, we knew that Christ was central in both our lives. Just how much Christ had played a role in my life, she'd not known for many years.

I was always greeted warmly by the elder members of St. Paul's, and this Sunday, I surprised them with a girl from the Midwest. The elder Efthimou brothers Ralph and Paul and their wives Helmi and Sarah were excited to meet who I had with me and learn a little about her. I introduced Darcy as my girlfriend from Iowa State University. It was silly, as I look back, but it was so important to me when they saw me choosing and dating a nice Lutheran girl from Minnesota. They were among the few who knew about my high school situation living in the wood alone. As Darcy was an impressive young lady, I wanted them to know I was making good choices. They were outstanding community members and always so gracious and patted me on the back with silent approval.

After church, I drove Darcy back to Honesdale and stayed with her as long as possible. I didn't want to leave, but the hour came that I should. I wouldn't see Darcy again until I returned to ISU in the fall. Seeing her and breaking up the lonely upstate summer was so good. I could hardly wait to see her again soon.

Chapter Forty-Two
Antics

Curt and Darcy at another Charity Dance Marathon Spring of 1983.

January 1983
Playlist:
Every Breath You Take, The Police
Billie Jean, Michael Jackson
1999, Prince

I was technically done with classes at ISU for winter graduation in December of 1982. I had met all my Bachelor of Science Degree in Journalism requirements for graduation. Darcy had one more semester left, and I would not leave her. She was among, if not the best, thing that ever happened to me. There was no way I was leaving Iowa, no way. Without getting a loan for school, though, I would likely drain the rest of my limited funds in my bank account. I needed to replenish my savings and prepare for interviews.

I had to be enrolled to qualify for a school loan to help with living expenses. I signed up for a minimum of six credits of classes. That was the minimum to qualify for the loan that would enable me to maintain my savings and help pay room and board expenses and tuition for one more semester.

I took the classes just long enough to meet the requirements to get the funds deposited into my account; then, I dropped them. I lost the tuition portion of the loan, and yes, I admit, it was an antic that I worked the system. It didn't matter, I was still going to have to pay it back, and I would. I'd heard of students scamming the loan systems for far greater injustices than mine, cars, down payments on homes, spring break vacations, and other items. I just needed a little time and money to keep moving forward, and no other source or bank would loan me any funds with the amount of school debt I had piled on.

My goal for the semester was to work as many hours as possible on Bob Fisher's farm, helping him control the hog disease devastating his herds. I could give him full-time attention and try to help him get through the difficulties he was having while at the same time helping myself. My part-time employment pretty much supported just my minor living expenses and books. In the coming months, I could work full time, and I wanted to put as much money into my account for living and interviewing costs, such as travel. This strategy worked and, more importantly, gave Darcy and me a lot more time to continue growing more deeply together as a couple.

We returned to her home in Lakeville one late spring weekend, and she took me to Crystal Lake Park. A swimming and gathering beach on the east side of the lake her parents lived on. We bought a bottle of Lancers wine and some cheese and crackers and had a picnic as we watched the sunset on the west end of the lake. As the beach emptied, we talked and chatted long into the evening. One of our favorite things together was and remained to look into the sky above and explore the stars as we spoke. We watched the moon rise, and eventually no one was left on the beach but us. Darcy is very witty and clever. She suggested we go skinny dipping. It was an odd suggestion, I thought, coming from Darcy. I'd taken her on picnics to Saylorville Lake south of Ames, and she never suggested swimming there.

"Seriously?" I asked.

"Yeah, come on, let's go; you go first and see how warm the water is," she suggested.

I stripped down and jumped in. "The water's fine," I said, "come on in."

"No way," she said as she sat giggling at me.

"What do you mean?" I asked.

"I'm not going skinny dipping! Are you kidding?" she laughed again. She just sat there smirking away at how she suckered me. Her antics were always fun, as she goaded me sometimes, but this one topped them all. She got me good and checked out all the goods in the moonlight. How did I fall for that? Even worse, when I came out to get my clothes, she stole them, ran to the car, and locked the door. Flush in the face and embarrassed for having fallen for this trick… I wouldn't chase her to the car through the parking lot. Can you imagine that scene if a Lakeville cop drove up… naked twenty-something guy trying to get in a locked car with a girl in it? I returned to the lake and waded into it waist-high until she returned and set my clothes back on the beach.

While I was half laughing inside at her antic, I so wanted to toss her in the lake, except I knew she was wearing her watch and other jewelry, and we'd have some explaining to do when we returned to her house. Laughing, she said, "Did you think I was going to go skinny dipping?"

I was more embarrassed at having fallen for her trick than standing naked in front of her. "You got me, Darcy."

"Yup," she said laughingly, "I got YA!" I dressed, and after I pulled my shirt back on, Darcy grabbed me around my neck and kissed me.

"I love you," she said.

"I love you too, Darcy." We sat chatting for about another hour and gazed into the stars until the mosquitos became unbearable. I had to dry off before we went back to her house.

When I first met Darcy's mom, I loved what I saw. I knew what kind of woman Darcy would be in the long term. Her mom Betty was a beautiful woman with a stately figure in her fifties. More importantly, she was a warm, sensual, sensible, humorous, and upright woman with a great personality and always gracious and filled with great appreciation for everything and everyone she met. I could see where Darcy could get her sweet devilish ways too. Betty was a little naughty and very competitive in card games. She always snickered or politely smiled at her husband's sometimes off-color jokes, and in a respectable reprimanding manner to some of his jokes, his short name of Bob would receive an extended pronunciation to "oh Boaaaaaaab!" If Darcy ever turned out to be what I saw in her parents, Darcy was the girl for me. It was a good weekend at her home, getting to know her parents more, and then back to ISU we went.

Iowa State University has an annual tradition each spring semester with a serenade of the bells from the Campanile. Near the end of the term, a concert of its bells would play on a pre-announced specific night. They would play all evening, and students and Ames residents would gather from all parts of the campus and community into the central campus square where the Campanile stood. There would be thousands gathered for the event. After the concert, everyone kissed someone, whomever you would be with, girlfriend or boyfriend, or just friend.

Darcy invited me to go. It was the second time we kissed under the Campanile, but this time I could genuinely look into her eyes and tell her I loved her. She is always the fire in the firefly, lighting the way for us both and introducing me to participate in one thing or another.

We once danced all night to raise money for the United Way Charity through a dance-a-thon. It was early in our relationship that I discovered her giving heart. We had such a blast. It was a costume theme, and we went as clowning farmers…my idea. I was always picking up short-term jobs in addition to farm work. I worked a second job in Ankeny for six months on a temporary project for the UDIA (United Dairy Industry Association). UDIA had small inflatable cows as promotion pieces. I borrowed one and took it to the dance with me, and we tossed it around the dance floor among the dancers. As the 24-hour dance lasted into the wee hours of the morning, I thought about the work ahead of me. It was Saturday morning, and I hadn't had any sleep. But I wanted to complete the 24 hours of standing and dancing with Darcy. I did not want to let her down. We were among a few remaining couples standing when the marathon officially ended. I had to bolt as soon as it did; my responsibilities were calling me. Darcy and I danced for a worthy charitable cause for 24 hours. It was our first philanthropic event together as a couple, and sharing, caring, and giving back to the world would continue to be a central theme in our lives. Darcy went home to sleep, and I went to work. She was so much fun to be around, even with and because of her antics.

Chapter Forty-Three
Leaving Ames

Spring 1983 – Summer 1984
Playlist:
You and I, Eddie Rabbit
Allentown, Billy Joel
The Girl Is Mine, Michael Jackson, Paul McCartney
Flash dance, Irene Cara
Hungry Like the Wolf, Duran Duran

Over the past couple of years, my skills and my responsibilities grew at Bob Fisher's farm. His trust in me and the flexibility he showered upon me were fascinating. I kept track of my hours and turned them in using another green ledger. I was given several jobs and told that I could schedule my own hours as long as I completed the assignments. I was entirely on the honor system. He gave me a wide variety of responsibilities: vaccination of hogs at various intervals, removing dead hogs from feeder pens, managing and spreading manure onto fields in winter months, power-wash empty barns and farrowing houses, hauling grain from the co-op to the farm elevator in the summer months, assist in the care of the farrowing hogs, castrate male piglets, sort and move hogs from pen to pen based upon their weight progress, administer antibiotics and more. He rounded out my skills in his livestock's daily animal husbandry care.

Unfortunately for the Fisher family, the whole hog operation was infected by various deadly diseases, spreading rapidly. I wasn't afraid to tackle any job he asked of me. The full-time employee's treatment of some hogs was not always acceptable. I'd seen some hogs abused so badly they expired. Some of these farmhands had been there too long or were simply stressed in other ways and taking it out on these poor animals. Hogs were not easy animals to consistently control and could test your patience. I understood that.

As a dairy kid, I more than once belted a cow that kicked me in the head while milking. I understood the frustrations, but beating a hog to death or killing it with a bat to make it simpler to remove the hog from a pit rather than struggle with it wasn't in the best interest of this farmer.

There were other management issues I brought to his attention in confidence. He noted them, and I did see a change in some activities. And I made some suggestions for efficiencies and better management that he could share with his farm manager.

Bob Fisher knew I would be leaving after graduation. He didn't want me to go and offered me a job in his operation. It was 1983 and the economy was still tough. The job prospects that I was interviewing for offered less than I made at the Yaphank County farm in New York when I had just a two-year degree. Here I had a four-year degree, and it felt like I was going backward and had four times the school debt.

Bob offered me a $40,000.00 annual salary, a pick-up truck, and housing. The forty-thousand-dollar salary was excellent for a graduate in 1983! How could I turn this down? I pondered.

Darcy and I talked for a long time about the possibilities of doing this for a few years and saving as much as possible toward getting into my farm or business. Darcy was a good listener, but she had many questions for me. We went on long walks through campus on several occasions discussing this opportunity. I was interviewing with ad agencies in Chicago, Minneapolis, Los Angeles, and Syracuse. None were offering salaries near this amount; most were at half or less.

Darcy coached me to finish interviewing at these agencies. She reminded me that these were some of the top ad agencies in the country, and she was impressed with how I got interviews with them.

I got them using those fifty rejections I received last year asking for an internship. I sent out another resume and the rejection letter I'd received from them earlier, seeking permanent work. I told them I was still interested in working with their firm. It had paid off. I'd traversed across America from sea to shining sea and had great success in my first round of interviews. Landing one of the jobs was a good possibility. I impressed each of them enough that by the time I returned to Ames, I had letters from them thanking me for traveling so far to visit and requesting me to schedule a second interview with the next round of higher-ups! My portfolio of works was modest, but they were impressed that I didn't give up and that I was driving hundreds if not thousands of round-trip miles to and from each interview.

Acknowledging that it was always my decision, Darcy cautiously coached me that though the pay was more than double what I might start with at any of the agencies, this would probably not open doors of opportunities in journalism and advertising as I had at the moment if I delayed moving forward.

As I listened to Darcy, I looked at my hands. They were huge. My fingers were thick from my teen and college years of hard, laborious work. They were farmers' hands. I could imagine them pecking away on a typewriter someday, recording my thoughts as a farmer, but already these hands had grown into two calloused claws that could probably break a man's hand if I squeezed it enough. That was a comment I often received when I shook someone's hand, not realizing my strength; my firm grip often caught people by surprise.

Over and over, Darcy and I talked about the opportunities before me. While discussing career choices financially, the best job prospect, for now, was right in front of my face. I'd already turned down one offer with John King, and given all the perspectives that Darcy and I talked about, I was about to turn down another with Bob Fischer. I even suggested temporarily taking the job until I landed some permanent opportunity, but that wouldn't be fair to Bob Fisher. "Don't focus on the money," she said, "focus on what you want to do, and the money will come. Farming will always be there for you, Curt," she said. "Now's the time to try the ad agencies you've interviewed so well at; look to that future," she coached.

That's what I have always done; kept looking forward. I looked past other opportunities, from girls to jobs. Darcy was a great reminder to stay steadfast. It paid off on the girl part, as I had Darcy now. Hopefully, it will pay off for me in the career field.

Darcy was a critical influence in my decision to let Bob Fischer know I would not be taking his offer. I was ever so grateful and flattered, and I told him so. It just wasn't meant to be, and God confirmed to me through these talks with Darcy that she had even more interest in us making a life together. I already knew this and wanted a life with her, but ongoing confirmation that kept coming from her was always comforting. More than ever, I was hoping to land a job in Minneapolis and be close to her, but my best prospects so far were elsewhere.

On graduation day, Darcy and I walked into two different ceremonies from each of our colleges. We sat, observed, and cheered each other on. Darcy's parents had come and graciously invited me to hang with them. They took pictures of us together, and I took many of them with Darcy. It was a good day, and though I was with Darcy and her parents, I'd be less than honest if I didn't acknowledge that there was a slight disappointment in my own family not being here to celebrate as I traversed the ceremonies and saw many graduates celebrating with their families. Still, given the negative letters I received from Loretta, it was probably best that they didn't come.

I was still interviewing and had not landed a permanent position. I made a large placard out of scrap foam mounting board and paper, which I hung over my body and marched into the ceremony. It said, Ad Man, hire me, and I had put my home phone number with a New York area code. A picture of me is prominently displayed in the ISU yearbook of 1983 with the caption, "Hard times as a student advertises for a job." *Ha,* I thought "hard times" were me since I was born. I was perennially stuck in hard times. The economy sucked in the 1980s. Interest rates on my school loans were high. An FHA home mortgage rate was upward of 20-25%. Inflation was killing my meager savings, and great-paying jobs were limited.

No one ever called regarding my placard. Or at least Loretta, who would have taken any call as it was her home phone number, never shared any with me. She didn't want me to stay in Iowa. Though she and I were estranged, she wanted her kids to surround her with the love she needed but couldn't command because of her actions.

I left Darcy with her parents for the rest of the afternoon. I didn't want to be too presumptuous, invading their victory and celebrating their youngest daughters' accomplishment. I was as proud of Darcy as they were. I saw firsthand how much work she put into her design major, and as much as she always encouraged me, I couldn't wait to see what she would do in her career. I would later join them at their invitation for dinner at the Hickory Park Restaurant.

When I reached my car in the Cy Auditorium parking lot, I took off my gown and cap and sat on the hood of my car. Here I was in the heart of the Great Midwest, a boy from New York City who'd lived with anxiety and fears most of his life under an umbrella of family dysfunction, and I graduated with a four-year degree on my own. I managed this, paid for it, owned it, and no one could take it away. I received $60.00 in tuition help over the last six years. Loretta sent me $20.00 three times in three different birthday cards with a note to use the money toward my education. I believed she was sincere but did not comprehend what it cost or what I had borrowed to accomplish this. And I never told her. My dad, of course, had helped me by fixing up decent cars for my transportation.

I hopped in my car and drove around Richardson Court Circle, where Darcy and I met. It was just two and a half years ago, but it seemed like an eternity. I parked my car and thought about some of my foolishness, my insecurities when we first met, the hilarious times we'd had, and the intense and caring conversations we engaged in for each other. The hallway kiss and my walk and talk with Janice one evening about it. I felt a little silly now over some of them, but I was glad for all of them. I thought about all the back rubs I'd given Darcy during her menstrual cycles to help alleviate her cramps, how much I truly felt sorry for the pain she had to go through, and the head rubs for her migraines. I always prayed for it to leave her body and, if it had to go somewhere, to enter my own. I loved her; I'd grown to cherish her.

I left my car parked in the courtyard at the RCA and walked to the Memorial Union. I picked up a soda and walked up to the Campanile. Many graduates took pictures on the lawn in front of it. I looked at the Campanile as if it were mine and Darcy's. It was! It was our own! And I'm sure many felt the same way. That Campanile is embedded in many hearts and rings for so many long before us and will after us. It's everyone's Campanile, but for a few moments in time, Darcy and I owned it as it rang out for our hearts. Every time it rings in the future, I thought it would ring for us.

It was a beautiful day. I took in all the smiles of the parents, the smiles of the graduates, many with worried and anxious smiles as they were heading home without jobs, and some with exuberant smiles as they landed opportunities in distant cities or furthered their education. But mostly, I saw smiles of accomplishment. The same smile I had on my face. Not only did I get a diploma, but I also got a prize worth all the diplomas in the world. God could not have guided me any better nor have been more generous to me the first day he whispered, "That's the girl you're going to marry." I got Darcy. We had grown into one.

I looked back on all those troubling years, the deeper periods of silent angst and self-pity, the embarrassment of being homeless and living alone in the woods, all those years of sharing and communing with my God in the Comet, and he had guided me to this day. It was my day, Graduation Day 1983, at Iowa State University for the boy from New York City.

I finished my soda, and my thoughts quickly turned toward packing and planning the move of my belongings. My apartment lease was up at the end of May. Everything I owned would have to fit in that kitchen table, the small trailer we used for a table: my mattress, textbooks, deceased brothers' guitar, which I never did master, notebooks, typewriter, and a few other odd personals.

Back at the apartment, one of my roommates was already moving out. It was time to get out the towing bar, bolt it back on the table, carry it out of the apartment, and turn it back into a trailer while he and my other roommate Mike were still there to help.

While I still hadn't found a permanent job, I did have three job prospects I was focusing on in Minneapolis. I had interviewed with Colle McVoy advertising, Land O Lakes Cooperatives, and CENEX cooperatives and had second-round interview invitations.

Feeling confident about my prospects with them, I asked Darcy's mom and dad if I could haul my trailer and belongings to his house and store them in a boat garage he had. Darcy's dad insisted yes, and they were glad to help. Through this sharing and request, they knew I had sincere and longer-term interests in their daughter.

After graduation, I helped Darcy and her dad pack all her belongings into their Ford van. I wished them a safe journey home, and I'd see them in a few weeks.

The following two weeks would be my last at Fischer's farm and, for that matter, in Iowa State for a very long time. I packed up my trailer and headed on I 35 north to Darcy's mom and dad's home in Minnesota.

I got about 50 miles past Story City when a trucker passed me by and blasted his horn loudly as he passed. I wasn't sure what that was about. Was it a warning of some sort? I looked in my rearview mirror. Everything looked normal, so I just continued moving forward. My mind was on all the upcoming momentum I had going the next day and in the next couple of weeks. I had to be in Chicago the following day for my second interview with D'Arcy McManus and Macius Advertising Agency.

Shortly after the last, another semi-trailer passed me and blasted his horn. One blast from the first trucker I thought was a fluke, but from a second was confirming that something might be wrong. I was oblivious to the fact there was trouble brewing behind me.

When this second truck passed, I looked in the rearview mirror on the driver's door as my center mirror was blocked by pillows and belongings stacked high in the car. Suddenly, I saw my trailer swerve wildly within sight and quickly out of sight. I immediately pressed the brake and pulled over to the highway's shoulder. As I did, the following trailer movement in my rearview mirror was more than a swerve. I saw my trailer leave the back of my car and tip over smack in the middle of the highway with my belongings strewn everywhere.

Upon inspection, I found the tow bar bolts had come undone from the trailer, and while it was still attached to the hitch on the car, the rest of my trailer was not. I must not have tightened them enough or forgotten to do so altogether.

I quickly gathered my things and brought them to the side of the road. I dragged the trailer there as well. It was all beyond repair. At first, I wasn't sure what to do. It certainly wasn't all going to fit in my car.

I gathered everything and packed it as best I could back into the trailer's box and whatever else would fit in the Chevette. I threw the mattress over the top of the trailer to cover my stuff. I left everything there, cut across the highway median, and headed back toward Bob Fishers' farm. My best hope was that Bob would loan me one of his pick-up trucks, and I could haul this stuff back to his farm and store it somewhere until I could get a new trailer.

Bob Fisher, of course, received me well. I explained what had happened, and he asked me how he could help. I asked to borrow one of his pick-up trucks to haul back my belongings and store them somewhere on his farm. "Take that truck over there, Curt. Can you fit everything in it?"

"Yes, sir, I think so."

"Well, if you can fit everything in it, why don't you haul it up to Minneapolis and return the truck when you can." Bob had a dozen pick-up trucks. Though he probably wouldn't miss this one, I didn't want to take advantage of him.

"Thank you, Sir, thank you. I'll return the truck tonight. I'll bring it right back."

"Take it as long as you need it, Curt,"

"Thank you, Bob, I very much appreciate it, but I will return it tonight."

As always, the keys were in the ignition of every pick-up truck on the farm. I parked out of the way and left the keys in the ignition of my car. I hopped in the pick-up and returned to my trailer within an hour. I had borrowed a few tools, so I could take the trailer apart and loaded it into the pick-up truck's bed first. Then I piled my belongings on top of it and headed for Minneapolis.

Minneapolis was a three-and-a-half-hour drive from Ames. I was a mess, covered with dirt and grease with a pick-up load of junk parts and damaged belongings. Upon arrival, Darcy's dad looked at me like I was Jeb Clampett from the Beverly Hillbillies. Still loving and wearing that red and white polka dot hat didn't help my hillbilly image either.

He was gracious, though, and understanding. I unloaded my belongings into his boathouse, hauled the trailer parts, and stored them behind his cabinet shop in a field he owned until I could later dispose of them.

Here we go again, I mused! At every turn, there was always a challenge. Always an uphill road and a curve, even here in the flatlands, but I had no time for self-pity. I had an interview in Chicago scheduled for the next day. My original plan was to drop my things off at Darcy's house, stay over, get dressed, leave about two o'clock in the morning, and drive to Chicago. The trailer breakdown changed that.

By all accounts, I surmised Loretta must have stuck a needle in her voodoo doll of me while I was driving, trying to keep me from reaching Minneapolis. Though I didn't believe in her antics, when I called home and told her what happened and asked her if she stuck a needle in my picture, she never denied it but confirmed it was another sign that I was not meant to stay in the Midwest. She was against my choice to stay.

Like always in my life—shit happens. It happens to anyone who is trying to do something. I was always trying to do something and get beyond Loretta and her own life of misery. She dragged everyone down.

I unpacked my suit, tie, and shoes, threw them in the pick-up, and returned to Bob Fischer's farm at nine pm. I arrived at half-past midnight and parked the truck where I had taken it from. I stopped at the gas station a few miles before the Story City exit and filled the tank with gas. I wrote a note of gratitude and thanks and left it on the dashboard.

I grabbed my suit and hopped in the Chevette. We headed south past Ames to interstate highway 80 and east to Chicago. I drove the next seven hours to arrive just in time for my 8:00 interview. I was a wreck, though. A speeding ticket added to the stress and anxiety I already had.

Driving through the night to make the appointment had me exhausted. A few miles from the agency, I pulled into a gas station, cleaned myself up in a restroom, and changed into my suit. I doused myself with deodorant spray and slicked my hair down with water, trying to shape my curly hair into some look other than that of a guy who'd been dealing with the stresses I was.

My first interview a month ago went well. I was interviewing with one of the top ten advertising agencies in the country. I needed to be in my prime. I wasn't. I was exhausted, stressed, and concerned.

While sitting in the waiting room to meet the gentlemen I would be interviewed by, I noticed I forgot to change my white socks! I suddenly became self-conscious. My shoes showed dust streaks from where I wiped them with a paper towel in the station restroom. I had sprayed my suit with deodorant to mask the slight hog smell it had acquired from travel in the pick-up truck. I now dreaded going through the interview and thought of faking sickness and leaving.

"Mr. Riess," the receptionist called, "this way, please." I took a deep breath, got up, and followed her to a conference room. There I met two account executives. We chatted casually for about twenty minutes. I was nervous as heck and not at ease at all. I was never asked to open up my portfolio. Not a good sign. They then had me wait again for another group interview.

After about three hours of interviewing three different groups of people, I left Chicago, knowing I would not be working there. Much of the interview focused on who I was and where I came from, family life not excluded. *I answered their questions honestly, maybe too honest,* I thought. There were a lot of questions about me growing up, what I did in high school, why I chose my major, my family and friend relationships, and why I had to pay for my schooling (I had that listed as an accomplishment on my resume). None of the groups asked me to see any portion of my portfolio. The interviews were an evaluation of my mental capacity and background. At one point, I wanted to let them know what had happened to me the day and night before to show how strong my mental state was after all that stress! But frankly, I didn't want to be in Chicago. I wanted to be in Minneapolis with Darcy. If I got this job, I thought. It would be too hard to be separated from her again like the summer before.

I sat through what seemed like a million questions till I became numb. I was eventually dismissed, and I thanked them for their consideration. I knew the interviews had not gone well, and I would not be getting an offer from them. I drove from the Northside of Chicago to Rockford, pulled over in a parking lot, and slept for a few hours before returning to Minneapolis.

Darcy's dad offered me some temporary work in his cabinet shop while I interviewed in Minneapolis and elsewhere. He also offered me a bedroom in his home until I found a permanent position and a place to stay. It was incredibly generous of him and Betty, and there was no doubt Darcy approved! They sensed that the two of us not only wanted to be together, but we belonged together. They knew their daughter better than I did and saw that our chemistry together was better than I even thought.

A week later, I drove to Syracuse, New York and interviewed for the Silverman Mower ad agency job. That interview went well, and I hopped back in the Chevette toward Minneapolis. I'd have a second interview with CENEX in just a few days and another with Colle McVoy advertising agency. Though Van Etten was just a hundred miles or less away from Silverman-Mower, I had no time to go south and visit my dad and Loretta. It would have to wait.

Both my interviews with CENEX and Colle McVoy were successful. Things had gone so well with Colle McVoy that they scheduled me to take some aptitude and psychology tests with a psychologist. If those went well, I was told I'd have an offer in hand. The psychological interview went well, but I wasn't so honest this time. I answered the questions positively regarding all my family relationships, never letting on to dysfunction within the family unit. In the tests and questionnaires, I did the same. When asked about stressful situations and how I'd handled them, I always referred to problems in my jobs, never my family. I now understood more why the D'Arcy McManus and Masius interview process was the way it was. They were testing to see how I would perform under pressure. These agencies had substantial multi-million-dollar clients. They couldn't afford a potentially unstable person and risk losing a client. I would be hearing from one, if not both, for a final interview within a week or so. In the meantime, Silverman Mower had written me an offer for a position. Loretta read it over the phone to me as all my mail was still sent out with her return address. She was thrilled, I somewhat.

In addition to Darcy, I fell in love with the Midwest and its culture. While I was happy about the offer and Syracuse was a place, I could see myself thriving in, I didn't want to leave the Midwest. In my interviews with them, there were hints that I'd frequently travel to an account in Manhattan. I wasn't too excited about that, either.

I shared the news with Darcy and told her I would pass on the offer. I was confident I would get an offer from one of the three companies I interviewed in Minneapolis. So far, I've had two offers, one from Silverman Mower in Syracuse, New York, and one from The California Milk Advisory Board in Los Angeles, California. I knew I could land one in Minneapolis.

I worked in Bob's shop for about three weeks as he allowed me to take time off for my interviews. It was a good thing I had worked all those hours my last semester in Iowa, as my cash was going fast for gas to and from these interviews. Bob asked if I was interested in the cabinetry business, but the dust kept my head and nose stuffy with my allergies. Bob had three girls and no son. There was some thought that I may be interested as a future son-in-law, but I honestly didn't, though I hated disappointing him.

I had my third interview with CENEX. Dave Cummings was the manager I interviewed with and he was the guy I would report to. The interview went well, except in concluding the interview, I asked him if he had any concerns.

He said, "Yes," as he leaned back into his chair, "After hearing all you have accomplished, you sound like a very ambitious fellow, and I think you might be a little bored in this job." I was interviewing for a copywriter's position within their internal ad agency.

I noticed he looked at my calloused hands when he said this.

I held my hands up for viewing.

"Sir, I am ambitious. As we discussed, I worked my way through high school and college, paying my way for the chance of an interview like this. These hands show evidence of that, but they would like a little boredom, boredom from the harder labors I've performed, and a chance at the keys on the typewriter within your department. If you give me a chance, I'll prove my value."

He looked me in the eyes as if he didn't care whether I came on board.

That week I received two letters of offer. Both were for less money than my job at the Yaphank County Prison Farm after I finished my two-year degree, and both were less than half that of Bob Fisher's offer.

One was from Colle McVoy, the other from CENEX. The offer from Colle McVoy was for a $16,000 annual salary, $5,000.00 less than my two-year degree landed me, and I'd have to pay $200 a month in downtown parking fees. The offer from CENEX was for an $18,500 annual salary, and there was free parking. Darcy and I discussed my options. She was all for the Colle McVoy position and the status of my working at a significant creative agency. With my school loan repayment soon to start, I gave up the status that came with being employed with a high-flying ad agency, and I opted for the free parking.

The first day I was on the job at CENEX, a human resource representative gave me a tour of the building and showed me to Dave's office, where he invited me in and welcomed me. He took me around the department and introduced me to the other copywriters and staff. Then he took me to my desk and said, "There is your desk; there is your phone; good luck, you are on your own." I thought it was an oddly sarcastic thing for him to say to a new employee, but it didn't matter; there I was with an opportunity, and a steady paycheck was soon on its way.

The following week Dave was gone. He'd given his two-week notice for a new job in Maine the week before I came aboard. I and 35 others now reported to his boss, a director named John Setala.

As I plodded through this new soon to be found rut of an opportunity at CENEX, I at least had a steady paycheck. Darcy's parents were generous enough to let me stay in their home while interviewing, but I knew I couldn't overstay my welcome. Tired of renting throughout college, I found a mobile home for sale not far from where Darcy lived. The sale price seemed reasonable, and I found out why. It didn't meet the current building codes so a mortgage couldn't be obtained for it.

Upon learning that I couldn't get a loan, Darcy's dad asked, "how much could you buy it for?"

"About half what it's worth, six thousand dollars," I told him, "If I had cash, but I don't have that right now. Maybe after a few months of work," I remarked.

"How much would it take to bring it up to code?" Bob asked.

"Not much," I said. "It needs a larger window in one bedroom, and the furnace room needs to be lined with fire retardant walls. If I did the work myself, I don't think I'd have more than $1000.00 into it," I added. Bob offered to loan me the $6000.00 and said I could pay it back in two years. He didn't know me very well yet, but enough to know that I'd do as I said.

I was elated. I told Bob I'd pay it back in less than a year, and I did. I fixed the home, brought it up to code, and lived in it through one of the coldest winters in history and my first in Minnesota. The mobile home had walls made with two-by-two-inch wall studs and just a thin paneling inside and tin siding on the outside. The lower third perimeter of the walls had a constant frost on the inside. With the heat on constantly and burning a wood stove for extra warmth, my roommate and I could hardly keep the inside temperature above 60 degrees. We piled more snow around the outside perimeter as insulation and wind barrier. I had to figure out how to make more money and buy a real house.

In Dave's absence, there was no departmental leadership. His job was internally posted for hire and my temporary boss Jon Setala interviewed external candidates, but none met his criteria. As months passed, I slowly began to fill Dave's shoes and lead our department, organizing our weekly meetings, coordinating our projects, and utilizing our internal resources to lead a group of 35 people. Jon noticed this and gave me the temporary lead supervisor position in the manager's absence with a small but appreciated bump in pay. As he continued to interview and the more, I performed as the lead supervisor, I asked for the job twice, which he refused. After I was rejected, one of the older employees told me that Jon's boss, vice president of Marketing Dick Siderius, would never allow such a young guy like me in the position. It was almost a year, and Jon could not find a suitable candidate to pass the interview with his boss.

One evening I lay awake thinking hard about my next choice. I was managing the whole department and had acquired the respect of the employees, including many who were years senior my age. Our department performed well and got praised by its internal customers under my leadership. I somehow had to convince Jon to get me an interview with Dick Siderius.

The following week Jon had two more interviews for the position. After completing the two interviews, I knocked on his door and asked If he had time to meet with me. He motioned me in. "How did the interviews go?" I asked.

"I won't be asking them back," he replied without a smile.

"Well, Jon, I want the job," I stated. "I want you to ask Dick Siderius to interview me for the job." Jon didn't say a word; he just stared at me, looking at me like a kid. "Jon, you can't deny that I have been handling this job for almost a year and handling it well. While you have been interviewing candidates, I have performed two jobs, that of my own and that of Dave Cummings! I feel I deserve serious consideration." Jon continued to stare at me. "Jon, you've already given me the chance to prove myself. Have I not succeeded? Has this department ever performed as well?"

He continued to look at me with a blank stare. "Jon, I don't want this to sound like a threat, it's not intended to be, but if I can't have the job, I will move on from CENEX. There are other opportunities." He leaned back in his chair, and his frown disappeared as he put his pencil eraser to his cheek.

To my surprise, he responded, "Let me think this through, Curt. Give me a day or two." A few days later, the secretary of Jon's boss phoned me to set up an appointment to interview with Dick Siderious.

Dick Siderious was a misplaced Montana Cowboy. He was large-framed, tall, and rough-looking. He had a stern demeanor and did not waste much time with anyone. I'd heard from field staff that he hated sitting at the ivory tower (as the headquarters was known) and longed to return to his former field manager position (a field representative working with the local cooperative board of directors).

"Come on in," he motioned with his hand. "Have a seat." As I sat in his office directly across from him face-to-face, he reviewed some notes, my educational history, and my college work history. "From New York!" he said under his breath. "Worked on a pig farm—heh! Went to Iowa State University? Why did a kid from New York go to a lame school like that?" he asked grumblingly. I didn't answer. He continued to review other documents, possibly my three-month, six-month, and annual performance reviews, notes from my supervisor, and who knows what else. After what seemed like an hour, but quite possibly only five minutes of me sitting face to face with him as he toiled through my employee file, he placed the stack of papers back into the file and closed it. I wasn't privy to the file. I sat motionless and didn't say a word. He leaned back on his executive chair, clasped his large hands together using his two index fingers to form a steeple, placed the steeple on his lips, and stared at me through his thick-framed glasses.

"Why do you want this job?" he asked.

"I already have the job, sir; I've been performing it for almost a year. I want to be recognized for the work I'm already doing with the rank and pay the previous manager had."

He looked at me with a poker face staring directly into my eyes. "Do you like what you are doing," he asked, still pressing his lips through the steeple made with his fingers.

"Yes, sir," I responded. "I hate my job," he said. "Can't wait to get back to Montana."

"Your boss Jon speaks pretty highly of you. Do you know he asked me twice if I would interview you, and I told him no?"

I placed my elbows on the chair arms, clasped my hands together, made a steeple with my fingers, and pressed them against my lips as he did. "No, sir, I was unaware of that," I spoke through my steeple.

"You're too young; most people in your department are twice your age."

"I have their respect, sir."

"Hmph, that's what I'm told," he grunted.

Keeping my hands clasped together but removing the steeple from my lips, I looked at Mr. Siderious directly in the eyes. I asked, "Sir, if you officially acknowledge me with the manager role and the pay grade level for the responsibilities I'm already performing, I'll continue to perform the copywriter role as well. I've done it all year with ease. We can save our department and company a position and salary!"

The vice president looked at me with astonishment. "Where were you born?" he asked.

"New York City," I responded.

"What part of New York," he demanded.

"Brooklyn, Greenpoint, to be specific."

"Hmph, a kid from Brooklyn," he murmured. "Does Iowa State produce much of your type," he asked.

"Only the ones that come from Brooklyn," I responded confidently and with the same poker face he had dealt me the whole time.

That response finally got his lips to form a smile behind his fingered steeple still pressed to his lips. "You'd be the youngest manager I've ever hired, the youngest in the company," he said with excited anxiety.

"My maturity is well beyond my years, Mr. Siderius," I pleaded firmly. "Hmph, I've been told that too," he said. "You don't have much experience, though," he insisted.

"My performance this past year, voluntarily, I might add, should speak for itself," I reiterated with steel nerves. "You're a pretty confident kid—a little cocky too," he stated matter-of-factly.

I wanted to exude confidence, but him telling me straight out that I was cocky felt like I had crossed a boundary. I sat still and waited nervously for his following comment.

"I don't have any more questions," he stated as he rolled around to a pile of files on his credenza behind his chair, and he dismissed me with a wave of his hand as if I had wasted a half-hour of his time. He kept his back to me, stared down at reports on his credenza, and didn't say a word. I got up from the chair, and thanked him for his time.

That evening Darcy asked me how the interview went. "OK," I told her. "It went just OK. I think they think I'm too young for the job," I said. I didn't want to elaborate much more. Siderius crushed the confidence I walked into his office with. I was too embarrassed to tell her how short it went, that he didn't give me more than 20-30 minutes, how he didn't ask me any serious questions about my work, his sarcastic remark that I attended a lame university, and he thought I was cocky. Darcy could tell I didn't want to be pressed anymore on the topic, and we moved our conversation to how her day was.

Three days later, Jon's secretary summoned me to meet with him at two in the afternoon after the coffee and donut cart rolled around to the fifth floor. It was our routine weekly departmental review, so I thought nothing more of it.

"Come on in," he summoned. "Close the door and have a seat." I sat. "Well, you sure impressed my boss," he lamented sarcastically. I sat motionless and dumbfounded, unsure if I was being chastised or praised, fearing I made an ass of myself and Jon to his vice president. Every management level at CENEX must have gone through POKER FACE University! They all wore expressionless, stressful-looking poker faces, and I never knew how to take the frown. Whether it was of approval or disapproval, the smirk was the same.

Jon stared intently at me, "Well, congratulations if you still want the job, you got it." My heart thumped with adrenaline as if I were twelve-hunting my first deer. "He told me you were willing to do both jobs, the management job and the copywriter job." My heart was still pumping with excitement as I nodded yes. "That won't be necessary, but I think you impressed him greatly with that offer," he said. "I want you to meet with human resources and get the process rolling for hiring a replacement for your role as a copywriter."

I was still stunned and somewhat speechless. "Yes, sir," I replied. "And thank you, sir."

"Curt, you've done a fine job this past year; you deserve this chance. As your superior, though, I want to tell you our company is having a rough time. There will be challenges ahead. While we will put you through some courses and seminars that will help you round out your managerial skills, I want to offer you one piece of personal advice," he said with a low and serious tone. "In times of trouble, always err on the human side of things." Jon and I stared into the eyes of each other. I couldn't yet grasp exactly what his advice meant or what he was trying to tell me.

Jon was a successful creative communication and advertising director with CENEX for many years. He and his team created the corporate identity and name of CENEX, the corporate logo, and the slogan "Where the customer is the company" for the formerly named cooperative, the Farmers Union Central Exchange. His whole corporate identity and communications package made the Farmers Union Central Exchange appear like the Fortune 500 company it aspired to be. He seemed well respected by the upper ranks, and I sensed that he knew something big was coming our way that he couldn't yet tell me.

That evening, I stopped by the liquor store on the way home, picked up a bottle of Mateus, and shared the news with Darcy about my recent promotion and that my salary would double to almost triple. "Come on, let's go to my mom and dad and tell them," she insisted. She was so proud of me and even more excited than I was. Her mom and dad, Bob and Betty, cheered us as a couple and celebrated by breaking out a bottle of scotch and making a perfect Rob Roy for themselves and for me. Darcy, as always, sticks to the wine. When they asked what my new role would entail, I was well equipped to tell them every detail as I had already been in it for over a year. "You've been doing the job for a year already," Bob asked, "why did you do that?"

"Because someone had to, we didn't have a leader; I stepped into the role and just started performing in it."

"Well, it paid off," Betty lamented enthusiastically, and the glasses were raised again. My Darcy, my beautiful Darcy, looked at me with her eyes of adoration and amazement. She was right in her council a couple of years back when I considered Bob Fisher's offer to manage his farm to not focus on the money. I gave up that opportunity for half the salary I was making at CENEX, but now, with this new pay grade and little more than a year from that offer, I'd be making more than I was offered at Fishers.

Just six months into my new role as Manager of the CENEX Advertising and Graphics unit, I'd learn just what a rats nest I landed myself into. Dave Cummings must have known or sensed at his departure that CENEX was in deep financial trouble and would soon have its first layoffs. Entire divisions within the organization that our internal ad agency supported were dismantled, and people were let go by the hundreds.

Dick Siderius did what he said he'd do, resigned from his post, and retreated to Montana to become a field manager. At age 25, I experienced one of the most trying internal re-engineering processes and corporate layoffs I could never have imagined in college.

Each department was tasked to become a "cost recovery" unit and threatened that we would lose our jobs if we couldn't succeed. Cost recovery meant we had to build and implement a plan to bill our work and worth back to the divisions we served. Corporate didn't replace Sideris and rolled his division under another Vice President. My boss Jon and all other managers temporarily reported to Maurice Miller, VP of CENEX Corporate Planning. As we sat around a table in an early meeting with him, he looked each of us managers directly and asked, "Do you think you can turn your department into a cost recovery center?"

Each manager he addressed one by one sheepishly nodded yes, but when he came to me, I looked him directly in the eyes and said confidently, "Yes, I can do anything."

He glared at me. "Who are you?" he asked.

"I'm the advertising and graphics manager."

"What is your name?"

"Curt Riess."

"Well, I want to see you do that, Curt," he said condescendingly.

Not long after that meeting, Jon Setala was terminated. Another manager within the Marketing Division was promoted into his position. His name was Larry. He was a pleasant guy with a great sense of humor and a contagious laugh, but I sensed he didn't know what he was getting into any more than I did.

Half of the second floor of CENEX housed a giant processing computer. Desktop computers were nonexistent. I brought my own Macintosh computer to work, a Fat Mac and used it to begin employing my department's cost recovery system. Our department had Compugraphic typesetting equipment which, I discovered could run some minor enterprise software, tracking time, billing, and receipts similar to an accounting package. I found room in our budgets to purchase the software and employ it. I developed a job jacket system for moving projects from one department area to another while tracking and recording billable hours for each role or task. I trained my staff on using it and practiced for weeks until we felt confident enough to start billing the departments and divisions we served.

Within four months of Maury's mandate that we become a cost-recovery unit, we sent out with our completed projects a notice announcing that we were now a cost-recovery center and began mailing invoices for our work. None of the other departments had made any progress toward cost recovery and took Maury's message as it was probably intended to be, start looking for a job.

The first week we invoiced our internal customers, I was summoned by several managers and directors to whom we served what this meant. I explained to them that we had become a cost recovery center and that the invoices we sent them had to be paid to our department for our work through the internal accounting system. They all looked at me like I was crazy and asked who authorized us to do this.

It didn't take long for our new vice president to hear what I had done from other divisional vice presidents as they voiced their anger against a department, they were already funding through budget allocations. I was summoned into Larry's office and asked exactly what did I accomplish? I explained what we had accomplished, laid out our small business plan, forecasted expected revenue toward profits, or at least minimally to break even for the first year. I also provided samples and copies of invoices already transmitted through the intracompany mail system for work performed. He was astonished and asked me for copies of all the invoices we had sent out to date and to whom and more samples of other protocols and procedures I had set up. He asked me if we could employ the same system for the rest of the marketing departments. "I don't see why not," I enthusiastically promoted. He complimented me and reported what our unit had accomplished to his boss.

A few days later, I was called into Larry's office and told to stop and halt all efforts at cost recovery immediately! He repeated it to be sure I heard him. I was told to stop billing the divisions and hold off on all efforts until further notice. I was stunned! Larry wasn't the typical poker-face managerial type. He was more open and more communicative, and he expressed that he had no idea why; he was just told to tell me to stop, and unlike other bosses who would protect the next level of authority, he let me know where the directive came from.

I was concerned. That son of a bitch never really thought we'd accomplish the task and to his amazement I had. Even more problematic was the task of going to my staff after all the work we accomplished to achieve what we did and explaining to them that without any reasons given, we had to halt all efforts toward our cost recovery mission. I was too naive to realize the task was given to us as a perceived task to which we would all fail and deserve termination. But I succeeded. The handwriting was on the wall.

As the coming months began to unfold, more departments we served in other divisions were being dismantled and laid off. With disappearing divisions and departments like hardware and others, demand for our services began to dwindle, and many of us were sitting idle. I now began to understand Jon Setala's advice "to err on the human side of things" and called my entire staff into a meeting. I could not share anything with them official, only discuss and confirm the obvious that they too could see that the demand for our services had been significantly reduced. Soon, our department wouldn't be needed at all. I encouraged them all to use the company equipment, typesetters, and each other after hours or as idle time within work hours permitted to develop resumes and prepare themselves for the possibility of finding a job. We had become a close team, accomplishing what they initially thought couldn't be completed and then being crushed for doing so. I felt the worst for three hired employees, one to replace me as the copywriter, who had only been on board for less than four months when all of the upheaval and turmoil began.

In the ensuing months, while all my staff developed resumes, only a few moved on to other job opportunities, and those who did thanked me for the insights, assistance, and recommendations. I didn't need to ask to replace them with internal job postings; our unit was idle.

The day came when I was instructed that I could choose three of the 35 staff people and myself to keep employed, and the rest would be laid off. I asked if I could forfeit my position to stay and keep a fourth employee and was told, no, that is not an option. I was being considered for another post.

Human resources instructed us on the procedures for laying off the people and how to perform the exit interview in a private conference room, one by one. It would be a Friday, so the laid-off could go home and be surrounded by family over the weekend who might otherwise be in school or working if it weren't a weekend.

Then Friday came. I had my stack of thirty or so pink envelopes to begin my exit interviews. The other department managers began immediately at 8:30 performing their layoffs. Employees would come bounding out of the private conference rooms in anger. Some returned to their offices screaming loud profanities; others pounded their desks. There was no privacy in the open-air office environment to conceal these actions. Some of my staff came to my office asking what was going on. I just gave them a reassuring look and put a finger to my lips to remain quiet, and that I'd communicate soon.

More employees began to make noise in the adjacent departments. Our unit's tradition was celebrating any staff's birthdays with a cake and coffee at 9:30 break time. We had planned to do so for a gal named Vivian. I devised a different plan against the guidance and advice of the human resources to perform the layoff notices individually.

At the 9:30 birthday celebration, we all assembled in a conference room. All eyes were upon me, and everyone was in a somber mood. "Err on the human side of things." Those words of advice have more meaning to me now.

"I'd like to have your attention," I asked. "First warm birthday wishes to Vivian and many happy returns." The whole staff applauded. "As most of you have seen, staff are being dismissed in the adjacent departments. We all anticipated this day was coming; we prepared as best we could, preparing our resumes." A large gulp was hanging in my throat. "We have developed over the last couple of years into a top-notch and very close working team. There is enormous talent in this room, but it's no longer needed here at CENEX for other failings within this company. I was asked to pick three employees I think could assimilate into other departments that might remain. I've chosen these three, and here are my reasons."

I gave the staff the reasons for the three employees, all three of which had only been on board for less than a year, had made moves from other parts of the country to relocate, and I thought they would suffer a more significant hardship because they had little time with the company to which severance pay was based. All the rest of you will receive termination notices today. I wanted to let you know this as a team rather than suffer through a one-on-one communication procedure we are seeing in the adjacent department.

I want to spare all of us the anxieties and emotional bewilderment of whether each of us is the next person to be called into a conference room.

After we have cake and coffee, I will be available in a private conference room for anyone with questions or concerns, but there are these things in each of your employment termination envelopes. You'll receive a notice outlining any severance pay to which you may be entitled. It is based upon your years of service to CENEX. You'll get a notice of continuing healthcare and other benefits, including outreach assistance, interview training, and resume-building services if needed. Of course, you will receive your official separation notice.

"I'll hand each of you your envelope, and again, I'll be in the conference room after this meeting for anyone who would like to discuss anything privately." My staff looked at me with a lack of surprise and proud calm. No one lashed out; broke down in tears; everyone had a calm look about them. "Are there any questions for me?"

One of the staff members asked me if I was staying employed. "Yes, I am," I said. "But I want you to know that I offered up my job to save one more of you, but I was told that was not an option. I don't know what is in store for me nor how long I may stay if I do."

"Are there any other questions?" I asked. There were none.

"Well then, Vivian, let's cut the cake and celebrate your birthday," and so we did. The staff was amazingly calm offering up a few jokes and polite laughter, reassuring each other that everything would turn out fine. They were prepared. I took a significant risk to err on the human side of things months before, and it paid off, all thanks to Jon Setala.

After Vivian passed out the last piece of cake, she stood and commanded our attention. "I just want to thank everyone for the birthday wishes, and I want to thank you, Curt, for all you've done for us." I received a standing applause from my staff.

"Well, Vivian, it's a birthday you'll probably never forget," I said laughingly to lighten the mood. Then I began to move about and hand out the termination envelopes, "but remember, for every door that closes, a new and better door of opportunity opens, and it begins with this envelope," I said, trying to put a positive spin on opening what most would consider being a most negative document to receive.

I was so proud of my staff as they returned to their desks. They were as pleasant as possible, still celebrating Vivian's day, and calmly began packing up their personal belongings. They were some of the most professional corporate staff I'd ever worked with. Managers and employees from the adjacent departments looked on with wonder! Only six employees needed some private time with me, mostly over questions related to benefits, and the three employees whom I chose to stay on board as they wanted more clarity as to what lay ahead.

Chapter Forty-Four
The Proposal

Winter 1983

Playlist:

The Search Is Over, Survivor

St. Elmos Fire, John Parr

We Are The World, U.S.A. For Africa

You Belong To The City, Glenn Frey

I Live My Life for You, Firehouse

Three and a half years after I first saw her, I asked Darcy to marry me. My employment with CENEX seemed secure as they assigned me new responsibilities. I bought and fixed up the mobile home and paid her dad back. Because I was aggressive with extra payments to the school loans, I didn't have too much money for the engagement ring. We expanded considerably from our five-dollar college dates having a corporate salary, and splurged a little here and there.

On one such splurge, I took Darcy to a fancy restaurant atop one of the hotels in Minneapolis. All the waiters and waitresses wore formal wait attire and would break out in opera as they served meals. It was fun, relaxed, and unique.

I ordered a bottle of wine, and it came wrapped in a towel chilled in a stand set by the table, first-ever for me! For an appetizer, we ordered a quail. "One?" the waiter asked. I looked at Darcy. "Yeah, just one…" we agreed we'd split it. One was enough at the price we had to pay for it too! We had no idea what a quail appetizer was. The waiter took our dinner order, and within ten to fifteen minutes, he rolled a substantial silver domed platter to the table. He set the tray in the middle of the table. As he lifted the dome off, he pronounced, "your quail, sir." Darcy and I looked at the thing in the middle of this massive platter. It was no bigger than a mouse! We both started laughing hysterically. We cut it down the middle and served it on our appetizer setting. We were sure the waiter was having a good time with the chef and others over two naive young lovers out on the town that night. That's how it was for us in our early years, learning about the finer things in life through mishaps and explorations into different venues and always having a good time. We were both motivated to learn and earn more.

One of the few kind gestures Loretta ever made was giving me my Nanny Riess' wedding ring when I told her I'd be asking Darcy to marry me. She heard me talk about Darcy's admiration for her Grandpa Henry, and Loretta knew I admired my dad's mom. Loretta told me she thought Darcy might appreciate it as an engagement ring and let her know it was my grandmother's. It had the most petite diamond other than the one I had mounted on that gold bracelet I gave her the night we first made love. I couldn't afford both an engagement ring and a wedding ring, and in my research, I'd heard they were often purchased in a pair, so I was hoping she'd understand this was just the beginning and that we'd shop together. I also wanted Darcy to explore what she would like. She had a designer taste, better than mine.

I had a hilarious and glorious plan to propose to Darcy. I would take her back to that restaurant and order the quail again. Darcy would, of course, refuse and tell me not to waste my money again, but this time I would have the ring sitting under the silver dome instead. I was going to cue the wait staff and ask them to sing some Italian love song the minute I got down on one knee there in the restaurant and ask her to marry me. Then we'd go to one of our favorite nightclubs and dance the night away, and I would explain that the ring was my grandmother's and only symbolic for the moment in that I'd like to shop with her for the actual ring.

Being absent from both of my hometowns in upstate New York, I wrote what might have been one of the very first Christmas Letters sharing my Midwest experiences with folks back home; the Kings, the Hansen family, Garlands, the Duke, and some members of St. Paul's church. I had written the letter before proposing to Darcy, anticipating she would say yes. I pre-stated in it that I was engaged to Miss Darcy Hoff. I had not sent any of the letters out, waiting until after the actual proposal to Darcy to be sure she said yes. I would mail out my Christmas greeting immediately after.

However, as the proposal went, it wasn't as romantic as I had planned. Darcy came to my mobile home right after work to hang out on the first Friday of December. She had a mild cold coming on and just wanted to stay in, snuggle up and watch some television. I made some mac and cheese, and then we retreated to my bedroom to keep warm. Hanging out in that mobile home was like being in a refrigerator cooler as the frost on the inside walls was now about ten inches up from the floor permanently. We kept warm by snuggling under the many covers I draped on my mattress on the floor, and those snuggles led to even more generous emotions and activities.

After our lovemaking, I sat pillows against the frigid wall so Darcy could prop her head upon my chest. We chatted about our work week when Darcy interjected in a polite but quizzing manner, "So what about us?"

I looked at her and said, "What do you mean what about us?"

"Well," she quizzed with some shyness but also directness, "Is there going to be a future with us?" I was silent as she lifted her head and looked at me blankly. "I mean, if there is no intent between us," she said, "then I don't want to hang around, you know what I mean?"

While I was surprised at Darcy's questioning, I shouldn't have been. I never once gave any hint in any form that I was planning to ask her to marry me. I assumed she knew I was committed based on the acts of love between us. It wasn't that, though; December is traditionally a month when many young couples get engaged, and Darcy, of course, deserved to be naturally wondering.

I looked at Darcy, and I said, "Well, of course, there will be a future for us! I mean, I'm here in Minnesota; in this trailer a mile from your house! We're one; you know there will be a future for us!"

The unuttered question on her face now was: When?

I was going to implement my plan in the next week or two just before Christmas, but this had to be the moment. With Darcy inquisitive and feeling low with a cold, with us fresh with passion from a lovemaking session, it seemed the right time for me to pop the question. To play dumb and try to avoid the subject to keep my plans a surprise wasn't the right thing to do. Here I was, lying with one of the most beautiful girls in the world. A girl from a crowd of thousands that singer-songwriter Cat Stevens selected and pulled from his concert audience at ISU to steal a kiss from and now she was staring at me with those beautiful blue eyes and soft lips as she pressed her hand firmly on my chest with the unspoken question of "when?"

"Well," I said hesitantly and with a sigh of having to fess up, "I'd like you to read something," I rolled over and pulled out my not yet sent first annual Christmas letter. As she read through my life news to my friends and family, I pulled out my grandmother's ring.

When she got to the last paragraph, tears came to her eyes, and she looked up and asked, "Really?"

"Yes," I said, "will you marry me?" and I presented my grandmother's ring. Darcy broke out in a joyful set of tears as we embraced. She loved the fact it had been my grandmother's.

The dinner idea was skunked; there'd be no silver platter, no opera singers, no bottle of champagne. I asked my bride to marry me on a floor mattress in a humble mobile home with frost ten inches higher than we were on the walls! I scrapped my planned proposal that I had rehearsed the past few weeks with these humble beginnings.

"With this ring," I asked, "will you love me every day of your life as I will you?" and still with tears, she nodded, "Yes."

"Darcy, I can't tell you how long I've been planning this, it just wasn't going to be here, but I have three promises to you I want to share."

Promise One: "My love, as I told you, this was my grandmother's wedding ring. I want to go shopping with you and pick a different setting to set this diamond in. I know the diamond is small, but if you would be patient with me and give me more time, I promise I'll work hard to double the size of it every five years the rest of our lives together."

Promise two: "My love, I'll always be faithful to you. I'll someday build you a different and unique house that we'll call our own, design together, and you'll decorate. I'll always try to be kind, gentle and help you with your dreams. I'll love you as we build a family, and I'll love you till I die."

Promise three: "Darcy, we both have our dreams. I'm sure we'll accomplish them together, if nothing else I promise you'll never have a boring life! You'll never be bored being married to me." Darcy teared up again and promised me herself and her unwavering support in everything we decided to do together.

Darcy was excited to tell her mom and dad. We got dressed and went back to her house. Her mom and dad were enjoying a lovely quiet Friday evening at home with a fire in the fireplace. Snow flurries were falling and were highlighted by the floodlights lit out their back windows. Their home overlooked a lake. Bob loved music and had some of his classical music on. They greeted us in their kitchen as we came in, and Bob offered us a drink.

"Well, we have an announcement." Darcy quickly and enthusiastically proclaimed! She could hardly wait. Her mom stopped in her tracks and turned forthright to us. Her dad also stopped midway to the liquor cabinet. Darcy then looked to me to make the announcement. "Well," I nervously hesitated, "I'd like to marry Darcy with your permission!"

"Well," gasped Betty as she must have been holding her breath, "it's about time!" she joyfully expressed as she headed for Darcy and delivered a big hug of congratulations. Betty had been wondering and waiting as anxiously as Darcy. "Congratulations!" Bob shouted, "I'll get the scotch! We have to celebrate." He proclaimed.

Darcy showed them the ring I gave her and explained that we'd go shopping together. Her dad fetched a bottle of Johnny Walker Red and made us all a perfect Rob Roy, even Darcy. "Cheers," he lifted his glass, toasted to us, and wished us much success and a long and happy marriage.

We all settled around the fire, sipping our drinks, and we would learn of Bob and Betty's proposal long ago. Bob first asked Betty's dad to marry her while he was milking a cow in the family barn. Henry looked up at Bob, told him he seemed like a nice fellow and said yes. When Bob announced to his parents that he would be asking Betty to marry him, Bob was given a vacant lot his parents owned in Minneapolis where he could build a home. Bob brought Betty to the lot and proposed to her. He asked her to marry him and shared the site where he promised to build her a house and start their life together. Betty said it was meaningful at the time, but she joked that it wasn't very romantic! Bob defended himself with his quick wit and said, "Yeah, but it was a "lot" of proposing!" As I was sure this conversation might be leading up to the story as to how I proposed to Darcy, using my quick wit, I said, "Well, I wasn't very romantic either; in fact, my proposal was over a mac and cheese dinner!" I surely didn't want to tell them the whole story!

After consulting with her mom, Darcy chose the date for us to be married. It would be a little over a year from now on April 20, 1985. Darcy and her mom planned everything, and her dad paid for everything; I just had to pick up the tab for the groom's dinner. A still traditional arrangement in those days, but times were changing, and I wasn't sure how much I would be responsible for. "Only the groom's dinner," Darcy told me, and I sure appreciated it as I was saving to prepare the start of a new life with my bride-to-be.

Chapter Forty-Five
Our Wedding

April 1985
Playlist:
Footloose, Kenny Loggins
All Night Long, Lionel Ritchie
Let's Hear It For The Boy, Deniece Williams Self Control, Laura Branigan
Hold Me Now, Thompson Twins Almost Paradise, Mike Reno feat, Ann
Wilson I'm So Excited, The Pointer Sisters

I was on a roll the last year and a half. I was paying down my school debt and saving for a home to start my life with Darcy. I sold the mobile home I owned, paid Darcy's dad back, and had a small profit to which I applied the rest to my school loans. My Chevette was having engine problems and was not reliable. Twice the engine was overhauled under warranty still on the car, but I still had to cover 1/3rd of the expense. I had suggested to Darcy that I help her buy a new car before we were married if I could use the vehicle on an occasional long trip back to New York. We purchased a 1984 Nissan Maxima, an expensive luxury car then, but planned we'd have it for a long time. Darcy's dad counseled me by asking me if we were sure we wanted to do this; he suggested we'd maybe want to buy a house. I told him we'd do that too… he looked at me with my confidence, dropped his council, and said, OK!

CENEX had a 401k program in which I had invested as many pre-tax dollars as their plan allowed. At the time, CENEX matched them dollar for dollar. The 401K had a provision that one could take funds out of the account without penalty for a first-time home purchase, and that is precisely why I was maxing out what I could put into it. I came out of ISU with twenty-eight thousand dollars of school debt. The government loan gave me an amortization whereby I would pay it off until I was forty-two. It seemed ridiculous to me, and that length of time was not on my list of goals. I had a different figure in mind for age 40, which didn't include still paying off school loans. I cut my school loans by a third with the profits from the mobile home sale, another third doubling the payments required, and paid it off using some extra earnings from various evening work in the next three years.

I lived temporarily in a rent-free room in exchange for gardening and maintenance for an elderly couple. Darcy and I began shopping for a future home. We found a double bungalow on 46th Street just two blocks north of Minnehaha Falls Park and one block from the Mississippi River road, a great Minneapolis location. The interest rate was 26-1/2%. The seller was willing to pay five points down on the mortgage as my affordability for this $79,000.00 property was capped at the 21-1/2% interest rate. And, even with that, I had to have the other side of the bungalow leased before we could close the loan with the bank.

The closing date for our new home was the morning before the groom's dinner and the day before our wedding. I drained my 401k funds for the down payment. It was now just over five years since we first met and dated. Some would say I took my time and I did, but there was a reason! Loretta and Harry and every one of my older siblings and my youngest were divorced. Loretta seemed to help influence their demise through her antics and interference, and I did not want to fall victim to the same dysfunction. I wanted to marry once and be sure we were rock solid together as a team against anything that would come our way, including Loretta.

Darcy had experienced enough of Loretta and my family to this point that she was comfortable moving forward, seeing how different I was from the rest. I needed that assurance that I thought only time could give us. I was excited to have her as my wife and live with her. To be by her side every night and begin building out our dreams. And she was excited to be with me.

April 19 came, five years and four months after we first met, and we closed on our first home together. The next day I awoke eager to get through the morning and onto the wedding ceremony. I could hardly wait to see Darcy and the dress she and her mom had picked. I was sure it would be something incredible, conservative, and sure, whatever kind of dress it was, Darcy would be a knockout. I was so honored and privileged to have this girl as my bride.

My older half-sister and brother, my younger sister, Loretta, and Harry, and my best man, the Duke, were the only attendees in my half of the family at the wedding, along with my best men. My King family was there as well."

It was a beautiful April day, and we were surrounded by good friends from college who stood with us at the altar. I still remember staring into Darcy's eyes, sharing my vows with her and her with me, but also reciting my own three promises under my breath. The ring she picked out was a beautiful setting, designed for a center marquee diamond I promised her down the road, but now set with the small round diamond from my grandmother's wedding band. Darcy was so gracious about it. She told me not to fret and that she would be satisfied if she never had more than that ring and diamond. I had lived frugally, and nearly all my net pay went into the 401K program and to pay off my student debt. I could have afforded a little more for that marquee diamond at the time, but I paid cash for everything, including the weeklong honeymoon we were about to embark upon in Hawaii. Loretta's credit card debt in our household was one of many significant sources of frustration and household strife. She always lived beyond the means Harry could afford, racking up high-interest credit card payments. I lived as my dad did, without credit cards and paying for anything I needed with cash.

Buying and repairing that mobile home taught me how to make some good money in addition to my salary from CENEX. One of the financial lessons I learned from my father was that you earn a living between eight and five, but you got all the extras in life between five and eight. In addition to my daily job, I began to find ways to make money in the evening and on weekends.

We married on Saturday, April 20, 1985. It was a beautiful ceremony and a grand evening celebration hosted by Darcy's parents at a country club they belonged to. I gave my toast to my bride in song. I brought her to the center of the dance floor, held a glass of champagne in my left hand as I held her right hand, and sang lyrics from a few songs combining them into a story reminiscent of my life up to meeting her.

In the song Something Good from the Sound of Music, I sang the lyrics; "Perhaps I had a wicked childhood, perhaps I had a miserable youth, But somewhere in my wicked, miserable path, there must have been a moment of truth. For here you are standing there loving me, whether or not you should, So somewhere in my youth or childhood, I must have done something good!"

No one in the audience except my own family knew a thing about my childhood, and as I glanced toward Loretta in the audience, she was sobbing. I hadn't thought about how she might feel about those lyrics, but they weren't for her. They were for my bride and me; I tossed away everything in my childhood past with those lyrics.

Then I transitioned to another Sound Of Music Classic titled Sixteen Going On Seventeen, but I changed the lyrics to have a little fun; they were as follows. "You are 23 going on 24, baby; you just married me; I am 26 going on 27. I'll take care of you. Totally unprepared were you to face the world of men, timid, shy and scared are you for things beyond your friends; you need someone older and wiser telling you what to dooooooo! (as I looked into her eyes, I cleared my throat and paused as I scanned the audience and winked. I backed the tune-up and changed the lyrics again to fit her parents and the audience that knew Darcy was a strong-willed and determined young woman way beyond her friends and who would never need anybody telling her what to do. I moved on to have some fun) I need someone younger and prettier telling me what to doooooo!" and with a pause and a few laughs from the audience, I transitioned and concluded with a tune I sang in my high school musical, Oklahoma, All or Nothing with a twist.

"With me, it's all or nothing. Is it all or nothing with you? It can't be "in-between"; It can't be "now or then" No half-and-half romance will do. I'll build you a house; all painted white, cute and clean and pretty and bright, big enough for two but not for three, but supposing that we should have a third one, he better look a lot like me, he can have your nose though, but he better looks a lot like me!"

Those lyrics reference my promise to Darcy that I'd build her a house, build a family, have as much fun as we possibly could together, and I'd never been boring. And I buried all the negative in my past, including the hallway kiss she never knew about forever.

We all raised our glasses to my bride.

After a magical evening, it was shortly after midnight when we got to our hotel in Bloomington. Just like the first night we made love, I had arranged for flowers in the room and some appetizers, but instead of our cheap college wine of Mateus or Lancers, I had a chilled bottle of expensive champagne waiting. As we approached the door, I lifted Darcy, carried her over the threshold, presented her with yet another beautiful bouquet of a dozen red roses, and popped the cork on the champagne. Just as I sang lyrics in my toast to her, referencing snippets of our life story up to our wedding day, one of the songs Darcy selected to play at our ceremony was Make My Life A Candle, written and sang by our then church music director, Handt Hanson. It was a religious song asking God to make my life (our lives) a candle to light the way every day for ourselves and others. Darcy had already been a candle to many in her life in warm and loving ways. She was already a candle in my life. "To our lives being a candle, Darcy," I toasted. "To our lives as a single candle, she toasted back."

The bed was already folded down. As we sipped our champagne, I proceeded to help Darcy undress from her wedding gown. While we had made love times before this night, it was always in the dark. I'd never seen Darcy completely undressed and naked except to the extent her bikini bathing suit exposed her beautiful body in daylight. She was always shy in our lovemaking and ensured the lights were off. It was the first time I saw her entire body fully nude, and she was beautiful. While I had brought condoms, she informed me we didn't need them as she was now on a birth control pill. I always suspected she hadn't been based on her very conservative make-out sessions with me, but now I had confirmation again that Darcy was not like the girls of my high school and early college years; I had chosen well.

Chapter Forty-Six
The Honeymoon

April 1985
Playlist:
Crazy For You, Madonna
Love Will Keep Us Alive

In the first act of keeping my promises to Darcy, I whisked her off to Hawaii to spend a week on our honeymoon. We spent two days in Oahu and found some nightclubs in Honolulu to dance our evenings away. I rented a condo on Maui and a car with plans to traverse and see nearly every square inch of the island. I was going to be sure she'd never get bored.

On the second day there, we tried to travel a road to the island's undeveloped side. Warning signs were posted at the entrance of the rough roads stating no rental cars beyond that point. When trying to cross lava fields on these undeveloped roads, I quickly learned why rental cars were not allowed beyond the sign stating so as I was scraping underbody on lava rock. We wouldn't get far around the island with the car, so we returned it and rented a jeep.

We drove around the island. We traversed creeks where bridges didn't exist, crossed ancient lava fields, and found beautiful vistas of inland valleys on the drier side of the island. It was a marvelous adventure, and some curious and brave tourists saw us drive past the restricted road signs and followed us.

We drove up to a herd of horses to which we stopped, and they curiously surrounded our small caravan and began poking their heads into the windows. Darcy began to feed one of them some Doritos,' and he yearned for more, sticking his entire head through the open roof and down into Darcy's lap, trying to capture the rest of the bag. She was laughing like crazy, albeit nervously. Everyone in the three vehicles behind us was in awe along with us. It was like a movie scene! We parked our jeeps, got out, hung out with the horses, and greeted each other to learn where we all had journeyed from.

We explored the seven pools at Hanna and various other tourist spots and hung out on the secluded beaches we found. Darcy was a knockout in her turquoise bikini and white see-through cover-up. I appreciated how beautiful she was outside, as I had already learned how beautiful she was on the inside.

We returned from breakfast at a local café one afternoon, and I tossed Darcy onto the bed. We began to make love when almost to a climax, Darcy started screaming wildly. Screaming wasn't the norm for her in making love, but I thought, wow, this honeymoon is going well! I looked into her frightened eyes and rolled over to see a giant tarantula sized spider above our bed on the ceiling! "Curt, Curt, look!"

"Holy crap," I said as I hurried under the sheets with her!

"Go get it," she demanded.

"Go get it!" I shrieked! "Are you crazy? I'm naked and hard as a rock!"

"You have to get it," she begged; "it could be poisonous!" I grabbed my shorts and slipped them on. As I tried to chase it with a shoe, it sped across the room at lightning speed. I started throwing my shoes at it, and each time I missed, the giant spider leaped across the room like a kangaroo. Darcy went undercover now, literally and completely. Finally, I nailed it with a deadly blow from the shoe. It lay listless and was about 4-5 inches across.

Darcy hurriedly dressed, and we called the condo maintenance man, left a message about the incident, and left the spider in the bathroom sink for him to see and identify. We left for another day of island exploration as he promised to inspect the unit and assure us there were no more spiders.

Upon our return, he informed us that our entire unit was inspected, and they found no other spiders or critters. They reassured us that I had killed a sugar cane spider, giant and scary looking but harmless. That was comforting, but anymore lovemaking was made with a watchful eye.

We enjoyed the rest of our week hanging out at beaches, attending luaus and doing what we loved most, having romantic evening dinners and great conversations about what we'd do in life together. In one evening, chat, I suggested that it was so much fun and beautiful here that we promised each other we should try to return every five years on our anniversary after I doubled that diamond. She chuckled and said, "Seriously, there is no need to double this diamond."

"No," I insisted, "I am serious about that promise. I will to do it, and we'll come back here every five years to celebrate."

After a week there we had a red-eye flight back to Minneapolis from Hawaii, arriving at 7 am. We immediately drove to the U-Haul dealer and rented a truck to move all our belongings into the home we closed on the day before our wedding. As soon as I returned from bringing the U-Haul truck back to the dealer, I called Darcy out to the front of the house, and then I lifted her again and carried her across the threshold. Barely unpacked and with boxes abundantly dropped everywhere, we went into our bedroom on the half-sheeted mattress and made love for the first time in our new home. Life was never, ever going to be boring. In our first week of marriage, we closed on our first home, vacationed in Hawaii, returned a week later, and moved into our new house the same morning we got off the plane. Promise three was already in the works!

Chapter Forty-Seven
Our First Three Years of Marriage

Curt and Darcy honeymoon in Hawaii

April 1985 – April 1988
Playlist:
Have I Told You Lately, Van Morrison
I Will Always Love You, Whitney Houston
The River of Dreams, Billy Joel

In our new home, Darcy and I worked feverishly every evening after work to create a new living space out of the unfinished attic. Darcy had landed a job as an in-house designer at an Ethan Allen Store, and though she was not practicing her college-acquired commercial design skills as job openings were scarce, she was helping me draft up our little space into a floor plan. As I constructed the new area, she made our tiny home exquisitely inviting with her choice of window treatments, furniture selection, and accessories. Barely occupying it for over a year, I suggested buying and moving to another home just a few blocks away I'd found. Darcy was crushed! We'd just completed the upstairs attic living area, and she looked forward to enjoying and decorating the new space. I convinced her that the double bungalow we were in would make a great rental property and help propel us toward something more interesting in the future. We moved, and we put her drafting skills to practice again.

Our next home had been completely updated and remodeled on the first level and had two good-sized bedrooms on the main floor, leaving three small bedrooms upstairs to revamp into a main bedroom suite. In less than six months, we had completed that project together, and by the following spring, I managed to acquire a third small home in the neighborhood, to which I performed some upgrades and rented out. Darcy and I were becoming a terrific team! I loved her before marriage, and my love for her grew even more in everything we did together. We made a great team in many things we worked on, and I kept my promises, mainly that she'd never be bored with me.

I performed well at my work with CENEX. With all the upheaval and layoffs during my first couple of years with them, I took on jobs, responsibilities, and roles left vacant from other terminations. I piled them upon myself without asking for additional pay. And each year, I received bonuses and promotions in income and stature for doing so. With each bonus and raise Darcy and I poured those dollars into paying off the home and rental projects we acquired. We continued to live frugally and on a minimal budget, careful not to increase our lifestyle to the total pay we earned. In fact, for the first five years of our marriage, we lived off only half of my income, and we used Darcy's salary and the other half of mine to pay off our house. We'd joke some mornings that maybe it's time to turn the heat on when we'd wake up to winter-like mornings and see our breath as we popped our heads above the covers! We kept everything to a minimum, even the temperature in our home.

My career was going well, but I sensed disappointment for Darcy because she wasn't quite where she wanted to be. I encouraged my love to keep pursuing her dream, sending out resumes to companies even if they don't have job openings and meeting with anyone who would take the time to do so for an informational interview.

It was difficult for her. The eighties remained tough economic years with high inflation still reeling from the President Carter years, but things were slowly beginning to change under President Reagan. I knew she'd land an opportunity if Darcy could get an open door in front of a potential employer. Her enthusiasm, grit, and skills would surely land her the first opportunity that opened. I encouraged her to stay in front of the doors of possibilities and that one would open. And when it did, she'd be walking through it.

For myself, opportunities poured upon me as people observed my work ethic and my use of L.U.C.K. One chance led me into a partnership where we developed two retail locations with a full-service car wash, quick lube, gas, and convenience store operation. Having observed my performance and confidence as an employee, CENEX invested nearly 2 million dollars in me and my partnership to build and brand these facilities with the CENEX flag. The demise of the corner gas station with a mechanic was already disappearing fast, and we were on the cutting edge of offering a different venue. As a petroleum company, CENEX was eager to see the models I would build in hopes of expanding them across their trade territory.

I worked my full-time career at CENEX while also building out the facilities, but operations began requiring more of my attention, so I resigned from CENEX to become a full-time entrepreneur.

Meanwhile, through Darcy's persistence in sending resumes out for commercial design work, she landed a job with Rosemount Office Systems as a commercial designer in their drafting department. She was so excited, and I was ecstatic and excited for her. I can still see the excitement in her eyes, that twinkling spark she's always had when something new and exciting came her way. We celebrated, of course, with one of our old standbys, a bottle of Mateus! Darcy performed well in her new career and proved herself beyond doubt with her capabilities.

Our convenience store models were running and performing well as new ventures. The first car wash had been up and running for several years. We were just barely occupied in the second facility for one year when the partnership bookkeeper quietly suggested to me one day that I should ask my partner to see the details of the books. I was running the daily operations and trusted the accounting and administration of the business to my partner, who was primarily absent as he also held another full-time job. "Why should I need to look at the books?" I asked. "Curt," she said, "things aren't right!"

"What do you mean they aren't right?" She began sobbing uncontrollably. "They haven't been for a long time, Curt," she said. "I see you working so hard…you're the one who brought in the investment money with your reputation when he couldn't (referring to one of my partners)," she broke down sobbing again. She was hesitant to say much, almost scared to death to do so, like she had a nervous breakdown.

"Can you give me a copy?" I asked.

She gained control of herself, "No, I can't; you need to ask your partner," she said. She flinched and didn't want to say anymore. The partner had previously done the bookkeeping in past years. As we grew, we hired a full-time bookkeeper and used an extra office in Darcy's dad's building where she could maintain an office and we all could hold weekly meetings.

I left the office and went home and talked with Darcy that evening. "What did she mean by all that?" Darcy asked.

"I'm not sure," I said. I was always a trusting person. "I don't know if the business is failing financially or if she was implying something else; she wouldn't say."

"Well, the partner tells you we are breaking monthly records!" Darcy stated.

"Yes based on the volume of cars going through our facilities, it doesn't make sense that we'd be failing."

"Well, maybe you should do as she said, ask to see the books?" Darcy suggested.

"Yeah, let me have another conversation about this with Luann first," I suggested.

Our weekly meeting with the partner and Luann took a very different turn after she suggested I ask to see the books. As we reviewed our weekly tasks, employee and hiring issues, head counts, and labor hours, we turned to our weekly sales and vehicle counts. They were all excellent numbers! Luan looked straight down at the table, never lifting her eyes. It was the first time I had observed this behavior from her. In her duties, Luann would often also serve as a part-time cashier at one of the facilities for a few hours a week as the bookkeeping was slightly less than a full-time position. She also handled the daily cash from the registers, made the deposits to the bank, and reconciled the checkbooks and bank statements. These tasks were always performed by my partner's wife in the past and still was occasionally.

Doubting any misdeeds and afraid that asking would break the trust that was always there among the partners, I let another week or two slip by without asking to see the books. Reporting the sales and vehicle counts in those weekly meetings was usually good news. I watched the nonverbals of the partner and Luan closely. At each meeting again, she lowered her eyes to the table to avoid eye contact with anyone and remained silent as the partners gave the numbers.

We ran a tight business, and our profits depended on labor control, so our labor force was substantially reduced on rainy days. With a few days of rain and some free time, I asked Luan if she'd go to lunch with me, and she agreed. I addressed the concerns she raised the past few weeks at lunch, and her body tensed. Her nonverbals expressed she was uncomfortable with the questions I raised. She insisted again that I ask to see the books. "Are we failing," I asked. "No," she responded. I waited with a long pause, and she offered nothing. We continued to eat our lunch, and she began to sob. "Curt, you're being cheated," she said. "Do you notice one of the partners always volunteers to cashier on our biggest days," she asked. Frankly, it was so typical I didn't think twice about it. "Watch the vehicle counts, Curt," she suggested as she sniffled and wiped her tears and nose with a tissue. "Watch the cashier and watch the vehicle counts; that's all I can tell you," She said.

I shared the hints of implied impropriety with Darcy. "What are you going to do," Darcy asked. "Well, the vehicle counts come from the register. We don't have vehicle counters in the wash tunnels. I will install vehicle counters in the washes and compare the counts to the register tapes," I said. "I'll also casually observe the register rings when one of the partners is there."

"What do you think you'll find," Darcy asked.

"I don't know, but Luan said to watch the register when the partner is there. I can't stand there all day and do that while managing the rest of the operation, but I'll figure out something."

Over the next two months, I recorded the vehicle counts for each day. Saturday and Sundays were our busiest and record-breaking days, and the days one of the partners volunteered to cashier given the reason we could always use an extra hand. The counts reported in our weekly meetings were substantially below what I recorded from the manual counters I installed. "Perhaps they are not working right," I wanted to think at first, always giving people the benefit of the doubt and being an optimist, but subsequent weeks proved the same. Worse, I observed the partner not ringing up paid cash for the car wash, asking the customer if they needed a receipt, and if they said no, the sale was not rung in the register. This proved to be a common practice. My best guesstimates were that 10, maybe 20% of sales didn't match the car counts.

After I collected my data and saw first-hand sales not being rung into the register, I did ask the partner if I could review the books. The shock on his face made me uneasy, and his nonverbal expression let on that he felt they might be caught. Luan looked straight down at the table.

"There is no need," the partner told me, "You focus on the work you do and leave that work to us." I didn't need to press the issue. I already knew what I knew. The next day, Luan told me she was reminded and instructed again, as previously, never to share "confidential" information with employees. Though I was a fifty percent shareholder, my partner also considered me an employee, which I technically and legally was. She inferred that the reminder was given to her because of my request.

Darcy was furious when I told her what I was finding. I was working around the clock and had taken a substantial salary cut leaving CENEX absorbing sweat equity in the venture. "What are we going to do," she asked. We both discussed what steps to take to address the situation in various ways for the next two weeks. We struggled internally and emotionally with every option. We had so much riding on my reputation. All the investment to build these two facilities came from my reputation and association with CENEX. Our pastor introduced my partner to me as a trusted congregational member. He had tried unsuccessfully to raise millions of dollars in investments from his friends and associations. I attended all these investment meetings, and while the Pro-forma and prospective financials looked great on paper, it was odd that he couldn't raise one dime from any of them, even some of his closest friends. Now we wondered, did they know and see a different person than we had?

Darcy and I felt obligated to visit with the pastor who recommended the partner. He was surprised and very disappointed. His council was to address it head-on. Since I asked to see the books and denied, I pulled the partner aside after one of our meetings and told him of my suspicions and that I thought I had observed that his wife was stealing from the company and witnessed that she didn't ring up some of the cash sales. Those were my reasons for wanting to see the books.

He immediately told me that I didn't understand the counts, that lots of cars and sales have to be voided for mistakes in the register, and he proceeded to give me many reasons for car count differences. I didn't tell him I had secretly installed car counters in the wash, and the car sales reported in our meetings were substantially different than the counters. Addressing all of this as only my suspicions head-on, as was suggested, I could tell from his body language that he was very uncomfortable. Without access to the books, an obvious camera to monitor the cash register tapes, and other tie-backs, it would be difficult to prove my suspicions without Luann's help. From my perspective, this partnership was over.

I went home and shared the day's activities with Darcy as usual. "What are we going to do?" She puzzlingly asked.

I had already given much thought to what I had to do. When I married Darcy, I enveloped her with love, my protection, my whole being, and just as a teen and young man who had to get away from his parent and his family to safely enjoy life with his bride as far away as possible, I now had to do the same with this partner.

I was now in my upper twenties but still very much a realist and too trusting of people. I'd had enough drama and dysfunction in my childhood that I avoided any kind of confrontation and didn't want to bring any pressure or associated trouble into our lives. "We have to get as far away from these people as possible, Darcy," I said. "Luan is stressed, she cries every day when she sees me, but she will never say anything. I think she's caught in the lies and deceit somehow!"

I was almost 29 years old. Darcy and I had come so far in such a short time. Not only had we amassed a few homes under our control, but I was also adept at making some money in the futures markets. This would be a huge setback. "Darcy, I must inform our CENEX partners I'm leaving. They have been so great to me, and I feel so bad, but I have to inform them that I'm leaving. We cannot stay and be a part of whatever misdeeds might be happening."

"What reason will you give CENEX for your departure?" Darcy asked. "I'll tell them the truth, that we have disagreements about how to operate," Darcy rubbed my shoulders, "I have faith in you, Curt. This will all work out."

"No matter what," I reiterated, "even if we have to start over, we must get escape from these people."

"I agree with you, Curt; let's get it over and move forward."

Darcy shared with her mom and dad what to expect in the coming weeks. When I told Luann I had addressed her concerns with the partner, she resigned. With Luann's resignation, the partner moved our office out of Bob's building taking all the files and records back to his home. This was all devastatingly embarrassing, but the worst was yet to come. The prominence of our facilities in the local community and our affiliation held stature, but being tied to them and the suspected devil of a partner wasn't for me. I was getting us out no matter what the personal cost to ourselves.

I met with the team of executives at CENEX that sponsored and supported our endeavor. I told them that my partner and I had philosophical differences in business operations. They expressed their concern and were not happy that I was leaving. They then asked me why our company was 30 days behind payments for gasoline inventories. I wasn't aware that we were. "Are you sure," I asked. "Yes, we are sure." They said, "and consistently."

"Well, I don't know, our business is flourishing, but I'll find out," I assured them.

The CENEX team requested a meeting with the partner, and I returned to work and presented that request. The partner agreed to meet with them. When I questioned him about why our company was late with payments, he insisted he had the money; he was floating the large sums in two-month T-bills to earn a bit more interest income for our operation. "That's a poor way to do business for such little incremental gain," I advised. "CENEX is a great company; these executives are my friends." "They've entrusted their investment to us and been very fair." My pleas for sensibility and an honest business ethic went on deaf ears.

Our meeting with CENEX was a complete disaster. The partner attended along with the executives, and the meeting lasted all but 15 minutes. As questions were asked of him, my partner remained silent, never uttering one word and remaining poker-faced, staring down at the table. Over and over, the team of executives asked him questions about late payments, if the business was sound, and other questions. He never answered, never said one word. As they looked at me, I reiterated a few of their questions to my partner, and again he never said a word. It infuriated the Vice President of CENEX Petroleum.

He clasped his hands and proclaimed, "Well, this meeting is over!" I was exasperated. How could my partner be so obstinate? He was already manipulating something within himself with silence! I was dealing with Loretta all over again, except the escape was even more difficult this time!

Several days passed, and I got calls from the CENEX credit collections department demanding past-due invoices. It was no use talking to my partner any longer. He wouldn't discuss the matter with me. I received a call from the CENEX team, who requested another meeting with us. My partner refused to attend. I did.

They were furious again when I showed up at the meeting without my partner and told them he couldn't attend. When questioned why he couldn't, I told them I didn't know. They were angry and said they didn't deserve this kind of treatment.

I respected them, appreciated them and their faith and investment in me, and agreed that they didn't deserve the treatment they were receiving. I gave them the same assurances and information the partner gave me that the businesses were flourishing. Still, I offered what he had told me, that he was delaying payments because of the investments in T-bills. Timely payments didn't seem to matter to him.

"Well, Curt, I'm sorry to say this, I think you are caught in the middle, and again I'm sorry, but you're about to get your Ph.D. in the hard school of knocks," The VP said. He then went on to tell me that if we didn't pay the entire balance in full of the past due invoices within three days, which had now grown to 60 days past due, he would send a fleet of trucks to lock the gas pumps and tear down all signage haling the CENEX flag! The rest of the CENEX team stared in silence at me.

Again, respecting this team and their investment they made in me, I looked after both our interests and advised him he couldn't do that and that an action like that was a breach of the contract between us. Using the word "can't" was the wrong word of choice on my part. "Don't tell me what I can't do," he raised his voice. "I'll do whatever the hell I want," he said in an angrier and more volatile tone. "I didn't mean you can't," I said, "but I'm advising you that what you plan to do is a breach of our contract. Read it," I pleaded. "There are other ways to solve this!"

He slapped his hands on the conference room table and repeated that we'd better have complete payment in three days or the trucks would show up

Friday, and he left the room. The rest of the CENEX team sat in disappointment and silence.

I returned to my partner and told him what I was told at the meeting. "Let them come and take the signage down," he said calmly. "That's perfect!" and he said nothing more. I couldn't believe what I was hearing. The egos of two men were at play: my partners and the VP of CENEX.

That Friday, true to the VP's word, trucks showed up as promised, locked the gas pumps up so we couldn't access the fuel in the tanks, and took down all signage containing graphics and the CENEX logo. The following Monday, my partner called to tell me we had a meeting with our company attorney.

We rehashed our discussions with CENEX while the attorney took copious notes. I shared all, including my conversations with my partner and the fact that I felt he had egged them on into doing this, and that I thought he was being deceitful in various ways, including holding payments for past due invoices.

Our discussions made it apparent that the attorney and my partner had already been meeting for some time. I was told that we would file a lawsuit upon CENEX for breach of contract, that any future losses we'd incur in our business would result from them breaching the contract, and that likely punitive damages could be obtained. I couldn't believe my ears. I viewed this as a total manipulation, even planned.

When I said I refused to allow this and then spilled my guts to the attorney about other suspicious acts I observed in the company and reiterating that since the attorney represented both my partner and myself, I wouldn't allow this to move forward, he continued to take copious notes and then looked up at me and stated, "Mr. Riess, let me make this clear; this firm and I do not represent you. We represent the corporation to which you hold stock, and we'll do what the corporation's directors wish us to do."

I was stunned; my partner stared at the floor. He couldn't look me in the eyes. I might be a 50% shareholder, but I was not a board member. Only the partner was a board member. If there was one childhood lesson that stuck with me from Loretta, it was a phrase she'd use on me when I was bullied: "When in Rome, do as the Romans do." Her advice may have been appropriate in other situations but I wasn't sitting with these Romans any longer. I said nothing more, got up from my chair, and walked out of the meeting. It was over. And the partnership would be over, too, one way or another.

The next day, I received a termination notice and was fired from my company. I was asked to turn in the car leased to me, keys, etc. I was in a state of several emotions, humiliated, defeated, helpless, and yet relieved.

I went home and told Darcy that I had to get a new car!

Life was not dull!

Chapter Forty-Eight
Babies

1988 – 1999

Playlist:

Have I Told You Lately, Van Morrison

I Will Always Love You, Whitney Houston

The River of Dreams, Billy Joel

I now had no job, no car and had taken minimal pay in our venture. I bought a slightly used jeep for transportation and then hired an attorney to deal with the partnership and its impending lawsuits.

With bleak employment prospects at the time and a possibility of a potential bankruptcy through the lawsuits, Darcy and I discussed my returning to school and obtaining my MBA. If we did face losing everything we'd financially gained thus far, what I could put into my mind was not something anybody could take away. We had the financial ability for me to do so.

I enrolled at St. Thomas University in St. Paul. Within months without my management, the partnership operations began to fall apart. My partner stopped paying our creditors, and I began to hate going to the mailbox. Each time I did, another certified letter demanded payment from me as I had been a co-signer and personal guarantor to the millions in loans the partnership took out. It was nerve-wracking to have zero control over what was happening on my behalf.

The MBA program diverted my mind from the daily worry about the future. In my second semester in the MBA program, my former boss and VP of Corporate Planning at CENEX called and asked me to lunch. At lunch, Maury asked if I'd be willing to share with him what had happened with the CENEX petroleum team. He also said if I didn't want to talk about what had happened I didn't have to, but if I were willing to share with him, he'd like to hear.

Maury was a great guy and a good mentor. I had developed a great relationship as superior and subordinate when I worked for him.

I had no problem sharing with him the truth, all the truth. The reasons I left my partner, and the truths about the CENEX team and those who made such poor decisions. A few days after that lunch, Maury asked me if I would voluntarily share all that I had shared with him with the CENEX attorneys in a deposition. I agreed to that as well.

Another month passed and I received another call from Maury. He offered me my old job back and some additional responsibility. I couldn't have been more appreciative but also surprised. "Maury, you know the whole story I shared with you?"

"Yes," he said.

"There is now a lawsuit pending and a future trial!"

"Yes," he said.

"Well, this is not going to be good for CENEX or me," I explained.

"Maybe," he said.

I was stunned and paused silently for a few moments. "Maury, why would you or CENEX want me to come back," I asked.

"Curt, after hearing your testimony and that of others from some of the petroleum team, you were the only person in the group who knew the right thing to do."

"We need people like you in our company, not just for what you know how to do, but more importantly for what you know what not to do." "What about the lawsuit," I asked.

"Let it take care of itself," he counseled.

"Oh my God, Maury, the whole organization knows about this." "I'm the Golden Boy that CENEX was willing to invest millions into; how could I walk around with my head held high?" "How am I going to respond to anyone who asks questions," I asked.

"Curt, you have nothing to hang your head low about, by my account, you are the only person in this debacle so far who can hold his head high," he said. "And if it helps any, I talked to several key people here who endorse my decision to offer you back your job. By the way, confidentially, a couple of guys on that team you worked with will be dismissed. And if anyone here or in the trade area asks you any questions about this issue, you tell them to see me and ask me."

I thanked Maury and asked if I could discuss this with Darcy and get back to him in a few days. Darcy couldn't have been more impressed and prouder of me. She expressed that despite what failings my partners and some of the CENEX team brought each other, my former boss saw through the whole debacle and saw that I was willing to share all the truth, even those truths that would hurt us financially.

I was hesitant and unsure that taking a job back at CENEX might be a mistake, but I took Maury up on his offer and returned to CENEX. It was the easy thing to do, and it provided a steady paycheck. Instead of the raise he was willing to give me, I asked if he would pay for the rest of my MBA, and I moved my classes to part-time status.

The certified letters kept coming every week with threats. I hated going to the mailbox. Our attorney advised us to sell all our rental properties but one and move all the profits into as expensive of a new home as we could afford as a proactive asset protective measure should a bankruptcy filing become necessary. We followed his advice, found a beautiful home and moved into it nearly debt-free using the sale proceeds and other investments I had made. We moved into a neighborhood of forty-somethings upgrading from their first home. We were in our twenties.

It was a troubling year receiving all the threats from my partner and the creditors he wasn't paying, but the one bright spot in our lives was that it was our fifth anniversary, which meant I'd take Darcy back to Hawaii as we agreed to do every five years. If there were a chance that we'd lose most of our investments and savings, at least we would enjoy a vacation, and I would keep my promise to her. And, of course, I doubled the size of her diamond.

Even better news came from Darcy just before the anniversary that she was pregnant with our first child. Darcy's announcement, with the sparkle in her eyes of our baby on the way, gave me a perspective to rid myself of some of the bitterness of the whole messy business situation out of my control and to continue forward, giving my employers my best performance. As I did in high school, I buried the problems surrounding me, focused heavily on what I could control, and tried to excel at my work. It paid off back then; I knew it would pay off again.

Despite the potential outcome of the lawsuit, which looked like it would favor the partnership, we prepared for the worst and there was nothing more we could do but live our lives as best we could.

With a rapidly changing technological economy, the demography I studied in college foretold the paradigm shifts like moving away from an industrial economy and toward a service and information-driven economy. I thought selecting corporate-oriented management classes in my master's degree would help me feel more comfortable settling into the corporate life at CENEX and Land O Lakes (the two companies had merged their agribusiness units within which I was employed). They didn't help. I became ever more doubtful about a corporate career, realizing that my young idealistic views would never materialize in a behemoth bigger than the Titanic and even slower to turn or adjust to the enormous icebergs ahead of them than I could wait for.

The Land O Lakes business was facing the demography shift of disappearing dairy farms across the Midwest, just as my instructors had foretold, and the pace was accelerating. Those dairies that remained would have to expand and get larger to survive. Land O Lakes' main milk supply for many of its small aging creameries was throughout the Midwest. They needed to source and produce near the markets where most of their finished products were shipped. And that was the coasts.

I wanted to help Land O Lakes and be a part of some forward-thinking solutions, but no one at the time would listen to some kid from New York! Especially some kid that cost CENEX two-plus million dollars in an investment gone sour.

The lawsuit occurred between my partners and CENEX. While I understood the case was likely to end in favor of my partner and our business, I wanted no part of what I saw as dirty money coming in the form of judgments or settlements because I suspected not all of the truthful facts had been shared. I sold my 50% stake in our corporation for $5.00 to release all personal liabilities and association with the company.

I'm sure my partner thought he screwed me again, as shortly after CENEX lost the suit, and damages were awarded to my partners and their creditors. Part of those damages was that CENEX had to purchase the real estate holdings we once held, and now CENEX owned my former businesses. They asked me if I was interested in owning them again, but I was not. It wasn't my dream, it was someone else's, and I wasn't going to focus on someone else's dream any longer, including CENEX's. Besides, I had a bitter taste for how both parties acted through the whole matter.

I was informed that I was mentioned extensively at the trial, yet I wasn't present as a critical witness in the lawsuit. When the judge asked why such a key witness was absent in the trial, the plaintiff and the defendant's attorneys stated that neither party felt it was to their benefit to have me (and my truths) bear witness.

Three months before our firstborn was due in December, and now free of any liability with the lawsuits, I gave a resignation notice for the second time to CENEX. I purchased some seminar licenses to teach finance and financial planning. Always having faith in me, Darcy never questioned my confidence or decision. Through all of our seemingly insane opportunistic troubles, she saw that I always came through and ensured we were always secure. On the other hand, my boss was concerned and couldn't believe I was once again leaving for what I was going to do. He coached me to stay on part-time caring for me and my best interest. He may have doubted my judgment that I could make a go of it.

I wasn't worried. We had a beautiful home in a beautiful neighborhood and it was now paid for 100% at age 32. My boss, of course, didn't know this and offered me part-time work that was too lucrative to refuse. I kept the job part-time with CENEX and built a steady income stream from my seminars, which enabled me to double the CENEX salary. Many of the workshops I taught were to blue-collar employees, and I had to deliver the seminars after the second or third shifts. It suited me fine as I worked three mornings a week at CENEX holding office hours for my staff.

I watched Darcy as her tummy grew with our first child. My bride changed physically and dramatically into a mature woman from the petite girl I first flirted with, dated, and then married. It was so unbelievable and radically fast to observe the changes in her body and wonder about parenthood as I lay next to her each evening. I loved her so much, and I loved it when she'd grab my hand and tell me to feel her belly as a movement of an arm or leg would kick. I couldn't imagine any of this in my life years ago.

I'd now known Darcy for ten years as we had dated for five years and were now in our fifth year of marriage. Our lives sped through the first ten years like a high-speed train with so much activity it seemed like a lifetime. Her mom and dad were ecstatic over the news of our pregnancy, and I heard Betty exclaim, "Well, it's about time," once again. Referencing our marriage together for five years before getting pregnant.

The oncoming baby, of course, had us both excited and Darcy, as mom and designer, couldn't wait to build-out a nursery in one of our bedrooms. Skillful as she is, she hand-painted wallpaper in the nursery and decorated it professionally. When she ordered the blinds, the blind rep saw her work and asked if Levolor Blind Corporation could showcase the blinds she ordered using the room in a photo shoot for a commercial they were planning.

Soon two stories of scaffolding and a film crew enveloped the outside corner of our home, with artificial sunlight pouring into the windows of the nursery. The film crew engulfed our house for a couple of days earning Darcy a nice rental stipend for her design skills and free blinds! She had unique talents and creativity, but none would be more important than guiding me in raising our children. None of what I knew from my parents was a repeatable option. I didn't want a repeat of it in any form. All I knew was that I wanted a loving, caring, and nurturing family, and I knew I could depend upon Darcy and her own experience with her parents to deliver that.

Darcy and I attended pregnancy and birthing classes together. It was an up-and-coming practice that initially seemed a little awkward for me, but it was an excellent experience to know and understand what a woman's body was going through. The calves, cows, and pigs I assisted as a farmhand never spoke of what I'd learn in these classes. The topics from birth to sex were covered, and I would know how to provide some aid, comfort, and coaching to Darcy as she endured the pain and discomfort of giving birth. Little did she know I had plans to aid the birth of our child in more ways than the classes taught!

On December 19, 1990, Darcy was induced to facilitate the birthing of our first son. It was a long hard labor of about 20 hours, and I felt so sorry for the person I loved most as she endured the labor pains her body delivered. I coached her into breathing and stretching skills and gave her back rubs and other comforts. Every minute, I was there by her side, trying my best to help ease her pain and maintain her confidence in me as I planned on delivering our firstborn. We had discussed this with our doctor beforehand. She asked me if I had any experience in the matter and said most men faint in the delivery room, and she couldn't have that. I proudly explained to her some of my chores at the pig farm, how I castrated piglets, and how I helped deliver calves over my high school and college years and explained the processes I had assisted in. Of course, I didn't explain all of the techniques, like the chains we'd sometimes have to wrap around the front hooves to assist in pulling the calf out, but she got the picture that I wouldn't be fainting at the table when the time came.

When Darcy finally approached the time to push hard and give birth, I got in my scrubs, sanitized my hands, and sat on a stool placed between Darcy's legs as she pushed. The elliptical tip of our firstborn's head began to appear. I was calm as could be and Darcy was working hard. With each push, Darcy could expel the baby inch by inch until I could firmly place my thumb and forefinger underneath the neck of its head. Dr. Lucas was to my left observing and admiring my skill when suddenly Darcy gave one big, long push, and pop came the weasel, all slimy and slushy, to which I quickly grabbed the rest of the baby with my other hand. "Don't drop it, don't drop it," Dr. Lucas nervously chanted as she jumped up and down, clapping her hands in the praying position. I stood holding our new son in my hands.

At first glance, the baby had a head shaped like a football from squeezing through the vaginal canal and looked like the alien in a movie called ET! I looked at Dr. Lucas as if to say calm down, then I joyfully announced it was a boy and laid him on her belly. Dr. Lucas sped to counting toes and fingers, wiping and inspecting his eyes, nose, and throat to ensure there were no blockages. We cut the umbilical cord, cleaned him up, wrapped him in a blanket, and cuddled him beside his mother.

We both shed tears of joy and wonder. Our first son would be named Austin, and he was beautiful with bushy bright eyes that twinkled like stars. He was alert, kicking with his tiny legs, and eager to see his new world. We both stared back at him in awe, and the image of ET faded away fast!

The very next day, I walked across the graduation stage at St. Thomas University with a banner over my shoulders announcing, "It's a boy" to receive my master's degree in business. I received polite and happy applause of acknowledgment. Darcy, of course, could not attend, and I had not invited anyone else to join me. I rushed back to the hospital to join Darcy and presented my diploma. "One day, a newborn son, another day, an MBA. What next?" I exclaimed. "And best of all, a beautiful wife!"

As is the hospital tradition for Christmas babies, Austin was wrapped in a stocking when we took him home. We stayed home with our newborn son for the next two weeks, marveling at how his football-shaped skull had miraculously readjusted into a perfectly round shape. His constantly twinkling eyes reminded us of a television Santa in various movies. He was constantly scanning and looking out into the big wide world with wonder and excitement at what he could be a part of or do next!

Our family grew. Darcy and I looked back upon our first five years of marriage. It was a trying time in our careers, but we still accomplished much. I kept my promises, and because of that adversity, Darcy had a dream home "all painted white" (on the inside), which locally famed Architects Watters and Bonner designed. The house was featured as a top contemporary design in an architectural magazine, highlighting its combination of modern, prairie, and nautical design elements. It was a fantastic home for us at our age. Darcy never expected such a fine home and appreciated it. She used her skills to appoint it magnificently.

We talked about our future and the economy. Interest rates had steadily declined, inflation was falling, and as I refinanced the remaining rental property we still owned, I continued to pay the mortgage down, maintaining the payment at the 21.5% payment level, which applied a lot to the principal. Darcy and I owned that rental free of any mortgage by year eight.

As we looked ahead at our next five years and established some goals together, I told Darcy that if I didn't get into farming (still always a first choice in careers) in the next year or two, I'd give up on that dream and look for something else. I knew it would be difficult to get started if I weren't in dairy farming by age 35.

In the spring of 1993, Darcy was pregnant with our second child. We negotiated on a dairy farm in Osceola, Wisconsin, a small community just northwest of St. Paul, Minnesota. It was an older dairy barn with cattle stanchions and a pipeline, but I could envision a new free-stall barn and milking parlor up on a hill across from the farmstead with plenty of ventilation for the herd in that location. But the old farmer and I were still a hundred thousand dollars apart in our negotiation. I wasn't willing to go up, and he wasn't ready to come down, citing some possible development capabilities of his land if it were parceled out.

In August, our second son was born. Dr. Lucas asked if I was getting into scrubs again; I had to decline as much as I wanted to. Darcy wasn't so sure I should do so either. I was exhausted from being up the day before and all night with Darcy before going to the hospital. I was mentally exhausted, too, after nearly four months of working on negotiations for the farm in Osceola, only for the deal to die. Still working part-time at CENEX, delivering full-time results, and giving my seminars in the evenings had worn me thin. Dr. Lucas delivered a beautiful baby boy whom we named Mason.

Though I was exhausted, it could not have been a happier and more exhilarating time to receive a second child from God. Unlike Austin, Mason was more significant in stature, chubbier, and had a perfectly round head. He was a more laid-back baby than Austin, cuddly, and quickly fell asleep upon my chest. Now two and a half years old, Austin adored his little brother and doted over him like a puppy. It was a pleasure to be a father to them, hold them, love them, and play with them. Mason was playful and took in everything, especially his older brother's antics, even as a baby. Darcy and I marveled at them and how instantly connected they became. One was born in winter, the other in summer, and while they were as different as the seasons, they soon became one soul in many playful ways.

Maury asked if I would consider returning to CENEX full-time, and I accepted a promotion to director level. I sold my seminar licenses. I was 34 at the time. If you achieved director-level status at CENEX, it was most probable that you were in your mid-forties. Unlike Land O Lakes, which had so many vice presidents, most with manager responsibilities, CENEX was a lean organization. My boss reported to one of two Sr. Vice Presidents, who reported to the President. A director level was only two levels of responsibility removed from the president, and with the status came a lot of responsibility and pay.

However, six-months back at CENEX full-time was enough to know that it was again a mistake for me to return. It was easy to do, but it was a mistake. Though I did well in my work, the constant internal politics drove me insane, and being the company's youngest director, there were many jealous employees, younger and older than me, shooting crooked arrows at my back. One afternoon, I was in the lunchroom with the new Vice President of Petroleum when a couple of his subordinates shouted from down the table to me in a joking manner to get some attention, hey, look, it's Teflon Riess inferring that nothing irresponsible ever sticks to me.

Since they were the VP's indirect reports and he was sitting across from me, I politely responded, "No Teflon is needed when you do good work." "Your accusations might stick if you boys could shoot a straight arrow instead of all the crooked ones you shoot."

The VP smiled at me as we continued our lunch. This childish attitude was a useless waste of everybody's time having to deal with adults who never matured beyond their high school diplomas. Their insecurities constantly warranted a babysitter. Most of them lived paycheck to paycheck, and everything they had depended upon that paycheck, so they lived in fear of losing it. They were always too fearful of taking risk and accomplishing great things, but all too eager to take credit for the accomplishments of others. I couldn't see myself babysitting adults at CENEX or LAND O LAKES for the rest of my career. But it wasn't time for me to make a change yet.

It was Darcy's turn now to enjoy her job. She'd proven herself a first-rate designer of commercial spaces like banks, medical facilities, corporate offices, and other establishments. She often accompanied a sales team in presenting her layouts and designs to potential customers. It didn't take long for the Vice President of Sales in her organization to see her enormous potential as a salesperson. She knew what she was talking about, had confidence, and believed in the new products the company was producing. He encouraged her to apply for an open position in the sales department. Darcy came home and told me about her doubts that she had the skills to sell and manage sales. I assured her she did, but she loved drafting and designing, and supporting the sales teams with her designs. She declined the offer.

After a few days, the sales vice president asked her to reconsider. She came home, and we discussed it again. "He's so adamant that I could succeed at sales," she said.

"I think you would, too, Darcy! I mean, why would you doubt yourself?"

"I've never been in sales," she said doubtingly. "The VP said the company would hold open my position for a month and allow me to have it back if I decided I didn't like it."

"Then try it, Darcy," I encouraged! "There isn't anybody who doesn't like you. You have talent, can design, and direct other designers in what you want for the customers you gain," I boasted to her. "I think you'll make an excellent Account Executive," I encouraged.

Darcy agreed to try the position with the option that if she didn't like it within a month or two, she could return to her previous role. Her boss agreed. Darcy took the job and never looked back. Her designs and space planning skills were selling the company product from day one, and she was on a roll.

Things for a bit finally seemed normal and steady. We continued to enjoy our weekend outings of camping with two young boys, but it was a bit wearing to be in a tent for Darcy with a second child. We were both doing well in our jobs, and the rental income was pouring in from our remaining rental. As we now had it paid off, all the revenue after expenses went into our savings and investments.

Darcy and I began to look for a cabin in the north woods of Minnesota and Wisconsin. I loved being in the country, and we soon bought a second home, a weekend retreat in rural northwest Wisconsin. While I was performing well in my career, the struggle of corporate life was still a stench. I thought the cabin life and the fun we'd have on the weekends would make the week's battle worth the trouble.

After looking at musty-smelling seasonal cabins one after another, one of our neighbors and friends learned what we were doing and asked if they could join us as partners. One would think I'd be done with partners after what I went through, but we seemed compatible and agreed. The joint venture with our neighbors allowed us to consider building a new structure from the ground up. It would be created for year-round use, making it more enjoyable to be there even if the weather was foul. I paid cash for our half the $130,000.00 price tag and spent another $100,000.00, being frivolous for the first time in our lives, purchasing an enclosed snowmobile trailer, four snowmobiles, two ATVs, and a suburban to haul everything. I paid cash for it all as we were able. I was earning a good salary at CENEX, investing it well, and Darcy was raking in commissions beyond her salary. Our first home, now a rental, packed another twenty-five to thirty-five thousand dollars of rent per year into our wallets too.

Our first year using the cabin was enjoyable, spending most of our weekends playing with our two little boys. It was bliss. Our partner had to exit within a year of cabin life as he took a job opportunity in Ohio and had to relocate. Darcy and I didn't blink or think twice, as we had paid off the partner's share and now owned the cabin wholly. It was a nice respite from the CENEX grind, the world at large, city life, and we began to frequent it more and more. We could escape on the weekends, leave the corporate world behind, get refreshed, and recuperate to make battle again for another week. Being in a comfortable year-round place and snowmobiling made the long Minnesota winters tolerable and passed quicker.

I was ever so grateful every minute of my life for the girl I married, and every weekend at the cabin was like a mini honeymoon with her. Our time there was always uniquely special as we focused on each other. It kept us having fun together playing games with the kids, and our love for each other grew more substantial and profound than one could have imagined on the wedding day. The bonds we were developing with our boys were also profoundly felt. We'd pinch ourselves sometimes, despite the adversity in our life, as to how near-perfect things had worked out for us so far.

The cabin weekends became our routine for a few years. We loved our days with the kids, our evenings together, watching the sunsets and the moon rises, grilling our evening meals perched high up into the trees on our deck, playing on the beach, fishing, and just being a family together. I was enjoying the traditional everyday family life I never had as a kid. And when Loretta and Harry would visit, though rare, she'd stare a lot at my interactions with my children and spouse. I often wondered what she was thinking. I could surmise happy, remorseful, and jealous thoughts in her facial expressions as her mind flitted back and forth in comparison to our lives versus her own.

While I was in love and content with my family, working at CENEX and Land, O Lakes, with their merger of petroleum and agribusiness assets, was a stressful job in a stressful environment. Working within a neutral corporate planning division serving both entities, I constantly had to manage a delicate balance of relationships between the Red Shorts Culture and the Green Shorts Culture, CENEX management being red and Land O Lakes management being the green. I succeeded in navigating and influencing a variety of personalities in working together among the upper management teams. Still, managing the climbers and their ambitious plans to displace people on the opposite side for their gain was a chore. And soon, I found myself bouncing back and forth into significant projects at both companies, eventually becoming a Land O Lakes employee as much of my work for a while was within Land O Lakes departments, only to be leased back to CENEX when they wanted me on a project of theirs.

My boss was a great mentor. And while he thought I was succeeding beyond his expectations, we developed an odd relationship, sometimes love, sometimes frustration. He promoted me just the same, but while he traveled excessively and had less and less touch on the projects I directed, his frustrations with me seemed to grow with every success I had. Some of my work surprised him, and while he admired it, he made it clear to me and others under his direction he didn't want to be surprised. In one accountability meeting, he directed me to run every major project I endorsed through him before proceeding. I would try. I would seek meetings to review with him when he was in town, and he'd say just put it in my "inbox" in an outline form. The problem is that Maury would return it to me with no comments, input, or sign-off, and he'd be off to travel for the company for two, sometimes three weeks. So that's what I did.

Time was never on our side to allow delays in communications and marketing materials we served to other divisions. He'd ream me in monthly staff and accountability meetings for not reviewing existing projects with him. To save face for him and me after he scolded me in front of others, he'd compliment me and say, "Riess, you're just so dam lucky your work is so good, but I want to see your proposals before you do them." I'd try to explain that I was running the project outlines by him, but he never commented on them, so I figured they were good to go. He'd get even more furious and insist I wasn't running them by him. He claimed he never saw any outlines. This love-hate developed over a few years to the point that he wouldn't grant me the "subjective" bonus pay I had earned.

There were other issues developing between us. I decried tasks and would not perform them coaching that I disobeyed his directives in his best "political" and career interest. He hated that side of me, citing in one debate he would not win with me saying, "Riess the trouble with you is you don't have a big enough mortgage!" He was right; little did he know I had none. Having no debts and no mortgage gave me all the power I needed to take suitable risks within work, say no to those I thought were detrimental, and be free to act like I didn't need the job and perform to the best of my ability, sometimes defying the direction given to take the risk toward a better approach. I always was financially free enough to have the attitude to say, "Take this job and shove it," though, of course, professionally, I'd never consider doing so. It was just freedom of attitude that I needed to do things right. Sometimes I felt what was asked of me was not the right thing to do, and I'd be insubordinate in not following through on some of those directions and orders.

The only saving grace for my discontentment and corporate culture frustrations was my growing apathy toward not caring how others fared anymore. Maury would mentor me saying, "People don't change; you just have to work around them." He was right, but it wasn't normal for me not to care.

My love, family, friends, and the cabin gave me solace. But having and living with that kind of apathy just wasn't me. Corporate America wasn't my destiny, no matter how successful I was or how much I was considered in the inner circle of upper management. Darcy and I agreed I'd look into a venture other than farming and get into business for myself, a lifelong dream.

Now thirty-four years of age I went to the James J. Hill Library in St. Paul and scoured the archives for SICs (standard industrial codes) that dealt with food and agriculture. If I couldn't be in the dairy business, which was going through rapid industry transformations during my career, I might find something related to food and agriculture. I created a list of companies from those searches and hired a broker to solicit the businesses on the list and see if they were interested in selling. I asked him to transcribe his calls to me for review. None of the companies on the list I'd given him was for sale then, but several offered an opportunity to talk and explore after talking with the broker. One particular business, The Melford Olson Honey Company (Mel-O Honey), located in Crystal, Minnesota, was an intrigue. In the transcript, one of the owners said they weren't interested in selling then but perhaps in two or three years. I visited the local chains of grocery stores and looked at their shelves dedicated to honey. Mel-O Honey held 90 percent of the shelf facings; they seemed to own the market. I was intrigued and did some more honey research. It was natural and organic, and I could foresee it becoming more and more mainstream in the future. I thought honey could become more of an ingredient sweetener for foods like cereals, meats, yogurts, and other foods. I found that honey didn't have an expiration date from the research I collected! It would last thousands of years and never sour if sealed correctly. That was a radically different supply chain and inventory issue than nearly any other food on the shelf.

I had the broker call the owner back three times to see if they would open the door for discussion. Each time the answer came back no, the broker would no longer call them for me and told me he was done calling them. It was a closed door, he said. I wasn't sure, so I visited the owners and introduced myself. I learned the company was owned by three brothers, Donald, Roger, and Eugene Olson. Their brand, Mel-O Honey, stood for Melford-Olson, their father, a Minnesota Beekeeper and founder of his company in 1918. Mel also happened to be the Latin word for honey. Melford was the first in the industry to market honey in bear-shaped bottles, first developing his little bear logo to set himself apart from all other competitors who used a bee on their labels. I shared with them that while they didn't have any interest now, they told my broker they'd consider selling in two or three years. It could take a couple of years to work out the details of any deal, and if they were interested, I'd be willing to visit with them and entertain some ideas. They said they would discuss it and get back to me.

Two weeks passed, and one of the Olson Brothers called to tell me they appreciated my visit but weren't interested. Darcy and I would visit and explore other business opportunities in the ensuing months and year, primarily within 200 miles of the twin cities. But as we dug into other options, the broker unearthed for me, more and more I thought about the honey company and its potential. I began revisiting that opportunity with regular visits to the Melford Olson Honey Company to open the door to discussions.

Chapter Forty-Nine
The in Box

1995

Playlist:

Have I Told You Lately, Van Morrison

I Will Always Love You, Whitney Houston

The River of Dreams, Billy Joel

April 1995 marked ten years that Darcy and I were married. At 36, I had a solid career at CENEX and Land O Lakes and was respected by upper management and those who counted. Equally so, Darcy was going gangbusters in her career as well. She exceeded her sales quota in the New Business category by 150%, sometimes 200%; even after her quota was raised yearly, she kept bringing on new business and exceeding her quota by huge margins.

Darcy won more big-screen televisions than our home could house, trips, and other perks to which we gave many away to friends. She was dynamite at what she did and a dynamite spouse and partner, always supporting me and my endeavors, and I did the same for hers. She made as much as I did with her bonuses and commissions and, in some years, even more! I loved her incredibly and was so very much proud of her as a spouse, businesswoman, mother, and lover. She had come so far from the girl I met in college. I encouraged her in every endeavor and decision and coached her in times of disenfranchisement and workplace politics as jealous employees coveted the prestige she held as the number one salesperson within the organization. She had access to the president, the owners, and the engineers, who all loved working with her.

As in any organization, though, she experienced bosses who were told to get more salespeople like Darcy and fired when they could not. When I first fell in love with her, I knew she was exceptional; that's why she had so many suitors. Now, as a career professional, she remained exceptional, and duplicating her skills, talents, and success was difficult for almost any sales executive within her company. Even the best sales managers she had could not perform themselves to her level. She, indeed, was exceptional at what she did. Sure enough, she got one crazy boss who came in and raised her quota to 300% of her allocation to destroy any bonus opportunity. Besides being an asshole and demanding accountabilities for every waking minute of the day, the control freak required daily sales meetings cutting into the time Darcy would otherwise be out selling. He was trying to drive out the person he knew he'd never be able to compete with. Darcy was so disillusioned by him and wanted to leave the organization, but she loved the product she sold. It was new, flexible, well-designed, and a leading product in her industry. She was bumming. I coached her to stop selling. "Just attend all of his meetings and stop selling. Let your sales plummet to zero or as low as you can."

"I can't do that," she insisted. "I'll get fired!"

"No, you won't, Darcy. The president of your company and the owner will never let him fire you. Hardly anybody meets their quota, much less 150% per year as you have. Do you think they will dare let you go? No way," I reassured her. "Do as I say, and this guy will fall flat on his face. You need to outlast the asshole, I insisted. I've had to do the same at times. The assholes try to prove themselves with all their bravado, but they don't last long. They sink eventually. When your quotas decline and upper management questions what's happening, you can be honest about your opinions and options."

"What are my options?" she asked.

"You can leave anytime, but I would be honest when they ask and tell them how you feel and why your sales have plummeted." After a few days of thought, Darcy agreed to do as I suggested.

To keep her spirits up, I laid some plans for our upcoming anniversary, and once again, we went to our favorite jeweler and doubled the center diamond of her wedding band. Then I whisked her off to Hawaii with our two boys, and we had one of the best family Hawaiian vacations on the big island we ever had.

Darcy did as I suggested taking a slight reprieve over the next year and letting her sales drop significantly. Halfway through the year, the president met with her and asked what seemed to be the matter. I coached her to be factual and frank and tell him that she wasn't motivated any longer and had stopped making any effort. She did.

After the meeting with him she came home and told me her president gave no reply or input; he just listened and thanked her for coming in as requested. She was nervous. I told her not to be anxious and be patient. Two months later, the newly hired Vice President of Sales was terminated for poor performance. Darcy was free to sell again, and by year-end, she made up most of the quota she was initially assigned and still exceeded it, though not by as much margin as in previous years.

Working with people is always an exciting affair. I also had plenty of experiences that seemed perplexing, and there were times when I recognized my own immaturity and misgivings. But throughout my career with CENEX and Land O Lakes, I steadily grew in my responsibilities and was often promoted for my great work. I had only one request from my boss, who understood my independent entrepreneurial nature: to keep him informed about what was happening. He traveled extensively for the company, often only being back in the office a few days a month. Each time he promoted me, I got a scolding for not keeping him informed and that the next promotion would depend upon me keeping him informed.

I'd explain to him that I was always running things by him, but he never took the time to comment on what I ran by him, and with his travel schedule, I had to keep moving along. "You never run anything by me, Curt," he'd strongly retort. I can't count how many times some of my staff would come to me waiting for an answer, and I'd tell them I ran it by my boss, but since he returned it to me with no comments, I'd instruct them, no comments must mean that he approves, move forward.

He and I developed a love-hate relationship over the matter. He loved my work but hated that I was arrogant (so he thought), and as he claimed, I wouldn't keep him informed. I loved him as a boss, mentor and eventually a friend, but I hated that he would lament to me in meetings how insubordinate I was by not keeping him informed. I'd run nearly everything by him through his inbox. Invariably, they came back with no remarks, approvals, or disapprovals. In the scolding he gave me when he said: "You know Riess, the problem with you is that you don't have a big enough mortgage." His real frustration was that he had no control over me financially! He couldn't have been more correct, but that wasn't why he was never informed.

It was my turn once again to rid myself of corporate life. I was tired of babysitting adults in other divisions too.

Because I was a director-level employee with significant responsibility, I wanted to give him ample time and notice that I would be leaving my post. I'd written a letter of gratitude to him for all the opportunities over the past 14 years, for his mentoring and what he taught me, for recognizing my entrepreneurial abilities, and for providing me with fulfilling work to be an intrapreneur within the corporate environment.

I was lucky to have someone who mentored me and loved me like a son and who understood my skills and desire to produce well. At times our corporate plants had labor strikes and some of us who were non-union had to take additional positions to cover striking employees. I was among the small percentage who were always willing to give more than was requested of us. I never stood in a line begging for more pay, more benefits, and less work. I always asked for more work and responsibility, and the income and promotions caught up with me. That's how it's done in corporate America. Please don't ask for more pay to do something; do it, and the rewards will follow. Time and time again, those who asked for the compensation and responsibility first and received it from me as a supervisor only turned out to take the pay and not put forth what they promised; soon they'd be on the list for the subsequent layoffs.

My boss confidentially discussed with me about possibly going to work for the then President of Harvest States. He confided in me that Harvest States was the next big merger with CENEX he was assisting with. He wanted to plant a trusted employee on the Harvest States side in anticipation he would bring me back through the merger. While I appreciated his complete confidence, I was working on other plans, and in December of 1996, I finally cut a deal with the Olson family. After nearly two years of pestering them to sell the Melford Olson Honey Company to me and working through negotiations, we signed a letter of intent to purchase and scheduled closing for May One, 1997. I was taking on 1.5 million dollars in personally guaranteed debt to acquire the company draining my 401K assets to zero.

I had corporate-wide visible projects assigned to me. As I still had four months before closing on the business, I pushed hard to ensure I could complete as much work as possible. In January, I worked feverishly every evening and weekend to move my projects to completion. I could have easily sloughed off, preserved my energies, and given my boss two weeks' notice before I left, but that wasn't me. I appreciated my time and career with CENEX and the people I served. I just couldn't see myself working in a cubicle for the rest of my life.

I slipped a personal note of resignation into Maury's inbox shortly after New Years Day. I wanted to give him plenty of time to transfer duties and projects or hire a replacement for me. In that note of resignation, I let him know what my intentions were, that I would be willing to stay on to complete my work, and that I was not leaving to work for another competitor; however, even still, if he felt it was necessary to terminate my services immediately, I would understand, and I was financially able to accept the termination.

Maury was always absent travelling and working with divisions and cooperatives in the field. A week after I submitted my letter to him, the letter I marked confidential to him personally was returned to my inbox unopened. He was already off on another trip when I got it back. I returned the envelope to his inbox, thinking there must have been a mistake. Another week passed, and the letter returned to my inbox again unopened. I called his secretary and asked if he was back in his office. She said he was here for one day and left again for Utah. I told her I had placed a critical piece of information in his inbox twice, and he returned it to me twice unopened. She had no explanation and said, "Just put it back in his inbox again, and I'll see to it that he gets it."

So again, I put my resignation, labeled confidential and important, back into his inbox.

Time passed, it was now the first week of February, and Maury had been in the office over the weekend, reviewed his mail, and headed out for field meetings in Montana. With all his travel and meetings catching him in his office was harder than one thought.

Once again, my resignation letter was returned to my inbox unopened. For nearly three and a half weeks, Darcy had asked me each night if Maury had gotten my resignation letter. I kept telling her the same thing; he returned it unopened. She suggested I hand deliver it to his office. I asked his secretary if she would unlock his office to put an important message on his chair so he could see it, and I wrote on it in large letters, "PLEASE OPEN IMMEDIATELY" She agreed, and I placed it on his desk chair assured he would see it the next time he returned.

A week later, Maury returned to his office. Wanting to be sure he read my letter, I swung by his office and knocked on his door. "Come on in," he responded. "Maury, I'm sorry to disturb you. I want to be sure you got my letter," I said. He reached over to the opened letter in the box on the corner of his desk and asked, "This letter?"

"Yes," I responded, and he asked me to close his door.

"Well, this time, I think you're leaving us for good and likely not coming back?" I nodded my head yes. "Curt, I wanted to promote you again with the opportunity at Harvest States."

"I know, and I appreciate that, Maury; I wanted to give you as much advance notice as possible. I sent you this letter three times over the past month, and you kept returning it to me unopened."

He looked at me puzzlingly. "I notice you dated this letter January 5, and I'm just getting it more than a month later," he quizzed.

"Yes, as I said, I put it in your inbox three times, and your secretary returned it to me unopened all three times."

Maury looked at me and stared at me in disbelief. "What inbox did you put it in?" he asked.

"Your normal inbox, the one I always put my mail to you in."

Maury glared at me. Suddenly I felt like something had gone wrong. "Where's my inbox?" Maury asked.

"Right outside your door," I responded.

"Open the door and show me," he said. I opened the door and pointed at his inbox. He looked at me and asked, "Have you been using that inbox all these years?"

We looked at each other, and it was as if a ghost of enlightenment had just swept into the room. We both had non-verbal revelations and expressions of "Holy crap" on our faces. I put projects for approval into his "outbox" for years. So much was silently explained in one swift second. All those years, he admonished me for not sharing my work and getting his approval before I went ahead because I was putting materials into his outbox, the wrong box! I was the adult who needed babysitting now! We both stared at each other in miraculous disbelief as neither of us said a word and then simultaneously, we burst out into laughter. We laughed and laughed and laughed until both of us had tears in our eyes. It explained everything and so much more about our working relationship for years. Among the divisions he was in charge of was the division of Corporate and Marketing Communications, of which I was a director. Ironically the most significant miscommunication of all, for years between us, had been my misdiagnosed in-box!

While I felt a little foolish as we settled our laughter, Maury was gracious and asked, "I suppose now that you know where my inbox is, it probably wouldn't change your mind." I shook my head no. "Well," he nodded, "I'm sorry to see you go, but I can see that you will do this no matter what. Since you aren't going to work for a competitor, there is no reason for me to terminate you immediately. Please don't communicate this to anyone yet," he asked. "I have to be out of the office this week, but I'm back next Wednesday." "Let's plan on lunch next Friday at the St. Paul Capital Grill and sort through your time here." I agreed.

That evening I went home and told my love what a fool I'd been. "Think where your career would have been had you known where his inbox was." She laughed and jabbed at me. I joked that it might have plummeted as had he had input, my work might not have been as great! It was all in jest as he was a talented guy, but it sure sheds light on so many meetings and a disgruntled boss telling me numerous times I was lucky my work was so "damn good" as he'd say all the time, or he would have fired me for insubordination. He obviously never meant it as he continued to promote me, but for a moment, I wondered how it might have been different had I known where his inbox was. These were the days of handwritten mail. Emails were not invented yet. I rehashed many times when I would receive a project of mine or my staff and send it to his "inbox" for approval, receive it back with no remarks, and tell them that since he didn't make any remarks, it was OK to move forward. I had suffered some bonus money for minor insubordination over not knowing where his inbox was.

I met Maury for lunch at the St. Paul Capital Grill the following Friday. Over lunch, I laid out my entrepreneurial plans for the Melford Olson Honey Company. He was so intrigued and had always known I was destined for entrepreneurship. Lunch soon rolled into the dinner hour as we talked and talked about all the years we had together and how I grew under his mentorship. He was so appreciative of the times that we worked together, all the work I'd done for him, even admitting a few times when we had disagreed strongly about some directives he gave me, to which I refused to follow through on and it was best that I hadn't. A few I insisted were not politically safe risks for his or my career. I used a payphone to call Darcy and leave a message at home that I was having dinner with Maury and wouldn't be home for dinner this evening.

The Capital Grille had a fine selection of scotch. We were both fans of single malts and, on occasion, had consumed a bottle here and there between us on travels together. Our dinner conversation rolled from years of past service together to looking ahead. He was in the middle of helping to make the Harvest States and CENEX mergers come alive. He appreciated that I worked diligently to complete my current projects before leaving. His recent work on the merger was strategically important, and my timing for going was inconvenient.

He proposed that I remain employed with full pay and full benefits as long as I gave my departments one day a week to check in, review their work, and keep them on track for success.

"That's all you work anyway," he joked. Since we had plenty of scotch, I asked him if this was a serious offer. He asked, "Am I ever not serious?" One thing about Maury, he always thought through his plans well before broaching them with anyone. He was a master at corporate planning, a real pro, and was responsible for many directions in which CENEX had grown into a billion-dollar organization. He had a lot of responsibility and didn't have time to do the babysitting I had done. If I babysat for him, he would look out for me again, possibly making up for some lost bonuses as to my misunderstanding of where his inbox was.

No matter what the real motive was, he was indeed once again helping me to succeed outside the corporation, and I would continue looking out for him within the corporation by assuring the many departments I was managing stayed intact. I completed their projects by meeting with them once a week while he focused on what he had to do. As we rolled past dessert, we continued to sample some of the finest scotch available as we laid out a plan on how I could assist him for the next two to three years, one day a week, as I pursued my new career with the Melford Olson Honey Company. We were at the Capital Grill from noon until eleven pm, having moved from the lunch table to the bar, back to a dinner table, and back to the bar again.

It remains one of the most enlightening evening discussions about career and fortune I've ever had. And the fact that the man paid me my entire full-time salary and benefits for three years for one day a week of service proved to me good guys don't finish last. They can finish first if they stay steadfast and true to doing what's right and give more than you take as a general course in your life. I was paid handsomely even though I was the adult who needed babysitting over an "in/out box". And, I am sure, though he never said so, that hanging on to me as an employee for the first three years while I pursued entrepreneurialism once again, was his fatherly love and insurance for me just in case I failed or changed my mind.

Chapter Fifty
Micayla

February 1998
Playlist:
Something About The Way You Look To, Elton John
You Were Meant for Me, Jewel
For You I Will, Monica
All Cried Out, Allure
All By Myself, Celine Dion
Let It Flow, Toni Braxton
My Heart Will Go On, Celine

I left CENEX and Land O Lakes for the third and final time in the spring of 1997. Though disappointed in my notice of resignation, Maury was happy I'd accepted his offer to stay on one day a week. He appreciated all my contributions throughout my 14-year "part-time" career as he joked about the leaves and sabbaticals, I took to try out entrepreneurship. He loved me in his way and looked out for me like a son he never had. It was too bad I didn't learn where his inbox was! But it probably wouldn't change my quest and desire for entrepreneurship.

I loved being a dad and nurturing our two boys. Darcy had wanted to stop at two children, but I dreamed of having a little girl. I dreamed of one day having a massive celebration of her life and walking her down the aisle to another man who would love and cherish her as I did Darcy. We made a great couple together. We made a lovely family unit. Almost perfect. "So how about trying for that little girl," I coaxed Darcy. She agreed we'd try, but it was the last child, no matter what sex child we received.

Harry and Loretta visited us once a year. They saw little of my family growing. We'd mail a few pictures sometimes, which they appreciated, but when they did visit, they were amazed at how different a life I had from them. My dad fondly interacted with my children, holding them, bouncing them, and acting like a grandpa. Loretta, too, would welcome them as babies but was more aloof. She seemed more interested in how Darcy and I were accomplishing so much as a couple. None of my children ever got close to her.

In May of 1997, I took control of the Melford Olson Honey Company. We were only an eight-person company, and I arrived every day at about 4:30 am to turn on blow molding machines that needed three hours to warm up before their operation. I would perform most accounting tasks during that time and start equipment to produce bottles for the filling line which ran from 9–4 with clean-up and the crew clocking out by five. While the line ran, I would make cold calls to drum up some sales. Whenever I could meet with customers, I would, and try to secure new business.

Traffic was horrendous for me as rush hour flowed in both directions of my commute. I often let the bottle machines continue producing and did the bookwork again until six when the traffic would clear. That was my life for the first five years, in addition to giving CENEX my one-day-a-week commitment. The CENEX pay enabled me to forego a salary from the business; I didn't take compensation for the first six years paying off the Olsons as fast as possible.

In July, Darcy announced that she was pregnant with our third child. I wanted a little girl, not just for myself but for Darcy. The boys would naturally gravitate toward me as their dad though I always coached them on appreciating their sports-minded mom. Darcy had an excellent relationship with our boys, but I wanted a girl in our lives for Darcy to do fun girl things. Now that we were pregnant, we crossed our fingers for a girl.

We enjoyed our beautiful home with no plans to leave it until Darcy's mom and dad offered us their home on Crystal Lake if we were interested. Her dad had wanted a cabin up north, and they planned to move.

It was a smaller home than ours, but located on a lake, and it would appreciate as an investment more so than where we were located. I thought through our finances that if we purchased it for what they were asking, we could free up about a hundred thousand dollars for reserves in our business from the sale of our home. It was again challenging for Darcy to give up our house, but she agreed it would be best to have some extra cash to help the new business grow. I had established a small credit line, but it wasn't enough to buy the inventories we needed as we acquired more customers and grow.

In September, Darcy shared with me that there was some concern that the baby she was carrying might have a disability, Downs Syndrome. She asked me to attend an ultrasound with Dr. Karen Lucas, our family MD. As she moved the ultrasound about Darcy's belly, a form of a tiny human being took shape on the picture screen. Dr. Lucas found all the limbs, fingers, and toes and told us everything looked normal and that the baby didn't appear to have any deformities, but the tiny size of the head and the body at this stage of pregnancy was a factor of suspicion. Along with this observation and a previous test, there was a 90 percent chance this baby would be born with Down Syndrome.

That news sunk in slowly as I wasn't educated as to precisely what all possible outcomes might be with a Down Syndrome baby. Dr. Lucas advised that we do some research and, if we had any questions, to let her know. She also professionally, discreetly, and politely let us know that we could still choose to abort the baby if we decided, and she left us in the patient room.

We both looked at each other with dead silence and concern in each of our eyes. I tried to smile at her and she wanted to smile back at me, but it was difficult. Neither of us said anything, but one thing was for sure: without it being spoken aloud, we would not abort the child whatever the outcome. That was not an option for either of us. It had never entered our minds until Dr. Lucas mentioned the possibility. After Darcy dressed, I hugged her, held her for a moment before we left, and said, "Well, it's a girl!"

In the following days, we began to gather some books from the library (the internet only existed for commercial, military, and academic uses at the time) and learn about all the possible deformities and abnormalities that were potential with Down Syndrome. I found nothing positive in the library, mainly the medical practice and scientific nature books.

As Darcy and I read through the books, I looked at her and asked, "Does all this matter?"

"What do you mean?" she asked.

"We're not going to abort the baby no matter what, right?" She agreed. "Well, why don't we forget this stuff for now, and let's just see what God gives us?" Darcy agreed. I didn't see any sense in building nervousness or pre-conceived perceptions for either of us through the pregnancy. As before, Darcy's bodily changes were enough to stress her and to contend with, and I didn't want her mind contemplating worst-case scenarios. Besides, we had two young boys to enjoy, and they kept us busy.

We weren't in business with the Mel-O Honey Company a year when the Hoffs vacated their home in January 1998, and we would move in the first week of February after our closing. Since we were just three miles away, I used the Mel-O Honey truck to move our furniture and belongings. We packed and moved a truckload each day after work beginning February fourth. On February eighth, with the last truck full of our bedroom furniture and clothes from our closet, we drove to the Crystal Lake home to unload. As we began, Darcy felt a little lightheaded and said she needed to sit down.

"Please do, sweetheart," I said as I continued to carry boxes in. With each box I carried into the living room, I glanced at Darcy. She was sitting comfortably, but I could tell something was amiss. I walked up to her and gently patted her cheek. "Darcy, I think we should go to the hospital."

"No, I'm OK," she insisted. "I'm fine. I'm fine."

"No," I insisted, "I think we should go to the hospital now." She again insisted that she was fine, just a little tired and wheezy from all the moving activity. I went outside and shut the doors to the truck. I had a strong suspicion that we would not get it emptied today.

I got Darcy's coat, helped her put it on, and said, "Let's go to the hospital and just check things out." She consented. Darcy was induced when Austin was born, so there was a planned birth there. With our second son Mason, we went to the hospital once as a false alarm, and Darcy thought we should go twice more, but I encouraged her that it wasn't her time yet. When it would be, somehow I'd know it, I tried to reassure her! And this time, though Darcy didn't think so, as the timing was at least three weeks earlier than her due date, I was sure we would have our third baby very soon.

We left the Mel-O truck on the side of the street, still fully loaded, and drove to the hospital. Upon arrival, I shared at the admissions desk the possibility that we might be having a baby, and Darcy looked at me as to how I could be so confident! The nurse got a wheelchair, brought Darcy in for an examination, and immediately told her not to push and that the baby could arrive any minute. They didn't want that to happen until Dr. Lucas could get there. Darcy was surprised at this news. I called her parents and our best friends Jo and Gary and told them we were at the hospital. They were outside our room waiting within a half hour. Dr. Lucas made it to the hospital just before the baby came and asked me if I wanted to get scrubs and deliver the baby. Once again, I was exhausted from moving. Also because of any potential complications that might occur with our knowledge the baby might have Downs Syndrome, I suggested she perform the delivery. OK, she agreed, and ten minutes later, we had a beautifully tiny, petite baby girl. Dr. Lucas counted all the toes and fingers and looked her over very closely.

I cut the umbilical cord and held our daughter in my arms, staring at her tiny head, ears, and eyes while the nurses attended Darcy. She looked normal, I thought, but something inside me confirmed that she was indeed born with Down Syndrome. Darcy had beautifully almond-shaped eyes, and tiny Micayla's seemed almond-shaped like her mom's. But was it from Darcy's genetic pass down or the Down Syndrome extra chromosome?

Diagnosing her with Down Syndrome was challenging to tell from the physical features, at least for us. Dr. Lucas confirmed too that she looked very typical, but perhaps because of the risk, we should run a test, or maybe she didn't want to pass us the bad news and let a day or two settle in with a confirming test.

It took two days for the test results to return, confirming Micayla had the extra chromosome. I handed our wonderful gift from God to Darcy and read the results. My eyes shut like steel doors. As Darcy peered into Micayla's beautiful eyes, already wide open and taking in the world, I turned to her, opened my eyes, and tried to smile. A tear or two slipped past my eyelids. Darcy began to shed tears, and as strong as I wanted to be for her, I could not hold back the tears. They were a mixture of tears of joy and love, and we wouldn't be honest with you without telling you they were also from natural feelings of disappointment, anxiety, and worry.

I thought a lot about how much more time Dr. Lucas spent looking over Micayla's features and measuring her head, arms, and legs than Austin and Mason. I was sure she already knew that Micayla had features of Downs Syndrome. Still, her ever-professional stature would confirm her assessment before she delivered the potentially sobering news.

When Dr. Lucas arrived at the hospital to go over the test results we'd already received, "The good news," she said, "is that she appears healthy and normal in every other physical way." The precautionary X-rays they performed on her showed no abnormalities or congenital disabilities like holes in the heart, twisted or other intestinal problems, and other deformities common in children with Down Syndrome.

Micayla was a healthy, already smiling, and spunky happy baby. We both sat quietly with lumps in our throats. It was still the most devastating news in what I considered my now perfect life with Darcy. I had to be strong for her, and she was being strong for me, but we both broke down again and cried together and finally said, "Well, look at her; she's just beautiful." God had a unique way of making us blind to the apparent features of a Down Syndrome baby.

Grandma and Grandpa had the boys and brought them to the hospital for visits. They immediately adored and loved the new baby, and neither could get enough time to hold and cuddle her. Austin was constantly tried to make her laugh, bringing out his brother Mason's infectious laugh, and Micayla fell in love with them both. The instantaneous bond between the three siblings in the hospital room was incredible. I admired my two sons and Micayla. I was inspired and in awe.

We hadn't shared Micayla's confirmed condition with anyone. When Darcy was released from the hospital, we returned home, where the Mel-O truck still lay parked, full of boxes. Jo and Gary and their daughter Bethany had brought over dinner, and Darcy's mom and dad came along with a couple of our other friends. Everyone ooohed and ahhhed over Micayla.

As we finished dinner and looked forward to the desert, I told everyone I had a small announcement to make, and informed them that Micayla was born with Down Syndrome.

The room went silent. I explained the good news that she is a healthy, happy child with no internal or external deformities that we could see now. No one else could either, or at least they never fessed up. Darcy's dad began to weep quietly. So did some of our friends and Gary. Darcy's mom Betty held back her tears; she would deliberately maintain composure for our family unit.

We had previously asked Gary and Jo if they would be Godparents to our baby when we first got pregnant. I am ashamed that I asked the following question in the now morgue-like atmosphere that swept over the room. My news about Micayla brought laughter and celebration to silence and mourning.

"Jo and Gary, would you still consider being Micayla's Godparents," I asked. And that turned out to be just the ticket that prompted Jo to stand up and say, "Listen, she is a beautiful baby, and she is going to grow into a beautiful girl, and we're all going to love her the same as any other." Darcy's mom Betty jumped all over that, and the chatter about the room turned back on and was upbeat as we all enjoyed our dessert with coffee and tea.

The next day I unloaded the rest of the Mel-O truck and made the last move of boxes from our old house to the Oak Shore house. We closed on our former home a week later, and I was back to my typical working 12–14-hour days at the Mel-O Honey Company.

Over the eight weeks of maternal leave, Darcy and I chatted a lot about Micayla and what her needs might grow into. Our pediatrician suggested we find and join some support groups with other parents of Down Syndrome children. The more I searched for information and learned about Down Syndrome, the more I became convinced the best thing to do for us was to give Micayla our utmost love and time to grow. There were so many varying degrees and levels of functionality among this population that I felt to observe other grown children might set an uncertain expectation or even dampen our own with fear. We had two boys to enjoy and help grow; a new business and another new home to organize. I convinced Darcy that it was best to give ourselves time and have no fewer expectations of Micayla for now than our boys at this age until we learned a little more about her as she grew. Darcy agreed.

Not knowing what Micayla's condition would be a year from birth, Darcy and I decided she would resign from her job and stay home with Micayla for a year. I felt terrible for Darcy. She loved her career. I knew she would miss it, but I offered that she could come and work with the Mel-O Honey Company in sales after a year and that her role with Mel-O Honey could provide flexibility. Since I had the income from CENEX and we had no personal debts other than the business debt, we could afford to do this.

A few weeks after Micayla's birth, Loretta and Harry arrived to see our newborn. Loretta held Micayla in her arms, and we informed her and my dad of Mic's condition. She was kind and gentle and held her for hours during her stay. My dad did as well. They were a little subdued and different after raising my sisters daughter for several years. She knew she would have to behave whenever she visited our home. We had a pleasant visit, and she seemed excessively calm. When I asked her if she was OK, she mentioned that she wasn't feeling very well lately.

When she returned home, she informed my youngest sister about Micayla's Down Syndrome, and my sister immediately called me to tell me that Loretta wondered what sins I made that God would punish me with such a child. Par for the course, I thought for Loretta, and sadly I thought, par for my little sister. Why would she even consider repeating what she'd heard? She was increasingly becoming more like Loretta, never having anything good to say about anyone and throwing condemnation at others' accomplishments or whatever she was jealous of.

Chapter Fifty-One
People Die as They Live

December 1998
Playlist: None

Loretta always wrote me letters. Since I'd been married, her poisonous pen became more subdued and I still constantly had to remind her to don't waste a postage stamp if she had nothing good to say in the letter. In her more recent letters she complained of a pain in her side. Since her visit too, shortly after Micayla's birth, she often complained about pain below her stomach. When I occasionally called home to chat with them, I suggested she go to the doctor and see what she could find out. She finally agreed to do so in June. She got some results: Cancer. The test results weren't what anyone had expected and weren't good. MRIs showed massive growth in her liver.

There was a sense of urgency; within weeks of her test results, she was scheduled for an operation to see if surgeons could remove the tumor from her liver. Harry wanted her to be in the best hospital despite his miserable marriage to her. The operation was scheduled at New York City's Sloan Kettering Cancer Center.

My work schedule was insane, but I flew into LaGuardia and was there for the operation day. Before the operation, the surgeons came into the room and explained what they would do. They told us if the cancer were only local to the liver, they would try to cut as much of it out as possible and then proceed with Chemotherapy to rid the liver of the rest of the cancer. If they found that cancer had spread to other parts of the body, they would sew Loretta back up so she could have whatever time she had left to say her goodbyes. That wasn't easy to hear. Despite how miserable a person she was, she gave birth to me. No son wants to listen to that kind of possible scenario for his mother.

It was a long, tense day. My older half-sister, myself, and my father were present. My older half-brother came in from Long Island after work to visit as well. We all wished Loretta good luck as she was wheeled into the operation room. She thanked us, but the expression on her face looked as if she knew this would not be solved.

The operation ended, and the surgeons were conspicuously absent for hours. They never said a word about the process or results except to send a nurse out and let us know the operation was over and Loretta was resting. I suspected that Loretta asked them not to give the operation results to her family until she was awake and ready to hear the news herself. That is precisely what happened. When she awoke and returned to her room, we sat with her as the Surgeon told us he was sorry, but they sewed her back up. There was nothing they could do for her.

With our questioning, they offered some life-extending care options. Still, they told Loretta it would only delay her inevitable death, not cure it. She had already made up her mind. She would not accept chemotherapy or life-prolonging treatments, preferring to live whatever time she had left in as quality away as she could.

I stepped out of the room and asked the surgeon if there was any chance of experimental treatment or cure in this hospital or elsewhere. Looking into his steady eyes, he said kindly and reassuringly that the best thing to do was to go home and let Loretta enjoy whatever time she had left.

It was July, and Harry packed up Loretta's things, and she went home to die.

I returned to my family and business. The company was new to me and it was very stressful. I still had much to learn and long days with limited time for anything, including visiting Loretta. I began to call her weekly, but that soon faded as the phone calls between us were horrible.

She ungratefully told me several times that my dad had offered everything, even to mortgage his home if some cure in some other part of the world could help her. "What the hell does he want from me?" she'd selfishly ask in response to his gestures as if he wanted something other than to help cure her. She was so ungrateful of his love all her life and even in her dying sickness.

She told him and everyone else she wanted to die. And she did. She remained a miserable person to her death. While Harry was still in love with her after all these years, she treated him miserably in her last dying months, and let him know how much she despised him to the very end. She moved out of their bedroom into my sister's former room. She told him she didn't want to sleep with him, and he was never to touch her, that she didn't wish for his care.

As fall approached and the cool weather began to set in, I asked her in a phone call how she was doing and if there was anything I could do for her. She told me she wanted to go to Florida one last time for some warmth and sun. When I arranged for them to go to Florida for the month and soak up some sunshine, she told Harry she didn't want him to go along. She deliberately hurt him again. She constantly bashed Harry for everything.

I flew down for a few days to stay with her in her last week. She seemed at peace. Little was said between us as I had already reduced my calls to her because every conversation was always mean spirited and with ill-hearted digs aimed at my personal life and my siblings. She was always trying to interfere with my siblings' marriages and relationships in negative ways.

In my first year of marriage as she began to do the same with me, I had to tell her that if she tried to get between Darcy and my relationship, if she put me to a choice in any way, I let her know that I would choose my wife and abort her as a mother. My siblings had already done this with years of absent communication with her. I was at least giving her a chance with a forewarning.

Darcy's mom and dad owned a condo in the same complex I had rented the condo where Loretta stayed. They graciously made dinner and looked after her when I wasn't there. I took her out for dinner a few nights, but she never felt well enough to eat. After I visited Florida, she returned to Van Etten, and me to Minneapolis.

The week before Christmas, I flew back to New York and visited Loretta for the last time before her death. By now, she was very ill and miserably sick. I slept in my old bedroom. I could hear her vomiting several times a night in the bathroom adjacent to my bedroom and her sighs of discomfort and pain. I was so sorry for her, and I wept hearing her suffer.

She lived a tragic life, treated people miserably, and was now dying a tragic death. I tried to shut out all her suffering I heard all night, but it was impossible.

During the day, she sat on the couch, just staring. Harry sat in his recliner staying with her all day. Whenever he offered her comfort, a cup of tea, a blanket, or some consolation, she snapped at him and told him she hated him and to leave her alone. She told me she didn't want any care from him and didn't want him touching her. I was angry about her remarks and how she treated him but said nothing. She told me all she wanted was to be held like a baby. Maybe Jesus could give her that when her time came I thought to myself. While I sat next to her and would put my arm around her and, at times, held her hand, I felt nothing but anger over how she continued to treat Harry. Her meanness drove any compassion I had out of me. I held her hand out of understanding, but not warmth or compassion. I was angry at how she treated a man who had loved her his whole life and how she treated him the same to her last dying day.

On my last morning with her, she called me into her room. As she sat up in her bed, she asked me to sit in a chair and looked directly into my eyes. She lectured me about life in nearly every aspect she could think of as if she had ever lived the perfect life! I sat quietly, disgusted at some of her propositions and the degradation of her other children. She asked what sin I had to deserve a child like mine, referring my disabled daughter. I kept silent, trying to chalk all of this up to her sickness, but frankly, it wasn't. It was just her. In my mind I turned the question on her. What kind of sin did she do that she had such mental anguish, depression, and anger at everyone close to her?

Harry walked up to the bedroom doorway while she continued to pour out all her misery and unhappiness to me. As he stood there listening in on the conversation, she became a tyrant on how she never had anything her whole life and that nothing was owned in her name that she could leave to anyone. But she had written in a letter what and to whom she wanted certain items to give and wanted her final wishes followed. Her voice, now loud and stern as she knew Harry was listening, she concluded by telling me that after she dies, I should expend all of my energies to get every last dime out of my selfish and mean-spirited father that I can. She told me that if I didn't, he would give it all to his other son, whom she despised all her life, but not unlike she did the rest of us at various times.

As she ranted on, I thought about how we all had tried to love her as a mother our whole lives. She was constantly distancing herself from us, especially her daughters. None of us, especially my dad's son from his first marriage, deserved the sick, meanspirited verbal's that she dealt us, even if she was dying.

In my few visits back to her, I'd tried to remain positive, and when she would begin her rants, I stayed quiet and compassionate in trying to understand she was a sick and dying woman. She had no appreciation of how difficult these trips to New York to see her were for me at a time in my life, running a new business and with a new baby.

I had finally had enough. I wouldn't sit any longer and listen to Loretta trying to divide me against my father. She had already succeeded with all the rest. I was the last one she wanted to break down.

I looked directly into her eyes and began sternly. "Listen to you. Just listen to yourself. You're dying, and in your last days, you continue to try and hurt people just like you've done your whole miserable life. Here, this man has offered you everything he has to find care for you, in love! And you continue to treat him so poorly. All you care about is dismantling his life, creating upheaval in ours, telling us to get whatever we can out of him as you sit here dying."

I couldn't help myself. The words kept pouring out of my mouth.

"I don't care about getting one penny from him or you. This house and possessions you put so much value on mean nothing to me, and should mean nothing to you. People are essential in life," I scolded her, "people, and all you have ever done was hurt the people who have tried to love you." "What have you done?" "I already have ten times your wealth because I spend my life caring for and enriching other people, not tearing them apart." "Don't ask me what I have done to deserve my children." "The question is for you; What have you done to deserve such a pathetic life?"

"I don't want anything from either of you. It would simply remind me of the misery you represent." "In your last dying days, all you can concern yourself with is material things, more importantly, dividing and hurting people." "You lived a miserable life, and are now dying the way you lived." "You even have voodoo dolls of your children."

Lorretta sat motionlessly. She said nothing. Harry heard all this and said, "Curt, I think that is enough."

"It's enough, all right," I said, and I got up from the chair and asked Harry if we could leave for the airport.

He reminded me that we still had three hours before we needed to be there. I responded in front of Loretta with, "I know, let's go for lunch. I'm not spending another minute here."

I was determined not to give Loretta the satisfaction that she'd won, and used some of her last breath to plant seeds of division and ill will and turn me against my dad.

I packed my duffle bag with the few things I had brought, grabbed my suitcase, and my dad and I started for the car. Loretta's door to her room was closed. It didn't matter; I said my piece. "Are you sure you want to go this early," my dad asked. I said, "Yes, dad. I'll buy you lunch."

From that moment on, Loretta was already dead. I wasn't wasting any more time or resources to spend my precious time on earth with the deceased. That's how I felt.

It was a cold and rainy December day with heavy overcast clouds. It looked as miserable as I felt. As Harry and I got into the car and he turned on the windshield wipers, I saw Loretta at the back porch window staring at us. I could tell she was sobbing terribly. I stared at her without emotion on my face as she stared at me, pouring tears from her eyes. *You miserable bitch.* I pondered. *You made us all dance through the rain from your eyes all these years, and you're still trying.*

My dad began to back out of the driveway away from the porch. Nothing swept away Loretta's tears or my feelings as the wipers swept away the rain. For a moment, I wanted to tell my dad to stop the car and let me go in and hug her one last time just because it was a compassionate act to do. It would have been the warm way to say goodbye for good, but nothing was in me. And if I did, she would interpret it as a win! A downpour had started. I was so empty. I wished my visit was different, that she was different. I couldn't give Loretta any satisfaction that she'd gotten inside of me to hurt my dad.

The car backed toward the garage and I stared at Loretta sobbing in the window. My dad turned the car down the driveway, and with it so did my head. I didn't look back. That was the last time I saw Loretta alive, the last time I talked with her while she was conscious.

As we headed for Elmira Airport, we drove past the cemetery where she would soon be buried. She had already made a statement of hate (and love at the same time) years before when she placed a stone for my older brother Gary and put the message "Beloved Son" on one side and her name and "Beloved Mother" on the other side. A clear and permanent display that none of us mattered, indeed not Harry. She wished to secure her place and marker in the world alongside her favorite child. She'd soon have her wish.

Harry's favorite fast-food chain was Wendy's. He loved their chocolate shakes and chili. That's where we went and sat for two hours before we drove to the airport. We chatted about this and that, and he told me how sick Loretta was and that, as usual, she didn't mean what she said. I told my dad it didn't matter, but he was wrong, she always meant what she said, and I warned him to beware of my little sister as Loretta shared the same things, she said to me with her.

Harry continued to defend her. He still cared and loved her, and I was sorry for him. He told me not to worry and he should get me to the airport so he could get back to Loretta.

I said my goodbyes to my dad and boarded the twin-propeller plane. As the plane took off and I looked across at the gray skies and brown hues of the hills surrounding Elmira Airport, I began to bleed with raindrops.

Chapter Fifty-Two
The Funeral

January 1999
Playlist: None

I called on New Year's Day to wish them a Happy New Year and a Happy Anniversary. They were married for 40 years. My dad told me Loretta's condition had worsened, and she mostly slept all day. I didn't speak to her. I asked my dad to keep me informed as to her condition. "She seems to be in a lot of pain," he indicated, "but she wants to die in her home and not go to the hospital." Some nurses trained my younger sister to give her some morphine shots.

For the following two weeks, I called daily to check-in. With my sister's presence, I could tell the home had a frantic atmosphere of hysteria and chaos. I heard her yelling obscenities in the background at my father as he tried to convey the situation to me, telling him he was f...g wrong at everything he was trying to say. She screamed in the background for me to hear her over his voice. "He isn't caring for her; I am."

I knew what was going on. My younger sister was trying to take control of a situation she had no experience, knowledge, or business to handle. My older sister was there trying to maintain a calm sense of order as my younger sister played Harry against everyone, just as Loretta always had.

Loretta had been unconscious for two days, only communicating with horrible moans of pain and discomfort. My dad asked if I could come out because he thought she might be waiting to see me. I didn't want to be there. I couldn't afford the time away from my business should her dying days drag out. She had her opportunity to say goodbye the last time I saw her and she used it horribly. But I told him I'd try to make some arrangements and call him daily to check-in.

I called him twice a day. In one call, I could hear my sister in the background with hysteria screaming, oh my God, oh my God, we're giving her too much morphine. Near the end of my call, I could hear a testament that she no longer emotionally could take care of Loretta but would not allow Harry to intervene in any way. My sister demanded with a hysterical scream that Loretta be moved to a hospital despite her wishes.

At first, my dad refused to call an ambulance and transport Loretta to the hospital against her wishes. I counseled him and suggested that given the circumstances and the lack of professional help, Loretta would be cared for properly and possibly not endure the apparent discomfort being expressed. The insaneness was still there in the background noise fostered by my sister.

My dad finally agreed. He told me he didn't think she had hours to live and asked if I wanted to say goodbye. He held the phone up to her ear, and I whispered a minor tune in her ear and suggested that it was OK to go to God. She should let go and go to heaven.

The ambulance toted Loretta away and settled her into a hospital bed, where she died within the hour.

I was empty—void of any emotions. I spoke with my dad, expressed my sympathies to him, and told him I'd be on my way in the next day or two as soon as I could arrange flights.

I flew back into the Elmira and Horsehead valleys to find the same drab gray-brown winter hues of color I'd left weeks before. They were depressing. I rented a car and stopped at the Pudgies Pizza at seven corners in Horseheads to pick up a sheet of pizza to bring to my dad's home. As I waited for the pizza to cook, I had a slice and a Coke and sat thinking about the last time I'd been here and the paradise night by the dim green light that ensued afterward.

Memories flooded into my soul of all those years of heartache and hell as I drove past the countryside where much of it took place, Cotton Hanlon, where I had worked, and up through the valleys and hills to my dad's home.

I opened my dad's door and greeted him and my older brother Harry with the pizza. I looked around; I could easily see that the house had already been stripped of most furnishings. Loretta's desk and chair were gone, as were other furnishings. Walking past where she slept during her dying days and the primary bedroom, I saw belongings strewn all over the room. Her jewelry boxes were gone, and her closet rampaged through.

After putting my suitcase and suit bag into my old room, I shared the pizza and learned what had happened. Harry Jr. told me the girls, but mostly Daffy, my youngest sister, had gone through everything of Loretta's and cleaned the house. They took it all over to her mobile home. When she began cleaning out the furnishings, Harry Jr. put down his foot and ordered her out of the house, explaining that the man still owned this house and its belongings and needed furniture to live with. My dad was oblivious to everything and said he didn't care and they could have whatever they wanted. He was in great despair.

I didn't see my sisters until the next day and addressed them about what I'd heard from Harry. Each had a different perspective on the story. However, Daffy's position was that Loretta had a will she gave her, which she would not share with me. Daffy said it was her right to possess anything she wanted. I explained that Dad still had to have furniture to live with and pressed her to produce their supposed will. She still would not share the Will with me. I figured she received the exact selfish directions Loretta gave me to take everything I could from Harry upon her death, except she took it literally and willingly.

Harry Jr. and I talked with my dad and put some sense in him to halt the scavenger and let a month go by before h let anyone commence taking anything more from his house. He agreed.

The funeral arrangements were made with the Allen-Manzar Funeral Home in Spencer. Loretta was laid out, and except for a few flowers I purchased out of respect and those of my older sister and my King family, there weren't any others. Darcy flew out to be with me; although I told her there wasn't any need as we had Micayla and our two young boys to care for, she wanted to be present for me, my dad, and my family.

There was a brief local obituary, and beyond that, relatives were notified by phone. None of Loretta's siblings' nor their spouses, cousins, or extended family from Long Island and New Jersey attended the funeral. Aside from my dad, two sisters, and brother, and my King family, only one friend of Loretta's from Spencer was there.

The service was as brief as the obituary. I sat through the Pastors sermon and heard nothing. I was numb and, out of respect for my dad, gave a eulogy he requested of me. My words were short, a matter of fact, and more historically oriented to where she grew up and came from. I tried to focus some attention on my dad, but what could I say? Anything truthfully nice was limited. Sure, she could be fun and pleasant to most outside the family, she raised children, and she was a wife, but the quality of her actions, in how she was a wife, were not those a person could exemplify and be proud of. I would not and could not provide a charade of complementary attributes.

After the service, I stayed in the parlor alone with her. I walked up to her casket and stared at her. After what she had directed me to do in her dying days, and seeing the very evidence of her instructions through my youngest sister, the extraction and theft of her and my dad's things from their home, all I could do was look at her with pity and disgust; her legacy of selfishness, dysfunction, meanness, and erratic behavior and thought, "Oh my God, she lives on in my little sister." I thought. I took one last look at her face. Her physical appearance showed no remorse; I wondered if her soul did. I couldn't thank her for anything except my birth.

Her body would remain in the morgue for a later spring burial as the ground was too frozen to dig the grave. Since her death, I called my dad every day to check in on him. He reassured me he was doing fine but sounded bitter in many calls. He was sorting through many pictures and tossing out things from the past. He was an atheist. He didn't believe in Christ or an afterlife. To him, Loretta was dead. To me, she was probably in hell. I hoped not and prayed not, and though I am a Christian and prayed for her forgiveness from God, I could not personally lay forgiveness on her. I saw the damage she had done. Her ill spirit and selfish actions now lived in my little sister.

Spring came, and I wasted my time flying home for Loretta again. My brother, my father, and I carried the coffin from the transport to the stand in the cemetery. As a pastor from St. Paul's Lutheran Church presided over the burial service, my dad began to weep and stepped off to the cemetery's north side. I walked over, put my arm on his shoulder, and asked if he was OK. He remained silent for a couple of minutes as he wept, then took a deep breath and said emphatically, "I wasted my whole f--king life with that woman." He always loved her, no matter how poorly she treated him. I wondered if he had come to some finality and point of realization, having just turned 70 a month before realizing what a terrible mess and time he had endured. I just stood silently with him until he could gather his composure.

After the service was over, we lowered the casket to the ground. The backhoe would return later to bury the coffin. We returned to my dad's house, except for my sister, who returned to her mobile home. I went into the garage, got a shovel, and returned to the cemetery.

I buried Loretta with it. With each shovel I threw on top of her coffin, I poured out every hurt, every sarcastic insult, every beating, every demeaning remark or insult, and every degradation she ever dealt me. After I filled the hole, I asked God to forgive her for all the same she did to every other child she had and her siblings and grandchildren. I asked for forgiveness, too, for whatever pain I may have caused her in response to her actions, for my lack of understanding…of so many things I still didn't know.

My Aunt Peggy's words and council telling Darcy and me once, "the difference between your mom and me is I forgave myself, your mother will never forgive herself," always haunted me. Now more than ever, I wondered, what hadn't she forgiven herself for? I might never know, but I could understand it because I couldn't forgive her.

Loretta's miserable life was over. She was buried. Her secrets were buried.

And I was free, almost.

Chapter Fifty-Three
It's Very Difficult to Escape

Playlist: None

After my first year in college, I bought my sister Daffy her first car. I didn't have much money, but I knew she would never escape the dysfunction at home without one. She seemed to make no effort to borrow a car to seek a job, or perhaps, Loretta was making it difficult for her.

Even though she helped to incite excessive arguments with Loretta in the household, I knew she needed a way to escape, get a job, and get out from under Loretta's control and influence. With all the household trouble Daffy caused and her obsessive lies about nearly everything, I began to see a pattern of behavior much the same as Loretta's and worse. She was a liar at home and had the same reputation in high school. Throughout high school, many kids had behaviors emanating from home and acted them out in school, and teachers saw it in Daffy. Teachers who knew me couldn't believe we came from the same household. They didn't realize that what they saw in my little sister was the natural consequence of the dysfunction in our family, which is so often learned and imbedded in another human being.

My sis caused such misery at home in high school that my dad refused to help her with anything, not even a car. So, from my meager savings, I bought her a used Honda Civic, which ran well and got excellent gas mileage for her budget. I painted it silver for her as I had car paint leftover from the Comet and put a black stripe down the side, like what I'd done years before with Comet. I hoped a good car like Comet might bring her luck, or at least some wheels of independence to help her make her luck. She never thanked me, just complained that it was an ugly car. I told her she didn't have to take it, but she did. She had grown into a mini-Loretta at an early age. I tried to love and care for her, even later in her troubled life, loaning her thousands of dollars after her first divorce to try and help her stave off some troubles with debt. Loretta always had credit card debt, and Daffy followed.

On one visit back to Van Etten, she informed me she was pregnant. She was still just a young woman with a whole life ahead of her, and while I would not choose abortion, I asked her if she considered it for herself. She told me that she had already had multiple abortions and that her doctor told her one more would likely damage her body and not allow her to have a child again. I was surprised and disappointed. She used abortion as a form of birth control! I couldn't imagine the guilt she might have for those abortions. She told me she wanted to have a child. I was glad about that. The child's dad wanted nothing to do with her or their child. I couldn't blame him or her first husband for not wanting anything to do with her. She was a product of Loretta, foul-mouthed, dysfunctional, a liar, a thief, and a manipulative soul.

She had no decent place to live. She was renting a room in a house in Elmira, so Loretta persuaded Harry to carve off five acres from his land and give her the two derelict trailers that sat on those acres near the cemetery just down the road from their home. He gave her the land and helped move the two trailers together to form a temporary home until she could afford to put a new home on the parcel. That never happened. She lived in them until they fell apart.

She moved into the trailers and had her baby. After a couple of years, she called me again, asking me for more money. This was now the third time she asked me for money to bail her out of some issue, and she would never honestly share why she needed the money. She was frantic, crying and begging as she did before. I asked her what the money was for this time. She refused to tell me but pleadingly begged me for the money.

Twice before, I had bailed her out. It wasn't just a few thousand. Each time, the amount approached nearly twenty thousand dollars. She told me she had a lot of credit card debt and could no longer feed her kid. I knew better than to believe that manipulative story. All my previous help enabled her to keep getting into financial trouble and spend wildly using the credit I freed up.

I asked her again what the money was for, but she wouldn't tell me. Upon my visits to Van Etten, I observed she was living large, serving lobster dinners to her friends while living in the shanty of the two combined mobile homes. She always seemed to be dressed in spendy brand-name clothes and jewelry. These observations raised remorseful reminders in my mind that she had never once made an effort to pay back any of the tens of thousands I loaned her. This time I refused her by telling her if she couldn't tell me the real reason and If this time I couldn't directly pay who or what she was in trouble for, instead of giving her the cash, I wasn't going to help.

Darcy and I were sensibly working hard, saving out of every paycheck for our own lives, and Daffy seemed to live high from our concern and care for her. No matter how much she pleaded and tried to manipulate my emotions toward helping her again, I reminded her that she had never attempted to pay me back. I wasn't going to loan her money again.

Less than a year later, she would be sentenced to time in jail for grand larceny theft. Rumors circulated that she had embezzled. Whatever she needed a loan from me for, she either got it by stealing or perhaps she already had stolen and needed it to pay it back to avoid her prison sentence. While I felt horrible that she had to serve time in prison, it was perhaps the best lesson for her to learn. "Sometimes a family has to let go and let the system handle an issue," I told Loretta. Loretta did not want to hear that from me and let me know. It was devastating to her and Harry, and they were embarrassingly disgusted.

The care of her toddler daughter now fell to them while she went to prison to serve her sentences, lest the child would have been placed into foster care.

For only the second time in my life, I saw them both working pleasantly together, raising my sister's daughter. I observed how they showered love upon her for two years and cared for her in a way they couldn't do for the rest of us. Loretta seemed calm and comfortable in caring for her granddaughter. It was like a second chance to raise a little girl and try to do it well.

Loretta was pleasant, and so was Harry. They visited us a several times in Minnesota, bringing my niece along. We could tell that this grandchild was a blessing in disguise. Raising her gave Loretta some other focus and reprieve from her grief over my brother and brought her and Harry closer together.

When I would visit for those two years, I thought a lot about how happy they seemed. Harry seemed delighted as this little girl genuinely loved him, and I saw the love he could give back. It was all bliss until my sister was released from prison.

Then a weekly battle between her and Loretta about raising her child became the norm. My little sister had become Loretta, the high anxiety, manic-mood switching depressant swearing and cursing at the small child as if she were a cellmate in prison. It was terrible to witness, and oddly enough, Loretta criticized the very behavior she bestowed upon all of us.

When my sister was released from serving her time in jail, her daughter didn't want to return home with her mother. That infuriated my younger sister, who feared the loss of her daughter's love while in prison, and the next few years brought hatred and anger back into Loretta's household. Her granddaughter constantly craved and sought back her relationship with her grandparents. The rotten apple that did not fall far from the tree did everything she could to drive a wedge between the love that developed over the two years her daughter lived with Loretta and Harry. The only silver lining was that I was no longer one of the dominant recipients of Loretta's wrath. Loretta's focus was now on Daffy with threats to have her declared an incompetent mother and secretly report her to social services out of concern for her granddaughter.

My poor dad was caught in the middle of Loretta and my sister's dual manipulation of each other over the care and love of her daughter. There would be punishable lengthy times for years afterward when my sister wouldn't allow her daughter to visit them, sometimes for months. If Harry refused to assist my sister with a car repair or some other request, my sister used her daughter manipulatively like a weapon to hurt Harry and Loretta by not allowing her to visit them.

It was a dysfunctional tornado that traveled back and forth almost daily, if not weekly, as she lived less than 100 yards away. My niece would sometimes sneak off to see her grandparents only to return, get found out, and suffer the same abuse Loretta had inflicted upon us. The apple definitely did not fall far from the tree, and unfortunately for the little girl, she'd be raised by one worse than Loretta, one that was rotten to the core.

On the few return visits, I would make to the homestead, almost always without my family so they wouldn't witness and experience all the dysfunction, I was always coaching and counseling them all to get along. It was useless. Dysfunction was embedded, reborn, and the norm among them. Harry regretted giving my little sis ownership of the property as he would have instead not had her living so close. Still, he could do nothing but endure her crappy attitude and manipulative personality because Loretta wanted to see her grandchild.

As long as their grandchild was still living nearby, he did whatever he could or was manipulated into doing whatever he could for his granddaughters' sake by Loretta and my sister, whether it was loaning her money that Harry would never see again, repairing plumbing or heating in her hut, or repairing her car. He did all sorts of tasks to enable peace between the families, and it only lasted until my little sis needed money again or the next item fixed. The dysfunction was so intense that I could never bring my family back to Van Etten to spend time where I grew up.

Darcy only had to experience one mild incident to dismiss all desire to return to Loretta's household. However, she was always willing for my sake. The dysfunction I lived with as a child and teen continued. I went home to pay visits alone. I wouldn't expose Darcy or my children to it for even a day.

Several years after Loretta died, Daffy was in trouble again. She lost her job, and now for the fourth time, she called me up and asked me for money. I had several conversations with her and flew back to Van Etten, counseling her that she should consider coming out to Minnesota so I could help her. A new place, environment, and a bigger city with lots more opportunities might help change her attitude and move forward. I helped some other friends from high school to do the same, and they seemed to thrive. It may work for Daffy.

She asked me for twenty thousand dollars to pay off some debt she owed for the third time. Fearing that if I didn't help her, she might land herself in jail again, I agreed to do so on one condition; get out of Van Etten and consider an offer I made. I offered her a job at my company in Minneapolis. I told her I would pay the moving expenses, lease her an apartment for one year, and if she liked living in the Midwest, I would help her buy a home, just as I did for another friend from Spencer.

I asked that she give it one year, just as Harry had coached me long ago. He told her it was a good idea. Seeing how well I flourished, he convinced her to accept my offer. Darcy had huge intuitive reservations about doing this, and so did I, but she supported the effort if I thought it would help Daffy. Through our example and associations, I hoped to coach her into a better life. I had only one condition for extending my help; I told her the deal was off if she used foul language in my home or business.

Daffy always had a loud and obnoxious tongue. As a teen, I cannot count how many times I wished she would shut her mouth to avoid antagonizing Loretta.

I gave her the money she requested. I couldn't believe what I heard next. As soon as I gave it to her, she told me she had second thoughts about coming out to the Midwest. The little bastard never really intended to follow through. I told her to return the money immediately and that the deal in providing her the debt relief was I would help her, not just with paying off her debts but help her start a new life.

I had offered her a job paying an annual salary of $40,000.00 in my company, more than twice what she had recently earned. I also told her I would help her buy a home after two years if she paid me back. In the worst-case scenario, I explained to her that if she didn't like working with me or my company, there would be lots more other opportunities she could apply for in the more significant metropolis of Minneapolis. It finally sounded good to her, and she agreed.

I found her a two-bedroom apartment in downtown Lakeville near our home, which I leased for a year. Harry picked up a U-Haul truck I paid for, helped her load all her belongings into it and drove it to Minnesota.

Daffy arrived, and Harry and I moved all her belongings up to the second-story apartment I leased and helped her settle. It was a Friday. She was keenly jealous of the home Darcy and I had made for ourselves. It was written all over her facial expressions and in her sly remarks. On Saturday, I drove her around some newly developed neighborhoods. I showed her where I thought she could afford a home in another year or two, coaching her that she'd have to keep her credit cards free of debt. I could tell she didn't want to hear that counseling. Her daughter was excited to be in Minnesota and saw being around us as a chance for a new life. My dad had encouraged the same message to her as a little girl, and eagerness and desire were written all over her face and in her eyes. She was a beautifully bright little girl, and I was hoping this chance I created for her mom would make a life-changing improvement for her too.

Daffy spent Saturday night in the apartment I leased for her and stormed into our home on Sunday morning, saying she wouldn't live there. She claimed it was noisy, which it might have been on a weekend as there was a bar called Babes just down the street. I told her it was temporary, and we could find something after the first year, that the noise was probably just a couple of people from the bar.

She insisted I had to find her some other accommodations in the neighborhoods I drove her around to see as a potential future home, or she wasn't staying; she was going home. Darcy looked at me with great concern and sat silently. She had cautioned me in several discussions about me helping her, but she always supported me in my efforts.

Once again, the dysfunctional bastard was trying to manipulate me. Having already paid off her credit cards, paid for a U-Haul for her, and signed a year's lease on an apartment, she was now threatening me that she was leaving if she didn't get her way with me. She acted as if she was some valuable commodity to me. I tried to reason with her quietly, and Harry did as well. She worked herself up to the point that she couldn't resist her natural tendency to use her foul mouth, accusing me of convincing her into coming to the Midwest, telling us she should have stayed home.

Darcy and I sat quietly as Harry tried to persuade her to calm down and try this. He insisted to her that what I had offered was the best opportunity she'd had her entire life.

Listening to her and Harry banter back and forth with her foul mouth spatting out as many F this and F that, my heart finally let go. She thought she could manipulate me with her threats to leave as she did with Harry and Loretta. She seemed to believe that all my generosity was because I needed her. It was a trait of a narcissist constantly trying to elevate her perceived value to others.

She had manipulated nearly $60,000.00 from me and not paid one cent back in principal. I thought about the apartment I just leased for a year for her. I'd lose another $15,000.00 if I sent her home. It didn't matter. I sat there looking at Loretta all over again; the only difference was that she wasn't lunging forward with her fists. My heart sank for her little girl, but for the sake of my own family, my children, my Darcy, my heart had to let go of her and the sympathetic care I had for her little girl, and I quietly said, "You're right. I think you should go home." She and Harry looked stunned, never thinking I would say so. "I gave you only one condition, and in one day, you broke that condition."

"You're right. It would be best if you went home, the sooner, the better. Tomorrow, I'll rent the U-Haul again and help you load your belongings back into it, and Dad can drive you home." As with my mother, I had to finally divorce my relationship with my sister.

The look on her daughter's face was heartbreaking. "Please, Mom, try it," her daughter pleaded.

"You shut up, come on, we're getting the f—k out of here," she shouted as she stormed out of our home and back to the apartment.

My dad looked at Darcy and me and said, "I'll talk to her."

"No, Dad," I instructed. "This will never work. I thought it could, but it won't. And I can't bring this kind of dysfunction into my family and life. I feel sad, but I can't have it." Harry looked more disappointed than anyone.

The next day Harry and I went to get the U-Haul truck, loaded everything back into it, and bid them farewell. With the unpaid tens of thousands of dollars, I loaned Daffy to bail her out of her debts and messes, I now added a year-long lease for $1250.00 per month; $15,000.00 down the drain trying to help her.

I asked her to return the money I just loaned her within six months. I never saw a dime. She stole that money from me as well.

Once a thief, always a thief. Once a liar, always a liar. Born into dysfunction, it is a very difficult climb out. I cared deeply for Daffy despite her thefts and mistakes. I genuinely wanted to and did try to help her. I saw her as a victim of Loretta while my siblings saw her as a liar and a cheat. While she never made any effort to pay Darcy and me back, I remained in touch with her and tried to coach her with advice as someone who cared for her. I found myself dealing with and cajoling Loretta all over again. She didn't die.

Chapter Fifty-Four
Diamond Darcy

2000

Playlist:

Have I Told You Lately, Van Morrison

I Will Always Love You, Whitney Houston

The River of Dreams, Billy Joel

Another five-year diamond upgrade was due. My best friend Gary suggested we go to a jewelry show in Las Vegas, where he shopped for his wife, Jo. What a great idea, I told him. Darcy and I both need a long weekend away. I arranged for the kids to stay with Darcy's parents for a long weekend, and the four of us took her to the Las Vegas Jewelry Show where we looked for a diamond. The problem was that the setting she had for her wedding ring had just about enough room for the last diamond I bought her. While exploring potential diamonds with a jeweler and realizing the difficulty of doubling the size of the existing diamond and using the current setting, the jeweler looked up at Darcy and asked, would you consider a whole new set?

"I have something special," he said.

Darcy looked at me, careful of the sentiment I may have had for the first wedding ring I bought for her. "Why not," I suggested, "let's look." The jeweler returned with a different and unique contemporary setting with a beautiful diamond three times what I intended to double. Looking at the new ring, I asked Darcy, "Would you be willing to give up the original ring I asked?"

"Well, not give it up," she said, "but I love this ring." Neither of us had looked at the price tag yet. We asked the jeweler to take it out of the case to try it on. It looked spectacular on her. The flared contemporary setting and design were all Darcy. The ring was designed for her, Diamond Darcy!

I looked at the price tag, *Oh my God,* I thought to myself, it was almost half the price of our first home. I looked into Darcy's eyes. I didn't need to ask again if she liked it. The soft, caring twinkling in her eyes was not the reflection of this multi-karat diamond and setting; they were the same admiration she always looked at me with. As she turned to look at me, I said, "Darcy, I want you to have it if you want it. You've been the greatest mother, career professional, and spouse I could have imagined."

Darcy now looked at the price tag and had second thoughts. She knew we were still in the early stages of growing our new business. "Don't worry about the price tag; I want you to have it." Putting another diamond in Darcy's original wedding ring wouldn't work. It would look too ridiculous. The new setting was probably about as big of a diamond as might look decent on her small finger without looking overly flashy.

Darcy looked at the ring again. "I'm pleased with the ring you gave me, Curt," she insisted.

"Yes, I know, but we are here to double that diamond. I'd like to buy that ring for you if you like it?"

"I love it, but," she hesitated as she pondered the price tag again. I reassured her it was OK. "OK, but on only one condition," she offered, "we're in a new business. Let's focus on that. You don't need to double it anymore."

"Deal," I agreed! I liked the idea, I thought to myself; I looked forward to adorning my love with other jewelry pieces as we moved through life. Besides, doubling the stone she was about to wear every five years would mean she'd be wearing a golf ball by the time she was fifty!

After the jewelry show, we once again headed to Hawaii. This time with two great boys and one adorable little girl for another fantastic family vacation on the Big Island. I needed it. The last three years were packed with stress.

Chapter Fifty-Five
Cat in the Cradle

2010

Playlist:

Cat in the cradle, Harry Chapin

Though Daffy and Harry were now talking, she lived with her boyfriend in North Carolina. The distance was as far away as I was to be able to observe Harry's everyday behavior. My dad's neighbors made it clear that my suspicions were right about the onset of dementia with him. We made plans to move him to Minnesota, closer to us. I'd fly back to New York and help him clean out his jam-packed, oversized six-car garage of tools, metal, filing cabinets full of nuts and bolts of every size, and miscellaneous parts and tools. It was an enormous undertaking, and I solicited help from John Kings' now grown-up sons to assist us. It took about six months of periodic cleansing. We had cleared just about everything: trucks, bulldozers, countless tons of steel and tractor parts, old farm implements, all but a tractor he wanted to give me, and some remaining tools. And, of course, Comet.

While the tractor was a nice gesture on my dad's part, I suggested to him, "Dad, why don't you give that tractor to the neighbor down the hill? From my calls to you, I know he has checked in and helped you many times these past three years." Harry liked that idea, and the neighbor, who had borrowed it on occasion, was thrilled to have it, and it made my dad feel good to give it to him. Harry was grateful for his help, particularly since his bout with Leukemia. My dad's last tools were given to the King boys for all of their help.

"Are you taking Comet to Minnesota," Harry asked. I looked at my dad in silence. We were planning to sell his house and ten acres with it, but not the land across the road he owned. "I don't have time to take it now. Let me think about it for a day or two."

My remaining time with him went by fast as we wrapped up some other details, met with a realtor and septic contractor to replace his septic system, and bring it up to code for sale.

After Loretta died, I helped my dad invest his meager savings of about $7,000.00. I multiplied it to almost fifty thousand dollars over five years. I had him open a Schwab account and told him what stocks to buy, sell, and when. He was thrilled at the whole prospect, and I made it look a little too easy for him to the point he began to pick some stocks. I wouldn't have recommended any of them, and he didn't do well with them. One of the holdings I had previously suggested, I told him to sell. That holding had tripled in value over two years, and he wanted to believe it would keep going up. I begged him to sell it, but I had now created a "genius" of the markets. The stock tumbled in a few months, and he lost most all his gains. Still, he had more than before and fell in love with the Chrysler 300 sedan that hit the market. He asked me if I thought he should buy it at seventy-eight years old. It was only the second new car he owned behind the one I bought him out of college and the first new car the man had ever considered buying for himself. He had nearly forty thousand dollars in his bank from our investments over the years, so I asked him why not. You only live once. Buy a new car. He hesitated and needed more convincing. "Dad, buy yourself the car. I'll help you invest the remaining fifteen thousand and help you grow it again." That offer helped tip him toward buying the car. "Will you do that again" he sheepishly asked. "Yes, Dad, go buy the car you want. "OK, but you take ten thousand and grow it in your account." I'll keep five here for any emergencies, deal?"

"Deal, Dad, go buy your Chrysler."

That Chrysler was to him like Comet was to me. It was a car that made him feel good, a car that made him feel important, a car he bought outright with his own money. In fact, it was an automobile better than Comet or any other vehicle he purchased in his life in that it was his first car purchase without having to piece it together from junkyard parts.

I was so happy he bought that car. If he had hesitated over money, I would have bought it for him. He only had three good years of driving it before I realized he shouldn't be behind the wheel.

The day before heading back to Minneapolis, Harry asked me again, "What about your Comet?" I had looked Comet over good. It was a unibody design (a design without a full frame). Since Harry sold the wheels off her, she sat on the ground for years, and some of the floorboards had rusted through.

"I don't think it's worth hauling back to Minneapolis, but I don't want to sell her either. Could we move her across the road and park it in the woods?"

"I don't think that is a good idea, Curt. You've seen abandoned cars in these hills before, the windows get shot up by hunters, and then if kids get into the car and fool around, someone could be hurt."

Harry was always worried about liabilities and someone suing him. "You know Curt, I know it was your first car, and if you want to keep it, you should haul it back to your place in Wisconsin." I did want to keep it, but I just spent the last two years of my available spare time from work nursing him back to health and helping him clean up his stuff, and I had no more time to haul a trailer out and pick up that car. Not now. I traveled extensively in my business, and I had several upcoming trips abroad to make.

I walked outside and sat behind the Comet steering wheel briefly. I thought about all the stuff I helped my dad get rid of. Why can't he just let me park Comet in the woods? But he was right. I didn't want to see Comet all shot up, and that's precisely what would happen. In that rural setting, no one respected other people's property that might look abandoned. Heck, even most public road signs had bullet holes in them.

I had thought her soul was dead, but then I heard her whisper! *"Darcy is your new Comet Curt; you told me so long ago; Let me go, let me go. Your dad let go of all his tools, tractors, and trucks, all of that iron that he loved for years; it served him well; I served you well. I'm just iron. In the scrapyard, they'll recycle me to make new cars. Let me go."*

Suddenly some yellow jackets, which had found their way through the rusted floorboards and made a nest in the back seat, began attacking me and chased me out of the car. I got stung and slammed the door shut, trapping the rest of them inside, buzzing about the windshield. At first, I watched them in anger, feeling the sting's pain. Of all the dangerous turns, skids, and miles we traveled together and the emotional pain; this was the first time I'd ever been physically hurt in Comet. I was a grown man with teenagers, but Comet talked with me like the boy I once was. Then a sudden calm came over me. I was in the bee business. Comet knew this from our talks over the years. From her soul, I heard her message. *"Give me new life, a resurrection—through the scrap yard."* And the bees were no coincidence, an earthy physical reminder of how far I had moved on from those days with Comet. I had built a honey import and processing business with sales in the tens of millions of dollars. From my earnings, I could buy any car I wanted. The bees and the sting were no coincidental message.

The sting reminded me of how I had worried and believed anyone who'd ever drive Comet again would get hurt. It's why I wouldn't let my sons have her and bought them new cars in high school. *"Let me go, let me go," she whispered again.*

Comet looked tired from sitting all these years idle and rusting away.

I went into the house and got a sheet of paper. On it, I wrote, "To whoever receives this car, know that it was the greatest car on earth to a teenage boy coming of age, but she's dangerous, and she should never go down a road again." I signed my name and folded the paper. I wanted some piece of Comet. I thought about removing the grill or the Ford Granada hood ornament I added for a touch of class or one of the scripted pieces of chrome that proclaimed her name Comet! But with her wheels already gone and one front fender damaged from my dad's snowplow getting too close one winter, she looked battered. I didn't feel right about stripping anything off her body. I respected that car; that car was my first love at a time in my life when I could love no one else. I had to let her sleep as dignified and whole as she could.

Later that evening, when the bees were asleep, I took the note I'd written, slipped it into the glove box on the passenger side, removed the registration, and tucked it into my wallet. *"Take my tags," Comet whispered, "your first plates!"* I got a screwdriver and a flashlight in the garage and first took off the rear license plate. Kneeling at the front grill and struggling a little with the rusted screws, I finally got the front plate off, and for the first time, I kissed her—on the front bumper—and said goodbye. Back in the house, I tucked the license plates into my suitcase.

That night I told my dad he was right. I never sold the car because I didn't want someone hurt. I asked him to call a junkyard to come to tow it away.

Chapter Fifty-Six
The Final Hurt

2013

Playlist:

A Mother Loves A Blessing, Susan McCain

After Loretta's death, I called my dad every day of his life to check in and try to enrich his day with some positive conversation. He and my youngest sister weren't talking because of more than one incident between them after Loretta's death.

The U.S. Food and Drug Administration banned the drug Loretta used to control her diabetes because it was discovered to have caused liver cancer. My dad had forwarded a class action suit document he received for me to review for him. I mailed it back, having filled out all the information except where my dad was to sign. I instructed my youngest sister to help him sign as the deceased's spouse and beneficiary. I shared the news with her and asked her for a simple task to ensure he signed it. He was getting forgetful. Instead, she signed her name and mailed the documents to the class action attorneys. My dad was awarded 10,000.00 dollars when the suit was settled. The check came to my dad's address, but it had her name and was payable to her when he opened it because she was the person who signed the document. She said she'd sign it, cash it and turn it over to him. We both trusted her to do so, but she didn't. She stole that money from him. That was one of the last straws of many that extended a nearly eight-year non-communication between them. He disowned her. They lived less than 50 yards away, and each time I returned to visit him, I'd try to patch up the horrible situation between them even though she was clearly at fault.

"Once a thief, always a thief," he'd describe her to me, and he wouldn't have anything more to do with her. He wouldn't help her when something needed fixing and shunned her from his life. "Pay me back my money," my dad would say, "and then I'll think about helping you." *Ha,* I thought to myself. *Good luck with that.* She owes me plenty of money and has never made one effort to make a payment.

He repeatedly regretted ever conceding to Loretta's request to give her five acres and the run-down trailers she lived in. The water supplying her shanty was from a spring and electric pump on his property. While he allowed the water to flow for years, she came at him one day in a rage, much like Loretta, over the money she stole, and he cut the water line to her and shut her off. I tried to reason with him over the phone, making excuses for her pathetic actions, pleading with him to forgive her for the sake of her daughter, but he was done. "Let her come and fill up pails," he said. "She can now spend that money on her own well." That was a spiteful side of my dad I'd seen before when he was pushed too far with Loretta. It was my sister's turn.

She didn't spend one dime of that money on a well. She'd met some boyfriend online from North Carolina to whom she took her sob story and suckered the money out of him to pay for a new well. Somehow, she'd learned to suck money out of everyone she could, not just me and my older sister.

I continued every day to visit with my dad over the phone. Since New York time was an hour ahead of central time, I often caught him at his dinner hour as I commuted home. We'd talk for a good hour, sometimes longer, depending on the traffic on my commute.

Harry tried to make some semblance of his life the first two years after Loretta passed. He was bitter and didn't want to honestly believe his life was wasted with a woman who despised him. He yearned to try and understand why she was the way she had been.

On more than one occasion, he visited Loretta's aunts, cousins, and sister quizzing them about pictures he'd found Loretta had hidden from him. Each time he found another picture or letter she had written or received that told more of Loretta's history, he'd visit her relatives with a curious mind to learn things he'd never known about her past. He began to share what he was learning with me. Some of what he shared began to help me piece together things Loretta would occasionally tell me in response to my questions that usually ended sharply with a snappy response of "mind your own business" when I pushed further. After several inquiring visits from my dad, my Great Aunt Helen finally asked him not to visit her with any more questions. He'd been there several times in the two years after her death. She told him everything she knew of Loretta's story and her complex and challenging life. She asked him to let it all lie, that the woman was finally at peace, and to let her rest without any more inquiry.

He took it to heart. He didn't need to hear anymore. He slowly began to fill the living room tables with pictures of Loretta that he had taken down. When I would visit him, he'd tell me that sometimes he felt like Loretta's eyes were moving, and he thought she was trying to tell him something. He was falling in love all over again with her. It seemed to comfort him.

What he learned from her relatives, he shared with me in our phone calls and visits. Not all of her secrets were buried with her.

Nine years after Loretta's passing, my dad at age 79 drove himself to a hospital. He had them call me and my older brother Harry Jr. and I immediately hopped on a plane, flew to Elmira and then drove to the Robert Packer Cancer Institute in Sayre, Pennsylvania, where he checked himself in. My brother Harry was already there. My dad was diagnosed with Hairy cell Leukemia, a blood cancer. Over the six weeks, he was in the hospital, I returned every two. Loretta had kept a journal, and while my dad was in the hospital, I perused through some old photos and her journal.

I didn't spend much time in her journal because I soon found that some of her writing was meant for us all to read after she was gone. It wasn't pleasant. I found a bundle of letters with a note wrapped around them with a rubber band that began with; Curt; I am dead if you are reading this. Covered underneath this statement was another letter addressed to me, placed on top of the bundle of unopened letters she had written while I was at Iowa State. They were the letters I had never read and had returned to her unopened as proof to her that I wasn't any longer reading her letters when I asked her to stop writing me. I just stared at them. All were postmarked almost 20 years ago, in 1981 and 1982. I wondered why my dad hadn't shared these with me. The letter was addressed to me and was intended to be opened after she died. I didn't open it. I put it and the rest aside momentarily and pursued flipping pages of her journal. In its pages in her handwriting were all kinds of her thoughts and emotions. One letter told of how her daughters meant nothing to her, but her sons were her pride and joy. Numerous entries compared Harry to previous lovers who adorned her with jewelry, coats, and other material gifts, and she called him Hitler, who gave her nothing.

Reading just a few pages of that journal was enough to know it was filled with hate from a disturbed mind. Some of it was deliberately written for her children and Harry to read after her death and meant to hurt them. She put to paper what I warned her not to express verbally on many occasions. I'd often warn her to be careful in her choice of words and condemnations. I would tell her, "your mean words cut to the core and will go to the grave with an individual."

I didn't think I'd glean anything from reading anymore. She was a sick woman. Loretta never took my advice, and what was in front of me was proof she was intent on having the last word and giving a final jab, a final hurt. I doubted I'd find any secrets left written among them and certainly no solace in reading much of what I already knew from Harry. I wrapped everything up, put the unopened letter addressed to me back on top of the unopened bundle of letters, and packed them back into the box my dad had them stored in. I wasn't going to be hurt by her anymore. If Harry hadn't wanted me to see them after all this time, I didn't want to see them either.

When Harry left the hospital, I convinced my little sister that now would be an excellent time to make amends with my dad as he would need some care. If she couldn't provide it, I would arrange to bring him to Minnesota and sell the homestead. Selling the homestead seemed to scare her. Knowing the house was always there, she internally rationalized that she'd never be homeless. Her shanties were falling apart, and she had no resources to purchase or build a new home. Though she'd stolen thousands of dollars from us, I always had sympathetic thoughts that eventually I would buy her a double-wide trailer home to replace the shack she raised her daughter in. But it wasn't time yet. She agreed to help him through this. And if she did so honorably, I quietly thought I would help her with a new home for her lot.

Sitting on the edge of his hospital bed on his release day, he looked at me and said, "Curt, look at me. Overnight, I've turned into an old man." He had. Before Leukemia, he was a muscle-bound, robust man jumping quickly on and off tractors and bulldozers. He'd lost so much muscle and was now a bag of bones. "Oh, come on, Dad," I said. "You lost a little weight and muscle tone from laying around here for two months, but you'll recover and be as good as new."

He never really recovered to his stature before his Leukemia. He seemed to have lost all interest in puttering around in his garage, working on tractors and cars. Depression set in. He sat around a lot more, and my daily phone calls in the next two years, I could tell that he was sleeping more often and dementia was setting in. Most days now, I was calling twice a day, and he'd forget that we had the same conversation earlier. He was still driving out to the Midwest to stay with our family twice a year for a couple of weeks. He'd sometimes arrive 6 to 8 hours later or a day later than he had planned, citing he made a wrong turn and lost his way. I became worried about him.

He was nearly two days late when he told us he would arrive on his last trip to see us. He didn't have a cell phone, so we had no way to contact him. When he arrived, it was apparent that he'd lost his way and that something wasn't right with him. He was thin and so weak he could hardly get out of his car or get up from a chair once he sat down. He'd have to rock his weight forward numerous times to launch up to a standing position. He swore he was OK and, as always, jested to any problematic concern we inquired about him that "it's just the blessings of old age." I suggested we visit our health clinic, and my doctor examined him and confirmed that he was in the early, if not the mid stages, of dementia and very underweight. He coached Harry that he should not live alone and consider moving closer to one of his children. Harry, of course, insisted that he was OK at first but acquiesced after considerable consultation with the doctor.

It was fall, and I convinced my dad that he should stay with us for a few months. He was frail and continued to act funny. We nursed him back to health through the winter, and I had a neighbor in Van Etten look after his home in his absence and ensure the heat was on and all was OK. He stayed with us for almost seven months. We were remodeling our home then, and Darcy left a meal for him to heat up every day in the microwave. Every day he never ate it, saying he wasn't hungry or had forgotten. I tested his skills on the microwave. He couldn't remember how to operate it. We wrote instructions, but if he got hungry, he simply ate an apple or some piece of fruit which we kept a bowl full for him. Some contractors working in our home asked if my dad was, OK? We were told he sits and stares the whole day, never leaving his chair and not even blinking.

I watched him more closely and noticed the same, even in the evenings. I thought he was watching TV with us, but he wasn't. He'd just stare without blinking and seemed to drift off. I'd approach him and wave my hand in front of his eyes to break the stare. I took him back to the doctor and explained he was also having horrible bowel movements and not making it to the bathroom. His mind was failing quickly. Not realizing his mess, he tracked it through the carpet. The doctor gave him a physical and noted that he'd gained some weight living with us. Still, without further examination, he said he couldn't discern what might be wrong. Hypothetically he said he might have had a mini-stroke or several, or it's just advancing dementia. He highly advised that he should not be living alone any longer.

My dad and I talked at length off and on over two months about the future. I advised him that he should come and live with us in Minnesota. He didn't like the idea of living in the suburb but asked if he could live in one of the seasonal cabins, we had up north. I agreed to that but told him I would buy him a small house close to us during the winter. There was one or two just up the street from us for sale. I told him he didn't have to use his money; he could bank it and maybe go south for a month in the winter. I knew of some places he could rent near Darcy's parents, and they would be willing to check in on him, and maybe I could hire a part-time aid for him.

He agreed that we would sell his home and the ten acres surrounding it and keep the property across the street on a separate deed if he ever changed his mind and wanted to return.

While he was still in Minnesota, we hired a realtor and listed his property for sale. As mentioned previously, several items had to be improved upon inspections, and we had to bring the septic to code. I paid $17,000.00 to put in a new septic and told him he could pay me back upon selling the property. He agreed.

In May, he drove home, and I soon followed him back to New York to help him clean out the remaining items in his garage. I could not afford to be away from my business for very long, but we got it done again with help from my King family.

Every day the septic contractors came, they called me to tell me that my dad was kicking them off his property as he would forget why they were there. I'd have to remind him that we were selling the property, a condition of the purchase offer was that we brought the septic system up to code. He would then remember and apologize that he'd forgotten.

Meanwhile, my little sister lived in the South with her new boyfriend in North Carolina. When she returned home to find the house sold, she was furious. All of a sudden, she wanted to care for my dad! She called and asked me what the hell was going on and what was the plan. I told her the goal was to move my dad to Minnesota, buy him a house near us, and spend his summers at our place in Wisconsin. I described his last seven months with us, to which she had no idea he had even been with us. I shared the doctor's assessment, and he suggested that he should not live alone any longer. I made the horrible mistake of being truthful with her. I told her about his failing memory, bowel movements, and eating habits and I thought he was only a couple of years away from possibly needing assistive living. He needed it already in my mind, but I would be patient in learning and observing more when he lived nearby.

After that call with my little sister, my dad told me he had changed his mind about moving to Minnesota within a day. I was exasperated…Dad, what do you mean? Why the sudden change? He wouldn't tell me. Dad, "You signed a legal document and sold your house; the closing is in two weeks! You can't back out now."

"Oh yes, I can," he said vehemently. "Daffy says I don't have to sell if I don't want to!" I was furious. I surmised what had transpired. She was nowhere to be found and didn't return the calls I left for her. She was off chasing money through another online boyfriend when he needed to have been cared for the last six months. Now she told him and convinced his ailing mind that I was moving him out to Minnesota and was putting him in a nursing home.

Within days all hell broke loose. The realtor, the broker, the purchaser, and the attorneys were all furious and threatened my dad with lawsuits. I was mad as hell at my little sister. I didn't need her bullshit 1200 miles away. My dad soon had cases against him because of my little sister's ill advice. Their costs drained most of the money, which I helped him invest and grow over the years.

I had it up to my ears, and while I still called my dad every day, half the time, him not remembering what was going on from one day to the next; I called my little sister, and I demanded that she take over resolving and fixing the mess she created. While I had argued with her repeatedly that he needed care, she insisted that he live independently. In several argumentative conversations, she admitted that she did not want the house sold, was insecure with her boyfriend, and counted on my dad's home to live in one day. I couldn't believe my ears. Little did she know she wasn't even in his will for a long time. As executor of his estate, I had his will and intentions filed with my attorney. My brother Harry and I were the only ones named in the will until, he was taken out through her accusations and false witness. It happened over a meteor!

On a visit home, I asked my dad if I could have the meteor that had once fallen in his backyard as a boy. It was used as a birdbath in his mom's and Loretta's garden for decades. I'd gotten nothing from Loretta except some crystal caricatures I had given her, which she gave back to me in sackcloth in our last fruitless conversation.

I asked Harry if I could have it when he was ready to give it up. I'd like to have it mostly in memory of his mom, one of only two women I ever had respect for. I saw it as a keepsake to pass along to one of my children someday. Meteorites were all the rage and selling like crazy on eBay then. The constant news about them falling from the sky and how people were collecting them made me think about it.

I wanted to secure it before it disappeared, but I was too late. My dad graciously said, "sure, I'd like you to have it; take it back with you this trip."

"Thanks," I said, and I went looking for it. Most of Loretta's gardens had now grown over, and I couldn't find it. Where is it, Dad? He showed me where it was, and there was the base it had sat on for nearly 30 years, but not the meteorite! He was furious that someone had taken it.

Later that evening, Daffy came over to say hello, and he asked her where the meteorite went with an implied tone that she had taken it. "I didn't take it," she immediately replied. "Harry Jr. took it!"

"How do you know that?" I asked.

"I saw him," she said emphatically. Guilt was written all over her face. The fact that she immediately had an answer and never said anything to my dad when he supposedly took it made her statement obviously suspicious that she was lying, but she convinced my dad that Harry Jr. had taken it.

While I highly doubted Daffy's story, I politely confronted Harry with a call as my dad asked me to. He knew nothing about it. He told me to talk to the neighbor above my dad about how broke my little sis was and what she did for him for money and in exchange for repairs on her trailer as proof of how desperate she was. "She probably took it and sold it for money," he said. "She always needs money, you should hear what she does for your neighbor up the hill." He continued. He was more descriptive of what actions she exchanged for help than I wanted to hear. I didn't waste my time on the matter any longer. My dad had stopped helping her long ago, and she stole from me, so I could easily believe she was desperate and stole it from him. She was always desperate for money.

As the meteor was the only thing I had ever asked for, and because it meant so much to Harry as a kid, Harry was furious enough to call the police and have them visit his son and request it back. I knew in my soul Harry Jr. didn't steal, but only my sister Daffy knew who did. I felt horrible I'd ever asked.

My dads' belief in my sister and her ever convincing story divided him and his son from his first marriage for the rest of their lives. I felt awful for Harry Jr.

Months later, still fuming over the disappearance of the meteor and only subject to Daffy's repeated story my dad consulted me about changing his will. He wanted Harry Jr. out. I tried desperately to convince my dad not to do this. I pointed out my sisters history of theft, her resulting prison sentence from it, that she never paid me back one dime I had lent her, how she manipulated the class action suit money from him and how she took things from his house she had no legitimate right to do so after Loretta's death. But his mind was already failing cognitively with reasoning and rationality. And the more he aged and failed in his mental capacity, the more prone he was to hear and believe repetitious lies.

He was adamant about removing Harry Jr. from his will, yet he wouldn't put Daffy in either. He wanted to leave everything to me. I was honest with him that my life was in Minnesota and Wisconsin, and I would never return to Van Etten permanently. I had no interest. I again suggested he leave Harry in the will. I encouraged him that he has some forgiveness and put all of his children, from his first marriage, Daffy, and my sister Candice one of Loretta's children, from another man, and to try and see past the poor history and dysfunction of our pathetic family life. He would have no part of that. He wanted to leave it all to me.

Again, I told him I had no interest and tried an alternative suggestion. I suggested he leave it to my little sister's daughter, whom he and Loretta raised for a while and loved. He softened to that idea and said, I'll leave it to all my grandchildren. When I coached him that I had three kids and my little sister Daffy had one, so that might not be fair, I reintroduced the idea that perhaps he should reconsider Daffy, Candice, and Harry Jr. again. I made some breakthroughs in his mind as he finally concluded that because my little sister and I were his and Loretta's children, we would be in the will along with the grandchildren. I let it be and promised myself I would surrender my share to Harry Jr. and Candice when the time came.

That's how the will was drawn up: that was the last will I had on file for my father.

Failing mentally fast but still living alone, I now called my dad sometimes three times a day to check in on him. He slept late and often till noon or two o'clock in the afternoon, only to wake up to my call. Daffy left him alone and pursued trying to get married. She was with her boyfriend, and though she'd often share with me lots of personal "issues" that were wrong with her relationship and him and how insecure she was with him, she seemed determined to get into his pockets through marriage and held my dad and his house hostage as a backup if her plans didn't work out. She knew she'd need someplace to live as her shanty trailers were falling apart. At one point, her toilet fell through the floor as it had rotted.

Concerned for him, I visited my dad on a trip every two to three months to check in on him. I'd photograph and document what I would find. His stove no longer worked. He used a countertop toaster oven to cook nearly all his packaged meals. The silverware drawers were overrun with mice and covered with their feces. He had rotted meat in the refrigerator and frozen milk in the freezer. He was often confused. His entire freezer chest in the basement was filled with his favorite ice cream. Every time he went to town, he'd forget he had some and buy a couple more containers. He loved ice cream. He drove right through stop signs and red lights when I rode with him. And when I questioned him each time, he'd say repeatedly, "I didn't see it, what stop light?"

With calls to my little sister, I began to share my findings. She would return once in and while to verify what I was saying. She'd call me a liar and say he was doing fine alone. The next time I visited my dad, I brought my friend and business associate, Paul Rath, took notes, and retook pictures with him as a witness. I also tried to get Harry some county assistance and help with welfare check-ins with no success.

Since Daffy had him convinced I would put him in a nursing home, I suggested that he move down to North Carolina near her. I suggested selling the house again and buying him a mobile home in a park adjacent to their neighborhood.

Once again, putting her interests first, she blatantly complained that she was insecure with her boyfriend and didn't want to sell my dad's house acting as if she already owned it. I'd had it with her selfish denial of his needs and care and told her I had documented all my visits to Dad last year. I let her know that I was his health care directive and that if she didn't take some action toward his care and stop her selfish nonsense, I would take this to court and do what I had to do. That threat scared her, and she said, I'll take care of it. "Let me talk to Peter," her boyfriend. My dad moved to and lived in North Carolina, in Peter's home, within a couple of months.

Although I felt horrible that he would have to live with her dysfunctional personality, even sorrier for the guy who let her move in, living with her was safer than living alone.

Now that he was living with her, she'd ask me for money to help with his care. I couldn't believe it. With a visit to her, I told her that she should charge my dad and his estate a monthly stipend equivalent to what an assisted living home might charge. I wanted to be fair to her. I told her to charge it and ensure she documented it, as several people were in his will. She questioned me as to who was in the will and I shared the truth. I made a huge mistake in telling her that whatever share I get, I would give to Harry Jr. and my sister Candice. She shared that information with my dad as one more item to turn him against me.

One afternoon I received a phone call from Harry's attorney's office. I recognized the number. Darcy and I were driving to our lodge, and as usual, I put him on the speaker. Daffy had brought him to Long Island, where his attorney was located. He could no longer drive as she had taken his car away. In the background, I could hear his attorney coaching him to tell me what he wanted to say. Out of nowhere, my dad said with an un-warranted undertone of anger, "Curt, I want you to know that I am changing my will and leaving everything to Daffy." Darcy looked at me in shock! Not because I wouldn't inherit anything. We were self-made financially. She was shocked my father would do this, and of the dysfunction she heard in his demeanor. I knew he was not in his right mind, and I was suspicious that Daffy had manipulated him into this. I looked at Darcy and put my finger to my lips to indicate not to say anything but listen. Calmly I responded, "OK, Dad, you're living with her now, and she should provide all of your care. I think you're making a good decision."

He or his attorney was stunned that I didn't put up a fight. I heard a voice ask him to repeat it to me. "Curt, I want you to know I'm giving everything to Daffy. I'm changing my will. You're out," he said with a tone as if he wanted an argument. I was not going to let my sister win my dad away. She could steal everything from him, she already stole from me, but I was not going to let her have the satisfaction of dividing us. I said again, "It's OK, dad."

Darcy and I were both saddened by the approach my dad took. It was confrontational and mean, like Loretta. He'd probably been subjected to Daffy's rants and raves and brainwashing of how I would have put him in a nursing home had she not taken him to live with her. I'm suspicious, too, she threatened him that he would no longer live with her if he didn't sign everything over to her. He wasn't in a good mental health state. His anxiety was up, and emotional feelings probably aggravated him. I knew the drive to Long Island, where his attorneys resided, was a seven-hours' drive from Van Etten and even longer from Calabash, North Carolina. He got there by Daffy driving him.

I didn't need his estate, and even if I did, I would never stoop to the low levels my sister did to transfer all his assets to herself before he died. A friend told me she might do that to make it difficult for me to contest the will and retrieve assets, as it would require a civil suit. I had no intentions of contesting the will, but I was determined not to let her win at dividing us.

"You are making good decisions, and I support you," I told him again. He was living and dependent on Daffy now. I feared any resistance from me and explanations to his attorney about his mental state would make my dad's life even more miserable than I suspected. Her home life was full of dysfunction; her husband was cheating on her, very narcissistic like herself, and she seemed to enjoy too much alcohol based on her social media posts of admission. I was thinking fast.

His life might have become even more unbearable if I had fought this action. He seemed to enjoy the warm climate of North Carolina, where he could walk every day. Darcy and I couldn't provide that for him in our environment. I suspected she would dump him like a piece of trash back into his house in Van Etten if his will didn't change. I didn't want that for him and didn't care about any of his assets. Harry seemed content to be where he was. He told me he liked the weather and not being in the cold of Van Etten winters. In that aspect, I was happy for him. When I visited, I often found him sitting on the front porch in a rocking chair and failing in cognitive and memory abilities. One and a half years into this situation, I suggested a dual power of attorney and that since he was living with her to change the health care directive to be her. She did. And it appeared she was doing more than that now, but it would all be in only her name.

I cared about him. Daffy could have whatever he wanted to give or she wanted to steal. I saw the real story, it wasn't about love and care. For the money, she enslaved herself and her soul.

"Bye," he said, and he hung up. That was the final hurt! Darcy was still in shock and feeling terribly for me.

It wasn't my dad's actions that crushed me; I knew his mind wasn't right. It wasn't even that my sister was suspiciously the instigator. What hurt was that Loretta was still living. Daffy is a living, breathing sidekick of her mother. Loretta was still alive; her dysfunction and dishonesty was inherited.

After he changed his Will she continued to drop hints for money for his care. I'd tell her to sell his house or some of the land to support better care for him. She would yell at me that she was not selling the home because she wanted it. I told her I was OK with her buying it someday, but his assets should be used for his care and not her desires. She had heard rumors of gas leases generating up to $6000.00 an acre for shale gas. With 60 acres, she saw a way toward retirement funds, and it seemed she was out to get my dad's property no matter what.

I was always suspicious Daffy kept the nursing home threat alive and well with him, manipulating everything out of him—his savings, his car, and eventually all of his assets before he even died.

I was no longer allowed to call twice daily, much less daily. Daffy would not let my dad answer their phone or talk to me without her ear to the conversation. She'd tell me they had too many personal and business calls, and she didn't want to waste time answering my two daily calls. When I suggested he use the cell phone I bought him, she told me she wasn't going to be somebody's "f...g tech coach like I already am to that f...g Peter!" I believe she mostly didn't want him the freedom of talking to me without her monitoring the calls and listening in. She denied him any calls, facetime, and communication with my family, me, and his grandchildren for an extended period.

Her narcissistic and selfish attitude and lack of allowing my calls to go through to my dad required me to call the police several times to check in on my dad. Too often, they found him left unattended for days as she and her husband left town on trips. Darcy and I recorded the police visits on the phone as they asked him questions like whether he could use a phone. He'd say yes, and then they'd ask him to show them.

"Show us," they asked, "call your daughter. If you were in trouble, could you call her for help? What day is it? Who is the president of the United States? What year is it? Do you know how to call 911 if you get hurt?" He could answer none of these correctly nor other similar questions. He didn't know my sister's cell phone number and didn't know how to use the phone. He didn't even know the address where he lived.

He needed assisted living. I should have never allowed him to move in with her and Peter. I had his healthcare directive control at the time. He also should never have been left alone, but Daffy manipulated him.

Now married to him, she called her husband a narcissist but didn't recognize herself as one. They both lived beyond their financial abilities, driving Cadillacs, sports cars and flaunting food and fare like they were millionaires.

Public records would show they made minimal payments on their home and rental properties, eventually losing them and being upside down on their home for more than it was worth from lack of making entire principal and interest payments. They were pathetic intentional thieves living high on the taxpayer's dollar, and credit others had given them.

She told me of their deliberate plan to not pay the mortgages on the rentals they were upside down on. He isn't even a U.S. citizen and through his defaults and the bank sales of his homes we the U.S. taxpayers paid for their high-flying life style through FDIC insured mortgages from their losses. When they eventually divorced, she told me that he filed fraudulent tax returns. When I told her that as a spouse and signer of those returns, and knowing they were dishonest, she was an accomplice, I suggested she visit an attorney. She became reticent.

Darcy grew up in a Cleaver household (Leave It To Beaver TV Family Series from the 60s). Ever-increasing contact with my sister over the last five years of my dad's life allowed Darcy to observe the dysfunction I had come through. It was unbelievable for her to have heard what transpired in several speaker conversations with Daffy and the conversation between me and my dad about his will. She felt horrible for me. I had to begin unraveling my upbringing and try to explain my childhood. "She is so different from you," she'd question. "Ha," I laughed, "I used to hear that from my high school teachers."

For the first time I began to open up and share with Darcy how I grew up and safely not be judged for it. Darcy had glimpses of Loretta's dysfunction through the years but hadn't realized the extent of the abusive household we all lived within.

"Why didn't you share this with me before," she asked. "I just buried it, Darcy, much like my older sister." "And what would be the use," I asked. Darcy was disappointed that I hadn't trusted her to share it. "I trusted you, Darcy," I said, "but would you have married me had you known this long ago?" I asked. "Probably not," she said. "I agree; you wouldn't have taken the chance worried that I might turn out like them."

"I wouldn't have either," I agreed. "Why do you think I've coached our sons to look carefully at the family of the girls they consider marrying? It's rare for a kid to escape the kind of dysfunction I grew up with. It's often repeated generation after generation."

"And look, while there are no ill feelings between my older sister and me, look how little we communicated, once a year, sometimes not for years! She's buried it deep. I think the more she could distance herself from everyone associated with her growing up, the healthier she was. I was no different."

"Is there more to all this? I mean, is there a lot more I should know," Darcy asked. "Anything else that you've buried," Darcy asked.

I was quickly tired of the subject. "There is, but how can I share a lifetime?" I choked.

Darcy was empathetic. "You know, because you're supposed to love people, or you think you should love people; I mean, honor thy mother and father. You do it."

"I couldn't love her as a kid. I wasn't just some petulant son dealing with a mother who reprimanded him. It was way more than that, she didn't deserve my respect, and I had none for her."

"How did you deal with all that," she asked.

"Maybe buried is the wrong term; You let go of what's dead and move on. Bad feelings and emotions and bad experiences are all a noose around your neck. You have to let them die. If not, and you choose to hang on, they hang you."

"I've never buried anything," she shared.

"Really?" I asked. "You are fortunate to have had the parents you had." Darcy couldn't grasp how the full extent of my experiences growing up could be forgotten and buried. "I haven't forgotten," I said; "I forgave and saw it for what it was, beyond my control. I moved forward with what I could control, the choices I made."

I wanted to change the subject. I honestly had let go, and rehashing it all was a bore, much like writing this novel.

"I let go of something about you when we first dated!"

Darcy had a look of surprise on her face when I turned the subject to her. "What?" she asked.

"Aaaah, nothing," I teased.

"You can't do that to me," she pleaded. "Was there something I did that hurt you?"

I eagerly opened that door, wanting to get off the subject of my family. Talking about us was always more fun! "Well, I was the boy from New York City, but who was the boy in the hallway?" I gestured and tried to lighten the mood from which I'd just been told I was out of my father's will!

"What are you talking about," she gasped.

I shared some of my naive blindness arriving at her room and thinking all the flowers were her roommates. I tried to laugh and told her how foolish I was in believing I was the only guy she was interested in during our early courtship. She smirked and began to laugh a little, explaining that she couldn't help it that lots of boys were interested in her. "That hurt you?" she asked.

"No, it didn't at the time because I was unaware that I had to compete. It wasn't until another incident that I began to decipher and understand how blind I'd been, and it was the hallway kiss that hurt," I told her.

"What are you talking about," she asked, confused. And I told her the story in a more jestful way than it happened at the time. She had no idea whom I saw and justified any kiss she may have given as nothing more than a peck on the cheek. "Besides," she began to defend herself, "At the time, I didn't think you would make it in the Midwest or even come back to Iowa State based upon our conversations."

"But, if I held onto that incident, that hurt, we'd probably never have moved forward, right?"

"Well, you should have shared that with me and communicated," she insisted.

"Perhaps," I acquiesced, "easier said than done, but I think I made the right decision for the time, and I let it go."

We laughed. The rest of our ride to the cabin was on the light side, about our five-dollar dating antics and fond Iowa State University memories that brought us together.

I was out of my father's will, and while the gesture and act itself didn't hurt, the final hurt from Loretta was that she succeeded in poisoning my sister's soul. The girl had grown up just like her. Loretta had accomplished after her death what she wished her whole life regarding Harry, to take what was his. She re-created herself in my sister, who legally or not manipulated my dad under duress and an unstable mind out of everything he owned before he died.

Chapter Fifty-Seven
The Find

2012 – 2018
Playlist:
Praying, Kesha
Castle On The Hill, Ed Sheeran
Stargazing, Kygo, Justin Jesso
I'll Be There, Jess Glynne

Not too many years after my dad had shared what he learned about Loretta with me, I began to seek out adoption records from the state of New York to find my lost siblings. The records remained sealed by law. I rehashed the stories he'd told me and wondered how I might connect the various dots and find other ways to reach out and find them.

On February 22nd, 2012, I joined Ancestry.com and sought ways to research lost relatives in hopes that my efforts might reach any lost siblings looking for my mother or me. I hired a professional genealogist to build out my family tree on Loretta's side of the family and then on my dad's side. They offered a DNA test to learn about your origins, and all of my immediate family members took the tests. Subsequently, my half-sister Candice also took the DNA test. It took a few years, but miracles began to appear.

On March 3rd, 2018, while I was in North Carolina visiting my dad in the nursing home, mistakenly thinking it was his 90th birthday, I received the following message on my Ancestry account: *1.59 PM I just got my results, and you and I have a strong match for first cousins. I would like to hear from you. Sally.*

The next day March 4th, 2018, at 5:27 PM, I received another note from (Sister #1):

Hi Curt, I have been in contact with Lucy (another potential sister), and I believe after reviewing DNA and family trees that You, your half-sister Candice, and I are half-siblings sharing the same mother. At the time of my birth, I obtained my original birth certificate, which lists my mother as Loretta Victoria Stellato, age 22. She had two other children before she had me, so that they would have been born before 1953. I was born in 1953.

Lucy said that you and Candice are half-siblings and younger than we are. Is it possible that Gary T. James-Riess and Candice are the two children she had before me? Sadly, I see from the records that Loretta died in 1999; it would have been great to have met her—hoping to meet any siblings that may be related to me. Any help you can give is greatly appreciated.

Sally

When I shared this news with Darcy, she was shocked, bewildered, and astonished. "You're dead on with the promise, Curt; life is never boring," she said with a smile. "What are you going to do?" she asked. "I'm going to give myself a day to respond. I think my first response should inform her about some history. She may decide she doesn't want to move forward. I'll give her enough to determine if she does."

On March 5th, 2018, I responded: *Dear Sally, This is amazing. Based on what you told me, we are siblings. My mom, Loretta Victoria Stellato, had eight children. She gave up two or three for adoption. The other children she had are these names in order of birth as I know them. Robert Stellato died a tragic death at about age five. I never knew him. We believe she gave up her first child before Robert at age 16. Then there was Gary T. James Riess; I believe born in 1949; I knew and loved him as a brother. He died a tragic death at age 30 in a car crash. I believe Candice was born in 1951 or 1952 and is my older sister, and I have to say you look remarkably like her and Loretta in her younger years. You and Candice may have the same father. I remember hearing from my dad that Loretta gave up a child for adoption when he first met her. Harry Riess, my dad, just turned 90 yesterday and is in hospice. I just returned from visiting him. I was born in 1959, and another sister I have was born in 1961. Loretta died in 1998 or Feb 1999 from liver cancer (due to a diabetic medication she was taking) and is buried in a small cemetery (annexed) on my dad's family property in Van Etten, NY, next to Gary. The home she and my dad built and made for themselves is on the same property. (Where I grew up as a teenager) There is much more you may want to know, and I'm very willing to share with you and anyone else, including pictures, but this is not the easiest way to do so. I will tell you this, and I hope you will feel happiness rather than sorrow… Giving up a child for anyone must be incredibly difficult and painful, especially for a mom who didn't want to do so but perhaps had no other choice. I never saw a day with my mother without tears as a child. She had pictures of a boy and some babies under a glass top of a small desk where she wept nearly every day. When I asked her who they were, she would sternly tell me none of my business and send me away. She was a troubled woman filled with sorrow, grief, and guilt, sometimes making for a somewhat dysfunctional household. She was a lovely lady to anyone who met her, but things could often be difficult for her own family. My Aunt Margaret (Stellato) Curtain told me once, Loretta's sister (she had two other brothers, Martin, And Michael Stellato), that the reason Loretta was so sad was that, unlike herself (Margaret also had to give up a child), she never forgave herself. There is more; they all grew up in an orphanage called Brookwood Hall in East Islip, except Michael. I have an extensive family tree and work performed by a pro genealogy professional that I will try to have placed on my account. My cell is XXX>XXX>XXXX if you want to connect. I am writing a book about her, but it is likely two years from being finished. I look forward to meeting you someday if you wish. I'm happy for you that you've found us. I was hoping through Ancestry that eventually, this very occurrence would happen. I only wish Loretta would have lived long enough to meet the children she shed tears for most of her life. It was not easy for her, and without this knowledge today, the children she was able to raise suffered her grief throughout her life. I think you should also know people with diabetes abound in the Stellato family tree, myself included, for your health benefit. Loretta suffered some depression at times, but perhaps because of the circumstances. I'll stop here for now. I hope you'll feel free to call. I have A Facebook page, but I'm not much of a user if you want to see your brother and his family. Warmly, your brother Curt.*

Sally had been anxiously waiting for a response, and she read it at 2:43 AM when she received the notification. I know she read it repeatedly, with excitement, with anxiousness, and with some depredation. She responded two hours later with the following:

Dear Curt,

I have waited 65 years for some word or information regarding my biological mother. When New Jersey passed legislation to unseal all adoption records from 1940 forward, I got my application in. I only just received my original birth certificate last month. I started DNA with 23 and Me and continued to cover all bases with Ancestry. Thank you… Thank you for your letter. It's a lot to process, and I will undoubtedly read it many times before it all sinks in.

You should know that my adoptive mother, Phyllis, told me when I was six months old, my biological mother came to visit me to make sure I was happy, and she made the right decision to give me up. Loretta told Phyllis that she would be getting married soon and wanted to be sure she made the right choice. I never once doubted that she loved me, and it wasn't until I had my own children that I could fully comprehend the love and unselfishness of this woman's love. It must have been the hardest thing to ever do. I had always hoped that one day I would get the chance to say thank you to her and let her know she was always a hero to me. I hope she would be proud of the woman I became because of her letting me go.

Thank you for the heads up on diabetes. My A1C has been in the past high, but so far, I can manage it with diet and exercise.

I also have a FB page. My photo is of me holding puppies. I volunteer for the Guide Dog Foundation and have raised two working dogs and taken care of a breeder. I home whelped all 5 of her litters, and she gave the foundation 37 puppies that are/ will be service dogs for the blind or disabled veterans. I will look you up on FB, and I will call, or you are welcome to call me XXX.XXX.XXXX cell

XXX.XXX.XXXX home.

I feel I should say something to you for reaching out to me, but thank you just doesn't seem satisfactory for someone who has given me the greatest gift of all… my family.

I will always stay in touch, and we will have that long-overdue call soon.

Your sister Sally

Sally wasn't the only sister I heard from. On March 6th, I received the following from a sister named Lucy:

Dear Curt…just in case you look here…I sent an email to you…

Be well,

Your maybe sister!

Lucy

01:36 AM

CR: Hi, again, Lucy. I did not receive the email. Here it is again in case I made a mistake:xxxxxxxx@gmail.com.
Read, 01:49 AM

L: I think I made a mistake! Lucy
02:51 AM

"Well, things are certainly going to get interesting," Darcy laughed uneasily after I read the communications above to her.

"Yeah, they both would like to have phone calls." "What are you going to tell them? I mean, how much are you going to share with them about your mother."

"I'm not sure," I responded. "I think I need to get a feel for who they are and how strong a person they are to share a lot. It couldn't have been easy never knowing who your parents were or why you gave them up. I think they deserve the truth, but I'm not sure at what pace."

I phoned my sister Candice right away. She didn't believe what I was telling her. She'd never heard that our mother gave up children for adoption, and she was skeptical. I asked her, "Candice, you are one of the older siblings, nine years older than me. These children came after you and before me. Didn't you notice Loretta was pregnant?"

"Well," she muttered, "you know mom always had a big belly," and she caught herself for a moment. She still refused to believe it. I shared almost everything Harry learned from our great aunts and uncles with her. She had suppressed so much of it and wanted to believe otherwise and at first didn't have the desire to meet new siblings, only because she doubted the validity.

On April 28th, 2018, I wrote to yet another sister. Sally had told me she was contacted by someone she thought was a half-sister to her. She told me she was very nervous about the whole finding and figured I could make her more comfortable reaching out. On April 28th, 2018, at 2:56 PM, I wrote to my sister Helen:

Hi Helen, It looks like you and I might be a match. I understand you are going to connect with my sister Sally today. If you would like to connect with me at some time, my preferred reach of communication is via xxxxxxxxxxx@.com or my cell number at XXX.XXX.XXXX. I'm happy to talk with you and help you in your search if I can.

Curt

The three new sisters brought us to more frequent and closer conversations about many issues. I offered phone calls to each of the new sisters and multiple phone calls with my sister Candice. It had been years since we talked, separated by the distance we lived and the shared pain which she suppressed.

For two of my sisters, Helen and Sally, I held back lots of information about Loretta and her life and doled it out as slowly as I could sense they were excited to have a new family. I didn't want to dampen their excitement and paint a dark cloud over it. Only with Lucy did I spill Loretta's whole sad life saga. She seemed strong enough to move forward with the conversation and shared with me that she hadn't really sought out family at the end of our discussion. She was comfortable with her adoptive parents and life and wasn't seeking new relationships. It had been her only son who sought out the DNA relationships seeking to know more about family. Now that she learned she was an unwanted product of Loretta's horrible life, she didn't want to open new chapters and understand anymore. I had to respect that. In a significant way, her choice didn't allow Loretta to hurt her.

In the summer of 2019, in New York City, Candice and her boyfriend, Sally, and her husband, Helen, Darcy, and I met for the first time.

Chapter Fifty-Eight
I'll See You on the Other Side

March 2013
Playlist:
Home, Phillip Phillips
Wake Me Up, Avicii
Somewhere Only We Know

When my dad lived with Daffy and her husband Peter, my little sister would constantly hint and ask me for contributions for his care, the taxes on his property, and other living expenses. She pretended she didn't know about my dad's conversation about the will change and she continued to try and scam me.

I'd remind her that she never gave me a copy of the dual power of attorney, and I assumed she had one for herself. So, I'd tell her to sell the house or some of the land for funds to care for him. She would angrily shout out that she was not selling the home because she wanted it. I repeatedly told her I was OK with that and she should buy it, but his assets are to be used for his care and not her desires. She was out to get my dad's property no matter what.

After only three years or less of him living with her, and needing in-home assisted care for him, which she denied he ever needed, she eventually put my dad into a nursing-home, exactly what she lied to my dad a few years before that I was going to do to him if he moved to Minnesota.

Her excuse was that she and her husband, Peter were getting divorced, and she couldn't take care of him anymore. During the course toward their divorce, Daffy told me she had previously put my dad's real estate in her name (that it was legal in some way for her to do so), and now it was possibly subject to dividing it along with other assets in the divorce. As usual, when she called, I'd wait to call her back while we were traveling for a couple of hours to our

Northwoods home so I could listen to her on the speaker. Unbelievingly, once again, the fool was asking me for money. She asked me for ten thousand dollars to hire a better attorney to fight her husband, thinking I would care about her possibility of losing my dad's property. As she often listened on these conversations with Daffy, Darcy was in awe and disbelief that this conniving, lying scam artist was at it again.

Giving me the silent motion of saying no-way and with my nod in agreement, we listened to Daffy proceed with her request calling it a business opportunity, and she began explaining how I would reap benefits.

She played me so many times with the "poor" me story. Who was she kidding? She proposed the craziest screw your brother and his family scamming sales pitch I'd ever heard. I cut her off in conversation and gently reminded her of the past three loans and the year of rent I paid for her. That amount, and had I charged her interest, which I did not, would amount to well over a hundred thousand dollars. I explained the time value of money lost to me for investing it and multiplying it, that surely, I would have turned it into a half million dollars or more. I said politely, "because of that experience and loss you caused me, I don't loan money to family or friends." The call ended, and both Darcy and I shook our heads in disbelief of the dysfunctional thinking that was so alive in my sisters' thoughts.

With my dad gone from her home and control, I was freer to call and visit as often as possible for the last year and a half of his life. I explained to him that his daughter had transferred his assets to herself, and he no longer owned his property. I explained that he was at risk of losing his real estate, which would be counted in her divorce settlement. I felt he had a right to know this. He questioned it confusingly.

He sat quietly for a few minutes, then turned to me and said: "Well, do what is best for me; you always have, do what is best for me." I thought long about his request. I talked with Darcy about the matter.

He had been in hospice when she first put him in the nursing home. She thought he was going to die within weeks. He lived more than a year and a half longer because of the proper care and nutrition Hospice afforded him. I looked at it as a gift in that it gave me more time and opportunity to visit with him.

While the nursing home she put him into was clean and friendly, he deserved better care. His pension, social security, and veterans' benefits covered his low-cost monthly nursing home bill. But had Daffy not confiscated all of his assets in the last three years for her personal gain but instead used them for his care, he could have enjoyed a better senior living environment and, I believe, would have lived a more fulfilling and longer life. I held her responsible for his decline, maybe even premature death.

I often visited my dad without her or Peter's knowledge. I'd slip into town and never called their house any longer. Now that he was free of their grip, I was OK with never having anything to do with them and thrilled that I no longer had to interact with either of them. I'd note the visitor's sign-in book and never saw either of them registered for the weeks before I arrived. They didn't care. They were concerned with one thing, money. And getting somebody else's into their own pockets.

When I visited, I'd take my dad out to breakfast. We'd go to lunch. I took him to some of the best steak and fish houses in Myrtle Beach for dinner. He enjoyed our meals together. We hung out on the beach and the pools in the hotels I lodged in. He enjoyed basking in the sun and listening to the sound of the waves.

With each visit, I saw a significant decline. I'd have to help my dad go to the bathroom and carry an extra adult diaper to enable us to go out. We had great conversations and memories, even though I did most of the talking at times. He didn't remember much that he had bulldozers, backhoes, and other equipment, but he was always alert and mindful of the present moment and asked about Darcy and the kids and how they were doing.

He remembered Loretta, and a smile came over his face when we spoke of her. I shared some good memories and reinforced his thoughts that she loved him, even though I knew she didn't. It didn't matter. He was less and less conversational with each new visit but always enjoyed a beer at lunch or the scotch we had at dinner. I bought him the best.

A few years before he died, Darcy and I had sold our company to a private equity group and retired. We had successful and lucrative careers in our corporate jobs and entrepreneurial endeavors. Our family was raised, and we had a great life void of anything reminiscent of the life I grew up with, except for the hours of bullshit I had to put up with my sister Daffy.

Our daughter Micayla finished schooling, and our periodic absence from her was a slow but easy transition for the independence we trained her to yearn for. Our sons, now living independently, would check in on her if she needed assistance, and we were usually just a three-hour flight away from somewhere if she needed us. Soon, she would move into her apartment and live independently. We had more free time to visit my dad.

A month before his actual ninetieth birthday, Daffy called me and told me she didn't think he had much time left, implying maybe a day or two. Since we were living in Florida, we immediately drove up to South Carolina to see him. He was in excellent spirits and seemed to rebound from what we were told. While our conversations were primarily one-sided, he did respond with short sentences. In my last conversation with him, I shared some details about the sale of our business. He told me "you did great," (and because of the proceeds, he joked that) "I'd like to hang around you a little more often!" We were hoping to still go out for a meal, but it was evident that he could no longer do so.

He'd chew his food and bunch it into his cheeks like a chipmunk until they were so full an orderly had to pull the food from his mouth and dispose of it to ensure he didn't choke. They fed him liquid protein shakes through a straw. Over the past few months, I observed him wither away into skin and bones until he had no muscle left to stand up. He used a wheelchair and often hung his head down to his chest with his eyes closed most of the time. I was sad for him.

The man was starving to death as his dementia couldn't instruct his throat to swallow. I questioned the staff about this. They told me, quietly that my sister was informed that if a resident couldn't feed themselves, they were not supposed to be at this facility. They were supposed to have been moved to a care facility that could provide appropriately for the condition. But through signing up for hospice, Daffy managed to keep him there. Rather than sell his assets for better or proper care and comfort, Daffy stood by and was letting him die. She held his healthcare directive and she was calling the shots.

While he told me to do what was best for him and his real estate, I felt the best thing at the time was to do nothing. Daffy had already confiscated it by decree or some legal power of attorney strategy. She was the one sinning, removing his financial assets that could be used for his care. It wasn't worth bringing up to him any longer. He never wanted to be in a nursing home like this, and my sis would not keep her promise to him that she'd never put him in one. He was close to death, and the best thing for him now was to let him be at peace in the final sunsets of his life. Daffy will pay for her sins.

March 3rd, 2013, was his ninetieth birthday. Darcy and I drove again back to South Carolina to celebrate with him. We brought him a small present and a cake to share with others in his unit. He always loved a cake and bunched it into his cheeks as usual. We sat with him for the afternoon, but the conversation was limited to yes or no questions he could answer quickly. He'd nod his head yes or say no periodically. It was evident he would only be with us just a little longer.

My sis knew we were in town for his birthday and showed up dressed with pink bows on her high heels and costume attire fitting a hooker. We figured she was already on the prowl for someone else's money. She only dropped by for about a half-hour to make a showing because she knew we were there. Darcy and I listened in disgust about the troubles she was experiencing with her divorce proceedings, but we were polite. We had planned to ask her out to dinner but a half hour with her had already been too much.

It had been a long afternoon of mostly silence and holding his hand. As evening came I leaned over to my dad and wished him a happy birthday again. I congratulated him for living to the ripe old age of 90. I told him we'd be back in two more weeks, but if by chance he left us, I told him I'd see him again on the other side! He nodded his head and replied, "I hope so." He couldn't lift his head; his muscles were too weak. Tears began to stream down my cheeks as I had a premonition this was the last time, I'd see my dad alive. As I got up, I embraced him and repeated goodbye. "Take care," he replied in his usual fashion. Darcy hugged him and said her goodbyes. As we walked toward the exit door, I retreated one last time to hug my dad and kissed him again goodbye. It was the last time I saw him alive. He passed away two weeks later.

My sister never called me with any service information for him or informed me of his will. After refusing to allow her to scam me out of the $10,000 she was seeking with her new "business" proposition to us, she was embarrassed, and we never heard from her again. If she had planned or held a service for him I was never informed.

I waited for a copy of the new will from Daffy, but never received a copy. I assumed I'd be receiving one soon. It never came. I made multiple requests to Daffy only because I had legal obligations if one didn't exist beyond the last one, I had.

It didn't matter to me if there was a new will until almost six months later when my attorney reminded me I'd better get a copy and verify that we didn't have to submit the will we had to probate. Technically, as legal guardians of Micayla, we had obligations to do so by state law. With that information, I gave Daffy the same information and reiterated I was tired of asking. I told her I would have my attorney submit the will I had of my dad's if I didn't receive a copy of this supposed will she claimed existed with her as the sole heir within 24 hours. In less than three hours from the message I left, she sent me an email copy of the will.

The memorial headstone he asked to be placed next to his wife Loretta with any cremated remains the science field didn't want never occurred. She never followed through on any of his last wishes. Her excuse for not donating his body to science as he wished was the cost of legal fees and paperwork his estate would bear. She had already confiscated everything. I waited more than a year to see if she would act on the man's request for a headstone. She didn't. She did nothing;. I honored my dad's request and laid a stone next to Loretta's, where I was told his ashes were placed. I've never heard from Daffy again.

The good book says you reap what you sow.

Chapter Fifty-Nine
Loretta

2020

Playlist:

Leave a Light On, Tom Walker

Loretta would suffer terribly because of her parent's choices, and then her own. Matteo Stellato, a son of Italian Immigrants, had fathered Loretta with his then-girlfriend, Margaret Hardy. They were married at 18 on February 23, 1930, four months before their child, Loretta Victoria Stellato, was born on June 17.

Matteo and Margaret had three more children in the next five years of their marriage. Alcohol consumption played a considerable part in Margaret's life, and at least two of her children were born with developmental disorders, likely due to alcohol fetus syndrome. Indeed, Loretta's youngest brother had learning disabilities, as well as a son from her second marriage.

Matteo and Margaret were divorced soon after the birth of their last child. While the reasons for the divorce are uncertain, family rumors suggest alcoholism and child abuse were the primary cause. The divorce court gave Matteo custody of all four children.

A young man in his mid-twenties and now single, he could not care for his children. He boarded them into the Brooklyn Orphanage Asylum. He housed his children at one of its facilities, Brookwood Hall located in East Islip, New York. With a developmental disability, his son Mike was adopted by his sister Rose. Rose had wanted to embrace all the children, but her husband, without a job then, could not see a financial way forward to care for them all.

Brookwood Hall, a former mansion converted into a home for juveniles, was well-funded by generous donors. Matteo also contributed handsomely to the care of his children. At barely 12, Loretta was dropped at the orphanage with her younger siblings, Margaret and Martin. Like other alums listed as inmates of Brookwood Hall, Loretta often spoke of her three years there as the best years of her life. We would eventually learn they were.

She was well cared for. She loved participating in the Victory Gardens planted to feed themselves. She had access to most of the modern luxuries of her day, like televisions, radios, and nice clothes. What she yearned for most was a mother's love. While her father visited her and her siblings as often as possible, her mother did not. She could stay at the orphanage until she was 16, but longing for a mother, she left Brookwood Hall to return to her mother's home at age 15.

She soon found a form of love as her mother encouraged her to help put bread on the table. Just three months past the age of 15, she became pregnant. When her first son was born, she named him Robert Martin Henry. Named for three men in the family lineage she seemed to admire. Martin is the American name for her Italian father, Matteo, Henry for her grandfather and Robert for an uncle. She gave him her last name of Stellato either because she had to protect the father, her son, or she didn't know who the father was.

A little over a year after giving birth to Robert, she gave birth to another child at seventeen. A baby girl. Her mother allowed her to keep her first son, but a second child was out of the question. Their flat was small, and Margaret had more children with her second husband. Loretta was forced to abandon the child and sold it through an illegal adoption managed by an unscrupulous attorney.

Loretta soon found prostitution outside her mother's home as a way of life. She was a beautiful young teenage girl who had movie-star looks in her youthful days. She was undoubtedly attractive to desiring men who adorned her with jewelry, clothes, furs, and money. Through public records, we learned that Loretta lived outside her mother's home in the Astral Building, one of the most sought-after addresses of her time on India Street in the Greenpoint neighborhood of Brooklyn. Rents for flats in this building were high and based upon the relationships we've tied her to through DNA, it was likely provided her free of charge for services as a kept mafia princess.

She was living on her own but as irresponsible as she was with her body, she was also an irresponsible young mother. She woke up one afternoon into a horrible living nightmare. She had brought her sister from the orphanage to live with her and as they often would do on sunny afternoons she and her sister went to the rooftop of their six-story building to sunbathe. As they sat chatting and reading, they both fell asleep.

Loretta was awakened by sirens howling from the street below. When she could not find her young toddler son who had been on the roof with them, she looked down to the sidewalk below where she heard chatter and saw the emergency vehicles; the small figure of a little boy was lying on the sidewalk.

At one month shy of her 19th birthday, she gave birth to another son named Gary T. James Stellato. Again, possibly named for people she admired or knew and giving him her maiden name to protect him or the father. After Roberts fall to his death she was not about to give this child up for adoption as she had done before. She was just nineteen, with one child dead and another never to be seen or her whereabouts ever to be known again.

Loretta kept this son, and fourteen months later, at age 20 and two months, she gave birth to another girl, my older half-sister Candice. She would not give this child up and again protected her with a name not connected to the man who fathered her. Continued to be supported by men of criminal means, Loretta went on to have a third child just 14 months after Candice at age 21-1/2. She already had two children in her flat. She was often out all night long with relatives sitting for her kids. She again gave a child up for adoption.

She managed not to get pregnant for the next three years. But with her promiscuous life, she became pregnant by yet another different man. She sold this child through an illegal adoption for money.

Three years later, she was pregnant again by another different man. It would be her seventh child conceived out of wedlock.

That child was me.

She would have one more child after me, the only child she'd conceive in marriage, and perhaps the saddest and most dysfunctional of them all, Daffy.

Loretta suffered terribly.

Some of her children connected with their half-siblings to learn about their fathers and families through DNA tests. We would learn of a father known to have run prostitution rings and who likely provided the apartment for Loretta in the Astral Building, a father who would change his name to hide from some hideous past or enter a witness protection program because of mafia associations, and a father who was related and associated with one of the most notorious crime families in New York, The Gambino crime family. All known fathers had connections to crime and crime families.

One of them, Joseph Guglielmo was nicknamed Dracula for his violent murders and butchery of his victims to conceal their bodies. He was a horrible man. Some of his relatives were murderers, themselves gunned down and murdered in the gangster wars. His name and more of his story appear in a book published by the Crown Publishing Group entitled For the Sins Of My Father, and he is listed as one of the most notorious mafia figures on Wikipedia. He eventually fled New York City and was never heard from again. No one knows whether he lived in hiding until his death or met his death being captured and killed by his mafia enemies.

Loretta knew whom she was associated with. Whenever there was evening news about a mob member who was gunned down, arrested, and news about their trial, we would all be hushed so she could listen keenly to the reported news. Perhaps some of them were her lovers. Some gunned down or some arrested. Her interest was always keen on reports about the New York Mafia.

As a teen, seeking stories from her about her life and why she hated my father so much, she would explain that "all the other men in her life gave her lots of gifts, your father gives me nothing. I only truly loved one man," she told me.

That slipped sentence to me set me on a path of yearning and discovery.

"Why did you leave him," I asked.

"I didn't," she said with a sigh. "He left me."

"Why did he leave you," I asked.

"He went to prison," she responded.

"Why did he go to jail," I asked.

"He did a bad thing," she said.

"I'm sorry," I told her, and the tears dripping from her eyes told me it was time to leave her alone.

Much of what we learned about her life after her death explained some behaviors. And it also left wide-open speculation on others. The pictures of the mysterious children underneath the glass top of her desk were now understood and known. They were the children she mourned.

Her ungrateful and unfair hatred of my father, Harry, a provider of a lovely home and car, but not much extra, who wanted to make "an honest woman" of her and loved her his whole life, suffered for it.

Her experiences explained the deep, dark sadness that engulfed her when my older brother Gary died in a car accident. She told us all that he was her favorite, and she loved him so much. She had to think that God again had punished her for her sins. The years of grieving that followed weren't just for him.

I know now that her son Robert's death and guilt for it had an immeasurable and irreversible pain in her heart. That and the shame of giving up three other children for sale/adoption (another sort of death) explain so much of her mental illness.

What we know now explains her acceptance of the cancerous fate that befell her, her willingness and even desire to die and rid herself of the unbearable burdens only she knew of and carried all of her life.

She suffered.

And so did we.

We all had to tiptoe between the raindrops living with Loretta, and when it poured, we had to dance and dance fast. She was a basket of emotions with minute-by-minute mood swings that could bring on a funny woman one minute and serve you with a nasty snipe in another. She developed high anxiety and anger over simple issues, was a chameleon while entertaining outsiders, and blamed my father unjustly for all her unhappiness.

Underlying nearly all of her moods was chronic depression. She lived her entire life grieving over her choices, which none of us understood.

It was apparent through occasional and subtle conversations or leaked stories of her past life from relatives that she held some deep, dark secrets close to her chest, but that was all suspect in our youth.

Later in my life, I learned of two disorders that best describe Loretta's personality and behavior as I knew her. She had many of the same symptoms of Bipolar Disorder and Borderline Personality Disorder (BPD), also known as Emotionally Unstable Personality Disorder (EUPD). She suffered from either or both of these afflictions, but worse, she suffered from her own actions; life itself, the shame, guilt, and pain she kept secret. She dealt with her pain by delivering cruelty to others, particularly those closest to her, her children, grandchildren, and her spouse. No one was spared "the poisonous pen," as we all called it, and her cruel letters of preaching and condemnation.

There really isn't a clear explanation for all her ill behavior except to repeat my aunt Peggy who once succinctly and wisely explained why Loretta behaved so severely and cruelly; "The difference between your mother and myself is that I forgave myself. Your mother will never forgive herself."

And she didn't.

I'm thankful for my turn in this world, which Loretta and Harry gave me. But I don't need to forgive her for the pain she put all of us through. Regardless of any excuses we could afford her, Loretta was deliberately cruel to people. I tried to help her when she was alive, but she'd refused. She had choices, and she chose.

I wish I had a second chance to try and help her again with what I know now, but I doubt I or anyone would succeed. People seldom change.

Loretta doesn't need my forgiveness. She needs God's forgiveness and, more than that, to have forgiven herself.

Her legacy is a daughter following in her footsteps.

Chapter Sixty
Academy Awards

2021

Playlist:

We Are The Champions, Queen

Eye of the Tiger, Survivor

I'm Still Standing, Elton John

Life's Been Good, Joe Walsh

After she re-read my manuscript without shock, Darcy and I had many conversations to explain some parts of my life more extensively and fill her in.

Darcy and I had built a beautiful life together. Our life included children, a great set of friends, travel, corporate careers, entrepreneurism, and philanthropy. It had limited interactions with Loretta, as it had to, but it did not dismiss her entirely. Darcy and I have always looked at our life in terms of time. Short-term and long-term planning was vital to us. We looked at our future in decades, the 30s, 40s, 50s, etc. Each decade became the center of many of our fireside discussions. We'd establish our goals and work the plan toward what we wanted them to look like ahead of us. Her mother, Betty, and her husband, Bob, were master role models in planning for their own decades.

In our twenties, we spent time getting to know each other and establishing a solid and continuously growing love. We dated for five years before marriage, working on our careers in preparation for our children. We set plans to pay for their college education before they were even born. It was a dream and goal of ours to deliver to them eventually. We got some travel into our schedules, worked hard, and went out on many date nights but lived frugally, living on less than half our annual take-home pay and investing the rest. With L.U.C.K., it paid off handsomely. We invested heavily in each other with love, affection, care, and encouragement. We carefully chose a limited number of friends to surround us and grow through life together.

In our 30s, we had children and were financially beyond a middle-class existence, enjoying an above-average lifestyle.

We spent many weekends embracing our time together as a family at our weekend retreat, fishing, playing on the beach, and water sports. We enjoyed many fireside chats and games in the winter, creating closeness for our family and visiting friends. When we were there weekly, we focused 100 percent of our time on each other, never allowing work to interfere with our time there.

Our weekly ritual of time with the family and invited friends was enjoyed by us so much that by the time we were in our forties, we'd built a second retreat that exceeded the size of our mainstay home in the twin cities by 4000 square feet.

In the twin cities, we lived on a lakeshore in a solid upper-middle-class community near great friends and neighbors. Instead of progressing onto a larger home in an upper-crust neighborhood in the cities, we built a private family lodge off the beaten path with the idea that it would be a luxury out of town and a place to share with everyone in our circle. And that's what we did for the next twenty years after Loretta's passing.

In our 40s, we continued to work diligently and resourcefully to grow our business. We saw our children off to college to help them begin to make a life of their own. We honed the skills of our third child, born with the disability of Downs Syndrome, to build independence into her life in as many ways as possible. As a sport of my own, driving was an essential delivery, and she learned how to ride a Yamaha P50 motorcycle years before she mastered riding a bicycle! We'd putter around on our dirt bikes. Snowmobiles soon followed, then a golf cart. As she got closer to graduating high school, she asked me what kind of car she would get. I bought each of my sons a new sports car in high school.

Without the ability to pass a licensing exam, I sought out a slow-moving electric car, a Gem car, with four doors, a radio, and as many luxuries as the Gem car offered. Classified as a slow-moving vehicle, she could drive on any non-restricted federal or municipality roads posted at 45 miles per hour or less where cities allowed. She loved it. As she scoped out the interior of her car, she had one question and pointed to a knob on the door and asked what that was? "It's to turn down the window, honey," I explained. "The Gem car didn't offer power windows!" She tried it and said, "OK, let's go!" We drove off! From years and years of teaching her three-point turns and parallel parking with her golf cart, she mastered her new car in no time.

In our 50's, work was beginning to burn me out. I had built the second or third-largest honey processing company in the United States, and we were on the path toward $100 million in annual revenues. Our company was operating like clockwork. I was a builder, not a maintainer, looking for a new project.

Turning some of my CEO responsibilities over to Darcy and another executive on our team, I began philanthropical work in Western Africa. I started a small company called Mel-O Africa. The endeavor focused on providing subsistence farmers with employment opportunities in beekeeping and establishing an apiculture industry in Sierra Leone. It was grueling travel in a third-world country with narrow roads. I often found myself sleeping in the same clothes for days and I slept slumped over the steering wheel of my pickup truck in sweltering humidity at night. Relief from significant company responsibilities enabled me to take long trips, upward to a month, to try and establish teams to build out our plans.

As the boys left for college at home, Micayla had our undivided attention and continued to enjoy traveling abroad with us sightseeing the world when she was off from school. Life was generally good, and I was enjoying a less intensive workday.

For nearly seven years, one equity group or another kept soliciting me to consider selling my company. I never planned to sell, and their interest was more than purely speculative. At age 55, I retired temporarily for a year and a half to see if I would enjoy the time off. Most entrepreneurs never quit because they make too much money or they can't sit still. I was definitely in the latter category.

In that year and a half, I spent more time in Africa and tore down an old dairy barn near my factory. I wanted to see if I could do it again as I did when I was fourteen. I could and did.

Disappointed that my human resource manager informed me that our company was not equipped with the leadership I had trained and hoped would take over, I sat down with my children and asked them if they had any interest in the business. I didn't want to wake up at age 68 and wonder what to do with it.

I had solid purchasing interest knocking at my door. My children told me to sell it and enjoy life. My board of advisors told me to do the same. They stressed how few businesses like mine ever sell across the country and how rare it was to have the pursuers' interest I had.

My business performed at ratios and margins well above the average food business. They advised me that most companies cannot sell even for the equity their owners built up and are often just shut down or given away.

"Academy Awards" came to me through my business and personal life. My competitors always wondered how I was acquiring their customers. They thought it was with cheap honey. The fact was it was with integrity. In my early business years, I couldn't understand why it was so difficult to compete with them. I wondered why my raw product, processing, and packaging costs were more expensive than some retail-priced products were selling on the shelves. I soon found out why. Adulteration. Economic adulteration, as well as other substances.

I found laboratories outside the United States and began to test their product. When I brought the product test to the retailer or bulk user and showed them the results, they switched to our company. I didn't sell honey. I sold integrity, and every drop of our honey was backed by traceability and the tests we had performed.

We served some of the most outstanding companies in the United States. Our product entered millions and millions of homes across the country as a bulk ingredient in snacks or cereals or through retail packs of bears and bottles.

One of those outstanding products was General Mills Honey Nut Cheerios. Our client list included companies that cared about the integrity of their product. Companies like CVS, Walgreens, Malt O Meal, Post, and more than one hundred others. And those we could not switch, as we only had so much capital to spread around, began advising their suppliers to duplicate the testing we initiated in the industry. We shipped across our nation. We were helping to clean up the fraud in our industry which was so rampant.

General Mills was one of our largest customers. We appeared as model suppliers in some of their annual reports and other communications. We taught them a lot about our product and secured pure products for them at a fair price. In return, they taught us a lot about supply chain safety and food safety manufacturing issues. For nearly 20 years, our company was the only company that served the plants where its cereals were produced, and we developed a partnership experience between us.

They held an annual recognition of their top suppliers. They gave just six champion awards out of thousands and thousands of suppliers worldwide. Still, only six would qualify for their esteemed champion awards. We were one of them. Our company received a General Mills Champion award, our first Oscar.

The second Oscar came from one of Deloitte's Auditing Teams. After we signed the papers to sell our firm, the equity group employed Deloitte to audit our accounting records, inventories, and systems. They were done in two weeks. The auditing team praised our firm's exceptionally legitimate, clean, and automated accounting system for its web-based simplicity and for its compliance with Generally Accepted Accounting Principles and ethics. Having a big ten accounting firm on board throughout my career and an excellent CFO attributed.

They told us that many entrepreneurial companies they often find two sets of books as many entrepreneurs live off the company corruptly to avoid paying taxes and to place a fair value on the company, often assets like condos, houses, boats, cars, etc., all had to be dealt with as an add-backs to accurately increase the company's value.

Our books were clean. Darcy and I never mixed business and personal expenses. We generously shared profit sharing with our employees: our financial books were open to them. I never took pleasure trips on the company. I visited many countries only to see the inside of a plane, cab, hotel, and meeting rooms unless we were in the field auditing traceability reports. I had a family to raise and a business to run, so I was about the world and back to my company as fast as possible.

Deloitte praised us for the integrity they found and that it only took them two weeks versus three months for a typical company of our size. That was my second Academy Award. In addition to ourselves, my CFO, Tim Harder, also deserves a mention of responsibility for this. He was an outstanding talent, and his performance went above and beyond. He and his wife Pauline would further our efforts in Africa, selling their home and moving to Sierra Leone to carry on the work I'd begun.

The third award came from my two sons. As our company did extensive testing, we began to find a contaminant called Glyphosate in American-sourced honey. Doing research, I hypothesized that Glyphosate would soon contaminate honey throughout the industry. The FDA was already quietly identifying it in many other foods. Faced with that threat and sharing it with my two sons as we explored the possible sale of the business, my sons reiterated a saying we always used, that we would not sell any honey that we would not eat.

I reminded them that the first generation builds a business to 100 million and the second to a billion. They could diversify from honey, but they wanted no part of it. As we always taught them, integrity is paramount; money is secondary. "We'll make it on our own," they each said. Their integrity and choice to forfeit this enormous opportunity with my company earnings of multiple millions of pre-tax dollars a year was my third Academy Award, and I am proud of them.

Most of our competitors sourced honey from India. We did at one time, but when tests revealed it to be contaminated with lead, even though it was small parts per billion and probably not harmful, we destroyed hundreds of thousands of dollars of the product we had already paid for in our warehouse and refused to import honey from India again. The contamination problem was widely known throughout our industry. Many of our competitors continued to purchase it and they blended it with other products to decrease the number of parts per billion. No parts per billion were legally acceptable and still aren't today. The same is true of Glyphosate.

My competitors tried to steal customers from us with cheap, contaminated honey. We shared openly with our customers to test our competitors' samples. We never lost a customer. Seven years post the sale of my company, I suspect one can hardly source commercial volumes of honey free of Glyphosate from Canada, Mexico, The United States, Argentina, and parts of Brazil, wherever commercial agriculture and commercial beehives are located near each other. I no longer eat honey, opting for pure maple syrup as a sweetener.

With idle time on our hands, Darcy and I began to travel. Our eldest son was back from five years of college and living at home. We continued our focus on building out Micayla's independence from us. She attended a community college post-high school graduation. As we traveled, we left Micayla to fend for herself with the aid of our son. With each trip, her independence and confidence grew more substantial. It was difficult for Darcy to let go, but she knew it was best. And what better way to divert Darcy's attention than that of travel?

Life was rolling along in our permanent vacation mode well. Our well-laid-out plans for our fifty's decade came to fruition and Darcy convinced me to buy another Comet. A car I'd love to drive and enjoy in my retirement. I did. I purchased a Porsche 911. She enjoyed driving it as much as I did. Since I wasn't your typical ego who acquired one of these cars on a low mileage lease and only drove it to the weekend restaurant outing and back, I had to buy her one too. I was driving mine every day and even into the winter months. At last count, I had 45,000 miles on it and almost as many rock chips! It's no longer showroom perfect, but it's a blast to drive every day! I also convinced my best friend who had his eye on a Corvette, his dream car, to abandon that idea and buy one too. He did and we enjoy occasional tours in the country together racing each other.

While I adorned Darcy with clothes and jewelry gifts most of her life, many pieces in an art form, I surprised her at Christmas with her personal custom-ordered Porsche 911. We flew to Germany and picked it up at the production plant in Stuttgart. That summer, we toured in the car all over Europe for over a month. We followed castled rivers and romantic roads mapped out by the Porsche organization.

We then journeyed through rural countryside from Mannerheim to Vienna, Prague, and as far east as Budapest seeing dozens of hamlets and every major city in between. We rounded out our trip through Croatia, following its coast back to Venice, Italy, then across the peninsula to the Black Forest and the Alps to a destination, we'd ship the car home to the States.

During that trip, we adjusted our plans for our 60s decade and looked further to our seventies. When we returned, Micayla had graduated from community college and high school, and we set her up in her own apartment to see how she'd do independently. With a bit of help, she has done wonderfully. Our fourth Academy Award!

Her boyfriend, a year behind Mic in college had asked me if he could marry her several times. I first took his inquiry with a grain of salt and chalked it up to puppy love. But as time passed and we watched their puppy love maturing, and he continued to ask, we began to take him seriously. Especially when in a talent show in front of the entire school audience, he sync-lipped the lyrics of Ed Sheehan's song Perfect, staring and pointing to his sweetheart sitting just below the stage. The whole audience was in tears.

I spoke to Adams's mom, and we came up with some responsible conditions he had to meet before he asked me again to marry my daughter. We explained to both of them at the time, most of all, of course, that he had to finish and graduate from college. He agreed. He worked at all the other conditions, found a job, got some training in some of the conditional areas, and succeeded.

After graduating, Adam pulled me aside one day and said, "Curt, remember you told me that if I got a job, graduated from college, and did all the other things you and my mom requested, I could marry your daughter?"

"Yes, I remember," I said.

"Well, Curt, I've done all those things. May I marry your daughter?"

Tears of pride poured from my eyes, and I said, "Well, Adam, if she says yes, you may marry her."

Adam took his time in planning his proposal. He saved for a ring, and on his 22nd birthday, he asked for a party and had a list of invites. We celebrated his birthday, and after he opened a few gifts people had brought for him, he got all of us to his attention. He said, "I want to thank you all for the party and all of these nice gifts, but. I want one more gift." He asked Micayla to step forward to where he stood, got down on his knee, and proposed to her. Our fifth Academy Award.

Chapter Sixty-One
Happy and Yaya

2021

Playlist:

Make You Feel My Love, Adele

Perfect, Ed Sheeran

Changing, John Mayer

Grow as We Grow, Ben Platt

Joy of My Life, Chris Stapelton

More, Chris Stapelton

I Will Spend My Whole Life Loving You, Imaginary Future, Kina Grannis

Amazing Grace, Anne Murray

Darcy and I recently entered our sixth decade of age and have known each other for over 40 years. Due to the pandemic of 2020 and 2021, we modified our earlier plans for this decade and used the idle time to begin establishing steps toward our seventies. We have great activities and creative projects planned for our present and future grandkids at our lodge in Wisconsin if they wish to partake.

In 2018 I had a 14-car carriage and hobby barn with second-story space constructed to build a creative center. We would use some of the space to create a miniature greenhouse and various small studios and workbenches for arts, including painting, wood burning, leather-working, silversmithing, pottery, and other art forms. Our grandkids would be toddlers in our early sixties, and most benefit from the studios as they become adolescents and early teens. In the meantime, we and our friends and neighbors will also enjoy the space.

Darcy and I will continue to travel to see more of our beautiful earth between creating in these studios.

We had plans to travel back to Europe for three months, starting on a real estate tour in Sicily just before the pandemic. Our main objective was to explore potential homes in some of the most southern climates of Europe in hopes of securing a small place with an ability to own and park a car for indiscriminate touring. We planned to rotate among our existing homes and add another somewhere in Europe.

Early spring of 2020, the outbreak of Coronavirus in China became headline news. Adam and Micayla were with us for a few weeks in Florida, just before we planned to leave for Europe. We escorted them back to Minneapolis on Valentine's Day preparing to embark to Italy a week later.

Visiting my doctor for a routine checkup, I asked him what his thoughts were on the virus outbreak in China as it appeared the Chinese government was taking this very seriously. He dismissed the worries because it was a virus and suggested moving forward with our travel plans. "Doc, I've traveled the world; the Chinese People are everywhere; that virus will soon be everywhere?" Again, he dismissed it as just intense flu. I shared what he thought with Darcy and others. I was still skeptical. "Let's delay this trip and go back to Florida and wait a few weeks and see how this pans out," I suggested, and she agreed. Within three weeks, Italy was the epicenter of the pandemic in Europe, and New York City was fast becoming the epicenter in the United States.

In the spring and summer of 2020 municipalities, significant cities, and states were locked down. We canceled our real estate tour and another previously planned family trip to New Zealand. We split our time in Florida and spent time in Wisconsin to work on that creative center.

Being a little restless and having pulled my hamstring lifting some heavy beams, we set out on an unintended 11,000-mile journey through the western United States in Darcy's Porsche, revisiting places we'd been to before, but this time, with fewer crowds due to the pandemic and more time to enjoy the scenery. We continued working on the carriage barn's interior studios when we returned to Wisconsin.

With nowhere else to go and no travel to consume our time that winter, we hung out on the vacant beaches of Florida.

That winter, we purchased a townhome sight unseen in a neighborhood we desired for Micayla and Adam. Faster than her car, Darcy acted as the general contractor, had parts of the townhome gutted, remodeled it, and moved Micayla in.

Our oldest son and his wife brought their firstborn (our sixth Academy Award) into this world. We became Happy and YaYa to distinguish us from the other grandmas and grandpas, the names Happy for me and YaYa the Greek word for grandma, for Darcy. Our second grandchild, a boy to our other son and his wife, arrived as our seventh Academy Award five months later!

Immediately after completing the townhome, Darcy began planning Adam and Mic's wedding. While planning the wedding, at the same time, Darcy and I met with architects to develop blueprints for a remodel of our lake home near Minneapolis with the condition that construction does not start until after Mic's wedding. This would be a home, close to our children to visit periodically and eventually live out our senior elderly years. As if all of that wasn't enough on our plates, God gives busy people plenty to keep busy!

On February 12, 2022, a fire tragedy struck our family's beloved private lodge in Wisconsin. We were there at the time, no one was hurt, and it was a total loss. Throughout our life, I periodically reminded my children not to get attached to the material things in life, especially our family retreat. It was located in a high forest fire hazard area, and often, lightning strikes hit trees surrounding it. While neither of these was the cause of the fire (the reason was a chimney fire), I'd always had a hunch that some loss might occur from fire and was always proactive with fire prevention measures. As well prepared as I tried to be with ample fire extinguishers and other preventative measures, still, no matter how well prepared I thought I was, a loss occurred. That's the way life is.

As condolences on the loss poured in from friends and family, I reminded them that it was just sticks and stones, glass and nails, and there are plenty of growing trees around us to replace the loss of the log structure. I also shared, "We come into this world with nothing and leave with nothing. This tragedy is a small reminder that everything we have in life is just rented."

Looking to rebuild, I adopted U.S. President Joe Biden's "Build Back Better" motto as it had a new meaning for us, and we'd borrow it to do that.

More interestingly, a message came to me from our good friend and famed wildlife artist Jerry Raedeke.

He wrote: "Curt and Darcy, we are sad to hear of your loss… genuine that it was wood and stone, glass and nails, but it was also a part of you. And any loss, no matter how large or small, is an experience of grief, and grieving is the emotional payment we make for the loss. I know that both of you have more than the usual inner strength and will turn this, in time, into another blessing in your life. At the same time, it is very unfortunate, and we are sorry that you are going through this challenging experience. – Jerry."

Jerry's message summed up my mother. She endured the emotional payment of pain for her losses every single day of her life. She wept for the children she gave up, the children lost through death, and unfortunately, because of such love and pain, failed to realize and appreciate what she still had. She grieved because she loved, and she grieved deeply.

As usual, I leave no second in a day to waste. With a beautiful daughter's wedding plans, two homes heading for construction, and one of our condominiums needing freshening for our temporary living quarters, I built a bunk house in our carriage barn for temporary quarters while construction of the lodge in Wisconsin ensues.

The pandemic has left little help to hire in this remote area of Wisconsin, and what contractors there exist told me they were out three years in projects, so I've taken some of the work into my own hands. I'm skilled, enjoy the building process, and unafraid to take on some of the construction challenges. I've had no problem fulfilling my marriage vow to Darcy that she'll never be bored being married to me, certainly not in 2022 and 2023.

Our eighth Academy Award in life to date was given to us through Adams's proposal to Micayla and their wedding. It culminated in a lifelong endeavor to raise these special children to live as normal and independently as possible. It takes a village to raise a child, it certainly took one to grow and help me, and Mic and Adam were no different.

They have an incredible village of friends and families. As Darcy planned their wedding I had only one criterion: their broad population of special needs friends and their families were included in as many ways as possible. As the plans progressed, Darcy kept coming back with ideas from the wedding planner hired to assist. Every new idea exceeded the last to make this a night to remember for everyone who attended.

Their wedding occurred in August of 2022. It was a fabulous event. An extensive guest list included lots of their friends with unique or special needs, and out of desire and some necessity, the parents of every one of them were invited as well. As the guest list approached the capacity limit of 450, we began to limit our own family members to enable priority to the unique needs families. This event was for them and to our family members we had to pass up on; we apologized but they all understood.

I did not know many of the guest's parents, but we know they share similar hopes and dreams of independence for their children. The wedding was not just a gift to Adam and Micayla, but to everyone in attendance; in more ways than one.

Many of our guests remarked how much love poured out at this event and how it was indeed a gift to them to experience and shared how they learned so much. That gift was not from us, that gift was from the special needs population themselves. You have missed something spectacular if you've never been to a Special Olympics event or dance. Downs people love to dance and share their emotions forthright. This population was no exception. They could hardly hold back their tears and emotions nor allow the wedding couple, the traditional father and bride and groom and mother dances, to occur without edging to the dance floor and waiting for their chance to join in. The parents of many of the special guests let Darcy and me know that this event was indeed an inspirational gift to them, also.

No wedding venue is perfect. In fact some funny things happened at this one. First, my beautiful wife and mother of the bride forgot to put her lipstick on. She didn't realize this till long after the pictures were taken, and I gave her a kiss on the dance floor. Second, as I was giving a toast on behalf of Mic and Adam, in the middle, Mic signed in ASL (American Sign Language) that she had to use the bathroom. Ten minutes later, we finished the toast. Third, when it was time to toss the bouquet, the dance floor was so packed that when we asked Mic if she wanted to do that, as much as she did, she said, in the interest of all the fun her guests appeared to be having she said let's pass on it. "Everyone is having so much fun," she said.

Fourth when it was time for Adam to pull off the garter and pass it, he too said, "Let's pass on it as everyone is on the dance floor having so much fun." Finally, it was time to cut the cake! Again, they both said, "let's do it tomorrow!" So we did! It was a good thing we had a dessert buffet! They did not want to leave the dance floor. From the moment the band started with the father and bride dance at 8:00 until 12.05 the following morning, the dance floor was a marathon packing smiles and moves of love and perfect imperfections, mainly referring to all our crazy bopping, hopping, and waving of laser sticks!

Just as my new sisters were put up for adoption, Adam, too was put up for adoption. While most of us receive a child through birth and some are born with special needs, a part of my toast on behalf of Micayla and Adam was to his parents, Brian and Monica, and all of the other parents like them who adopted a special needs child. They are the true .01 percent of the world's most admired people and will sit on the left hand of God when that time comes. Additionally, we had at least one parent at the wedding who donated a kidney to give his special needs son a chance at life! No percent describes the love that father has for his son. The only word to describe it is "God." God dwells within us and will shine with brilliance if we allow and ask God to do so.

The pandemic has changed the world; it has changed us too! But in one thing, we remain the same: always grateful… for everything and everyone.

I've always looked at our life in seasons. Each year since they were born, I counted how many Christmases we had left with our children before they went to college. It kept time and priorities in perspective.

I look at my whole life as a blessing of lessons. Every event, challenge, make-out and makeup session, holiday, disappointment, graduation, anniversary, failure and success are a chapter of life. It's called living. Making a life! I indeed felt self-pity as a teen, but I was always up with the sunrise and feeling the warmth of God's soul within. I'll continue to do so.

The only constant thing in life I have seen is change. And we must embrace it. We can change for the better or change for the worse. There is no in-between. We must choose, even for that which we sometimes have no control over, like the weather. We either embrace it or suffer it.

We live in a beautiful world where we should all strive to live happily and harmoniously. It is imperfect, dynamic, at times peaceful, at times turbulent and demonic, not unlike my mother, Loretta.

As children, Loretta kept us dancing through the rain in storms of anxiety, despair, and depression. But being forced to dance through the rain and sometimes between the raindrops helped me develop a relationship with the unseen powers available to us all.

Though not perfectly, I danced with the Grace of the Holy Spirit and tried to maintain accountability to God above all. Through that Grace, I did honor my mother and father in that I did all I could to help them physically, financially, and mentally. But in my childhood years, living with them and living like them was not a path God forced me into. He gave me a free will, a choice.

From that near-fatal day when I made the most critical decision in my life to leave home while still in high school, I embarked on a choice… my own, a journey to somewhere else, a better life. I drove onward with confidence, ambition, a solid work ethic, and faith. Through faith my Comet took me down roads I'd never imagined. I was led to Darcy. The great Comet in the sky was always with me.

And who introduced me to the great Comet in the sky?

Loretta.

I never danced alone.